Impact of Financial Technology (FinTech) on Islamic Finance and Financial Stability

Nader Naifar
Imam Mohammad Ibn Saud Islamic University, Saudi Arabia & University of Sfax, Tunisia

IGI Global
DISSEMINATOR OF KNOWLEDGE

A volume in the Advances in Finance, Accounting, and Economics (AFAE) Book Series

Published in the United States of America by
IGI Global
Business Science Reference (an imprint of IGI Global)
701 E. Chocolate Avenue
Hershey PA, USA 17033
Tel: 717-533-8845
Fax: 717-533-8661
E-mail: cust@igi-global.com
Web site: http://www.igi-global.com

Library of Congress Cataloging-in-Publication Data

Names: Naifar, Nader, 1976- editor.
Title: Impact of financial technology (fintech) on Islamic finance and financial stability / Nader Naifar, editor.
Description: Hershey, PA : Business Science Reference (an imprint of IGI Global), 2020. | Summary: "This book examines the impact of FinTech on Islamic financial services industry and global financial stability"--Provided by publisher.
Identifiers: LCCN 2019015722 | ISBN 9781799800392 (hardcover) | ISBN 9781799800408 (softcover) | ISBN 9781799800415 (ebook)
Subjects: LCSH: Finance--Technological innovations--Islamic countries. | Financial services industry--Technological innovations--Islamic countries. | Finance--Religious aspects--Islam. | Finance--Islamic countries. | Financial services industry--Islamic countries.
Classification: LCC HG187.4 .I56 2020 | DDC 332.10917/67--dc23
LC record available at https://lccn.loc.gov/2019015722

This book is published in the IGI Global book series Advances in Finance, Accounting, and Economics (AFAE) (ISSN: 2327-5677; eISSN: 2327-5685)

British Cataloguing in Publication Data
A Cataloguing in Publication record for this book is available from the British Library.

Advances in Finance, Accounting, and Economics (AFAE) Book Series

Ahmed Driouchi
Al Akhawayn University, Morocco

ISSN:2327-5677
EISSN:2327-5685

Mission

In our changing economic and business environment, it is important to consider the financial changes occurring internationally as well as within individual organizations and business environments. Understanding these changes as well as the factors that influence them is crucial in preparing for our financial future and ensuring economic sustainability and growth.

The **Advances in Finance, Accounting, and Economics (AFAE)** book series aims to publish comprehensive and informative titles in all areas of economics and economic theory, finance, and accounting to assist in advancing the available knowledge and providing for further research development in these dynamic fields.

Coverage

- Applied Accounting
- International Economics
- Development Economics
- Behavioral Economics
- Wages and Employment
- Evidence-Based Studies
- Taxes
- Stock Market
- Field Research
- Economics of Migration and Spatial Mobility

IGI Global is currently accepting manuscripts for publication within this series. To submit a proposal for a volume in this series, please contact our Acquisition Editors at Acquisitions@igi-global.com or visit: http://www.igi-global.com/publish/.

The Advances in Finance, Accounting, and Economics (AFAE) Book Series (ISSN 2327-5677) is published by IGI Global, 701 E. Chocolate Avenue, Hershey, PA 17033-1240, USA, www.igi-global.com. This series is composed of titles available for purchase individually; each title is edited to be contextually exclusive from any other title within the series. For pricing and ordering information please visit http://www.igi-global.com/book-series/advances-finance-accounting-economics/73685. Postmaster: Send all address changes to above address.

Titles in this Series

For a list of additional titles in this series, please visit: www.igi-global.com/book-series

Financial Technology and Disruptive Innovation in ASEAN
Muhammad Anshari (Universiti Brunei Darussalam, Brunei) Mohammad Nabil Almunawar (Universiti Brunei Darussalam, Brunei) and Masairol Masri (Universiti Brunei Darussalam, Brunei)
Business Science Reference • ©2020 • 331pp • H/C (ISBN: 9781522591832) • US $195.00

International Trade Policies in the Era of Globalization
Ahu Coşkun Özer (Marmara University, Turkey)
Business Science Reference • ©2020 • 363pp • H/C (ISBN: 9781522595663) • US $205.00

Management Accounting Standards for Sustainable Business Practices
Ionica Oncioiu (Titu Maiorescu University, Romania) Gary Cokins (Analytics-Based Performance Management LLC, USA) Sorinel Căpuşneanu (Titu Maiorescu University, Romania) and Dan Ioan Topor (1 Decembrie 1918 University, Romania)
Business Science Reference • ©2020 • 360pp • H/C (ISBN: 9781799801788) • US $215.00

Handbook of Research on Economic and Political Implications of Green Trading and Energy Use
Ramesh Chandra Das (Vidyasagar University, India)
Business Science Reference • ©2019 • 421pp • H/C (ISBN: 9781522585473) • US $225.00

Emerging Research on Monetary Policy, Banking, and Financial Markets
Cristi Spulbar (University of Craiova, Romania) and Ramona Birau (Constantin Brâncuşi University of Targu Jiu, Romania)
Business Science Reference • ©2019 • 322pp • H/C (ISBN: 9781522592693) • US $195.00

Modernization and Accountability in the Social Economy Sector
Augusta Ferreira (University of Aveiro, Portugal) Rui Marques (University of Aveiro, Portugal) Graça Azevedo (University of Aveiro, Portugal) Helena Inácio (University of Aveiro, Portugal) and Carlos Santos (University of Aveiro, Portugal)
Business Science Reference • ©2019 • 351pp • H/C (ISBN: 9781522584827) • US $215.00

Foreign Business in China and Opportunities for Technological Innovation and Sustainable Economics
Anna Visvizi (Deree – The American College of Greece, Greece) Miltiadis Lytras (Deree – The American College of Greece, Greece) Xi Zhang (Tianjin University, China) and Jie Zhao (Anhui University, China)
Business Science Reference • ©2019 • 284pp • H/C (ISBN: 9781522589808) • US $195.00

IGI Global
DISSEMINATOR OF KNOWLEDGE

701 East Chocolate Avenue, Hershey, PA 17033, USA
Tel: 717-533-8845 x100 • Fax: 717-533-8661
E-Mail: cust@igi-global.com • www.igi-global.com

Editorial Advisory Board

Table of Contents

Detailed Table of Contents

In the literature, it is argued that there is an agency or incentive problem in the Mudarabah Interbank Instrument (MII), an instrument where the depositor is the rabbul-mal (capital provider or investor) while the counterparty is the mudarib or entrepreneur. It is to the receiving bank's advantage to 'declare' a lower profit rate. To solve this problem, the Malaysian Central Bank revised the rules by setting a minimum benchmark rate for the MII. This practice is quite similar to the fixed interest rate in conventional financial system which may trigger several Shariah issues. In this chapter, the authors argue that the blockchain technology is a better way to address the issue and propose and how it overcomes the issue in the Islamic interbank money market. As implication of the study, Islamic banks can start using it as a testing process for the future businesses, and in accordance with the analyzing test results, they can implement the system for every occasion.

The purpose of this chapter is to examine the factors that influence small and medium-sized enterprises' (SMEs) intentions to use the investment account platform (IAP) based on technology acceptance model (TAM). The central hypothesis for this chapter was that SMEs' intentions to use IAP were a result of perceived usefulness and perceived ease of use. This chapter also suggested that perceived ease of use and intention was mediated by perceived usefulness of the IAP. Using primary data collection method, 163 questionnaires were collected from SMEs in Kuala Lumpur, Malaysia using the purposive sampling technique. The data were analysed using SPSS and SmartPLS. The chapter found that perceived ease of use had significant influences on SMEs intention to use the IAP while perceived ease of use significantly affected perceived usefulness and the relationship between perceived ease of use and intention was mediated by perceived usefulness of the IAP. The results of this chapter suggested strategies to promote the platform as a fund seeking platform for SMEs.

The disruption of innovations in the banking sector continues to indicate a positive trend among bankers and customers. The innovations of technology that stand with speediness and fast track transaction effectively support the spread in using banking system without barriers. Recently, the financial services industry continues to be surprised by the latest technology's innovation that is known as artificial intelligence. By looking into the ecosystem for the future sustainability of Islamic banking and finance in Southeast Asia, Islamic financial services may learn and adopt several best practices of A.I. from global banking practices. With a focus on the Islamic financial services industry in Southeast Asia, an exploration on the readiness of such industry and advantages of artificial intelligence are made. This research depends on the qualitative investigation from documentary materials. The leadership of Islamic banks shows their readiness in accepting artificial intelligence.

Financing small and medium enterprises (SMEs) is one of the most important mechanisms to boost economic growth in both developed and developing nations. The contributions of SMEs in many countries' gross domestic product (GDP) have been overwhelming. SMEs improve job creation in all sectors of the economy and contribute to the people's economic wellbeing. However, many SMEs are not getting financing from their respective counties due to strict regulations and interest rate hike. With this kind of regulations and high interest, many brains are wasted, and many ideas are vanishing with the job opportunities attached them. Government agencies are therefore in need to innovate different ways to facilitate SME financing and support new businesses for achieving and maintaining sustainable economic growth. This chapter proposes an Islamic FinTech and its mechanisms to achieving this vital initiative using the Islamic benevolent loan "Alqard al-hasan."

and to highlight how FinTech contribute to enhance the financial and social inclusion, by providing convenient and accurate digital financial services (DFS) to the excluded population.

The chapter attempts to test the hypothesis that cryptocurrencies are real independent financial instruments that pose no danger to global financial system stability. For the empirical analysis, the authors use data related to bitcoin and widely traded asset classes. They also utilize the copula approach as well as the CoVaR model. The results show a significant role of crypto-asset market in the stability of global markets. Precisely, they find a dependence between bitcoin and oil prices defined by a normal copula model. The empirical results regarding the systemic risk show that extreme changes in bitcoin prices may have an adverse effect on equity and gold markets. There are positive and significant effects of EUR, JPY, and WTI markets when bitcoin goes down. The authors have also shown that after 2016 the virtual market sudden changes are more likely to raise the whole regular financial system losses, except the energy market. These results are important for policymakers and investors.

The digitization of payment and the development of private digital currencies have constrained central banks to examine the issuance of their own central bank digital currency (CBDC) in order to face the competition of the new peer-to-peer payment system and the decline of cash use. This chapter addresses the topic of CBDC and places the discussion within the context of dual banking intermediation and financial stability. The design of CBDC in term of accessibility, anonymity, interest rate, and payment mechanism depends on the cryptocurrency use and money characteristics regarding the use of cash and deposit. The CBDC Sharia compliant, free of interest or PLS-based, fulfilling money value stability might be a solution. The effects of CBDC on banking intermediation and financial stability depend importantly on the CBDC design and switch significance of banks deposit to CBDC but remain an open question given the pros and cons arguments. In a dual banking system, Islamic banks could limit the disintermediation effect and maintain financial stability under Sharia compliance.

This chapter deliberates on the effects of FinTech on economic performance in the context of political instability in MENA zone countries. Using a multiple regression model to estimate time series data based on a sample of 10 MENA zone countries for 2011, 2014, and 2017, the study contends that FinTech's lending activities increase inflation and that this effect could be interestingly moderated by sound policies and regulations. In addition, the authors find empirical support for the FinTech's role as a driver of economic growth and a breeding ground for innovative projects in a context of freedom of expression, association, and media. In terms of practical implications, decision makers are asked to formulate and implement sound policies and regulations that permit and promote the positive role of FinTech in terms of economic performance.

Preface

FinTech is one of the most topical areas in the global financial services industry. The emerging of distributed ledger technology, smart contract and biometrics, new digital currencies, and new payment platforms has motivated the innovation in financial services. The adoption of FinTech by the Islamic finance industry is the most natural way to achieve a strong position in this digitalization era. The development of artificial intelligence, machine learning, and blockchain technology will redesign Islamic financial services and products. However, the increasing use of FinTech can affect the potential financial stability system. While the development of regulatory technology, cybersecurity, and identity security could help the global and Islamic financial services, there exists a need for an edited collection of original research in this area.

This book aims to offer valuable insights into the current state of Islamic finance and financial stability in the era of FinTech. It provides relevant theoretical frameworks and the latest empirical research findings in the area. The target audience of this book will be composed of professionals, researchers, investors, and regulators working in the field of Islamic finance and FinTech.

This book is divided into three interconnected sections. The first section, entitled "FinTech as a Distributive Technology for the Islamic Finance Industry." Five chapters are included in this section (Chapter 1 to 5) dedicated to exploring the application of ledger technology, Artificial intelligence, peer-to-peer lending, and other technologies in Islamic finance.

In the first chapter, the authors study the advantages and disadvantages of using blockchain technology in Islamic Interbank Monetary System. They explain the role of distributed ledger technology in eliminating misleading investment information, improving the sharing of every outcome of the investment, and then increasing the trust of customers. They propose a private blockchain system in the Islamic Interbank Money Market. By using private blockchain, rather than a public blockchain system, Islamic banks can avoid the unfavorable elements of the blockchain system while retaining information specific to customers.

In the second chapter, the authors examine the factors that influence Small and Medium-Sized Enterprises' (SMEs) intention to use Financial Technology and Islamic Crowdfunding Platforms. Crowdfunding brings the Internet platform to the financial industry to connect fund providers and investors. The projects listed in Islamic crowdfunding must be compliant with Islamic law. Using data collected from SMEs in Kuala Lumpur (Malaysia), the authors found that perceived ease of use has a significant relationship towards intention, while perceived ease of use has a significant relationship towards perceived usefulness and perceived usefulness mediates the relationship between perceived ease of use and intention to use investment account platform.

In the third chapter, the authors discuss the perspectives of enhancing Islamic Banking and Finance in Southeast Asia through the Application of Artificial Intelligence. They attempt to study the attitudes of Islamic banks' leadership in Southeast Asia in accepting artificial intelligence. While the leadership of Islamic banks shows their readiness towards accepting the technology's innovations and artificial intelligence, they are still tied down to the regulatory requirements, the readiness of their employees, acceptance of their shareholders, and awareness of their customers.

In the fourth chapter, the authors propose a benevolent Islamic loan known as Qard al-Hassan (Islamic interest-free loan), by using Fintech facility. The proposed loan SMEs Qard Al-Hasan Facility (SQAF) is designed to facilitate loans with a bit longer maturity than the SmartQard, as it is attempting to boost stronger businesses and startups. The payment and reimbursement are based on a digital system, that comprises the mobile payments, online payments, and in-store payments capabilities, offering solutions that are multi-country, multi-currency, and multi-sales channels.

The fifth chapter is dedicated to the study of the development of FinTech practices in Turkey and explores FinTech application in Islamic finance. The author assesses the viewpoints of the sector participants about Islamic finance and FinTech and discusses whether the share of Islamic finance in the sector can be increased by FinTech applications or not. Based on interviews with the participants from influential stakeholders operating in Turkey, results show that new technology products and services, such as peer-to-peer or new payment networks, open banking applications, digital currencies, blockchain-based practices, and artificial intelligence will dominate the banking sector, and these will change the way of doing business in the near future.

The second section, entitled "FinTech Risk Management and Regulation." Four chapters are included in this section (Chapter 6 to 9) dedicated to understanding the regulation and risk management in the finance industry with the disruption by FinTech.

In the sixth chapter, the author provides advanced quantitative risk management modeling techniques and simulation strategies that can be applied to equity trading portfolios. In this chapter, the author attempts to incorporate and compute the impact of asset liquidity trading risk into L-VaR models by explicitly integrating the impact of the time-volatility dimension of asset liquidity risk instead of the movements in the bid-ask spread. Using an extensive daily data of the GCC stock markets, the author examines different equity trading portfolios and determine the potential risk exposures and risk-budgeting allocations, with unlike correlation factors, under different illiquid and intricate market perspectives and with the imposition of operational constraints based on fundamental investment considerations. The proposed quantitative risk management techniques and optimization algorithms can have important uses and applications in expert systems, machine learning, smart financial functions, and financial technology (FinTech) in big data environments.

The seventh chapter intends to document the various ways that the nascent technology, blockchain, and other forms of distributed ledger technology can provide both increased and decreased risk as well as offer FinTech industries a fertile environment to pursue key technological advancements that can help shape almost every facet of the financial world. The author discusses blockchain technology as a source of both trustlessness and trust. This dichotomy represents the truly unique world that blockchain opens up within FinTech.

The eighth chapter explains the steps taken by Malaysia's financial regulators to deal with FinTech based companies. It provides an overview of FinTech regulations issued by the Bank Negara Malaysia and Securities Commission Malaysia. The authors also provide a critical review of regulations and propose solutions and recommendation to improve the FinTech ecosystem in Malaysia.

In the ninth chapter, the author discusses the Shariah issues of cryptocurrencies and study the risk associated with Bitcoin. The author examines the characteristics of a Valid cryptocurrency from the holders' and Shariah perspectives and discusses Shariah rules for dealing in Cryptocurrency. The author also investigates if Bitcoin fit the Shariah standards of valid currency. The author finds that dealing in Bitcoin is driven by reasons other than the use of regular currency, and hence, it is not within the boundaries of the acceptability needed to obtain the necessary Shariah recognition.

The third section, entitled "Financial Inclusion and Financial Stability in the Era of FinTech." Four chapters are included in this section (Chapter 10 to 13) dedicated to exploring the effect of FinTech on financial inclusion and financial stability.

The tenth chapter highlights the impact of FinTech adoption on the enhancement of financial inclusion. The authors discuss the theoretical framework of technological innovation adoption, including Innovation Diffusion Theory (IDT), Technology Acceptance Model (TAM), United Theory of Acceptance, and Use of Technology (UTUAT). The authors also examine the way of improving financial inclusion using digital channels.

The eleventh chapter aims to study dependence structure and risk spillover between Bitcoin, stock, and bond indexes, exchange rates, Gold and crude oil WTI futures contracts. Using a copula approach, the author finds significant and symmetric dependence structure between Bitcoin and WTI daily changes. To measure the contribution of the virtual market to systemic risk, the author uses dynamic VaR, CoVaR, and ΔCoVaR measures. The results show that after 2016, the virtual market sudden changes are more likely to raise the whole regular financial system losses, except for the energy market that exhibits positive spillover effects from the virtual system. The debt market appears without reaction in the face to Bitcoin price losses.

In the twelfth chapter, the authors study the Central Bank Digital Currency (CBDC) characteristics and its implications in a dual banking system. They investigate the issues of CBDC related to its issuance and design and the impact of CBDC on banking intermediation and financial stability. The authors also discuss the potential emergence of CBDC with a focus on its motivations and design, mainly the differences between CBDC and other money forms and private cryptocurrencies. Besides, the CBDC is examined in the view of Sharia, considering the principles of Islamic finance. The third section discusses the implications and challenges of CBDC on dual banking intermediation and financial stability.

The thirteenth chapter aims to analyze the impact of Fintech on economic performance and financial stability in MENA countries. By using data including Mobile Money, Digital Payment, Debit card, and Regulatory quality, the authors study the impact of Fintech on macroeconomic variables such as inflation rate, unemployment rate, investment, and financial freedom. The empirical results show that Fintech increases Inflation and decrease unemployment. Also, Fintech increases investment and financial freedom while it significantly decreases when the authors consider Political Instability.

I hope that this challenging book can help academics, professionals, researchers, investors, and regulators to better understand Islamic finance and financial stability in the era of FinTech.

Nader Naifar
Imam Mohammad Ibn Saudi Islamic University, Saudi Arabia & University of Sfax, Tunisia

Acknowledgment

I want to thank the authors and reviewers of each chapter for their time and efforts in contributing to this challenging book. Thanks to everyone on the editorial advisory board who helped me so much. Special thanks to the professor Mohammad Al-Suhaibani for his ongoing support and recommendations. I also specifically appreciate the continuous assistance of and Ms. Jan Travers (Director of Intellectual Property and Contracts at IGI Global).

Nader Naifar
Imam Mohammad Ibn Saudi Islamic University, Saudi Arabia & University of Sfax, Tunisia

Section 1

FinTech as a Distributive Technology for the Islamic Finance Industry

Chapter 1
Eliminating Trust Issues in Islamic Interbank Monetary System by Blockchain Technology

Muhammet Furkan Yavuz
Istanbul Sabahattin Zaim University, Turkey

Buerhan Saiti
Istanbul Sabahattin Zaim University, Turkey

ABSTRACT

In the literature, it is argued that there is an agency or incentive problem in the Mudarabah Interbank Instrument (MII), an instrument where the depositor is the rabbul-mal (capital provider or investor) while the counterparty is the mudarib or entrepreneur. It is to the receiving bank's advantage to 'declare' a lower profit rate. To solve this problem, the Malaysian Central Bank revised the rules by setting a minimum benchmark rate for the MII. This practice is quite similar to the fixed interest rate in conventional financial system which may trigger several Shariah issues. In this chapter, the authors argue that the blockchain technology is a better way to address the issue and propose and how it overcomes the issue in the Islamic interbank money market. As implication of the study, Islamic banks can start using it as a testing process for the future businesses, and in accordance with the analyzing test results, they can implement the system for every occasion.

DOI: 10.4018/978-1-7998-0039-2.ch001

INTRODUCTION

Banks need to hold liquidity (cash) for a given period for liquidity management or managing the asset and liability mismatch. To achieve this, banks borrow money from other banks via money markets. This incurs interest whereby the banks agree on a rate of interest depending on the maturity. This practice is prohibited in Islam.

In the case of Islamic Financial Institutions (IFIs), they collect deposits and raise funds from individuals or companies, and government bodies or private sectors, to finance the deficit. The deposits or liabilities of the bank are normally held on a short-term basis (Saiti et al., 2016). Furthermore, the money deposited in normal savings and current accounts can be withdrawn upon the customers' demand. On the other hand, the financing or receivables which are recognised as assets will normally be for a longer term. The question that arises in this regard is how IFIs can manage the duration gap between its liabilities and assets?

In order to address this important issue, IFIs adopt several Islamic contracts such as partnership based (like *Mudarabah* and *Musharakah*), sale-based (*Murabahah* and *Tawarruq*) and service-based contracts (for example, *wakalah*). In the case of partnership contracts, Islamic banks agree on a predetermined profit-sharing ratio. The bank that accepts the funds agrees to pay some of its profit from its investments to the investee bank. For example, the *Mudarabah* Interbank Instrument (MII) is an instrument where the depositor is the *rabbul-mal* (capital provider or investor) while the counterparty is the *mudarib* or entrepreneur. The profit ratio will be predetermined by both parties, while the investor will bear losses. The tenure of MII ranges from as short as overnight up to a year. On maturity, the principal plus profit will be paid to the investor.

Bacha (2008) argues that there is an agency or incentive problem in this structure as it is to the receiving bank's advantage to 'declare' a lower profit rate. To solve this problem, the Malaysian Central Bank (BNM) revised the rules by setting a minimum benchmark rate for the MII. With this revision, the minimum rate of return for the MII was set to equal the prevailing rate of the Government Investment Certificate (GIC) plus a spread of 0.5% (Bacha, 2008). The benchmark rate serves to ensure that only banks with reasonable rates of return participate in the MII. This approach reduces the uncertainty in the profit rate as it is calculated as follows:

1. The prevailing rate on the Government Investment Certificate (GIC) of the same tenor + 0.5% (annualised), if the declared profit is lower; or
2. The declared profit adjusted for PSR; if it is higher than the GIC + 0.5% annualised;

This practice is similar to the fixed interest rate in the conventional financial system, which may trigger several *Shariah* issues. For example, waqf is facing challenges in enhancing its governance structure to ensure Shariah compliance as well as economic efficiency. A potential alternative approach to address the Shariah compliance issues that arise from lending and borrowing in the Islamic interbank money market is blockchain technology. Abojeib and Habib (2019) examined the importance of such innovation in Islamic finance, particularly Islamic social finance. They argue that Islamic social finance is facing several challenges that could be solved by such innovations. In this chapter, we argue that blockchain technology is better able to address the issue of understating the profit or advantage to one party and propose how it overcomes the issue in the Islamic interbank money market. The remaining sections are organised as follows. Section 2 will explain blockchain technology, section 3 proposes how the blockchain technology overcomes the trust issue in the Islamic Interbank System and section 4 concludes the chapter.

Blockchain Technology

Crosby et al. (2016) explained that a blockchain is essentially a distributed database of records or public ledger of all transactions or digital events that have been implemented and shared among involved parties. Each transaction in the public ledger is verified by the consensus of a majority of the participants in the system. Once the information is entered, it can never be erased or destroyed. The blockchain contains a certain and verifiable record of every single transaction ever made. Bitcoin is a decentralised peer-to-peer digital currency and one of the more popular examples of blockchain technology. Zyskind and Nathan (2015) emphasised that third parties should not be trusted with personal and sensitive data as it could render a person or institution susceptible to attacks and misuse of data. Instead, users should own and control their data without compromising security or limiting the ability of companies and the authorities to provide personalised services.

Bitcoin is a system that could be highly useful in today's day and age (Bitcoin Wiki, 2018). As the name suggests, it is a chain of blocks that keep a record of the transactions of the system. It could also be termed ledgers. Every block contains the information of the preceding block and locks itself. After one block is closed, the upcoming block writes the preceding information. This process continues as new information is recorded and new blocks created, thereby constituting a chain.

One of the biggest concerns about this system is double-spending potential as the system is artificial. However, this clever system prevents this to happen. If someone has 1 million pieces of information on the system and wants to send it to another person on the system, he or she states a sending request which needs to be confirmed by the system's miners. When the transaction is complete, all the ledgers or blocks update themselves such that the sender has no information (blocks) and the receiver has 1 million pieces of information. In this system, the owner of the information is protected (Ray, 2018).

This explanation unveils the second unknown term, 'the miners'. In short, they are individuals who use their Central Processing Units (CPUs) to contribute to the system and accelerate the transaction time (Getting started with Bitcoin mining, 2018). They do this by connecting their hardware into the system. In a way, they constitute the physical element of the system without whom the system would not be able to operate on a global scale. When a send request is made, the transaction is encrypted and sent to the blockchain system. The miners' hardware is then used to solve the encrypted transaction's password using the power of the hash-rate. When the password is unlocked, the transaction happens. This is the confirmation phase of the transaction.

Miners are rewarded for their efforts by earning the blockchain's currency, which differs according to the blockchain system the miners are using. If it is Bitcoin's blockchain system, the reward is Bitcoin. If it is other crypto currency's blockchain, they are rewarded with the currency of the respective system. Miner's are rewarded based on the number of transactions they solve. The more encrypted transactions they solve, the more reward they earn. The rate of compensation changes, which means that profitability may also change (FAQ – Bitcoin, 2018).

This system is highly transparent. This is evidenced by the ability for everybody to see all transactions in the system; they are all public. Everyone has a unique code like IBAN but is more complex. Secondly, people need other people to be able to make a transaction. Lastly, everybody accepts the transaction so that double-spending or cheating can be prevented. In other words, the system is alive and evolves with its users. As such, the system is constantly updating itself with the transaction information of all the users, and everybody can see what is happening in the system.

As for the banks' transaction system, there is much ambiguity surrounding transactions. Recently, Iran declared that they left SWIFT as the US controls the entire system, and no other organisation is authorised to see the workings of the system. It is a system that lacks transparency. The US alone is in a position to allow or deny transactions. Given such limitations, we must question whether this system is suitable for a global money market.

Advantages and Disadvantages of Blockchain Technology

Morabito (2017) explains that the blockchain system subsides in a mentality of distributing transactional data into several nodes that are represented by computers. These nodes merge and act as a single chain of information. Businesses can benefit from this system in several ways, such as empowering users. It means that users can manage their information as part of the transaction. It offers durability, sustainability and reliability because the blockchain system cannot fail with a single mistake and does not require someone to fix the problem because the information is stored in every block. Also, among the advantages of not having a centralised computing system is that trust is cultivated by allowing users to view every transaction. The transactions cannot be changed. Hence, the sustainability of transactions is guaranteed. As for the drawbacks, the three main disadvantages are redundancy, signature verification and consensus mechanism.

The conventional banking system has its mechanism of verifying transactions. It differs from bank to bank, but the main logic is similar. They are the third party in the money transaction process. Whenever someone wants to send money to an another, they simply type the amount and send it to the receiver. The banks then approve the transaction and send it to the receiver account. The only validation mechanism is the bank. However, in blockchain, there are many validation mechanisms and all of them must approve the transaction. This situation comes up with a problem. It means that so much work has to be done. In addition to this, so much energy, electricity, consumption be needed. That means lots of work should be done for the same result. Also, it means that the whole system should update itself for only one transaction to be done. This infrastructure of blockchain deduces the redundancy of the system.

Secondly, every blockchain transaction must be digitally confirmed using a public-private cryptography scheme such as ECDSA (Elliptic Curve Digital Signature Algorithm). Confirming these transactions is complex, which results in bottlenecks in the system. In contrast, in centralised databases such as banks, once a connection has been established, there is no need to individually verify every request unless any alarms are triggered. The complexity of blockchain verification could be regarded as a disadvantage compared to the bank's signature system. In a distributed database or distributed ledger system like blockchain, effort must be expended in ensuring that nodes in the network reach consensus. Nevertheless, Iansiti and Lakhani (2017) argue that the blockchain technology can reduce the cost of transactions if it is adopted widely and reshape the economy.

To sum up, blockchain has advantages and disadvantages. Morabito (2017) explains that "blockchain governance has tremendous transformative potential for our societies". However, the risks and benefits associated with its practical applications, must be cautiously evaluated, avoiding unrealistic hopes, as well as the drawbacks of a technocratic way of thinking. If correctly managed, decentralised government services through blockchain are promising and desirable since it could support more transparent public administration. The decentralisation of governance through open, distributed blockchain like Bitcoin, nevertheless, presents severe risks and drawbacks, which offset the benefits. While initially designed as disintermediation tools, fully distributed blockchain is categorised by a huge amount of third parties and money-making businesses contributing intermediation services, with strong asymmetries of information and power between developers and users.

The free nature of existing distribution networks calls into question factors such as digital divide, unaccountable power of core developers, and lack of clearness in the decision-making process, thus making some blockchain advocates' expectations overestimated and unrealistic. Hence, there is cause to investigate the role of blockchain-based governance as a large catalyst of individual power in a complete sense. Furthermore, the promise of empowering individuals is likely to stay unfulfilled due to the prevailing role of markets and the tentative verification systems of fully distributed blockchain. On the other hand, the process of undermining public institutions, the superiority of economics over politics, and the change of citizens into custumers with the promise of more autonomy, effectiveness, and fairness may conceal yet an additional dangerous process of the corporatisation of politics, which perpetually empowers markets to the disadvantage of citizens. Far from being innovative, such transfer of power from the public to the private sector has been ongoing in different forms for decades, with vast social and economic costs. For instance, the steps necessary to complete a securities trade are the same today as they were 50 years ago; computers only improved the trading speed. In contrast, blockchain primarily reorganises the operations of financial transactions in ways that were not envisioned just a few years ago.

It will take time for institutions to completely account for the profits and risks that blockchain-based governance offers. Some organisations cannot afford to wait for total clearness as the technology evolves and is deployed by their competitors. The swiftness of innovation will accelerate as technology, and financial services continue to come together, and success will repeatedly be determined by the ability to take sensible action founded on knowledgeable experience. Consequently, it is crucial for institutions to vigorously partake in this cycle of innovation and disruption to guarantee that they comprehend how technology is dynamically influencing the sector and that they are well-positioned to recognise and track opportunities as it evolves. Equally, it will be essential to realise that working to build up a perfect solution will be pointless if the challenge changes prior to the implementation of a suitable solution.

In the nearest future, we predict a reasonable multitude of changes and developments from Blockchain-based governance solutions. At the moment, the dawn of the blockchain revolution produces challenges that lie ahead for financial services that will require new and innovative thinking. Blockchain is a radical technological innovation that offers a great amount of potential and opportunities to organisations. Success will depend on the risks that firms are ready to take as well as on the speed of their actions and decisions. It becomes apparent that the most successful firms will be those that will be able to outperform and distinguish among competitors during this blockchain revolution."

Working System of Blockchain Technology

Blockchain offers numerous benefits such as transparency, efficiency, fast transactions, solid data storage and easy access to data. The infrastructure of blockchain technology allows all information to be kept by every member of the system and prevents anyone from changing the data. Ensuring the safety of data is the most advanced feature of blockchain. On the other hand, it is an open source technology, which means anyone can contribute to the system. Any person or corporation can develop a solution to make the blockchain system better. It may seem confusing that while everyone can enhance the system, they cannot ruin the information. This is an appealing feature. Blockchain lets everyone detect every transaction and at the same time, prevents them from fraud.

This being the case, blockchain is becoming more popular in every sector for different purposes. Recently, French President Emmanuel Macron proposed that the European Union use blockchain technology for agriculture so that we could track every step of the supply chain and keep up with bigger rivals (Paluch, 2018). This will allow them to track the transactions from raw materials to the end products. By giving codes to every starting block, it can be tracked similar to barcoding products. This offers the ability to analyse the productivity of raw materials. By tracking from the very beginning of the raw materials, they can compute their productivity and come up with solutions to make more efficient end products. It would allow tracking products to control the supply chain and produce more efficient products.

Blockchain leading area of application is finance. While it promises many opportunities, the main actors in finance (i.e. banks), should take advantage of blockchain. Islamic banks should invest more in this area. Without interest rate, they can reach the masses by using blockchain whole also using it as a platform to develop new products. Supporting such innovation would reflect positively in Islamic banks as being open-minded to new technologies.

Even though blockchain is readily associated with Bitcoin, its potential exceeds far beyond cryptocurrency. Blockchain promises secure transactions in a virtual world. Utilising this opportunity will attract the attention of individual customers and corporations. Using an uninterruptible system will provide continuous service for customers, unlike Visa and Mastercard, which suffered service interruption in 2018 (Paluch, 2018). Transactions controlled by a single authority may cause system failure for payments to their customers. With the advanced technology of blockchain, this type of outage cannot occur because of a distributed verification system. Each participant of the system can act as an authority to verify the transaction, and with the help of that system always keep functioning.

This chapter does not advocate that Islamic banks try to hide their real investment profit from their customers or lenders. Rather, it emphasises eliminating misleading investment information. Sharing every outcome of the investment will certainly increase the trust of customers. Shariah compliant banks should prioritise this delicate issue. As mentioned earlier, banks do not have to share their information with everyone. In dealing with sensitive business about money and money derivatives, they certainly want to keep secret information to themselves. Like any other business, banks also have confidential business information about how they make a profit.

A private blockchain system could be ideal for classified transactions. Only certain members can follow the processes during the investment. No one will be able to intervene in the process. Establishing a digital wallet for each party and naming each investment means the process is classified while also being able to be tracked. Some may argue that, if banks create this system, it would be anonymous and identifying which wallet belongs to whom is not possible. However, in a private blockchain system, banks can declare which wallet belongs to them and which wallet belongs to their investments. On the other hand, when they want to create a new wallet for themselves and their customers, they can inform the other parties, wait for the approval in order to prevent any misunderstanding, and then start the investment process. If anyone creates a new wallet, it can be detected because every member knows the number of wallets of the system. By doing so, every party would have knowledge of which wallet belongs to which bank and investment.

Figure 1. Public and private blockchain network
Source: Mobiloitte Blog (2018)

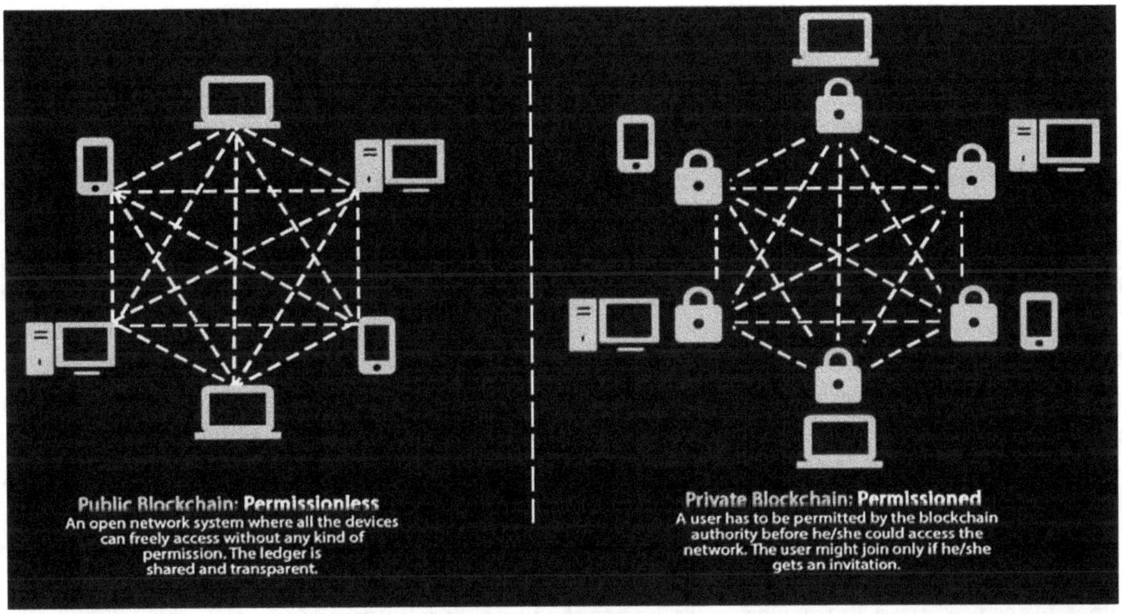

There is no denying that the public blockchain system has some adverse characteristics. Dedicated software developers such as the Lightning Network team are trying their best to minimise these features. The focus should be on the capacity of eliminating trust issues that may occur in transactions like the Islamic interbank lending processes. By using private blockchain, Islamic banks can avoid the unfavourable elements of the blockchain system while retaining information specific to customers. As shown in Figure 1, only certain members can participate in the system and execute their job. It is a restricted area for any outsider. With a limited number of participants, the system will surely work more efficient compared to the public blockchain, and reduced likelihood of system failure would mean that the system functions more efficiently.

Applying Blockchain Technology in the Islamic Interbank System

Swan (2015) emphasises that blockchain's main area of application is integrating cryptocurrencies to businesses due to its efficiency. According to Swan (2015), Ripple Lab is seizing the blockchain technology and reinventing the banking system by giving opportunities to conventional financial institutions to establish businesses more efficiently. Reinventing the banking system is a bold standpoint, but she supports her idea with the explanation that on the Ripple network, payments can be made through banks bilaterally without an intermediary. Also, Ripple is developing a smart contract system to be used on blockchain. It is safe to say that banks realised the benefits of the blockchain system and started to invest in this area. For example, in Turkey, Akbank started to use Ripple's network (Ripple, 2019). Similarly, JP Morgan has established its cryptocurrency to demonstrate its efficiency starting with selected industrial customers (Julia Horowitz, 2017). JP Morgan's cryptocurrency is planned to work as a stable currency. There will be no fluctuations in the price.

Nakamoto (2008) also proposed a system for electronic transactions without relying on trust. He started with the usual framework of coins made from digital signatures, which provides strong control of ownership, but is incomplete without a way to prevent double-spending. To solve this, they suggested a peer-to-peer network using proof-of-work to record a public history of transactions that quickly becomes computationally impractical for an attacker to change if honest nodes control a majority of CPU power.

Similarly, Shariah compliant banks' income mentality is mostly based on profit sharing. This applies to borrowing and lending cash between banks. In the Islamic perspective, corporations, banks or individuals cannot charge the other parties a fixed income rate. The payback should at least be the same amount unless loss occurs. Nevertheless, this could be manipulated if Islamic banks become consumed by making a profit.

As mentioned earlier, banks borrow money from other banks to meet their cash needs. Islamic banks have a system that differs from conventional banks. They agree on a profit-sharing rate from a certain investment. The profit sharing ratio may differ accordingly to investment type, investment risks and capital. This may seem a burden to the borrower bank, which can mislead the outcome of the investment and can pay less profit to the other bank by hiding the real return of the investment. It is easy to forge a document and hide the real results. Parties may also declare no-profit and pay only the capital. In order to prevent this situation, banks can use a shared, transparent system to remunerate each party. The blockchain system would suit this purpose, as all transactions are transparent.

To clarify how it could be done, in Figure 2, Bank A and Bank B make a deal on investment and investment's profit sharing. Lender Bank A will send the lending amount from its wallet to Borrower Bank B's wallet. The amount will be known. Then Borrower Bank B will make its investment and send it to the investment wallet. In that stage, a transaction number (TX number) will be created automatically. By giving the code to the Lender Bank A, they will be able to detect if the right amount of money was sent to the investment wallet. They also can see Borrower Bank B's wallet account before and after the investment. After the investment is completed, the sum will be resent to Borrower Bank B's wallet. Lender Bank A is still able to follow all these processes and will have information about how much profit was made as a result of the investment. When the amount is sent to Borrower Bank B's wallet, Lender Bank A can demand its capital and profit share. If Borrower Bank B sends less money to Lender Bank A, Lender Bank A can demand its real share based on the evidence gleaned from tracking every step of the investment and know how much profit resulted from the investment.

Step 1: Lender Bank A sends money to Borrower Bank B.
Step 2: Bank B invests the amount and Transaction number (Tx number) generated.
Step 3: Generated Tx number is shared with Bank A to watch the process.
Step 4: Investment's outcome collects and Bank A can detect how much profit was made by tracking the Tx number of the investment and demands their profit share.
Step 5: Main capital and profit share sent to Bank A.

With the use of blockchain, banks, especially Shariah compliant ones, have a transparent and trustworthy system. This would cultivate trus, which would attract more participation and generate more Islamic capital. Unless banks prove their trustworthiness, they will lose customers, especially given the recent global financial crises. This is particularly true for emerging markets which entail greater levels of risk. Transparency and trust are core characteristics of banks and the capital market. If capital is to growing, Islamic banks need to keep growing as well.

Figure 2. Proposed blockchain system in the Islamic interbank money market

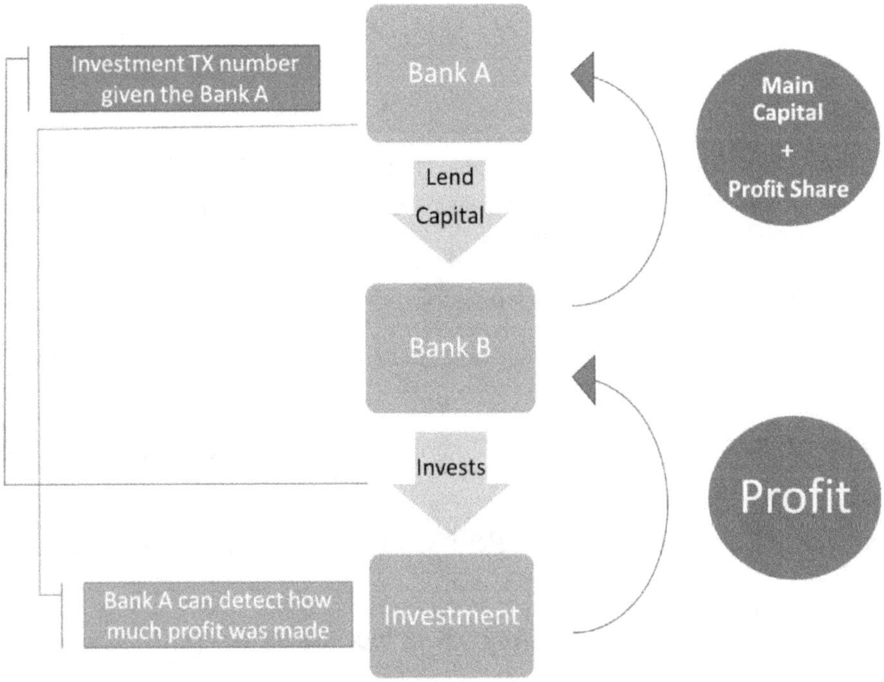

CONCLUSION

When blockchain is articulated, people start to imagine a public system whereby everyone can see everything users do. Blockchain does not have to be public. There is no obligatory use of a public blockchain. Banks can create a private blockchain to eliminate the trust issues about profit sharing. The lender can see how much profit the borrower bank made from the money they lent them. No third party should be involved. From the viewpoint of audit companies, it would be much easier to determine current account balances and transactions between parties. There would be no need for copious documents to show a single transaction. Just a simple transaction code would help auditors track and control the cash flow. From that perspective, blockchain can save the environment by decreasing the need for paper while also easing several job functions.

Islamic banks should consider using the blockchain system to remove suspicion from bank and financing operations. Exploiting the system promises several positive outcomes. Islamic banks can start using it to test the process of future business and develop products suitable for an evolving business landscape.

REFERENCES

Abojeib, M., & Habib, F. (2019). Blockchain for Islamic Social Responsibility Institutions. In *FinTech as a Disruptive Technology for Financial Institutions* (pp. 221–240). IGI Global. doi:10.4018/978-1-5225-7805-5.ch010

Bacha, O. I. (2008). The Islamic interbank money market and a dual banking system: The Malaysian experience. *International Journal of Islamic and Middle Eastern Finance and Management, 1*(3), 210–226. doi:10.1108/17538390810901140

Bitcoin Wiki. (2018). Retrieved from https://en.bitcoin.it/wiki/Main_Page

Crosby, M., Pattanayak, P., Verma, S., & Kalyanaraman, V. (2016). Blockchain technology: Beyond bitcoin. *Applied Innovation, 2*(6-10), 71.

FAQ - Bitcoin. (2018). Retrieved from https://bitcoin.org/en/faq#what-about-bitcoin-and-consumer-protection

Getting started with Bitcoin mining. (2018). Retrieved from https://www.bitcoinmining.com/getting-started/

Iansiti, M., & Lakhani, K. R. (2017). The truth about blockchain. *Harvard Business Review, 95*(1), 118–127.

Julia Horowitz, C. (2017). *JPMorgan's move into crypto puts the rest of the industry on notice.* Retrieved from https://edition.cnn.com/2019/02/19/business/jpmorgan-jpm-coin-banks-blockchain/index.html

Mobiloitte Blog. (2018). *Public Vs Private Blockchain: What's Right For your Business?* Retrieved from https://www.mobiloitte.com/blog/public-vs-private-blockchain-whats-right-for-your-business/

Morabito, V. (2017). *Business innovation through blockchain.* Cham: Springer International Publishing. doi:10.1007/978-3-319-48478-5

Nakamoto, S. (2008). *Bitcoin: A peer-to-peer electronic cash system.* Available at: https://bitcoin.org/bitcoin.pdf

Paluch, D. (2018). *CryptoMonday: Russia, Ukraine, France, And Thailand | Blockchain24.co.* Retrieved from https://www.blockchain24.co/cryptomonday-russia-ukraine-france-and-thailand/

Ray, S. (2018). Blockchains: The Technology of Transactions – Towards Data Science. *Towards Data Science.* Available at: https://towardsdatascience.com/blockchains-the-technology-of-transactions-9d40e8e41216

Ripple. (2019). *Solutions to Send Money Globally, Using Blockchain Technology.* Retrieved from https://ripple.com/ripplenet/

Saiti, B., Hasan, A., & Ali, E. R. A. E. (2016). Islamic interbank money market: Contracts, instruments and their pricing. In *Islamic Capital Markets* (pp. 67–100). Cham: Palgrave Macmillan. doi:10.1007/978-3-319-33991-7_5

Swan, M. (2015). *Blockchain: Blueprint for a new economy*. O'Reilly Media, Inc.

Zyskind, G., & Nathan, O. (2015, May). Decentralizing privacy: Using blockchain to protect personal data. In *2015 IEEE Security and Privacy Workshops* (pp. 180-184). IEEE.

Chapter 2
Adoption of Financial Technology in Islamic Crowd-Funding:
Predicting Small and Medium-Sized Enterprises' Intention to Use the Investment Account Platform

Maizaitulaidawati Md Husin
https://orcid.org/0000-0002-2789-8274
Azman Hashim International Business School, Universiti Teknologi Malaysia, Malaysia

Razali Haron
IIUM Institute of Islamic Banking and Finance, IIUM Institute of Islamic Banking and Finance, Malaysia

Shahab Aziz
Azman Hashim International Business School, Universiti Teknologi Malaysia, Malaysia

ABSTRACT

The purpose of this chapter is to examine the factors that influence small and medium-sized enterprises' (SMEs) intentions to use the investment account platform (IAP) based on technology acceptance model (TAM). The central hypothesis for this chapter was that SMEs' intentions to use IAP were a result of perceived usefulness and perceived ease of use. This chapter also suggested that perceived ease of use and intention was mediated by perceived usefulness of the IAP. Using primary data collection method, 163 questionnaires were collected from SMEs in Kuala Lumpur, Malaysia using the purposive sampling technique. The data were analysed using SPSS and SmartPLS. The chapter found that perceived ease of use had significant influences on SMEs intention to use the IAP while perceived ease of use significantly affected perceived usefulness and the relationship between perceived ease of use and intention was mediated by perceived usefulness of the IAP. The results of this chapter suggested strategies to promote the platform as a fund seeking platform for SMEs.

DOI: 10.4018/978-1-7998-0039-2.ch002

INTRODUCTION

Financial technology (Fintech) is a combination of an innovative business model and technology solution in facilitating daily financial services. Fintech is a complex ecosystem that covers a large scope of techniques from data security to financial service deliveries (Gai, Qiu, & Sun, 2017; PwC, 2016). The emergence of Fintech has brought about tremendous development in the digital economy, especially in China, India, the United Kingdom, Brazil, and Australia (EY, 2017). The common products of Fintech that include e-wallet, crypto-currency, Peer-to-Peer (P2P) financing, crowd-funding, and Insurtech have become major financial alternatives for consumers and businesses (Capgemini, LinkedIn, & Efma, 2018; Jin, Seong, & Khin, 2019). As of May 2018, global investment in Fintech companies had hit US$57.9 billion, and this number is expected to increase annually (KPMG, 2018).

In the context of Islamic finance, Fintech is believed to offer various advantages to the industry namely increased efficiency, reduced costs and a wider range of products (Bakar & Rosbi, 2018; PwC, 2016). Fintech can also attract more customers and help the Islamic finance industry become more competitive against its conventional counterpart (Reuters, 2018). According to EY (2017) and PwC (2016), out of the four financial sectors that are likely to be the most disrupted by Fintech over the next five years are consumer banking, fund and transfer payments, investment and wealth management, and also small and medium-sized enterprises' (SMEs) financing.

In Malaysia, the Islamic crowdfunding platforms known as Investment Account Platform (IAP) has been initiated with an aim to provide investors the opportunity to invest and share the profits from Shariah-compliant investment activities (Mohamed Asmy & Hassanudin, 2017). In addition, with the elements of crowd-funding and microfinancing, the introduction of the IAP enables SMEs to get their capital in a shorter time with more simple terms and conditions, and also with shorter loan periods (Reuters, 2014; SME, 2016a). However, despite various advantages the IAP may offer, almost 60 per cent of SMEs are not aware of the availability of Islamic business financing facilities and are also still adopting conventional financing (Zahid, 2018). According to SME (2016), there is an estimated financing gap of RM21.8 billion that can potentially be met by alternative financing, including the IAP. The gap could exist due to little understanding and awareness among the SMEs on the development of Fintech (Ghazali & Yasuoka, 2018). Therefore, before further efforts are taken to promote and expand the use of the IAP platform as an alternative financing for SMEs, it is essential to explore and identify what may actually drive the SMEs' intention to use the platform. Utilising the technology acceptance model, the central hypothesis for this paper is that the SMEs' intention to use the IAP is a result of perceived usefulness towards participation in the IAP. In this paper, subjective norm, experience, and voluntariness are integrated into the model.

The remainder of this chapter is organized as follows: literature review and hypothesis development were presented in the next section. Thereafter, the theoretical framework is presented. Subsequently, methodology section is presented which provide details of the procedure, sample, and measures of the empirical study, followed by the study's results. This paper concludes with a discussion of the implications of the findings and by offering directions for further research.

LITERATURE REVIEW

Small and Medium Enterprises (SMEs) in Malaysia

As with any other countries, Malaysia recognises the important role of SMEs as an economic agent. SMEs in Malaysia are governed by the SME Corporation of Malaysia. As of 2017, SMEs accounted for 98.5 per cent of the country's total registered companies and 65.3 per cent of the workforce in the private sector. SMEs are also the engine of economic growth, with the contribution of 36.6 per cent of country gross domestic product (GDP) as of December 2016. In addition to that, SMEs also contributed to the increasing employment rate in the country. In 2015, SME employment grew by 5.6 per cent to 6.6 million workers compared with the employment growth of large firms of 3.4 per cent. As a result of the higher employment growth of SMEs versus large firms, the percentage share of employment by SMEs to total employment increased from 57.5 per cent in 2013 to 65.5 per cent in 2015 (SME, 2016b). In terms of location, SMEs are mostly concentrated in Selangor (19.8 per cent) and Kuala Lumpur (14.7 per cent), followed by Johor (10.8 per cent) (SME Corporation, 2017a).

SMEs are divided into two broad industries: 1) manufacturing, 2) services and others. Companies in manufacturing with 5 to less than 75 employees and recorded sales turnover between RM300 thousand to less than RM15 million are considered as a small enterprise while companies with 75 to and less than 200 employees and sales turnover of 15 million to 50 million are considered as a medium enterprise. In services and other industries, companies with a number of employees between 5 to less than 30 with sales turnover between RM300 thousand to less than RM3 million are considered as a small enterprise, whereas companies with sales turnover between RM3 to less than RM20 million and from 30 to less than 75 employees are considered as a medium enterprise (Auzzir, Haigh, & Amaratunga, 2018; SME Corporation, 2016). Table 1 below shows the detailed definition of SMEs by category:

Malaysian government has placed a high priority to SME development. SME policy framework, future development plan and various initiatives have been introduced to bring the industry forward. Over the last decade, SME and entrepreneurship development have emerged as a national agenda following the setting up of the National SME Development Council (NSDC). Since its inception in 2004, NSDC has continued to steer SME development in Malaysia by setting the strategic direction and formulating policies to promote the growth of SMEs across all economic sectors. As the highest policy making body, the Council has been crucial in promoting a more holistic and coordinated approach in SME development. Various activities have been conducted by NSDC including developing SME database and statistics,

Table 1. Detailed definition of SMEs

Size	Small		Medium	
	Sales Turnover	Employees	Sales Turnover	Employees
Manufacturing	RM300,000 to less than 15 million	5 to less than 75 employees	RM15 million to less than 50 million	75 to less than 200 employees
Services & other	RM300,000 to less than 3 million	5 to less than 30 employees	RM3 million to less than 20 million	30 to less than 75 employees

Source: SME Corporation (2017b)

monitoring and analysing SME performance to facilitate policy formulation, streamlining dissemination of information on SMEs, developing the SME financial infrastructure and endorsing the formulation of an SME Masterplan (SME, 2016b).

Financial Technology and Islamic Crowdfunding Platforms for SMEs

Financial technology (Fintech) is the latest technology and innovation that aims to contend the conventional financial approaches in the delivery of financial services. According to Kpmg (2018, pp.57), Fintech refers to "businesses that are using technology to operate outside of traditional financial services business models to change how financial services are offered". In other words, Fintech applies the use of information technology with other financial services. The applicability of Fintech is able to improve the performance of financial services in the country (T. Lee & Kim, 2015). According to Lacasse et al. (2016), Hong Kong has the highest adoption rate of Fintech (29.1 per cent), followed by the United States (16.5 per cent), Singapore (14.7 per cent), the UK (14.3 per cent), Australia (13 per cent) and Canada (8.2 per cent). Other than that, Islamic Fintech is also growing steadily around the globe. Malaysia, Indonesia, the GCC, the US, the UK and Germany are among countries with growing Islamic Fintech (Maierbrugger, 2018).

Islamic crowdfunding is one of the elements in Islamic Fintech. According to Islamic Financial Services Board (2017), crowdfunding brings the Internet platform to the financial industry to connect fund seekers and fund providers (investors) without the intermediation of a bank. The main focus of crowdfunding is to gather funds from a crowd in order to finance a particular project or venture of SMEs (Alonso, 2015). There's two aspects that makes a crowdfunding platform Islamic; the compliance and the structure (Karim, 2016). In terms of compliance, Achsien and Purnamasari (2016) stated that the projects listed in Islamic crowdfunding must be invested in halal-related projects only and are free from *riba* (interest), *maysir* (gambling), and *gharar* (speculation). In addition to that, Wahjono et al. (2015), Achsien and Purnamasari (2016), and Saiti et al. (2018) indicated that several parties must be involved in the Islamic crowdfunding project including project initiator, potential funders, crowdfunding operator, trustee, and Shariah Supervisory Boards. In terms of structure, there are several Islamic based-crowdfunding structures that have been introduced in the market. For example, Saiti et al. (2018) presented the *salam*-based crowdfunding structure for financing agricultural activities. According to them, *salam*-based crowdfunding structure offers various advantages including risk sharing, possibility to generate a large sum of capital, higher dividends, and minimum regulatory requirements. Aqidah, Mohd, and Palil (2016) introduced *waqf*-based crowdfunding as a collaborative fundraising tool for Islamic crowdfunding. Earlier, Lutfi and Ismail (2016) presented the *sadaqah*-based crowdfunding model for entrepreneurs using the *qard al-hasan* contract. In addition to that, there are several other Islamic crowdfunding structures that have been initiated including *zakat*-based, *infaq-sadaqah-waqf*-based, *qard-al-hasan*-based, *syirkah*-based (*mudharabah* and *musyarakah*), and lending-based (*murabaha*, *ijarah*, and *istisna*) (Achsien & Purnamasari, 2016).

The Advantages and Challenges of Crowdfunding Financing for SMEs

Crowdfunding offers various advantages to SMEs. According to De Buysere et al. (2012), the main advantage of crowdfunding is that the investors, who invest a specific amount of money for a particular project, are also ambassadors of the project they support. It is good marketing for the SMEs as the investors are able to help in promoting the project to their own networks. Crowdfunding also offers flexibility in a way that it allows investors to join the business venture with just a minimum amount of investment (Bloomio, n.d.). With the help of crowdfunding, SMEs are no longer required to go through the hurdles of applying for traditional loan from banking institutions, which will subsequently reduce cost and time spent on these activities. Furthermore, this will reduce the funding gap for SMEs (Association of Southeast Asian Nations (ASEAN), 2017). In addition to that, the concept of crowdfunding, which allows investors to invest their money in the company of choice, is able to decrease the cost of product development and pre-marketing, while at the same time, generates revenue before production, and therefore provides SMEs with a positive cash flow prior to product launching (De Buysere et al., 2012).

While crowdfunding is rapidly bringing the physical and digital worlds closer, SMEs face several challenges and threats such as lack of information technology (IT) security and compatibility, inadequate infrastructure, expertise insufficiency, and unsupportive government regulations (ASEAN, 2017; Capgemini et al., 2018; KPMG, 2017; Padmanaban & Soo, 2016). According to the Association of Southeast Asian Nations (ASEAN) (2017), the gap between regulatory frameworks and the advancement of digital economy is one of the major challenges to be addressed, especially in ASEAN countries. Therefore, in order to further boost the SME industry, regulators and industry players need to work towards addressing the challenges.

Technology in Fintech

Fintech brings about a new paradigm in which information technology drives innovation in the financial industry. The enabler in Fintech development is the use of technology and infrastructure. According to Life.SREDA (2015), the application programming interface (API) technology has been extensively used by start-ups across the world. API is a critical technology that offers application integration between platforms, innovation as well as client connectivity. According to Hines (2018), API is the latest evolution in integration technologies, enabling fast performance, reliability, and reuse of components that can be frequently and easily managed and updated. With the use of API, Fintech start-ups are able to extend their business model with specific banking services such as credit, payments, cards, and escrow accounts. Other than API, several other technologies are also associated with Fintech. Among them are backend as a service (BaaS-platform), blockchain, augmented reality (AR), and artificial intelligence (AI).

BaaS-platform is an approach for providing web and mobile app developers with a way to connect their applications to backend cloud storage and processing (Lane, 2013). The advantages of BaaS-platform are that it is able to provide common features such as user management, push notifications, social networking integration, and other features that mobile users demand from their apps these days. With the present emergence of mobile apps, BaaS-platform is able to help Fintech start-ups to expand their business and market their service not only to the local market but to other countries as well. Blockchain is another technology in the Fintech wave. It is a distributed digital ledger that is capable of combining a number of mathematical, cryptographic, and economic principles in order to maintain a database while continuously recording and documenting every and each transaction that occurs across a peer-to-peer network (PricewaterhouseCoopers (PwC), 2016). In other words, blockchain is a shared list of continually updated transactions, which allows multiple participants to maintain a database without the need for third party validation or reconciliation (Padmanaban & Soo, 2016). The technology behind blockchain eliminates the validation and verification friction for transactions associated with a centralised system, allowing for a safer, simpler, and faster exchange of digitally represented assets. For Fintech start-ups, including SMEs, blockchain is expected to become the basis for smart contracts in a way that automated processes are enforced without human intervention.

Several other technologies such as AR and AI also play a big role in supporting Fintech start-ups. AR is a new technology that involves the overlay of computer graphics in the real world, whereas AI refers to the technology used by computer systems to perform tasks that traditionally require human intelligence (Financial Stability Board, 2017; Silva & Laboratório, 2003). The applicability of both of these technologies is able to transform Fintech start-ups to achieve the status quo.

Background of the Malaysia Context

Malaysia is a Southeast Asian country occupying parts of the Malay Peninsula and the island of Borneo, which comprises 13 states and 3 federal states. Since gaining its independence back in 1957, Malaysia has successfully diversified its economy from agriculture and commodity-based to manufacturing and services sectors. Gross domestic product of the country increased from 4.1 per cent in Q1 2016 to 5.4 per cent in Q1 2018, with private consumption remaining as the main contributor to growth (World Bank Group, 2018). Malaysia is categorised as one of the most open economies in the world and is on track to achieve its transition from an upper middle-income economy to a high-income economy. In year 2019, the government aims to have more stable employment and wage growth, conducive financing conditions and benign inflation to support private consumption, which was forecasted to expand by 6.8 per cent (PwC, 2019). In addition, to support responsible innovation and economic development in the financial sector, the Malaysian government has been supportive of technological innovation including accelerating Fintech growth (Capgemini et al., 2018; ICLG, 2018).

The Inside Story of Financial Technology in Malaysia

To accelerate the Fintech growth, several initiatives have been taken by the Securities Commission Malaysia or SCM (a statutory body entrusted with the responsibility of regulating and systematically developing the capital markets in Malaysia). SCM's responsibilities include facilitating peer-to-peer (P2P) lending, assisting equity crowdfunding, and launching digital-free trade zones to help local SMEs get into cross-border trade by leveraging on technology (International Comparative Legal Guides (ICLG), 2018). Furthermore, Malaysia also allows foreign Fintech companies, namely Alipay and Telenor, to set up partnerships in the country to facilitate onshore and cross-border payments (ICLG, 2018). In addition to that, earlier in October 2016, Bank Negara Malaysia, the Central Bank of Malaysia, has introduced a financial technology regulatory sandbox framework. The framework is presented with the aim of enabling the innovation of Fintech to be deployed and tested in the country in a live environment, within specified parameters and time frames (Central Bank of Malaysia, 2016). The sandbox framework received high attention from the financial institutions in Malaysia. Maybank, the largest bank in Malaysia with branches overseas, launched its Maybank sandbox in June 2017, offering its customers a real banking API to connect and make use of existing banking functions (ICLG, 2018). The efforts in accelerating Fintech do not stop there. In November 2018, SCM also approved the first robo-advisor for the Malaysian market. Named as ERAA (Economic Regime-based Asset Allocation), it is a digital investment manager that works based on data, which is able to imitate the work of human portfolio managers to plan investors' portfolio investments. The robo-advisor is able to reduce the costs of human labour while still offering personalised portfolios, and can usually be accessed as long as one has Internet connection (Pikri, 2018). All the above initiatives have created awareness on the importance of Fintech for making business processes more efficient and effective.

Bank Negara Malaysia also ensure SMEs are not left behind and immerse in the advancement of fintech. In February 2016, an Islamic crowdfunding platform known as Investment Account Platform (IAP) has been initiated. The IAP formulate the efficiency of technology to channel funds from investors to viable economic ventures. The platform also targets ventures which include those from SMEs and others in innovative and new growth areas, and aims to provide investors the opportunity to invest in and shares the profits from Shariah-compliant investment activities (Mohamed Asmy & Hassanudin, 2017). With the assistance of crowd-funding and microfinancing elements, the introduction of the IAP enables SMEs to get their capital in a shorter time with more simple terms and conditions, and with shorter loan periods (Reuters, 2014; SME, 2016a). With a minimum requirement for fundraising of RM500,000, this initiative is expected to encourage the development of SMEs, which will, in the long run, positively affecting the economy (M. A. Aziz & Che Wan, 2016). In short, the establishment of IAP is to offer ventures including alternative ways for SMEs to get funding through a Fintech platform.

The Technology Acceptance Model

The technology acceptance model (TAM) developed by Fred Davis is one of the most important theories in the field of technology acceptance (Granic & Marangunic, 2015). TAM was adapted from two main theories in the field of psychology namely theory of reasoned action (TRA) and the theory of planned behaviour (TPB). Both of these theories link one's beliefs and behaviour. Specifically, TRA is a theory indicating both attitude and subjective norm will influence intention, which in turn influences behaviour (Ajzen & Fishbein, 1980). An additional variable known as perceived behavioural control has been introduced by Ajzen (1991) to the theory to account for behaviours that are not under complete control. Both of the theories has been widely applied in technology-related studies (Chu & Chen, 2016; Gamal Aboelmaged, 2010; Hassan, Iqbal, & Iqbal, 2018; Mishra, Akman, & Mishra, 2014; Moore & Benbasat, 1996; Yousafzai, Foxall, & Pallister, 2010). For example, Yousafzai et al. (2010) used TRA in predicting consumers' behaviour in the context of Internet banking while Chu & Chen (2016) investigated e-learning technology adoption by extending TPB with another variable. In addition to that, Gamal Aboelmaged (2010) utilised TPB to predict e-procurement adoption in the United Arab Emirates. In recent studies by Hassan et al. (2018), they examined the factors that affect the adoption of internet banking in Pakistan through the theoretical lenses of two theories including TAM and TPB.

In order to develop a reliable model that could predict the actual use of any specific technology, Fred Davis adapted the TRA and TPB and proposed the TAM (Granic & Marangunic, 2015). Based on TAM, behaviour (actual technology use) is determined by one's intention, and the intention can be predicted by two primary determinants perceived usefulness (PU) and perceived ease of use (PEOU). While perceived usefulness is defined as the degree to which a person believes that using a particular system will enhance his or her job performance, perceived ease of use refers to the degree to which the person believes that using the system will be free of effort (Davis, 1989). Further, technology adoption intention refers the degree of willingness to use technology continuously (Davis, Bagozzi, & Warshaw,

1989). In the context of understanding technology-related behavior, TAM was found to be superior than TRA and TPB (Yousafzai et al., 2010) and the main reason it was adapted in this paper. The TAM is illustrated in Figure 1.

Due to the applicability of TAM to predict technology acceptance's behaviour and its usefulness in identifying factors in determining behavioural intentions, this theory has been applied extensively in various research papers on intention-related research including on financial technology (Alaeddin & Altounjy, 2018; Cham, Low, Lim, Aye, & Raymond, 2018; S. Y. Lee & Park, 2016; Lou & Li, 2017; Mohamed Asmy & Hassanudin, 2017). For example, Alaeddin & Altounjy (2018) investigated the factors affecting Malaysian Generation Z's attitude and intention to use cryptocurrency in their financial decisions while Lee & Park (2016) explore the factors that affect the intention to use mobile payment services. In addition to that, Lou & Li (2017) explore the research and application landscape of blockchain technology acceptance. Using a comprehensive approach, they proposed that TAM is able to explain the adoption of blockchain technology. In the next section, each of the relationships between variables will be further discussed and hypothesis will be proposed.

Development of Research Hypotheses

The Relationship Between Perceived Usefulness and Investors' Intention

Davis (1989) defined perceived usefulness as the degree to which a person believes that using a particular system will enhance his or her job performance. This proposition is justified from the perspective that people's intentions to use the technology will be greater if they expect a technology to enhance their performance on the job. In the context of this paper, if SMEs believe that the use of IAP is able to increase their chance to get funding, they will be likely to use the platform. In short, perceived usefulness is about the effectiveness of the platform in helping SMEs to get their funding.

Literature provides a considerable amount of academic research examining the relationship of perceived usefulness and intention (Cham et al., 2018; Cho & Sagynov, 2015; Chu & Chen, 2016; Gamal Aboelmaged, 2010; Hamid, Razak, Bakar, & Abdullah, 2016; M. C. Lee, 2009). In the context

Figure 1. The technology acceptance model
Source: Davis (1989)

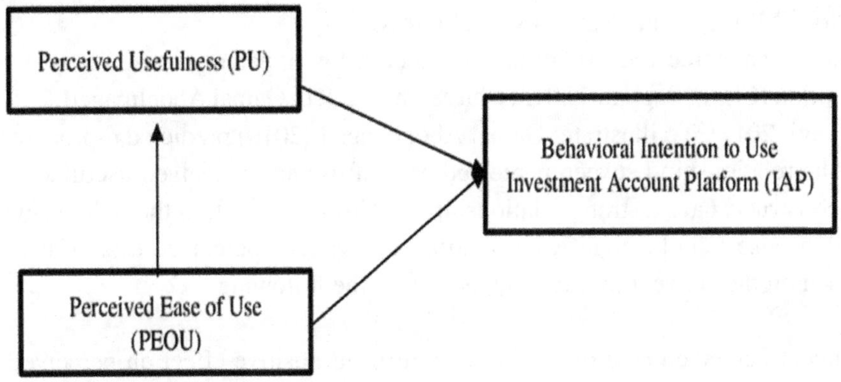

of new Fintech, Kim & Kim (2018), S. Lee (2016), and Mohamed Asmy & Hassanudin (2017) found the significant relationship between perceived usefulness and intention. Based on the above, this paper hypothesised the following:

Hypothesis One: Perceived usefulness has a significant positive effect on investors' intention to use the investment account platform.

The Relationship Between Perceived Ease of Use and Investors' Intention

Perceived ease of use refers to the degree to which the person believes that using the system will be free of effort (Davis, 1989). In the context of this paper, it refers to the extent to which users believe that the use of IAP is free of effort. According to Hamid et al., (2016), if a system is relatively easy to be used, individuals will be more willing to learn about its features and finally intend to use it. In other words, if SMEs believes that the IAP is relatively easy to be used, they will be likely to use the platform.

Many existing studies have assessed the relationship between perceived ease of use and its influences on the intention to use technology (Cho & Sagynov, 2015; Chu & Chen, 2016; Hamid et al., 2016; Tanduklangi, 2017). For example, Hamid et al. (2016) investigated and found that perceived ease of use was positively related to continuance intention to use e-government. In addition to that, many has uncovered that perceived ease of use affected intention in the context of new Fintech (Kim & Kim, 2018; S. Lee, 2016; Mohamed Asmy & Hassanudin, 2017). For instance, Kim & Kim (2018) investigate consumers' continuous intention to use one of the most commonly used Fintech, the mobile ease payment services. They found that perceived ease of use has a positive effect on continuous use intention in adopting the new technology. Consequently, this paper proposes the following hypothesis:

Hypothesis Two: Perceived ease of use has a significant positive effect on investors' intention to use the investment account platform.

The Relationship Between Perceived Ease of Use and Perceived Usefulness

TAM suggests that perceived ease of use influences the perceived usefulness of the technology. To explain further, the easier it is to use a technology, the greater the expected benefits from the technology. With regards to IAP, perceived ease of use can impact its usefulness to the extent that the platform must be easy to use for SMEs and thus realise its' usefulness.

Studies indicate that perceived ease of use is associated with perceived usefulness in the context of technology adoption (Cho & Sagynov, 2015; Chu & Chen, 2016; Gamal Aboelmaged, 2010; McCloskey, 2011; Tanduklangi, 2017). To illustrate, Gamal Aboelmaged (2010) predicted e-procurement adoption and measured the relationship between perceived ease of use and perceived usefulness. He found out that these two constructs have a strong relationship. In addition to that, in the online environment, Cho & Sagynov (2015) also found a significant relationship between perceived ease of use and perceived usefulness. Based on the above, this paper hypothesised the following:

Hypothesis Three: Perceived ease of use has a significant positive effect on perceived usefulness of investment account platform among investors.

The Mediating Role of Perceived Usefulness

One of the main advantages of the crowdfunding platform is that it offers speed and accessibility. Compared to conventional financing that requires more time in applying for a loan or seeking out accredited investors by themselves, listing up the businesses in the crowdfunding platform is far easier, efficient and effective in promoting the businesses out to the investor (Bakar & Rosbi, 2018; PwC, 2016). With regards to the crowdfunding platform, if the platform is relatively easy to be used, the businesses will have an enjoyable experience seeking for a fund and thus will improve the perceived usefulness of the platform and facilitate the intention to use. In other words, having a good perception of a crowdfunding platform as a useful tool to find the investor may lead the SMEs towards using the platform. Hence, the higher the perceived ease of use, the greater the intention to use the platform, who will perceive higher usefulness when using the platform. In sum, if the SMEs think that using the platform is easy, their intention of use the platform will increase. Several studies have considered perceived usefulness as a mediator for intention (Matute, Polo-Redondo, & Ana Utrillas, 2016; Moslehpour, 2018). Based on these arguments, this paper proposed the following hypothesis:

Hypothesis Four: The relationship between perceived ease of use and intention is mediated by perceived usefulness of the investment account platform

THEORETICAL FRAMEWORK

The proposed relationships between the variables are illustrated in Figure 2.

Figure 2. The theoretical framework

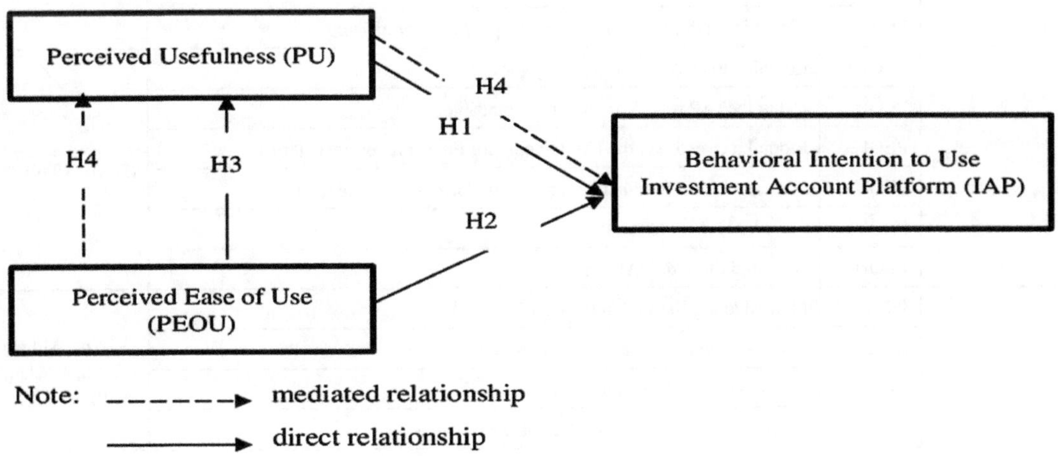

METHODOLOGY

Primary data in the form of questionnaire were collected from 163 SME owners in Kuala Lumpur, Malaysia using the purposive sampling technique. A self-administered questionnaire was developed to measure the research variables and to collect demographic information. The questionnaire consisted of two sections. Section A contained questions pertaining to the respondents' demographic information namely age, business type, and financial information on the SMEs. Section B consisted of a five-point Likert scale measurement questions ranging from strongly disagree (1) to strongly agree (5) to measure the variables. The measurement of each construct was adapted from Davis (1989) and SME (2016). Table 2 shows the items used in the questionnaire.

The hypotheses were tested by applying structural equation modeling. Statistical Package for the Social Sciences (SPSS) and partial least squares – structural equation modeling (PLS-SEM) via Smart-PLS were used to examine the hypothesised relationships among the proposed variables. According to Rasoolimanesh & Ali (2018), partial least squares have less restrictions about sample size and construct measurement, as well as its capability in handling both formative and reflective measurement models. PLS-SEM has been utilised extensively in technology adoption-related research (Alaeddin & Altounjy, 2018; Hassan et al., 2018; Kassim & Ramayah, 2015).

Table 2. Items used in the questionnaire

Variable	Item	Question	Source
Perceived Usefulness (PU)	PU1	Using the IAP would save my time in looking for financing.	(Davis, 1989)
	PU2	Using the IAP allows me to seek financing more quickly and efficiently	
	PU3	The IAP allows me to track the amount of financing subscribed for my enterprise	
	PU4	The IAP enhances the effectiveness in looking for financing	
	PU5	The IAP makes it easier to search for and seek for financing	
	PU6	I would find the IAP to be useful in applying for financing.	
Perceived Ease of Use (PEOU)	PEOU1	Learning to use the IAP was easy for me.	(Davis, 1989)
	PEOU2	Using the IAP was clear and understandable.	
	PEOU3	I found it easy to get the IAP to apply for financing for my enterprise.	
	PEOU4	It is easy for me to remember how to perform tasks using the IAP	
	PEOU5	The IAP is flexible to use	
	PEOU6	Overall, I think the IAP is easy to use	
Intention (INT)	INT1	I intend to use the IAP in the near future	(S. Aziz, Md Husin, Hussin, & Afaq, 2019)
	INT2	I am likely to participate the IAP in future	
	INT3	I plan to use the IAP in the next months	
	INT4	I predict I would use the IAP in the next months.	

FINDINGS

Characteristics of the Sample

SMEs from the manufactruring industry were made up of 45.4 per cent of the sample while the remaining 54.6 per cent were from services and other industries. As for the entire sample, 36.2 per cent of the sample are from small companies and 63.8 percent from medium companies. About 7.36 per cent of the businesses obtained funding from individual investors and family offices, 12.88 per cent funded by insurance companies, 15.95 per cent funded by pension and provident funds, 15.34 per cent funded by funds and other asset managers, 24.54 per cent funded by corporate investors, 12.88 per cent funded by government agencies, 7.98 per cent funded by sovereign wealth funds and government investment companies and the remaining 3.07 per cent from other sources of fund.

Reliability Analysis

Assessment of measurement model includes convergent validity (loading), average variance extracted (AVE), composite reliability and discriminant validity. All assessments are confirmed by the PLS algorithm. All factor loadings exceeded the recommended 0.7 threshold except for an item (PEOU6) (see Table 4). However, this paper kept both items in the model since Bagozzi & Yi (1988) suggest that factor loading greater than 0.60 is acceptable in an exploratory research. Discriminant validity was assessed using the Fornel-Larcker criterion and heterotrait-monotrait ratio of correlations (HTMT). In Fornell &

Table 3. Overall profile of respondents

Variable	Frequency	Percentage
Industry		
Manufactruring industry	74	45.40
Services and others industry	89	54.60
Type of enterprise		
Small	59	36.20
Medium	104	63.80
Financial source of business fund		
Individual investors and family offices	12	7.36
Insurance companies	21	12.88
Pension and provident funds	26	15.95
Fund of funds and other asset managers	25	15.34
Corporate investors	40	24.54
Government agencies	21	12.88
Sovereign wealth funds and government investment companies	13	7.98
Others	5	3.07

Larcker (1981)(Fornell & Larcker, 1981)(Fornell & Larcker, 1981)(Fornell & Larcker, 1981)(Fornell & Larcker, 1981)(Fornell & Larcker, 1981)(Fornell & Larcker, 1981)(Fornell & Larcker, 1981)(Fornell & Larcker, 1981)(Fornell & Larcker, 1981) criterion, the root square of AVE and all inter-construct correlations were compared while in HTMT, the mean value of the item correlations across constructs relative to the (geometric) mean of the average correlations for the items measuring the same construct was measured (Joe F Hair, Risher, Sarstedt, & Ringle, 2018). According to Fornell & Larcker (1981), to pass the discriminant validity assessment, each construct's AVE should be higher than its squared correlation with any other constructs while Henseler, Ringle, & Sarstedt (2015) suggest that to clearly discriminate between two constructs, the HTMT should be significantly smaller than one. In this paper, both Fornel-Larcker criterion and HTMT were met and thus confirming that the discriminant validity is not a problem (see Table 5 and Table 6).

Table 4. Factor loadings and reliability

Construct	Item	Loadings	AVE	CR	RHO
Intention (INT)	INT1	0.862	0.768	0.930	0.904
	INT2	0.854			
	INT3	0.899			
	INT4	0.890			
Perceived ease of use (PEOU)	PEOU1	0.774	0.599	0.899	0.876
	PEOU2	0.827			
	PEOU3	0.817			
	PEOU4	0.820			
	PEOU5	0.764			
	PEOU6	0.624			
Perceived usefulness (PU)	PU1	0.732	0.612	0.904	0.879
	PU2	0.840			
	PU3	0.817			
	PU4	0.836			
	PU5	0.701			
	PU6	0.757			

Table 5. Fornell-larcker criterion

Construct	Intention	Perceived Ease of Use	Perceived Usefulness
Intention	0.876**		
Perceived ease of use	0.681*	0.774**	
Perceived usefulness	0.429*	0.531*	0.782**

Notes: Main diagonal** elements are the square root of the AVE for each reflective construct. Off-diagonal* elements are the correlations between constructs

Table 6. Heterotrait-monotrait ratio (HTMT)

Construct	Intention	Perceived Ease of Use	Perceived Usefulness
Intention			
Perceived ease of use	0.765		
Perceived usefulness	0.468	0.580	

Model Evaluation, Path Analysis and Hypothesis Testing

Predictive power of the model is determined using the R-square (R2) and (Q2) value. According to Chin (1998) R^2 values of 0.67, 0.33, or 0.19 for endogenous latent variables in the inner path model are described as substantial, moderate, or weak. As shown in Table 7, R^2 for intention to use IAP was 0.472 indicating that 47.2 per cent of the variation in intention may be explained by perceived usefullness and perceived ease of use. In addition to that, R^2 for perceived usefullness was 0.236 indicating that only 23.6 per cent of the variation in perceived usefullness can be explained by perceived ease of use. This suggests that the model has a moderate explanatory power. Furthermore, blind-folding technique was used to assess the predictive relevance of the model. According to Joseph F. Hair, Hult, Ringle, & Sarstedt (2017), Q^2 values larger than zero are recommended as theytehy showed that the path model exhibits predictive relevance. As seen in Table 7, Q^2 value for intention was 0.322 while Q^2 value for perceived usefullness was 0.149.

Effect size (f^2) is another criterion used to examine the unique effect of each independent variable on the dependent variable. According to Cohen (1988), f^2 values of 0.02, 0.15 and 0.35 are classified as small, medium and large, respectively. In this paper, the effect sizes (f^2) of perceived usefullness and intention was 0.016 (small), while for perceived ease of use and intention was 0.547 (large). The perceived ease of use and perceive usefullness also had large effect (0.357). Hence, it is concluded that the research model has an adequate predictive relevance.

H1 and H2 examined the influence of perceived usefullness and perceived ease of use on intention to use IAP, respectively. H3 examined the influence of perceived ease of use on perceived usefullness while H4 examined the role of perceived usefulness as a mediator on the relationship between perceived ease of use and intention. Three (H2, H3 and H4) hypotheses were statistically significant. More specifically, perceived ease of use towards intention ($ß= 0.626$, $p< 0.001$), perceived ease of use towards perceived usefullness ($ß= 0.513$, $p<0.001$) and mediating role of perceived usefulness on the relationship between perceived ease of use and intention ($ß= 0.058$, $p< 0.10$) to use IAP were statistically significant. Table 8 shows the results of hypothesis testing while Figure 3 shows the results of the PLS analysis.

Table 7. Predictive relevance

Construct	R^2	Q^2
Intention	0.472	0.322
Perceived usefullness	0.236	0.149

Figure 3. Results of the PLS analysis

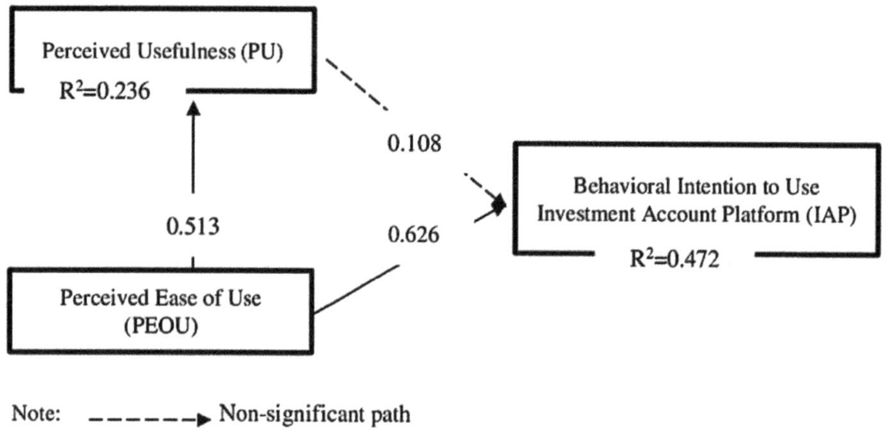

Table 8. Results of hypothesis testing

Hypothesis	Relationship	Standard Beta (ß)	Standard Error	t-Value	Results	f^2
H1	PU → INT	0.108	0.072	1.503	Not significant	0.016
H2	PEOU → INT	0.626	0.076	8.218**	Significant	0.547
H3	PEOU → PU	0.513	0.062	8.252**	Significant	0.357
H4	PEOU → PU → INT	0.058	0.039	1.426	Significant	---

* statistically significant as at p < 0.05 (t >1.96)
** statistically significant as p < 0.001 (t > 3.29)
***statistically significant as p < 0.01(t > 2.576)

Model Fit

Model fit was assessed using Goodness of fit (GoF) index. GoF has been developed by (Tenenhaus, Vinzi, Chatelin, & Lauro (2005) to assess the overall measure of model fit for PLS-SEM. The GoF is computed as the geometric mean of the average communality index and the average R2 value (Tenenhaus, Amato, & Esposito Vinzi, 2004). The GoF index is bound between 0 and 1, whereby the model with a higher fit is the better or more valid model. As a benchmark, Akter, D'Ambra, & Ray (2011) mentioned that the GoF value of 0.10 is considered as small while GoF value of 0.25 and 0.36 is considered as medium and large, respectively. In this paper, the model generated GoF value of 0.48, which indicates that the model has a better prediction power in comparison with the baseline values (GoF criteria).

Importance Performance Map Analysis

The importance of performance map analysis shows perceived ease of use emerged as the most importance factor in determining intention to use IAP. The construct also performed better in the given model. Perceived usefulness was found to be less important and also less in terms of performance within the model. Figure 4 shows the IMPA results.

Table 9. Goodness of fit (GoF) index

Constructs	Average Variance Extracted (AVE)	R^2
Intention	0.768	0.472
Perceived ease of use	0.599	
Perceived usefullness	0.612	0.236
Average score	0.66	0.35
Average x R^2	0.23	
GoF = (AVE x R^2) $^{1/2}$	0.48	

Figure 4. IMPA results

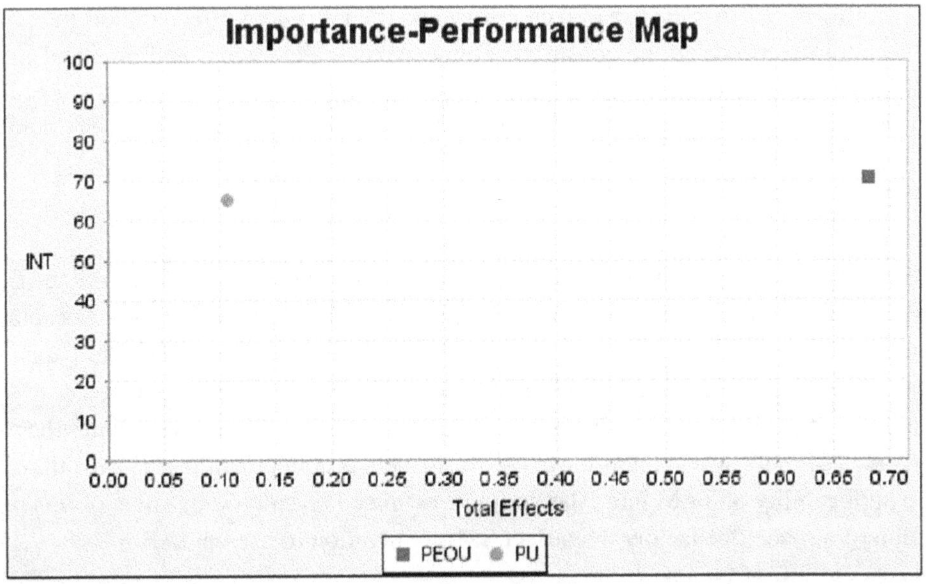

DISCUSSION

Based on the findings, three hypotheses were supported while one hypothesis was not supported. Perceived ease of use was found to have a significant impact on SME's intention to use IAP. The result indicated that the higher number of users believe that the use of IAP is free of effort, the higher their intention to use the platform. In other words, the easier for them to use the platform, the higher intention of users (SMEs) to use the platform. Therefore, in order to attract SMEs to use the platform as an alternative channel to get funding, the policy maker needs to ensure the platform is easy-to-use. User's training and system manual should be provided to the user's and potential users. The significant relationship between perceived ease of use and intention has also been found in previous studies (Cho & Sagynov, 2015; Kim & Kim, 2018; Mohamed Asmy & Hassanudin, 2017; Tanduklangi, 2017).

This paper also found a significant relationship between perceived ease of use and perceived usefullness. The results suggest that users are likely to perceive the platform as useful when they believe that their platform is easy to use. The result is consistent with Tanduklangi (2017), McCloskey (2011) and

M. C. Lee (2009). This result implies that when users think that using the platform is easy, they tend to believe that the platform is useful in facilitating them to seek for funding. This paper also found the mediating role of perceived usefulness on the relationship between perceived ease of use and intention. Obviously, the influence of intention to use IAP is strongly meditated by the practicality of the platform. Therefore, practitioners should focus on promoting the the practicality of the platform to SMEs that would lead them to use the platform. Practitioners may organise workshops and use the power of media in delivering the benefits of using the platform.

According to the original TAM, perceived usefulness is hypothesised to affect intention to use. However, this paper found the contrary. Perceived usefulness is found to have insignificant effects on intention. Although the insignificant effect of perceived usefulness is unexpected, it shows the same pattern as shown in several prior TAM research (Park, 2009). In sum, usefulness of the platform could not directly affect the user's intention to use e-learning. In a study by Park (2009), perceived usefulness affected users' attitude towards the use of technology and their attitudes affected their intentions to use. Future studies could incorporate the construct. This paper has theoretical and practical implications, which are discussed in the implication section.

CONCLUSION

The purpose of this paper is to examine the factors that influence Small and Medium-Sized Enterprises' (SMEs) intention to use the Investment Account Platform (IAP). Using Technology Acceptance Model (TAM), four hypotheses were developed where three were supported. In brief, the paper found that perceived ease of use has a significant relationship towards intention, while perceived ease of use has a significant relationship towards perceived usefulness and perceived usefulness mediates the relationship between perceived ease of use and intention to use investment account platform. The results of this paper highlight the applicability of TAM into Islamic finance-fintech research. The value of this paper lies in its presentation of a model for factors that affect SMEs' intention to use the IAP.

Theoretical and Practical Implication

This paper will be useful to researchers and professionals, including policy makers. Practically, this paper guides the strategic decision-makers of the banking industry especially in Malaysia to develop strategies that will help to increase the intention to use IAP in Malaysia. To attract SMEs to use the platform, policy makers need to ensure that the platform is convenient to be used in a way that the user is able to achieve the objective to use the platform with effectiveness, efficiency, and satisfaction. In other words, the platform should be easy to use by the SMEs. Few key features could be considered simplicity, functional yet reliable.

This paper also contributes to the body of knowledge. First, this paper provided insight into the effect of perceived of use and perceived usefullness in explaining SME's intention to use IAP, the crowdfunding platform based in Malaysia. Using TAM, this paper also investigates the mediating role of perceived usefulness on the relationship between perceived ease of use and intention. Previous studies have yet to utilise TAM in investigating intention to use IAP from the fund seeker perspective.

By bringing the theory from another perspective, this paper is not only helping policy makers in the development of better crowdfunding platform, but also provides a new insight into how to foster the platform to such users.

LIMITATIONS AND FUTURE RESEARCH

This paper has several limitations. First, it focused only on SMEs' intention to use the IAP; as a result, therefore, it cannot be generalised to other fintech-related platform. Thus, there is a need to commence further studies in other fintech-related settings, such as blockchain and other crowdfunding platforms. Second, this paper only considered two factors that influence the intention, and the factors selected may not include all other factors that could influence SMEs'' intention to use the IAP in Malaysia. Hence, further research could take into account other relevant factors. Future research should include the measure of actual behaviour and explore the decomposition of perceived ease of use and perceived usefulness so that more in-depth insights could be obtained. Third, the insignificant relationship between perceived usefullness and intention is worth investigated in future research.

REFERENCES

Achsien, I. H., & Purnamasari, D. L. (2016). Islamic Crowd-funding as The Next Financial Innovation in Islamic Finance : Potential and Anticipated Regulation in Indonesia. *European Journal of Islamic Finance Voluntary*, *5*, 1–11. doi:10.13135/2421-2172/1771

Ajzen, I. (1991). The theory of planned behaviour. *Organizational Behavior and Human Decision Processes*, *50*(2), 179–211. doi:10.1016/0749-5978(91)90020-T

Ajzen, I., & Fishbein, M. (1980). *Understanding Attitudes and Predicting Social Behavior*. Englewood Cliffs, NJ: Prentice-Hall.

Akter, S., D'Ambra, J., & Ray, P. (2011). An Evaluation of PLS Based Complex Models : The Roles of Power Analysis, Predictive Relevance and GOF Index. In 7th AMCIS Proceedings (pp. 1–7). Academic Press.

Alaeddin, O., & Altounjy, R. (2018). Trust, technology awareness and satisfaction effect into the intention to use cryptocurrency among generation Z in Malaysia. *International Journal of Pure and Applied Mathematics*, *120*(2), 7–10. doi:10.14419/ijet.v7i4.29.21588

Alonso. (2015). Crowdfunding in Islamic Finance and Microfinance: A Case Study of Egypt. In *Access to Finance and Human Development – Essays on Zakah, Awqaf and Microfinance.* (Vol. 1, pp. 85–94). Academic Press.

Aqidah, N., Mohd, S., & Palil, R. (2016). Crowdfunding: a Collaborative Waqf Based Internet Platform. *International Journal of Business, Economics and Law, 11*(5), 41–46. Retrieved from http://ijbel.com/wp-content/uploads/2017/03/IJBEL-57.pdf

Association of Southeast Asian Nations (ASEAN). (2017). *Facilitating Equity Crowdfunding in the ASEAN Region*. Author.

Auzzir, Z., Haigh, R., & Amaratunga, D. (2018). Impacts of Disaster to SMEs in Malaysia. *Procedia Engineering*, *212*, 1131–1138. doi:10.1016/j.proeng.2018.01.146

Aziz, M. A., & Che Wan, B. A. (2016). Platform Akaun Pelaburan – IAP Alternatif Baharu Usahawan Raih Teroka. *Berita Harian*.

Aziz, S., Md Husin, M., Hussin, N., & Afaq, Z. (2019). Factors that influence individuals' intentions to purchase family takaful mediating role of perceived trust. *Asia Pacific Journal of Marketing and Logistics*, *31*(1), 81–104. doi:10.1108/APJML-12-2017-0311

Bagozzi, R. P., & Yi, Y. (1988). On the evaluation of structural equation models. *Journal of the Academy of Marketing Science*, *16*(1), 74–94. doi:10.1007/BF02723327

Bakar, N. A., & Rosbi, S. (2018). Robust Framework Diagnostics of Blockchain for Bitcoin Transaction System : A Technical Analysis from Islamic Financial Technology (i -FinTech) Perspective. *International Journal of Business and Management*, *2*(3), 22–29. doi:10.26666/rmp.ijbm.2018.3.4

Bloomio. (n.d.). *The State of Equity Crowdfunding: Equity Crowdfunding Insights and Analysis*. Author.

Capgemini, LinkedIn, & Efma. (2018). *World Fintech Report 2018*. Authors.

Central Bank of Malaysia. (2016). *Financial Technology Regulatory Sandbox Framework. Central Bank of Malaysia*. Retrieved from http://www.bnm.gov.my/index.php?ch=57&pg=137&ac=533&bb=file

Cham, T. H., Low, S. C., Lim, C. S., Aye, A. K., & Raymond, L. L. Bin. (2018). Preliminary Study on Consumer Attitude towards FinTech Products and Services in Malaysia. *International Journal of Engineering & Technology, 7*(2.29), 166. doi:10.14419/ijet.v7i2.29.13310

Chin, W. W. (1998). The partial least squares approach to structural equation modeling. In *Modern methods for business research* (pp. 295–336). Mahwah, NJ: Lawrence Erlbaum Associates.

Cho, Y. C., & Sagynov, E. (2015). Exploring Factors That Affect Usefulness, Ease Of Use, Trust, And Purchase Intention In The Online Environment. *International Journal of Management & Information Systems, 19*(21–36), 7763–7769. doi:10.1021/acs.inorgchem.8b00815

Chu, T. H., & Chen, Y. Y. (2016). With Good We Become Good: Understanding e-learning adoption by theory of planned behavior and group influences. *Computers & Education*, *92–93*, 37–52. doi:10.1016/j.compedu.2015.09.013

Cohen, J. (1988). *Statistical Power Analysis for the Behavioral Sciences*. Hillsdale, NJ: Lawrence Earlbaum Associates.

SME Corporation. (2016). *Guideline for New SME Definition*. SME Corporation.

SME Corporation. (2017b). *SME Annual Report 2017/18*. Author.

Davis, F. (1989). Perceived Usefulness, Perceived Ease of Use, and User Acceptance of Information Technology. *Management Information Systems Quarterly*, *13*(3), 319–340. doi:10.2307/249008

Davis, F. D., Bagozzi, R. P., & Warshaw, P. R. (1989). User acceptance of computer technology: A comparison of two theoretical models. *Management Science*, *35*(8), 982–1003. doi:10.1287/mnsc.35.8.982

De Buysere, K., Gajda, O., Kleverlaan, R., Marom, D., Klaes, M., & De Buysere, K. (2012). *A framework for European crowdfunding. European Crowdfunding Network (ECN).* Retrieved from https://d21buns5ku92am.cloudfront.net/26522/documents/17930-1351284179-FRAMEWORK_EU_CROWD-FUNDING.pdf

EY. (2017). *EY FinTech Adoption Index 2017: The Rapid Emergence of Fintech.* Author.

Financial Stability Board. (2017). *Artificial Intelligence and Machine Learning in Financial Services: Market Developments and Financial Stability Implications.* Financial Stability Board. Retrieved from http://www.fsb.org/2017/11/artificial-intelligence-and-machine-learning-in-financial-service/

Fornell, C., & Larcker, D. F. (1981). Evaluating Structural Equation Models with Unobservable Variables and Measurement Error. *JMR, Journal of Marketing Research*, *18*(1), 39–50. doi:10.1177/002224378101800104

Gai, K., Qiu, M., & Sun, X. (2017). A Survey on FinTech. *Journal of Network and Computer Applications*, *103*, 262–273. doi:10.1016/j.jnca.2017.10.011

Gamal Aboelmaged, M. (2010). Predicting e-procurement adoption in a developing country: An empirical integration of technology acceptance model and theory of planned behaviour. *Industrial Management & Data Systems*, *110*(3), 392–414. doi:10.1108/02635571011030042

Ghazali, N. H., & Yasuoka, T. (2018). Awareness and Perception Analysis of Small Medium Enterprise and Start-up Towards FinTech Instruments-Crowdfunding and Peer-to-Peer Lending in Malaysia. *International Journal of Finance and Banking Research*, *4*(1), 13–24. doi:10.11648/j.ijfbr.20180401.12

Granic, A., & Marangunic, N. (2015). Technology Acceptance Model : A Literature Review from 1986 to 2013. *Universal Access in the Information Society*, *14*(1), 81–95. doi:10.100710209-014-0348-1

Hair, J. F., Hult, G. T. M., Ringle, C. M., & Sarstedt, M. (2017). *A primer on partial least squares structural equation modeling (PLS-SEM)*. Academic Press. doi:10.1016/j.lrp.2013.01.002

Hair, J. F., Risher, J. J., Sarstedt, M., & Ringle, C. M. (2018). When to use and how to report the results of PLS-SEM. *European Business Review*. doi:10.1108/ebr-11-2018-0203

Hamid, A. A., Razak, F. Z. A., Bakar, A. A., & Abdullah, W. S. W. (2016). The Effects of Perceived Usefulness and Perceived Ease of Use on Continuance Intention to Use E-Government. *Procedia Economics and Finance*, *35*, 644–649. doi:10.1016/S2212-5671(16)00079-4

Hassan, M. U., Iqbal, A., & Iqbal, Z. (2018). Factors affecting the adoption of internet banking in Pakistan: An integration of technology acceptance model and theory of planned behaviour. *International Journal of Business Information Systems*, *28*(3), 342–370. doi:10.1504/IJBIS.2018.092530

Henseler, J., Ringle, C. M., & Sarstedt, M. (2015). A new criterion for assessing discriminant validity in variance-based structural equation modeling. *Journal of the Academy of Marketing Science, 43*(1), 115–135. doi:10.100711747-014-0403-8

Hines, P. (2018). *APIs in Banking: Unlocking Business Value with Banking as a Platform*. BAAP.

ICLG. (2018). *The International Comparative Legal Guide to: Fintech 2018*. ICLG.

Islamic Financial Services Board. (2017). Islamic Financial Services Industry. *Stability Report, 2017*. doi:10.1017/CBO9781107415324.004

Jin, C. C., Seong, L. C., & Khin, A. A. (2019). Factors Affecting the Consumer Acceptance towards Fintech Products and Services in Malaysia. *International Journal of Asian Social Science, 9*(1), 59–65. doi:10.18488/journal.1.2019.91.59.65

Karim, N. A. A. (2016). *Islamic crowdfunding for social-impact housing (Pt 1)*. The Edge Malaysia.

Kassim, N. M., & Ramayah, T. (2015). Perceived Risk Factors Influence on Intention to Continue Using Internet Banking among Malaysians. *Global Business Review, 16*(3), 393–414. doi:10.1177/0972150915569928

Kavitha, P., & Baag, P. K. (2018). *Crowdfunding for Entrepreneurs- Analysis of the Institutional Work*. Academic Press.

Kim, S., & Kim, C.-B. (2018). A Study on the Factors Affecting the Continuous Use Intention of Easy Payment Services. In *International Academic Conference* (p. 216). Academic Press. 10.20472/IAC.2018.042.030

KPMG. (2017). *Forging the Future: How Financial Institutions are Embracing Fintech to Evolve and Grow*. KPMG International. doi:10.1093/acprof:oso/9780199742745.003.0007

KPMG. (2018). *The Pulse of Fintech 2018: Biannual Global Analysis of Investment in Fintech*. Author.

Lacasse, R. M., Lambert, B. A., Osmani, E., Couture, C., Roy, N., Sylvain, J., & Nadeau, F. (2016). A Digital Tsunami : FinTech and Crowdfunding. In *International Scientific Conference on Digital Intelligence* (pp. 1–5). Academic Press.

Lane, K. (2013). *Overview Of The Backend as a Service (BaaS) Space*. Retrieved from http://www.integrove.com/wp-content/uploads/2014/11/api-evangelist-baas-whitepaper.pdf

Lee, M. C. (2009). Factors influencing the adoption of internet banking: An integration of TAM and TPB with perceived risk and perceived benefit. *Electronic Commerce Research and Applications, 8*(3), 130–141. doi:10.1016/j.elerap.2008.11.006

Lee, S. (2016). User Behavior of Mobile Enterprise Applications. *Transactions on Internet and Information Systems (Seoul), 10*(8), 3972–3985.

Lee, S. Y., & Park, J. (2016). A Study on the Intention of the Use of Mobile Payment Services: Application of the Technology Acceptance Model. *Korean Management Science Review, 33*(2), 65–74. doi:10.7737/KMSR.2016.33.2.065

Lee, T., & Kim, H. (2015). An Exploratory Study on Fintech Industry in Korea : Crowdfunding Case. In *2nd International conference on Innovative Engineering Technologies* (pp. 58–64). Academic Press.

Life.SREDA. (2015). *Overview of APIs and Bank-as-a-Service in FINTECH*. Author.

Lou, A. T. F., & Li, E. Y. (2017). Integrating Innovation Diffusion Theory and the Technology Acceptance Model : The Adoption of Blockchain Technology from Business Managers ' Perspective. In *International Conference on Electronic Business* (pp. 298–302). Academic Press.

Lutfi, M. A., & Ismail, M. A. (2016). Sadaqah-Based Crowdfunding Model for Microfinancing and Health Care. *The Journal of Muamalat and Islamic Finance Research*, *13*(December), 32–51.

Maierbrugger, A. (2018). *Fintech on Track to Shape Future of Islamic Finance*. Gulf Times.

Matute, J., Polo-Redondo, Y., & Utrillas, A. (2016). The influence of EWOM characteristics on online repurchase intention: Mediating roles of trust and perceived usefulness. *Online Information Review*, *40*(7), 1090–1110. doi:10.1108/OIR-11-2015-0373

McCloskey, D. W. (2011). The Importance of Ease of Use, Usefulness, and Trust to Online Consumers: An Examination of the Technology Acceptance Model with Older Consumers. *Journal of Organizational and End User Computing*, *18*(3), 47–65. doi:10.4018/joeuc.2006070103

Mishra, D., Akman, I., & Mishra, A. (2014). Theory of reasoned action application for green information technology acceptance. *Computers in Human Behavior*, *36*, 29–40. doi:10.1016/j.chb.2014.03.030

Mohamed Asmy, M. T. T., & Hassanudin, M. T. T. (2017). The Behavioural Intention of Investors to Use Islamic Banking's Investment Account Platform (IAP) As A Source of Investment Portfolio: A Structural Equation Modeling Approach. *Journal of Islamic Monetary Economics and Finance*, *3*(1), 113–138. doi:10.21098/jimf.v3i1.712

Moore, G. C., & Benbasat, I. (1996). Integrating diffusion of innovations and theory of reasoned action models to predict utilization of information technology by end-user. In *Diffusion and adoption of information technology* (pp. 132–146). Boston, MA: Springer. doi:10.1007/978-0-387-34982-4_10

Moslehpour, M., Pham, V., Wong, W.-K., & Bilgiçli, İ. (2018). e-Purchase Intention of Taiwanese Consumers : Sustainable Mediation of Perceived Usefulness and Perceived Ease of Use. *Sustainability*, *10*(1), 1–17. doi:10.3390u10010234 PMID:30607262

Padmanaban, P., & Soo, H. K. Y. (2016). *Catching the Fintech Wave: A Survey on FinTech in Malaysia*. Retrieved from https://www.pwc.com/my/en/assets/publications/2016-pwc-aicb-catching-the-fintech-wave.pdf

Park, S. Y. (2009). An Analysis of the Technology Acceptance Model in Understanding University Students' Behavioral Intention to Use e-Learning. *Journal of Educational Technology & Society*, *12*(3), 150–162. doi:10.1145/3108421.3108432

Pikri, E. (2018). *StashAway is The First Robo-Advisor The SC Has Approved for The Malaysian Market*. WEALTHTECH.

PwC. (2016). *Global FinTech Report: How FinTech is shaping Financial Services*. Author.

PwC. (2019). *Budget 2019 overview: What's in store for the economy and impacted sectors*. Author.

Rasoolimanesh, S. M., & Ali, F. (2018). Guest editorial. *Journal of Hospitality and Tourism Technology*, *9*(3), 238–248. doi:10.1108/JHTT-10-2018-142

Reuters. (2014). *Planned Malaysia investment platform to expand role of Islamic banks*. Author.

Reuters. (2018). *Fintech, a global boost for Islamic Finance?* Retrieved from https://www.reuters.com/article/idUSWAOAPHREBLWW18A3

Saiti, B., Afghan, M., & Noordin, N. H. (2018). Financing agricultural activities in Afghanistan: A proposed salam-based crowdfunding structure. *ISRA International Journal of Islamic Finance*, *10*(1), 52–61. doi:10.1108/IJIF-09-2017-0029

Silva, R. L. S., & Laboratório, J. C. de O. (2003). Introduction to Augmented Reality. *National Laboratory for Scientific Computation*, 1–11. doi:10.3169/itej.66.53

SME. (2016a). *Access to Finance*. Retrieved from http://www.smecorp.gov.my/images/SMEAR/latest/Chapter6.pdf

SME. (2016b). *SME Annual Report 2016*. SME.

SME Corporation. (2017a). *Economic Census 2016: Profile of SMEs*. Retrieved from http://www.smecorp.gov.my/images/SMEAR/latest/2/Census English_FINAL.pdf

Tanduklangi, A. (2017). Determinants of User Intention in Using e-Learning Technology in Indonesian Context: An Empirical Study. *Mediterranean Journal of Social Sciences*, *8*(3), 69–77. doi:10.5901/mjss.2017.v8n3p69

Tenenhaus, M., Amato, S., & Esposito Vinzi, V. (2004). A global goodness-of-fit index for PLS structural equation modelling. In *Proceedings of the XLII SIS scientific meeting* (pp. 739–742). Academic Press.

Tenenhaus, M., Vinzi, V. E., Chatelin, Y. M., & Lauro, C. (2005). PLS path modeling. *Computational Statistics & Data Analysis*, *48*(1), 159–205. doi:10.1016/j.csda.2004.03.005

Wahjono, S. I., & Marina, A., & Widayat. (2015). Islamic Crowdfunding : Alternative Funding Solution. In *1st World Islamic Social Science Congress* (pp. 1–12). Academic Press.

World Bank Group. (2018). *Malaysia Economic Monitor: Navigating Change*. Author.

Yousafzai, S. Y., Foxall, G. R., & Pallister, J. G. (2010). Explaining internet banking behavior: Theory of reasoned action, theory of planned behavior, or technology acceptance model? *Journal of Applied Social Psychology*, *40*(5), 1172–1202. doi:10.1111/j.1559-1816.2010.00615.x

Zahid, A. Z. M. (2018). *Assistant Governor's Welcoming Remarks at the Islamic Finance Rendezvous Series*. Academic Press.

KEY TERMS AND DEFINITIONS

Adoption: Readiness to perform a given behavior.

Crowd-Funding: The practice of funding a project or venture by raising small amounts of money from a large number of people, typically via the internet.

FinTech: The new technology and innovation that aims to compete with traditional financial methods in the delivery of financial services.

Small and Medium Enterprises: Businesses whose personnel numbers and profits fall below certain limits.

the application of artificial intelligence can be observed based on the practices of international banks that have many branches around the globe. The observation of the micro level can be done by viewing the local banks' practices which may be valued from aspects of regional or within a specific country.

Based on the macro level, the majority of international banks are depending on the usual conventional practices of financial services. They can be considered as secular banks that rely on the practices of usury. Their relationship with their customers depends on the creditor-lender relationship. In adopting artificial intelligence in their financial services system, these international banks are more willing to become the pioneers of the practice. They are supported with strong monetary profits that they gain in every single day. The Royal Bank of Scotland and City Group were among the first pioneers that adopted an artificial intelligence platform in their banking operation (Computerweekly, 2016). They used cognitive solutions in the delivery of their banking services, especially in improving their customer services. An artificial intelligence called Luvo is adopted by the Royal Bank of Scotland to service the Bank's customers by providing answers for their questions. Luvo also has the ability to pass any request made by the customers to other rightful agents of the Bank. Luvo is basically a cognitive chatbot that utilises the service of IBM's cloud-based Watson conversation. Luvo is available to the said Bank's customers in Scotland since 2016.

Meanwhile, City Group adopted Behavox with a venture of US$20 million in 2017. Behavox is a software fintech that relates to behavioural analytics. It utilises natural language processing or NLP that improve the interactions between the employees and customers. Additionally, the Behavox's NLP ability efficiently converts the audio conversation into texts. Thereafter, Behavox applies sentiment analysis algorithms to the texts in order to detect positive (such as jokes) or negative interactions (such as anger) (Memminger, 2016). Behavox can also trace the negative pattern in selling and buying of products and stocks. After such tracing, Behavox will provide a remedy or takes action to overcome such negative pattern.

Another practice of adopting artificial intelligence's function can be traced from the SEB Bank of Sweden. The SEB Bank of Sweden is also recognised as the first bank that utilised IPsoft cognitive technology to improve their customer services (Lacity et. al, 2017). The IPsoft cognitive technology deploys a robot named Amelia that has the ability to understand 20 languages, apply logic and infer implications, and learn through experience by observing the interactions between human agents and customers. By having a multi-lingual artificial intelligence, the gap of understanding between the bank and their customers can be lifted and makes the communication better between the parties. By using Amelia, this can be attractive to attract any potential customers to engage with the bank. Furthermore, the customers can gain different experiences in communicating with the bank through Amelia as an artificial intelligence rather than a normal human agent of the bank. From a macro level of practices, it is observed that the majority of financial institutions that actively adopt and apply artificial intelligence in their operating systems are from the conventional banking industry.

At a micro level of practices, the application of artificial intelligence depends on the support of the governments, the readiness of the banks themselves to adopt the artificial intelligence in their financial services system, and the culture of their local finance market. Since the application of artificial intelligence is expensive, local banks may not have such a huge monetary budget to allow a total renovation within their financial services system. Moreover, the culture of the local finance market may be different from the competitive nature of the global financial market that has strong financially international banks. Majority of these local banks are still depending on their governments' supports, policies, and legislation. In a secured and regulated financial market, any change that tries to be made by the local banks must obtain a certain degree of approval from their governments or at least from their Central Bank as the regulatory authority. This is necessary to make sure that the local finance market is safe from any shocks that may cause uneven liquidity flow in the market. The micro level of practices relating to artificial intelligence can be seen from a regional practice or a practice from a specific bank.

Looking into the Gulf Cooperation Council or GCC countries, the latest development relating to artificial intelligence can be traced in the United Arab Emirates. There is an administrative movement made in the United Arab Emirates through the appointment of a specific minister of state for artificial intelligence (The Malaysian Reserve, 2017). Such an appointment is made to place the United Arab Emirates as the forefront country in catching up with global technological developments. Moreover, the development of artificial intelligence is taken as one of the United Arab Emirates' Centennial Objectives of 2070. By doing so, the United Arab Emirates becomes the first country among the GCC countries that take a serious measure in adopting artificial intelligence. As such steps are taken by their government, it is predicted that artificial intelligence will be utilised in all sectors available in the said country, which may include the banking and finance sector. This is taken as a positive step in the adaptation of artificial intelligence in both conventional and Islamic financial services industries in the United Arab Emirates. As one of the pioneering countries of Islamic financial services at a global scale, the step that has been taken by the United Arab Emirates is hopefully able to boost up the use of artificial intelligence in the said industry.

The application of artificial intelligence in the financial services industry of Southeast Asia can be considered slow and majorly depends on the aggressive movement made by the banks themselves. In relation to the Islamic financial services industry, the majority of Islamic banks are currently adapting to the advancement of technology (including artificial intelligence). This is impacted by the practices of the global banking industry. In comparison to their counterpart i.e. the conventional banks, Islamic banks can be considered slow in their adaptation to the advancement of the technology. However, they are certainly progressive in developing their systems and continuous efforts are made to catch up with the latest trend.

Based on the recent practices, it is identified that the Islamic subsidiaries or branches of conventional banks that are allowed to offer Islamic banking products are much faster in adopting the advancement of technology, including artificial intelligence. When a new operating system that cooperated with artificial intelligence is applied by the conventional bank, their Islamic subsidiary (or branches of conventional banks that are allowed to offer Islamic banking products) follows their parent bank to align with the systemisation of their operation. Moreover, the Islamic subsidiary is bound to follow the operation and technical conducts of the parent bank without disturbing any Shariah-compliance requirements. For example, HSBC as an international bank has spent around US$ 2.3 billion globally to increase the efficiency of artificial intelligence and digital capacities in their financial operating system. By making such improvement, all the branches and subsidiaries of HSBC (that including their Islamic subsidiary i.e. HSBC Amanah) will follow their parent company in time.

Depending on factors such as high cost, expertise, and skills in adopting artificial intelligence into their operational system, the Islamic subsidiaries of international banks have more opportunities to advance in applying artificial intelligence. Islamic banks that have an international linkage or their parent banks are rich international banks are also adopting technological advancement (including artificial intelligence) at a fast pace. This can be seen from practices as carried out by Al-Rajhi Bank and Kuwait Finance House; while the local full-fledged Islamic banks are catching up to such development.

In the 9th International Conference on Financial Crime and Terrorism Financing (IFCTF) in 2017, Al-Rajhi Bank's Chief Compliance Officer Mr. V. Maslamani highlighted that the said bank is at advanced stages in developing their artificial intelligence programme in combating money laundering, improving their customer due diligence, and refining transactions monitoring (NST, 2017a). Mr. V. Maslamani explained:

A.I. is the future and we believe that we can become the first bank in the country to roll out an A.I. programme for anti-money laundering (AML), customer due diligence, and transactions monitoring because of our smaller size, which allow us to be more nimble on technology development. With the implementation of this A.I. programme, we can save as much as 50 percent of the cost of handling all these three areas. I expect to see more implementation of A.I. in banks in 2018 and 2019, as A.I. can help to reduce cost, take away possible errors and speed up efficiency. (NST, 2017a).

Meanwhile, the Kuwait Finance House will initiate a robotic process automation programme (RPA), together with a collaborated partnership by EY in optimizing business quality and operational efficiency. The RPA programme that is enhanced with artificial intelligence system will work to evaluate the creditworthiness of the bank's potential customers, while it digitalises the rest of the banking process on behalf of the customers.

According to EY Partner Mr. Houssam Itani, he said: "RPA will enable quick and visible results – usually in weeks as opposed to months – in terms of cost efficiency and customer experience. In line with global and regional trends, RPA will form a stepping stone for the Kuwait Finance House (KFH)'s intelligent automation program" (IFNFintech, 2019). Additionally, Kuwait Finance House's Group Chief Officer of retail and private banking emphasised that:

A.I. technology is in line with KFH's growth strategy and our mission of delivering superior innovation and unparalleled customer service, whilst protecting the interests of stakeholders. KFH has made great strides in introducing a wide range of innovative e-services in different sectors at group level. (IFNFintech, 2019).

Currently, the introduction of RPA was done in Kuwait and it is believed that they will be extended to all branches of Kuwait Finance House as available around the globe.

LEADERSHIP IN FINANCIAL SERVICES INDUSTRY

Leadership is a complex notion that needs to be appreciated as its own unique nature when it comes to the financial services industry. Leadership, in general, can be understood as an influence (Kouzes and Posner, 2003; Ikpefan and Agwu, 2015). In relation to the followers, it is an ability to influence a certain group of people to work voluntarily to reach a certain set of goals (Ikpefan and Agwu, 2015; Bass, 2000). In accepting such indication of leadership, Stoghill (1974) explained that "leadership is a process of influence between a leader and those who are followers". With a similar connotation, Cohen (1990) described that "leadership is the art of influencing others to their maximum performance to accomplish any task, objective or project". In facing a new situation such as the disruption of technology in the financial services industry, the attributes of the leader must be dynamic enough to face the changes in the financial market.

The attributes of a leader in leadership are important. In relation to his followers, Koontz described that "leaders act to help a group to attain objective with the maximum application of its capabilities. They do not stand behind a group to push and to prod; they place themselves before the group as they facilitate progress and inspire the group to organizational goals" (Koontz, 1978). In recognising talents, a leader trains his followers and without shutting down their uniqueness in achieving their common goals. On this attribute, Caramela (2017) said a "leadership is the ability to not only understand and utilize your innate talents but to also effectively leverage the natural strengths of your team to accomplish the mission. There are no one-size fits all approach, answer key or formula to leadership".

Effective leadership will not be a success without good followership. In a structure of a financial institution or bank, the directions from the board of directors must be fulfilled by the management and their related officers without fail. In an Islamic bank, a similar situation can be found but with a bit extra requirement. The board of directors must not only concern with the decision making but also to achieve the Shariah compliance's requirements. Majority countries that established their local Islamic financial services industries have set up strict regulations that need to be followed in ensuring the nature of Shariah compliance. This is necessary to distinguish the operation of Islamic banks and conventional banks.

Good followership must have a strong communication strategy with their leadership, especially in facing any new challenges and to ensure transparency of information. Here, the corporate governance system within the bank becomes crucial to be evaluated. The same goes to the bank's internal control in managing internal and external threats to their operational system. The relationship between the leader and the followers should lead to positive action. This is similar to an observation made by Ogubunka (2004) on corporate management and leadership challenges where he said, "the leadership we desire is one that breed's positive influence… it is about transformation of value into actions, vision into realities, obstacles into innovations, separateness into solidarity, and risks into reward". In reality, good leadership and followership will not guarantee success in achieving the required goals; however, they can minimize poor corporate governance, mismanagement, and unrealistic objectives of the project.

In relation to the Islamic financial services industry, there are several influential leaders at the global scale that moves the said industry forwards. According to Abdul Alim (2014), leaders such as Khurshid Ahmad, Hajj Saeed Bin Ahmed Al Lootah, Prince Mohamed Al Faisal Al Saud, Tun Dr. Mahathir Mohamad, and Sheikh Nizam Yaquby have huge influences not only in the establishment of Islamic financial services industry locally but also globally. The Islamic financial services industry is a revolution that separated the banking system with interest (riba) and other prohibited elements as provided under Shariah. At the early stage of transformation in the 1970s, Hajj Saeed Bin Ahmed Al Lootah said, "I was raised on Islamic teachings and these say that riba (interest) cannot be touched. Travelling to many countries I saw how people transacted with banks and did their business and trading. Over here in Dubai, there were also these riba banks. And nobody said anything, nobody objected. That made me think: Why do we have to accept their banking and financial system? Why don't we use Islamic principles? People can buy and sell and do financing, all of that without involving riba" (Abdul Alim, 2014). Later, he went to consult Sheikh Rashid bin Saeed Al Maktoum, the ruler of Dubai.

According to Prince Mohamed Al Faisal Al Saud that established two earliest Islamic banks in GCC region, "As a Muslim, I have no choice but to combat riba (most often translated as interest). The task was to find alternatives, Islamic alternatives, which nobody believed was there in the beginning. In the beginning, everybody was laughing at us and saying what does religion have to do with economics?" (Abdul Alim, 2014). Even though the Prince was assassinated before he managed to see the spread of Islamic financial services industry globally, his leadership in establishing the earliest Islamic banks becomes an example to the rest that is holding the leadership in the industry.

Tun Dr. Mahathir Mohamad can be considered as the giant figure that moves the Islamic financial services industry in Southeast Asia. After his appointment as the Prime Minister of Malaysia in 1981, Tun Dr. Mahathir Mohamad directed the establishment of a national steering committee for the sake of exploring the chance in starting a local Islamic bank. As a direct result from the recommendation of the national steering committee, they established the first Islamic bank in the region that is known as Bank Islam (M) Berhad. In relation to the legislation process of Islamic Banking Act 1984, Tun Dr. Mahathir Mohamad mentioned that "When Malaysia became independent, we adopted the administrative system of the West. We adopted that and we became familiar with having rules for everything. If you want to do something you must have a law for it. So, we had to provide a law for Islamic banking. Of course, the law was passed by parliament and not passed by some Islamic authority. Islamic authorities in Malaysia do not have the standing to pass any law, so it has to go back to the parliament. In this same manner, you administer everything. It has to be systematic, for that is the way we used to" (Abdul Alim, 2014).

The leadership among Shariah scholars is also essential to make sure that the practices of Islamic banks are consistent with the tenets of Shariah. According to Abdul Alim (2014), "The first generation of Shariah scholars in Islamic finance had to learn very quickly how to this. This first generation of scholars advising the new Islamic financial institutions included such prominent Muslim religious figures as the former Grand Mufti of Egypt, Sheikh Mohamed Khater Mohamed Al Sheikh; the former Mufti of Sudan, Sheikh Professor Al Siddiq Mohamed Al Amin Al Darir; the Saudi Arabian Mufti Sheikh Abdul Aziz bin Baz; and Sheikh Yusuf Al Qaradawi". According to Sheikh Nizam Yaquby, he said, "Honestly, half of the questions I hear from people concern finance and money, like zakat [tithes] and inheritance. These are all about numbers and accounting. I think scholars who work as Shariah board members have more access to real problems of finance. I would advise scholars and imams who do not have all the answers to their community's concerns about money and finances to please, please, research it first or go to a scholar who is more knowledgeable. It is a specialisation" (Abdul Alim, 2014). Islamic financial services industry is dynamic in nature. Thus, the Shariah scholars that involve in this industry need to continuously upgrade their knowledge and learn from the expertise from others such as in accounting, economics, and finance. In reaching towards a more comprehensive resolution, the exchange of knowledge across fields is important and necessary to be done.

Thus, in facing the transformation and changes relating to the financial services industry, leadership and followership are essential to be considered. Persistent and positive attitudes towards facing such transformation and changes must be maintained at all time. This is necessary to ensure the sustainability of the financial services industry and their related institutions. So, they can continue to be viable in offering best services and financing products to their customers while adapting to the transformation and changes.

LEADERSHIP OF ISLAMIC FINANCIAL INSTITUTIONS IN ACCEPTING ARTIFICIAL INTELLIGENCE

In making any changes in certain sectors, the leadership plays a prominent internal factor in shaping a new movement in relation to practices and policies. While the demands from the market and customers are the crucial external factors. In analysing the importance of artificial intelligence and Islamic financial services industry, Kmeid is in the opinion that:

As customers become more sophisticated and knowledgeable, A.I. becomes extremely critical to Islamic finance. Like other aspects of life, the smart use of A.I. is a game-changer for the industry. When it comes to technology, what applies to conventional finance also applies to Islamic finance. ... Customers of financial institutions will conduct 85% of their financial transactions with no human interaction by 2020. With changing customer needs and a growing generation of millennial, a bigger challenge for Islamic financial institutions is the fierce competition of conventional banks offering financial services that are both attractive and popular among millennials. Today's customers of Islamic financial institutions require greater transparency, personalized products and seamless experience across all channels. ... A.I. is able to influence the speed and accuracy of this experience too. (Wahed Invest, 2017).

The use of technology in the financial services is attractive to the millennial customers, and extend the banks' services across borders and space. With such a trend among the customers, there is huge potential for Islamic financial services institutions to grab and utilise through the innovations of technology (including artificial intelligence).

In relation to the leadership of Islamic financial services institutions or banks in accepting artificial intelligence, a positive trend can be traced among the practitioners in the industry. In catching up with the disruption of technology including artificial intelligence among the countries in Southeast Asia, the development is at a slow pace with high committed efforts. This is happened due to the careful approach taken by the banks. Moreover, there is an apparent need to change the legislation in order to support innovative changes due to the use of technology by the banks. The competition among the Islamic financial services institutions in adapting to such changes is apparent and can be considered positive since such competition allows them to grow and innovate further.

In catching up with such technological development, Indonesia is not left out to adapt to the recent trend. Furthermore, according to a recent study conducted by Forrester Consulting on behalf of Appier, they found that Indonesia was ranked at the first place in the Asia Pacific region in applying artificial intelligence (Jakarta Post, 2018). With rapid business ventures are involved in adapting to the artificial intelligence in their operation and system, it is a good motivational factor to influence the Islamic banks in Indonesia to move further in adopting artificial intelligence and other technological development (Jakarta Post, 2018). Meanwhile, observation is done by Macky (Imark International, 2018) in relation to the practice in Philippine, he said:

In the Philippines, the demand for automation in the local market has started rapidly. Even the small enterprises need to automate operations to ensure that their goals to double and triple their revenues are met. Tech companies like IMARK help a number of Philippine companies to leverage high-tech tools that the world's most innovative companies are deploying to their own systems. Making the Philippines more technological like the rest of the first-world countries is slowly happening this year. By 2030, it is not impossible to see the biggest Philippine brands running without machine learning technologies integrated into artificial intelligence. (Imark International, 2018).

This is a good indication of the increase in the use of artificial intelligence in the local market and thus, may influence the rest of the business sectors which includes the banking sector. By having such view, it is encouraged here for the Government of Philippines to look into the potentials of Islamic financial services industry in their country.

In Brunei, Professor Lee Soo-young from Korea Advance presented the proposal during the Brunei-Korea ICT Conference to Promote New Industry in 2016, which took place at the Prime Minister's Office (PMO) Building (Brudirect, 2016). In his presentation, he spoke about exploiting artificial intelligence and the establishment of an Artificial Intelligence Institute in Brunei. The role of the said institute would be education, research and development, and business incubation for Bruneian institutes. The artificial intelligence would be the strategic area of focus. It would involve collaboration with domestic and international organisations. Moreover, Brunei is also one of the leading countries that actively involved with global Islamic banking and finance industry. Such a trend of leadership in accepting artificial intelligence can be considered positive and good for further development of artificial intelligence in the global Islamic banking and finance industry. Based on the proposal made by Professor Lee Soo-young, it is also suggested here to the Government of Brunei to progressively collaborate with their own local Islamic banks to explore the potentials of artificial intelligence in the operation of the Islamic banking system.

Malaysia is among the progressive countries in Southeast Asia that adapting towards embracing the use of technology in their financial services market (NST, 2017b). Moving forward in introducing digital banking and forming their own Shariah digital framework, Malaysia aims to be actively involved in the global halal market and halal tourism destination. Moreover, a vital improvement of the Islamic financial services system with artificial intelligence is inevitably a must to continue to catch up with the continuous technological development in the global banking industry. The newly elected Government of Malaysia continues to take a progressive step in maintaining Malaysia as the leading country in the development of Islamic banking and finance globally.

During the 15th Kuala Lumpur Islamic Finance Forum 2019, Tun Dr. Mahathir Mohamad the current Prime Minister of Malaysia encourages the Islamic banks to make an investment in technologies (NST, 2019). Tun Dr. Mahathir Mohamad said:

Moving forward, Islamic banking and finance players must also be intensely invested in technologies in order to transform the way they conduct their banking services and disseminate their products more effectively and efficiently. ...Fintech has also penetrated the Islamic finance space despite it being considered in still a very early stage. However, the potential disruptions to traditional Islamic finance should not be underestimated. The disruptions can swing both ways. From the Islamic finance consumer perspective, fintech disruptions are largely positive. Fintech innovation provides choices which are more aligned to individual needs. With more options, consumers enjoy more competitive financial services cost. Latest technology embraced by fintech leveraging on Internet, mobile devices, social media integration, big data analytics and artificial intelligence (A.I.) make financial transactions more automated, user-friendly and more convenient, thus a superior customer experience. (Prime Minister Office, 2019).

Thus, towards achieving the true value-based intermediation, such investment on technology innovations including artificial intelligence is necessary to strengthen Malaysia's position as the leading country. Simultaneously, it is also essential to enhance the growth of the Islamic banking sector while impacting positive growth to the economy, community, and environment in Malaysia and other countries.

CHALLENGES IN ADOPTING ARTIFICIAL INTELLIGENCE IN ISLAMIC FINANCIAL SERVICES INSTITUTIONS

The leadership of Islamic financial services institutions that has a positive attitude towards adopting artificial intelligence is a good stepping stone in shaping the financial market. In adopting artificial intelligence in the said industry, there are apparent challenges that need to be overcome by the Islamic financial services institutions. These challenges can be traced from (a) cost of implementation; (b) working skills of employees; (c) adequate legislations; (d) storage of the collected information; and (e) objectives in using the artificial intelligence.

(a) The cost of implementation: artificial intelligence is among the latest technologies depending on the capacity of machine learning. It is a new technology. Thus, it is apparently expensive in relation to its implementation in the financial services system. Without an adequate budget, the Islamic financial services institution may not able to adopt artificial intelligence completely in their system. This is one of the reasons as to why the practice in adopting artificial intelligence has only been carried out mainly by the bank's subsidiaries that have international linkage. In the case of failure, they will not feel so much impact due to their huge capital and profit gains.

The (b) working skills of employees: with the application of artificial intelligence, there is a tendency that the artificial intelligence may remove a number of tasks that are traditionally done by human employees such as accountants, data administrators, and market analysists. Instead of losing their jobs to the application of artificial intelligence, the employees must be equipped with versatile working skills that they may utilise in completing their tasks while working along with artificial intelligence. By having the application of artificial intelligence in the Islamic financial services industry, a new dimension of professional skills may be developed and trained among the employees. Depending on the leadership of the banks, the employees must be equipped with enough training and opportunities to increase their versatile skills and talents.

The implementation of artificial intelligence is also depending on the existence of (c) adequate legislation. In facing the rapid development of technology and artificial intelligence in the financial services system, there are loopholes in the existing legislation to capture their usage in the practice. This is crucial especially for the protection of customers and information. Any kind of misuse of information from the customers may disturb their privilege and open the banks for legal claims. Moreover, without any adequate legislation, the application of artificial intelligence may go against the laws and this may disturb its implementation in the operational system.

In the implementation of artificial intelligence, the (d) storage of the collected information must be considered carefully. The artificial intelligence may collect and processes large amounts of information and data at an expeditious rate. In the short amount of time, artificial intelligence may produce the financial data in an efficient manner which is productive for the Islamic financial services institutions. However, it is important to consider the storage of such collected information. Despite the advantages of efficiency and productivity, artificial intelligence may consume much information from organisations and customers that may deal or conclude transactions with the bank. Such information or data may be sensitive in nature. Islamic financial services institutions may also need to spend a certain cost to upgrade the security in their system and deal with the data from their customers with extra due care and diligence. Moreover, they have to guarantee that such sensitive information may not be used for any other reason, except for the purposes of the related transactions.

The application of artificial intelligence can be versatile in nature. Subject to the approvals from the relevant regulators, the application of artificial intelligence may be used in many segments of the banking system. However, the Islamic financial institutions themselves need to be clear on their objectives in using such an application. Instead of having any kind of wastage of resources and information, the banks may maximize the application of artificial intelligence with such clear objectives. For example, if the banks want to improve their customer services, they need to be clear on the level of satisfaction that their customers have towards their existing customer services. They also need to be aware of which channels of communication that their customers frequently contacting them. If the customers frequently contacting them through their official websites and emails, may be the most suitable application of artificial intelligence that the banks may introduce is a chatbot. If the customers frequently contact the banks by using phone calls, the banks may use artificial intelligence that can pick up the calls and providing the answers or directly connecting the customers with any appropriate officers.

Artificial intelligence may possibly cover a lot of data-driven functions in the financial services system. Nevertheless, it does not mean the implementation of artificial intelligence can replace certain functions that require sense, intellectual, and talent. With the increase of artificial intelligence in the said industry, the connectivity and relationship between humans as the employees and artificial intelligence may require advanced skills and flexibility in the working environment. In relation to Islamic financial services industry, the roles of Shariah advisors in making Shariah-compliance resolution may not be replaced by the artificial intelligence since such resolution making process is depending on the ever-growing knowledge of Shariah, the evaluation of morals, and intellect.

CONCLUSION

The financial industry is currently experiencing a transformation. These disruptive financial technologies and newly founded financial start-ups are taking hold and challenging the current way of traditional banking and finance sector. However, these technologies and start-ups are increasing in size and influence. Accessibility towards financial solutions is made possible with these financial technologies, especially to those who stand unbanked due to geographical factor. The incumbent players i.e. the Islamic banks still play a central role in the industry. Facing this current scenario, Islamic banks need to adapt to remain relevant and competitive in the future.

Looking into the use of artificial intelligence in the Islamic and finance industry of Southeast Asia, the leadership of Islamic banks portrays their readiness towards accepting the technology's innovation or artificial intelligence. However, they are still tied down to the regulatory requirements, the readiness of their employees, acceptance of their shareholders, and awareness of their customers. HSBC (with their subsidiary HSBC Amanah), Al-Rajhi Bank, and Kuwait Finance House seems to be at the front sit in implementing technology's innovation of artificial intelligence.

REFERENCES

Agrawal, A., Gans, J., & Goldfarb, A. (2019a). Economic Policy for Artificial Intelligence. *Innovation Policy and the Economy*, *19*(1), 139–159. doi:10.1086/699935

Agrawal, A., Gans, J. S., & Goldfarb, A. (2019b). Artificial intelligence: The Ambiguous Labour Market Impact of Automating Prediction. *The Journal of Economic Perspectives*, *33*(2), 31–50. doi:10.1257/jep.33.2.31

Aitken, R. (2018). *Global Financial Services Bullish on AI, the 'Disruptive Tech' Frontrunner*. Retrieved from https://www.forbes.com/sites/rogeraitken/2018/11/28/global-financial-services-bullish-on-ai-the-disruptive-tech-frontrunner/?source=post_page---------------------------#5ed3b85f2311

Ala, A. A. (2014). *Islamic Banking and Finance in the Philippines*. Retrieved from Inclusive Insurance Asia Website: https://www.inclusiveinsuranceasia.com/docs/landscape-study-2013/session6/MLSAO_S6_Takaful_BSP_Arifa.pdf

Alim, E. A. (2014). *Global Leaders in Islamic Finance: Industry Milestones and Reflections*. John Wiley & Sons.

Asian Development Bank. (2018). *Republic of the Philippines: Islamic Finance for the Philippines*. Retrieved from https://www.adb.org/sites/default/files/project-documents/50325/50325-001-tar-en.pdf

Basilico, P., & Attanasio, R. (2018). *A preliminary overview of RegTech*. Retrieved from https://www.politesi.polimi.it/bitstream/10589/142407/5/A%20preliminary%20overview%20of%20RegTech.pdf

Bass, B. M. (2000). The Future of Leadership in Learning Organizations. *The Journal of Leadership Studies*, *7*(3), 18–40. doi:10.1177/107179190000700302

Belanche, D., Casaló, L. V., & Flavián, C. (2019). Artificial Intelligence in FinTech: Understanding Robo-Advisors Adoption among Customers. *Industrial Management & Data Systems*, IMDS-08-2018-0368. doi:10.1108/IMDS-08-2018-0368

Britannica. (2019). *Artificial Intelligence*. Retrieved from https://www.britannica.com/technology/artificial-intelligence

Brudirect. (2016). *Brunei-Korea ICT Conference held to promote new industry*. Retrieved from https://brudirect.com/news.php?id=11167

Caramela, S. (2017). 4 ways to define leadership. *Business News Daily*. Retrieved from https://www.businessnewsdaily.com/3647-leadership-definition.html

Cohen, W. A. (1990). *The Art of a Leader*. Englewood Cliffs, NJ: JosseyBass.

Computerweekly. (2016). *Royal Bank of Scotland to use A.I. platform for customer services*. Retrieved from https://www.computerweekly.com/news/450400525/Royal-Bank-of-Scotland-to-use-AI-platform-for-customer-services

Engel, C. (2018). *Artificial Intelligence: The Weapon of Choice in Banks' Fight for Survival*. Retrieved from https://thefinancialbrand.com/71108/artificial-intelligence-banking-machine-learning/

Finews Asia. (2016). *Ant Fortune: Wealth Management with Several Scenarios*. Retrieved from https://www.finews.asia/finance/22965-ant-fortune-offers-wealth-management-with-scenarios

Fintech, I. F. N. (2019). *Islamic Bank becomes the First in Kuwait to integrate AI*. Retrieved from http://www.ifnfintech.com/eng/article-detail.php?guid=26EE62DB-F106-4880-851C-1ACB022FB5C6

Gokul, B. (2018). Artificial Intelligence in Financial Services. *Sansmaran Research Journal*, *8*(1), 3–5.

Ikpefan, O. A., & Agwu, M. E. (2015). Leadership of modern financial institutions and the changing paradigm of Banking in Nigeria. *Journal of Internet Banking and Commerce*, *20*(3), 1–17.

Jakarta Post. (2018). *Indonesia leads Asia-Pasific in AI implementation, study shows*. Retrieved from https://www.thejakartapost.com/news/2018/09/05/indonesia-leads-asia-pacific-in-ai-implementation-study-shows.html

Kaplan, J. (2016). *Artificial Intelligence: What everyone needs to know*. Oxford University Press.

Kmeid, R. (2017). Will Artificial Intelligence Rejuvenate Islamic Finance. *Wahed Invest*. Retrieved from https://journal.wahedinvest.com/will-artificial-intelligence-rejuvenate-islamic-finance/

Koontz, H. (1978). *Essentials of Management*. New Delhi: Tata McGraw Hill Publishing Co. Ltd.

Kouzes, J., & Posner, B. (2003). *The Leadership Challenge*. San Francisco: Jossey-Bass.

Lacity, M., Willcocks, L. P., & Craig, A. (2017). *Service automation: cognitive virtual agents at SEB Bank*. Retrieved from http://www.umsl.edu/~lacitym/LSEOUWP1701.pdf

Mackenzie. (2015, December 15). The future military artificial intelligence complex? *Financial Times*.

Macky, M. (2018). Artificial Intelligence 2017: AI age has begun in the Philippines. *Imark International*. Retrieved from https://www.imarkintl.com/artificial-intelligence-philippines/

Maddox, T. M., Rumsfeld, J. S., & Payne, P. R. (2019). Questions for Artificial Intelligence in Health Care. *Journal of the American Medical Association*, *321*(1), 31–32. doi:10.1001/jama.2018.18932 PMID:30535130

Malaysian Reserve. (2017). *A.I. and Islamic Financial Institutions*. Retrieved from https://themalaysian-reserve.com/2017/12/18/ai-islamic-financial-institutions/

Memminger, M., Baxter, M., & Lin, E. (2016). *Banking regtechs to the rescue*. Retrieved from www. bain. com/Images/BAIN_BRIEF_Banking_Regtechs_to_ the_Rescue. pdf

NST. (2017a). *Al Rajhi to roll out Malaysia's first Artificial Intelligence programme for Anti-Money Laundering*. Retrieved from https://www.nst.com.my/business/2017/10/287718/al-rajhi-bank-roll-out-malaysias-first-artificial-intelligence-programme

NST. (2017b). *Malaysia introduces the first Islamic digital framework*. Retrieved from https://www.nst.com.my/business/2017/12/316538/malaysia-introduce-first-islamic-digital-framework

NST. (2019). *PM: Islamic Banking Players must Invest in Technologies*. Retrieved from https://www.nst.com.my/news/nation/2019/04/478016/pm-islamic-banking-players-must-invest-technologies

Ogubunka, M. U. (2004). *Corporate Management and Leadership Challenges*. Lagos: The Nigerian Banker CIBN.

Prime Minister Office. (2019). *Media Release the 15th KLIFF*. Retrieved from https://www.pmo.gov.my/wp-content/uploads/2019/04/Media-Copy-Speech-YAB-Tun-Mahathir-Mohamad-at-the-Kuala-Lumpur-Islamic-Finance-Forum-2019-on-10-April-2019.pdf

Stogdill, R. M. (1974). *Handbook of Leadership: A Survey of the Literature*. New York: Free Press.

The Digital Finance Institute. (2018). *Global Review of Commercial A.I.: Artificial Intelligence and Machine Learning Report for Business*. Retrieved from Digital Finance Institute Website: http://www.digitalfinanceinstitute.org/?post_documents=ai-report

Wahed. (2017). *Will Artificial Intelligence Rejuvenate Islamic Finance*. Retrieved from https://journal.wahedinvest.com/will-artificial-intelligence-rejuvenate-islamic-finance/

Welling, M. (2019). *Artificial Intelligence Versus Intelligence Engineering*. Harvard Data Science Review.

Chapter 4
Financing SMEs Through the Islamic Qard al-Hasan:
A Proposal of Islamic FinTech Interest-Free Lending for Government Initiatives

Auwal Adam Sa'ad
International Islamic University Malaysia, Malaysia

Anwar Bin Allah Pitchay
Universiti Sains Malaysia, Malaysia

ABSTRACT

Financing small and medium enterprises (SMEs) is one of the most important mechanisms to boost economic growth in both developed and developing nations. The contributions of SMEs in many countries' gross domestic product (GDP) have been overwhelming. SMEs improve job creation in all sectors of the economy and contribute to the people's economic wellbeing. However, many SMEs are not getting financing from their respective counties due to strict regulations and interest rate hike. With this kind of regulations and high interest, many brains are wasted, and many ideas are vanishing with the job opportunities attached them. Government agencies are therefore in need to innovate different ways to facilitate SME financing and support new businesses for achieving and maintaining sustainable economic growth. This chapter proposes an Islamic FinTech and its mechanisms to achieving this vital initiative using the Islamic benevolent loan "Alqard al-hasan."

DOI: 10.4018/978-1-7998-0039-2.ch004

INTRODUCTION

Small and Medium Enterprises (SMEs) financing is growing rapidly and are becoming one of the most important mechanisms to help create jobs in the private sector economy. Financial technology is one of the most important mechanisms for enhancing people's well-being and can also lead to the achievements of financial prosperity in almost all economies, big or small and developed or developing. Islamic economic system is more than ever in need of modern technology enhancement to develop its unique techniques of doing business and digitalize its financing contracts for better application in modern societies. *Qard al-Hasan* (benevolent debt) is one of the most important mechanisms initiated to help those in need or with the good business ideas to engage their businesses by offering them interest-free loans for societal development and public enrichment purposes. MSE's can find this a way to go in every society as it is meant for their personal business development and economic well-being of the society.

SMEs Financing Initiatives

Small and Medium enterprise financing has gradually improved throughout the years, according to the investigations initiated by the Organization for Economic Cooperation and Development OECD's the findings on the development of SMEs financing shows a very encouraging development. Lending to SMEs generally improved in 2015, with a significant upward trend in new SME loans. While in 2013, only 6 out of 20 countries reported an increase in new SME lending, this number increased to 9 in 2014 and to 11 in 2015. For example, the volume of new SME loans in Finland rose by more than 23% in 2015 after seven consecutive years of decline. The median value of the annual growth rate of participating countries rose from -2.6% in 2013 to -0.1% in 2014, and then to 6.4% in 2015, illustrating a significant recovery in new lending to SMEs over this period.[1]

In 2015, the average interest rate charged to SMEs reduced for many countries, it may be, however, due to lose monetary policies in place. SME interest rates in 2015 were less than half of their level in 2008 in Belgium, France and Luxembourg peculiarly as low as one third.[2] Demand-side surveys also suggest a continued easing of credit conditions in a majority of participating countries, including a decline in loan rejection rates. At the same time, large cross-country differences persist, with credit standards remaining comparatively tight and interest rates relatively high in the economies most affected by the financial and ensuing sovereign debt crisis, such as Greece, Hungary, Ireland, Portugal, and Slovenia. Moreover, in emerging economies with relatively high inflation rates, including Brazil, Chile, Colombia, Georgia, Malaysia, Mexico, the Russian Federation, Serbia and Thailand, 2015 interest rates remained on average more than twice as high as the median value of participating countries.[3]

In our world today, SMEs in the industrialized countries managed over ninety percent of the existing firms employing almost two third of the labor force, such firms have very important role to play in growing the economy with further creation of new segment of employment. (Ronel Harel, 2016)

Identifying SMEs Financing Pain Points

SMEs always experience several pains in their fight to secure funding and execute their businesses amicably. SMEs are constantly hassling to physically rushing to their multiple funding banks accounts; manual paper work, check issues and many troubling payments procedures. Fintech is determined to be solving all these worrying pain points. And one of the most daring revelations was that of RSA group

Figure 1.
Source: Cesar J. Richardson, 2016

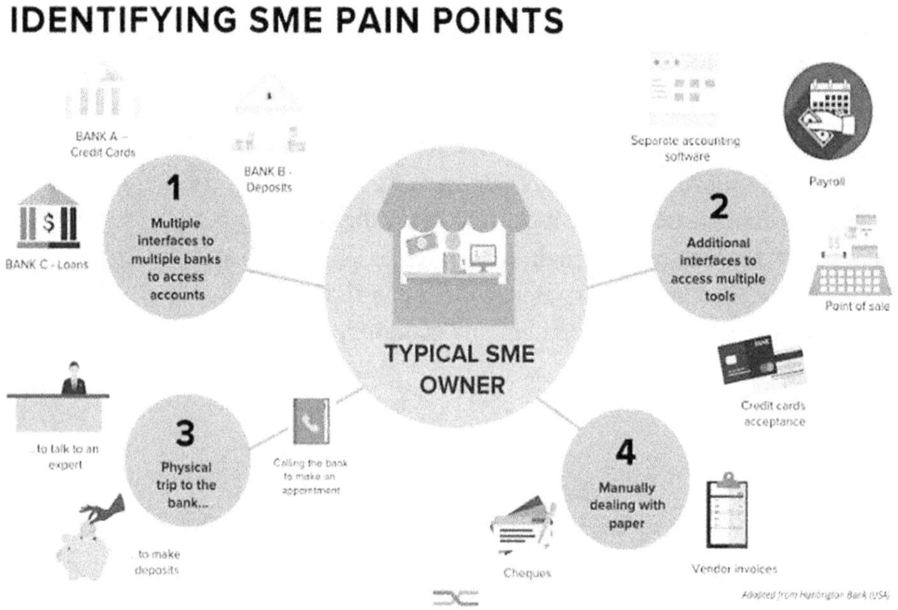

which reports that the majority of nearly (55%) of small and medium-sized enterprises (SME) don't actually survive over five years in business activities, RSA is a UK big commercial insurer, according to its new research, the research study "Growing Pains" uncovers the latest nature of the economy and barriers to developing SMEs, the study reveals a sinking development in one to five year business survival rates since 2004. Despite a recent improvement in economic conditions, survival rates remain worse than before the financial crisis.[4] The diagram below exposes the common SMEs pain points.

SMEs have the economic status in which government and other agencies are trying to solve their funding difficulties. Particularly those SMEs pursuing actual innovative projects which carries imminent potentials for economic growth.

The economic importance of SMEs and the funding difficulties described in the literature present a clear interest for governments to solve the funding problems facing these firms, particularly those firms with significant innovation potential in traditional sectors which lack alternative funding solutions. In this study, we explore the scope of available funding solutions in the Israeli market, including government programs, in order to discover if a market failure exists for funding innovation in traditional SMEs. In fact, our findings point to a profound market failure, with a complete absence of relevant funding sources for these types of companies. Through in-depth interviews with executives from a wide range of potential funding sources, we show that the main difficulty stems from a lack of financing schemes intended for ISTS and that in fact, the entire financing industry, be it based on debt or on equity, is geared toward serving either large companies which can provide sufficient collateral, or hi-tech companies. These problems, we claim, constitute a market failure and will ultimately hurt the growth potential of these small innovative companies working in traditional industries. Furthermore, lack of access to funding causes these companies to base their innovation activity on informal funding sources (Kaufmann *et al.*, 2014) which could lead to a focus on merely incremental innovation as a way of minimizing the inherent risks of innovation.

Benevolent Lending (Qard al-Hasan)

Qard refers to a contract of lending money by a lender to a borrower where the latter is bound to repay an equivalent replacement amount to the lender.[5] *Qard al-Hasan* is an Islamic interest-free loan which is given by the lender to the borrower on the basis of benevolence and kindness. According to the *Shari'ah*, *Qard al-Hasan* loans are not profitable loans, the lender should not whatsoever benefit from the loan given by getting an extra amount in return. The borrower is obliged to pay only the principal amount. However, since the benevolent loans are meant for assistance kindness and compassion, the borrow might do the same if he wishes, by paying better than the amount he has collected, but that should not be with prior arrangement, and must not be included in the contract, it is by the initial interest of the borrower and his generosity. The reason why it is lawful for the borrower to do so was the action of the Prophet Muhammad peace be upon him, the prophet was reported to have borrowed camels of young ages from his companions, when the repayment comes he discovered that has only the older camels, the prophet peace be upon gave the older camels and said the better among you are those who gave better than what they have taken"[6]

For that reason, *Qard al-Hasan* is a costless loan extended to people in need, for a specified period of time. At the end of that period, the face value of the loan *(asl al-qard)* is to be paid off. *Shari'ah* prohibits the stipulation of an excess for the lender, as it amounts to *riba*, whether the excess is expressed in terms of quality or quantity, or whether it is a tangible item or a benefit. *Qard al-Hasan* initiative shows the spirit of cooperation and brotherhood which will help improve the societal wellbeing and social security. If the Islamic Banks are required to attain certain socio economics objectives, then it will be vital for them to provide *Qard al-Hasan* products instead. Moreover, this will boost the corporate social responsibility of the Islamic banks.[7]

Qard Al-Hasan Shari'ah Regulations

Qard comprises three important components, contracting parties, offer & acceptance and the money to be lent. These three components are essentials for an Islamic acceptable Qard contract. There should be no contractual advantage that will benefit the lender in *Qard al-Hasan*, therefore there will be no pre-agreed periodic rebate (*ibra*) to the contract in which the buyer in an installment of a deferred selling price that has link to the *Qard al-Hasan* contract. There should be no any benefit whatsoever, including *hiba* that is given by the borrower to the lender be it in cash or in kind or any benefit if it is conditional to the *Qard* contract. However, any contractual benefit which is generic and has no any connection with the *Qard* and not special to the lender is permissible. Likewise any *Ibra* which has been given after settlement of a full selling price of an independent contract of sale that has no connection to the *Qard* contract shall not be regarded as a contractual benefit to the lender.[8] It is also not regarded as contractual benefit to the lender, any specific services, privileges or facilities provided by the borrower which are not exclusive to the lender, and they are allowed.[9]

Qard contract is considered completed once the following are fulfilled, if the *Qard* amount has been paid in full at the maturity or an early settlement via a mutual agreement of the contracting parties or by a transfer of the *Qard* payment obligation to be paid to or paid by a third party. Or by a complete waiver which has done voluntarily by the lender or by settlement via *al-Muqassah* with another *Qard* of the same value and maturity between the contracting parties. If the *Qard* contract is completed through any of the methods mentioned above, the contract of *Qard* is considered completed and the parties are free from any liability.[10]

Fintech Facility and Islamic Qard al-Hasan

Fintech has rapidly grown in the middle of the new millennium, with a huge growth in the last few years. However, Fintech is still signifying a very small share of business funding. One of the most important concerns here with that instrument is that it mostly assists to finance some particular projects other than an enterprise. It has been used in specific non-profit organizations and the entertainment industry, where non-monetary benefits or an enhanced community experience represent important motivations for donors and investors. Yet, over time, crowdfunding has become an alternative source of funding across many other sectors, and it is progressively used to support a wide range of profit-wise undertakings and businesses.[11]

In the Fintech industry, many technologies are feasibly active in various areas, some use tested tech to fulfill markets and consumer requirements, while others chased more experimental technologies like blockchain systems that store and remembered series of transactions that led to efficiency and cost friendly. Some Fintech used a robo-advisory system of technologies which gives automated advice by minimizing human impute. Furthermore, Fintechs are actually moving beyond business finances to offering a wider range of services for expanding industry's boundaries. The following diagram has illustrated more than thirty areas emerging as new norms in banking with the Fintech solutions.

The Smart Qard

Smart Qard is a short-term loan for small businesses that aimed at helping the entrepreneur's pay off their immediate bills in order to move their businesses faster so as to facilitate better growth and sustainable income. One of the examples of Smart *Qard* was SmartloansUK; the interest based smart loans firm gives away short-term loans for a twenty percent interest, one of the uniqueness of smart loans is that they are very fast, once lender's requirements are fulfilled, the approval will not last more than thirty minutes and the borrower will get the loan in the same working day.[12] This diagram illustrates how it works.

Furthermore, a similar platform was initiated in Singapore called smart funding; this is a platform that links local investors with SMEs who wants to trade their unpaid invoices for loans, this platform was initiated in order to create an alternative investment platform that gives high returns to local investors and also facilitates the preferred funding opportunities for SMEs and support their growth. This facility works very well for the Singaporean economy as investors secured 1.7% and 2.5% a month, or around 20% and 30% return per annum. The diagram below shows how the Smart funding platform works.[13] Below diagram shows how the Fintech facility works for invoice sellers in Singapore.

Figure 2.

Figure 3.
Source: https://apx.ac/investment

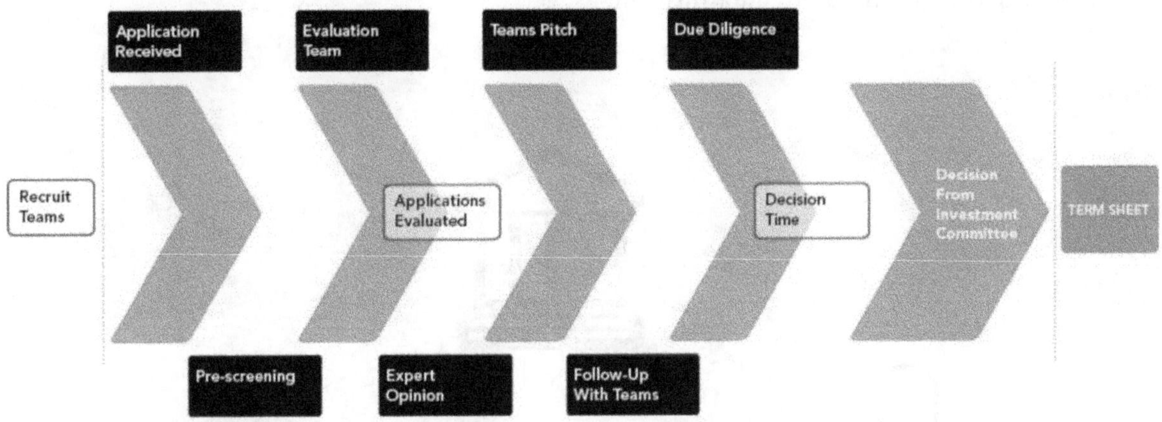

Figure 4.
Source: http://fintechnews.sg

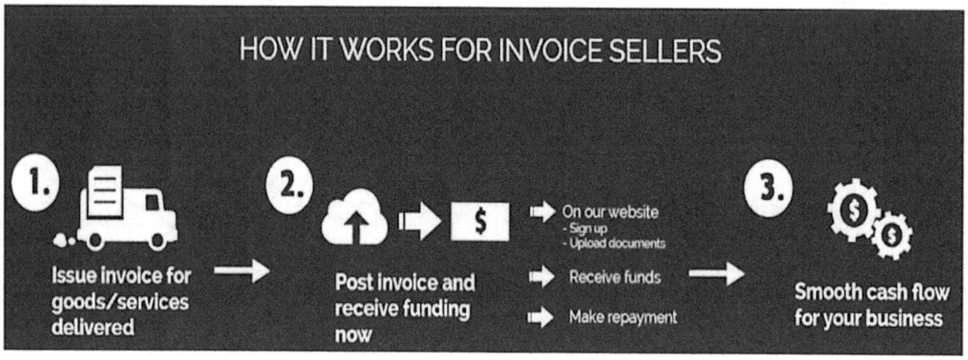

However, the *SmartQard* has a different approach as it is based on Islamic *Qard* which is "not an interest-bearing loan", the *SmartQard* will be given benevolently by the government to the borrowers whose businesses are experiencing slow in growth; this is to accelerate their business capabilities that will lead to and better returns. *SmartQard* will not charge any interest or fee, and by using Fintech, the *SmartQard* will be very fast and deliver the needful for SMEs growth and development. The following diagram illustrates how the *SmartQard* works.

Diagram for Smart Qard

1. The entrepreneur who has constraints of cash will receive *Qard al-Hassan* financing from the government.
2. The entrepreneur will operate his/her business as usual which to offer products and services to their customer.
3. The entrepreneur will pay back the financing to government which the amount of payment is the same with the amount received for financing.

Figure 5.

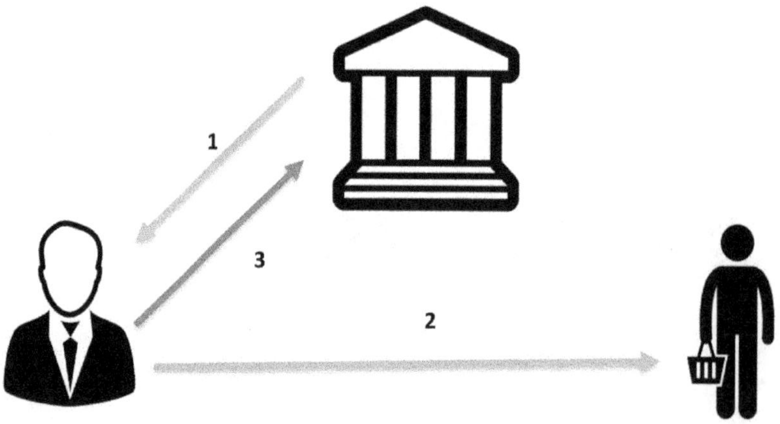

Islamic Fintech Solution for Qard al-Hasan Financing

Qard al-Hasan is a benevolent instrument used to help the needy but not a free donation, the beneficiary/bowworwer/SMEs should repay back the *Qard al-Hasan* at the repayment schedule. In this initiative, an SME will be applying for the *Qard al-Hasan* through the Government related agency, in which the evaluation process will be done by the relevant experts of the investment comity of the facility, the *Qard al-Hasan* will be paid directly to the SMEs account in a single click. SMEs *Qard Al-Hasan* Facility SQAF is designed to facilitate loans with a bit longer maturity than the *SmartQard*, as it is attempting to boost stronger businesses and startups. The diagram below shows how the *Qard al-Hasan* Financing works.

1. The government will be providing the fund for SMEs funding purposes.
2. The Government channels the fund to the Fintech facility
3. The Facility identifies the eligible SMEs for funding Purposes
4. The facility will distribute *the Qard al-Hasan* funds to the selected SMEs
5. After the maturity, the SME company will reimburse the *Qard al-Hasan* to the facility
6. The profitable SME may pay an extra amount to the facility by its own choice; the amount to be paid shouldn't be a fixed amount and will be determined prior to the Qard al-Hasan contract, as this is aimed at showing appreciations only.
7. In the case where were SME experiences lose and do not profit from it business, no appreciation amount will be expected.

Figure 6.

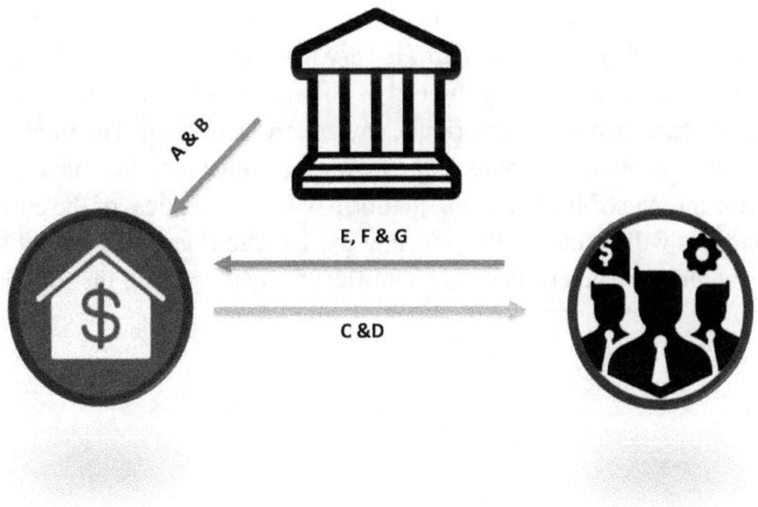

Payment and Reimbursement of Qard al-Hasan Financing

The payment and reimbursement of *Qard al-Hasan* should be designed based on the electronic and digital system, the system should comprise the mobile payments, online payments, and in-store payments capabilities, offering solutions that are multi-country, multi-currency and multi-sales channels. However, most of the developed payment technologies available are there to facilitate mostly interest based payments and deals, a new Islamic driving payment technology should be created from the scratch which will be supported with the Islamic principles and Shari'ah based contractual obligations. The new payment technology should support Islamic business to business supply chain and Islamic e-invoicing platforms for suppliers and traders, an Islamic mobile point of sale solutions should also be in a place where traders and retailers get consumer payments easily. These technologies could be used to enhancing the deals between SMEs and the Investors or the Government funding initiatives platforms, it will also help SMEs overcome many business hassles and elevate their market strategies and push for a stronger and faster economic growth.

CONCLUSION

Qard al-Hasan has proved to be one of the most important mechanisms that facilitate SMEs funding in the era of financial technology advancement. 'Fintech' will thus be playing an imperative role in achieving most of the Governments initiatives and do the needful for job creation, economic growth, business enhancement, and social development. The Islamic *Qard al-Hasan* is an answer to the difficulties experienced by a large number of SMEs in securing funds that will support to flourish their business ultimately leading to the GDP growth of the country. The Islamic *SmartQard* can be one of the most efficient methods of enhancing and funding small and medium businesses that often stuck in paying their immediate bills. This is because *SmartQard* is very fast and the refund will not take much longer, most of the developing nations are actually in need of some kind of *SmartQard* so as to touch the very small businesses out there, which never experience any government hand. The implementation of *Qard al-Hasan* using 'Fintech' technology can be a way forward in enhancing Islamic concerned businesses and drag many players into the SMEs financing platform who are skeptical of the current SMEs financing mechanisms, and this will be the way to boosting the Islamic financial system by moving together with the modern technology, which is playing a significant role in shaping the future of world banking and finance industry.

REFERENCES

Abidin, Alwi, & Ariffin. (2011). A case Study on the Implementation of Qardhul Hasan Concept as a Financial Product for Islamic Banks in Malaysia. *International Journal of Economics, Management & Accounting, 19*, 18-100.

Alnajdi. (2010). *Accounting and Auditing Organization for Islamic Financial Institutions "Shari'ah Standards."* Alimtiyaz Investment.

Bank Negara Malaysia. (2018). *Qard Application to Islamic Banks and other Islamic Financial Institutions*. Bank Negara Malaysia.

Capital, F. (2018). *Fintech Prediction. 3rd annual edition for financial technology prediction*. Author.

Harel, R., & Kaufmann, D. (2016). Financing innovative SMEs of traditional sectors: The supply side. *EuroMed Journal of Business, 11*(1), 84–100. doi:10.1108/EMJB-02-2015-0007

Haron, Saniza, & Ishak. (2015). Factors Influencing Small Medium Enterprises (SME) in obtaining Loan. *International Journal of Business and Social Science, 4*(15).

International Trade Administration. US department of Commerce. (2016). Top Markets reports financial Technology. International Trade Administration, US.

Ismail, M. B. (2001). *Albukhari "Aljami' Alsahih" [The book of debt]. In Husn al-Qada' Dar Duruq al-Najah*. Al-Qahira.

Organization for Economic Co-operation and Development. (2015). *New approached to SME and Entrepreneurship Financing: Broadening the Range of Instruments*. OECD.

Organization for Economic Co-operation and Development. (2017). *Financing SMEs and Entrepreneurs 2017 and OECD Scoreboard*. OECD.

ENDNOTES

1 OECD report "Financing SMEs and Entrepreneurs 2017": AN OECD SCOREBOARD p.1
2 OECD report "Financing SMEs and Entrepreneurs 2017": AN OECD SCOREBOARD p.2
3 OECD report "Financing SMEs and Entrepreneurs 2017": AN OECD SCOREBOARD p.3
4 https://www.rsagroup.com accessed 23/09/, 2018 at 2:40pm
5 Bank Negara Malaysia, "Qard application to Islamic Banks and other Islamic Financial Institutions" 26th February, 2018, p.4
6 Hadith reported by Imam al-Bukhari, the book of debt, vol.3 p.117 Hadith No.2392.
7 Ahmad Zainal Abidin, Norhayati and Arifin (2011)
8 Bank Negara Malaysia, "Qard application to Islamic Banks and other Islamic Financial Institutions" 26th February, 2018 p.16
9 AAOFI Shari'ah Standard, 2010 standard No.1-7 p. 270
10 Bank Negara Malaysia, "Qard application to Islamic Banks and other Islamic Financial Institutions" 26th February, 2018 p.17
11 SME report, OECD 2015 p.6
12 https://www.smartloansuk.com accessed 23/09/2018 at 3:18pm
13 http://fintechnews.sg accessed 25/09/2018 at 11:44pm

Chapter 5
The Path to FinTech Development Research on Islamic Finance in Turkey

Musa Gün
https://orcid.org/0000-0002-5020-9342
Recep Tayyip Erdogan University, Turkey

ABSTRACT

The concept of FinTech, which is the combination of finance and technology, aims to facilitate many services offered by financial institutions. This chapter examines the development of FinTech practices in terms of Islamic finance in Turkey. The chapter assesses the viewpoints of the sector participants, including participation banks, corporate customers, and FinTech companies operating in Turkey, about Islamic finance and FinTech. In this regard, the ultimate goal of the study is to present a projection to the market actors and decision makers in order to be able to enhance the share of Islamic finance in the sector. The interview findings of the study indicate that (1) new technological products and services will dominate the banking sector and these will change the way of doing business in the near future; (2) perception, knowledge, infrastructure, service network, and campaign factors affect the Islamic banking preferences of the customers; and (3) the challenges of legal acts, confidence, competition, and human resources primarily influence the development of the financial ecosystem.

DOI: 10.4018/978-1-7998-0039-2.ch005

INTRODUCTION

Nowadays, rapid developments in the field of technology have brought about great changes in every aspect of life. The financial technology called FinTech is seen as a compelling technology that will enable companies to compete effectively in the current century. The Financial Stability Board defines FinTech as "*technologically enabled innovation that could result in new business models, applications, processes, or products with an associated material effect on financial markets and institutions and the provision of financial services*".

The financial sector is undergoing a major transformation thanks to "FinTech", which means innovative financial technologies. FinTech, which takes its name from the combination of finance and technology, aims to facilitate many services such as payment, deposit storage, the financial consultancy offered by financial institutions, and makes them faster, accessible, cost-effective and secure at the same time. In other words, even when FinTech is thought of as only financial technologies, FinTech actually refers to companies that combine technology with innovative business models that make the financial services sector more accessible and easier. This means, in a sense, the toppling the banks from the throne, which is the most important actor of the financial system, and reminds Bill Gates' famous saying that "Banking is necessary, banks are not" in 1994. Financial technology companies, which emerged with this idea, have made great progress with the advancement of technology after the 2008 global financial crisis. The newly established technology companies have carried out the birth of FinTech with the efforts to change the banking system radically. In addition to offering new opportunities to customers, FinTechs, which pioneered the development of banks, continue to significantly change their traditional banking and personal finance approaches.

Banks in Turkey follow the technology closely and offer innovative products and solutions to the customers in many different areas of technology for years. This also allows Turkey to be a significant position in the banking sector in the world. Turkey using technology intensively has begun to generate awareness in this area together with the spread of technology. For example, ING Survey (2015)'s research results on the use of mobile banking show that the use of mobile banking in Turkey is at an advanced level compared to many European countries. While the mobile banking usage rate is 53% in Europe, this ration is determined as 65% in Turkey. Furthermore, due to Turkey's young and dynamic population, the use and appeal of technological products with the effect of internet penetration are increasing every day. With the interest of this attraction, the banking sector consumes intense energy to differentiate itself by offering products that will make life easier for the young and dynamic audience. In the same way, this young and dynamic group clearly shows that their interest in new products and services and their enthusiasm for using new technologies are in this direction.

In developing countries, and especially in Turkey banks have an important share in the financial ecosystem. Banks constitute approximately 80% of the financial markets in Turkey. In addition to the commercial banks carrying out traditional banking activities, participation banks aiming to increase their market share in recent years have started to take part in this ecosystem. On the other hand, although participation banks, which are operating in accordance with Islamic principles, grow faster than the commercial banks, their share in the sector is around 6 percent. However, in both Islamic countries and other countries around the world, Islamic banking is becoming widespread and these banks are adding new financial instruments in order to increase their share in the sector.

Within this context, this research study aims to examine the development of FinTech practices in Turkey and it especially explores FinTech application in Islamic finance. The paper assesses the viewpoints of the sector participants about Islamic finance and FinTech and discusses whether the share of Islamic finance in the sector can be increased by FinTech applications or not. In other words, the contributions of the financial technology in order to be able to enhance the share of the Islamic finance sector in Turkey will be assessed, claims and deficiencies related to the sector will be tried to be determined and suggestions will be put forward. Together with this objective, we will search whether the FinTech can expand financial inclusion or not. We discuss how the evolution of FinTech could trigger Islamic finance industry players for innovations and creativity by supplying new perspective and practice in financial transactions. Along with these, we believe in that technological infrastructure and several advantages owned by Turkey could support other Islamic countries and in this regard, Turkey could contribute positively to the development of Islamic finance in the world. Also in the scope of the study, we figure out recommendations and the needs to be done to improve the market further.

The discussions presented in the study are the results obtained through interviews with the participants from influential stakeholders including participation banks, corporate customers, and FinTech companies operating in Turkey. In this context, the goal of the study is to present a projection to market actors and decision-makers, as well as to contribute to the literature by providing a comprehensive perspective to academicians and researchers.

The structure of this paper is organized as follows. Following the introductory section, we provide a broad discussion of the topic incorporating the literature review under the background title. Next section discusses the development of Islamic finance in Turkey. After that, we present the data set and methodology of the research. And lastly, the study ends with the findings, conclusion, recommendations, and future research directions sections respectively.

BACKGROUND

Financial development has become an important component of economic growth. Today, the key to growth is the knowledge economy, in other words, the innovation. Harrison et al. (2014) examine the effects of innovations in the manufacturing and services companies and they point out that technological innovations excite the improvement and growth in the economy. Thus, technological development affects many industries and forces them to change the way of doing business as well as it has a similar effect in the field of financial services. The financial sector could benefit from technological developments and these developments could be considered as a serious competitive element for the sector.

The banking sector is the driving force of the finance sector in the economies. The banking sector leads to microeconomic and macroeconomic impacts through the mobility of savings, risk diversification, facilitation of exchange and allocation of resources. That is to say, the banking sector has a positive impact on economic growth by increasing savings and contributing to the transfer of funds between savers and investors. For these reasons, the banking sector can be regarded as the lifeline of an economy. Therefore, efficiently and healthfully functioning of the banking sector is crucial for the whole economy.

According to Gabor and Brooks (2017), the digital revolution of financial literacy will expand financial inclusion globally by adding new layers. This will transform the banks into producers of new financial products. In other words, the new financial concepts to be developed will be shaped around the applications of financial technology. The application of information technology in the finance industry is a field with great potential for innovations. Therefore, both enterprises and investors are highly interested in it. Pollari (2016), analyses the main factors of FinTech growth and its impacts on the financial services industry. The most important elements which make the FinTech a current issue are the developments in technology, the rapid increase in mobile applications and internet usage in recent years.

FinTech breaks the sovereignty of the banking-centric monopoly for financial services and allows companies from different markets to operate in the financial world. For example, Apple, the world's largest market-worthy company, entered the payment industry with Apple Pay in 2014, and the largest retail chain, Walmart, began to work in the banking and payments services. Another example from Turkey is MenaPay, which is a blockchain-based system, makes all payment records through QR coded mobile payment infrastructure. MenaPay offers a much faster payment system than traditional credit card methods. Especially the investors in the Middle East and Africa region show great interest in MenaPay[1].

The products developed by FinTech companies acting on the technology axis have characteristic features such as being simple and innovative, customer-oriented, scalable and not depended on the traditional systems. The participation of FinTech companies in the sector has accelerated due to the low-cost services provided to the customers as compared to the banks. These institutions, partially supported by banks and investors, will be in serious competition with the traditional banking sector. And it is foreseen that the traditional banking approach, especially the branches, will be changed by the effects of FinTech companies. According to the World Retail Banking Report in 2016, the rate of preference for FinTech services is 54.9% and on the other hand, the rate of preference for banks is only 38.4% (Capgemini, 2016). In another study, customer satisfaction for FinTech was 8% higher than traditional banking, and this level of satisfaction is in an upward trend compared to previous years[2]. For the year 2020, it is expected that 28% of banking and payment companies and 22% of insurance, asset, and capital management companies will be at risk. These mentioned shares are expected to be transferred to FinTech in the global financial sector (Lines, 2016). In short, FinTech is a significant tool which will fundamentally change the financial industry especially the banks that are currently seen as the main actors in the sector (Wonglimpiyarat, 2017). And, the banks are aware that the solution and business models offered by FinTech companies will radically change the dynamics and ways of doing business in the financial services sector. Therefore, banks want to adapt to these changes by cooperating with FinTech companies or by investing in FinTech companies and renewing their processes and infrastructures in the technical and business sense. The business and technical infrastructures of banks that cannot adapt to these changes can become obsolete in a brief period of time and as a result of this, it becomes inevitable for the financial services sector to lose customers in today's competitive environment.

In fact, finance and technology are very close concepts. Both the world of finance and the world of technology are very dynamic, and it is possible to face new products and services in these sectors almost every day. The financial sector, especially the banking sector, is trying to keep up with the ever-changing and developing technology, while there are financial products and services as a new main artery on the technology side. As a result, it is inevitable that these two dynamic structures come together. Financial technologies were continuously developing with introducing bank mainframe computers, more sophisticated data, and record-keeping systems in the 1980s. Internet and e-commerce business models flourished in the 1990s. Now, in the early part of the 21st century, retail financial services are being further digitized via mobile wallets, payment applications, robot-advisors for wealth and retirement planning, equity crowdfunding platforms for access to private and alternative investment opportunities and online lending platforms. Therefore, FinTech innovations are looking at a good platform in the financial industry (Desai, 2015). In other words, developments in technology are transforming consumers' access to financial services. By means of the internet, people can easily perform financial transactions from anywhere. Even, customers can communicate with their customer representatives online via internet banking and determine the most suitable services and products for them (Malaysia International Islamic Financial Center, 2016). In fact, it is possible to accept every area that technology touches on finance as a sample of FinTech. Financial technology initiatives such as mobile payment systems, online saving tools, daily budgeting practices, personal financial consolidation, financial solutions for small and new businesses, accounting solutions, robot investment advisors and mass funding are encountered. The combination of more powerful and fast chips, programming languages and operating systems, cloud technology, large data, application programming interface (API), broadband and mobile internet factors have created many changes in the finance, economy and the world. In this context, banks also make use of technology and invest in this area in order to provide better products and services to their customers and to increase customer satisfaction. In addition, banks can achieve both competitive advantage and cost advantage through advanced technology.

There are many studies such as Ferrari (2016), Romānova and Kudinska (2016), Vives (2017), Wonglimpiyarat (2017), Navaretti et al. (2018) and Thakor (2019) in the literature about the effects of financial technologies on the banking sector. Banks and financial services organizations can benefit from financial technologies in payments and transactions, digital wallets, mobile and retail banking, peer-to-peer (P2P) lending, crowdfunding, digital and alternative currencies, trading and foreign exchange, commodities markets, risk and compliance, security and privacy, financial advisory services and insurance. (National Digital Research Center, 2014). Unlike traditional banks which have a considerable amount of overheads and commitments, FinTech companies are able to generate savings through innovation and adaptation since they are smaller, more agile and quicker than banks. Thus, FinTech companies can help banks strengthen their competitive advantage by enabling them to reduce their operating costs significantly (Munch, 2015).

Although FinTech is a subject of many studies, we believe that there are many aspects that could be evaluated in the field of Islamic finance. Alaabed and Mirakhor (2017) study the role of Fintech in accelerating the implementation of risk-sharing Islamic finance. Firmansyah and Ramdani (2018) study one of the Islamic Fintech firms in Indonesia and assert that the Islamic Fintech innovatively provides a solution for encouraging financial inclusion and solving a specific social problem. Meanwhile, according to the study of Ulya (2018), the rule of sharia regulating the Islamic Fintech, specifically, peer-to-peer lending is not sufficient yet. Thus, there is a need for future improvement in the regulations which benefit the involved parties. Bakar and Rosbi (2018) evaluate the blockchain technology from Islamic financial perspective. Rusydiana (2018) attempt to reply to the most basic issues faced in the development of Islamic financial technology in Indonesia. The analysis result shows that the main problems which should be solved and improved are the policy instruments and human resources for Islamic Fintech development. Firmansyah and Anwar (2019) discuss the challenges and prospects of Islamic financial technology. They analyze Islamic Fintech firms in Indonesia and Singapore by using an online questionnaire in a descriptive approach. Their study findings show that the policymakers should provide favorable regulation to thrive in the sector.

According to the Global Findex Database, 73 percent of the adult population in the world who do not have access to bank services is concentrated in 25 countries. 22 percent of those who do not receive any financial services are located in Muslim countries and most of the people state religious reasons as one of the most important obstacles to accessing financial services (Demirguc-Kunt et al., 2018).

It is observed that Islamic banking, named participation banking in Turkey, and traditional banking are similar in private equity, free-market competition, and export of financial derivatives issues. Despite these similarities, there are fundamental differences between these two banking systems. This fundamental difference is that participation banks carry out their activities based on an interest-free system. While traditional banks collect deposits and give credit with interest, participation banks carry out interest-free banking activities based on Islamic rules. This difference brings a variety of diversity, vitality, and richness to the financial sector, as well as providing a qualitative and symbolic option for savings holders in different segments. It is thought that Islamic finance can offer a solution for individuals and businesses to overcome existing financial access problems by taking advantage of FinTech developments (Sidlo, 2017; Khan and Anuar, 2018).

Technology can reduce the asymmetric information and transaction costs and enable the development of financial products and services based on asset-based and risk-sharing. It is considered that the development of Islamic innovative financial platforms such as crowdfunding and peer peer-to-peer lending (P2P) can contribute to the reduction of financial inclusion problems. The potential of participation banks to develop mobile banking technologies by taking advantage of FinTech development is crucial because there is a limited number of Islamic FinTech service platforms. The best example is the "Your Bank" project which is the world's first interest-free digital banking platform developed by KuveytTurk Participation Bank in Turkey. By using this banking practice, people can open an account, apply for a credit card, get all banking and insurance services without going to the bank branch. Participation banks reached a certain infrastructure and customer confidence in the current system. They will be able to allow the Islamic financial sector to grow faster and more robust through a structure that supports technological financing mechanisms.

Turkey's strong internet infrastructure and a wide audience of users provide many opportunities for innovative companies. Besides, Turkey has the capacity to meet growing demand, new business models and innovation in the digital world thanks to the well-educated young population, who has worked in different parts of the world and is technology-oriented. Turkey is Europe's most advanced and competitive country in the payment systems market. For example, it is the first county offering contactless card payment technology services to the customers. The factors that improve the banking sector in Tukey are the technology and the ability of the banks to adapt themselves to the new technologies very quickly (Khalilov and Gündebahar, 2012). Digital wallet, biometric ATM, unmanned branch XTM, and wearable technology products are some of the examples in the sector. This dynamic FinTech sector in Turkey has attracted the attention of overseas companies and some companies which offer payment systems and mobile solutions were bought by foreign companies that want to expand the operations in Turkey and the surrounding area in recent years.

The presence of a strong financial sector in Turkey ensures an active and fast-growing structure of FinTech ecosystem. Turkey's financial sector and the banking system can remain strong despite the global and local economic and political fluctuations. The banking sector is one of the most powerful branches of industry in the country also performs the main driving task for the development of FinTech. The strengthening finance and banking sector within the framework of Istanbul Finance Center vision and talented human resources in the technology, finance, and banking sector play key roles in the rapid growth of the FinTech ecosystem in recent years. In Turkey, the FinTech market recently has a size of approximately $ 20 billion and is growing at 14% per year. The number of FinTech companies is over 200 in Turkey. It is possible to predict that the FinTech sector in Turkey could become a regional financial technology center by means of the geopolitical advantages in the near future. According to the global index performance score calculated by looking at the indexes such as the World Bank's Doing Business Index, Global Innovation Index, and Global Financial Center Index, in a sense, FinTech's growth and innovation opportunities are so high, although the economic development is at a limited point in Turkey. In other words, although Turkey is in the back according to the index performance, it is a place that far ahead in terms of FinTech growth and innovation in the worldwide.

Together with the advantages, the use of FinTech almost in all areas of life, especially in the banking sector, has also some drawbacks. The problems, which are subject to many studies such as Kim et al. (2016), Saksonova and Kuzmina-Merlino (2017), Kerényi and Molnár (2017), and Claessens et al. (2018) could be grouped under operational risk, security risk, system design, implementation and maintenance risks, abuse of products and services by the customers or firm personnel, reputation risk of the firm, and lastly, the risks of sanctions arising from legal violations.

Within the scope of this study, we hope that the findings of this research which evaluates the opinions of the stakeholders in the sector including participation banks, corporate customers and FinTech firms in Turkey will help government agencies, public, investors, and academicians to notice the future of FinTech in the lights of Islamic finance. And, also we believe that the Islamic financial industry can be able to outperform its competitors and can provide sustainable competitive advantage among their competitors by engaged with high technology system. The high Muslim populations in the world also give advantages and opportunities in promoting Islamic banking products and services. Islamic banks that used the FinTech system can easily and quickly advertise their new products and services in the world. This can attract customers to participate in Islamic banking products and services. In other words, FinTech looks like innovation in promoting Islamic financial products and services. As a result, FinTech is able to become a key enabler for future business.

DEVELOPMENT OF ISLAMIC FINANCE IN TURKEY

Establishment of Islamic Banking in Turkey

The private enterprises especially located in Central Anatolia form a different model similar to the cooperatives established against traditional banking since the mid-1960s. These structures, which are defined as "Workers Company", are the companies with a large number of partners starting to be established with the savings of Turkish workers abroad, especially in Europe. By the 1980s, the number of workers' companies exceeded a thousand (DESİYAB, 1981). Although this business structure model does not include directly banking, it is seen that the conservative people who have religious sensitivity have established with the aim of evaluating the funds in an alternative way without spreading the interest in commercial areas, industrializing and removing the regions and providing employment. These developments in the labor market have been an important motivating factor in the establishment of interest-free banking. Despite the failure in the majority of these companies, the experience gained in this field and the discovery of capital resources have strengthened the formation of interest-free banking model in the financial system. Support for the interest-free system was also provided by the entrepreneurs who formed the workers companies.

With the strengthening of the idea of interest-free banking, the first initiative was the establishment of the State Industry and Worker's Bank in 1975 (Asutay, 2013). The purpose of the Bank was to evaluate the savings of the citizens working in the country and abroad within the understanding of profitability and efficiency and to provide industrialization throughout the country by serving small and medium-sized enterprises (Yılmaz, 1993). This initiative model, which is not a direct Islamic bank, is noteworthy in that it is based on the principle of profit partnership which is one of the Islamic principles. The bank was known as the bank of the heavy industry since various workers' companies became partners in the bank. This interest-free banking model, which provided an important experience to the financial system, was able to continue its activities until 1978 due to the political and economic instability. It was transformed into the Development Bank of Turkey in 1988. These experiences have been substantial in terms of interest-free banking initiatives and applications in subsequent years. Economic and political developments in the national and international arena provided a roadmap for a banking system based on Islamic principles.

Turkey has moved to an economic system based on outward-oriented and competition in the early 1980s. With this transition, the financial system has begun to liberalize. Thus, the idea of "interest-free finance" has been matured in terms of socio-cultural, economic and political aspects. In addition to this evolution, Turkey is acquainted with interest-free banking model, by taking part among the founders of the Islamic Development Bank (IsDB). In this way, Turkey has gained the possibility of increasing the effectiveness within the structure of IsDB which is one of the world's leading financial institutions and plays a major role in the development of various financing techniques such as the realization of the economic cooperation program between the Islamic countries. As a result, getting into the international market for the Turkish businesses and organizations and the establishment of Islamic banking in Turkey have been facilitated. The historical process of Islamic banking in Turkey could be drawn in Figure 1 below.

The basis for the institutionalization of interest-free banking in Turkey which was started in 1983 by the Decree No. 83/7506 dated 19.12.1983 with the establishment of Special Financial Houses[3]. First, AlBaraka Turk and Faisal Finance Special Financial Houses started their activities in 1984 and they introduced a new model to the Turkish financial system. Then, new special financial institutions have gotten

Figure 1. Historical development of Islamic banking in Turkey

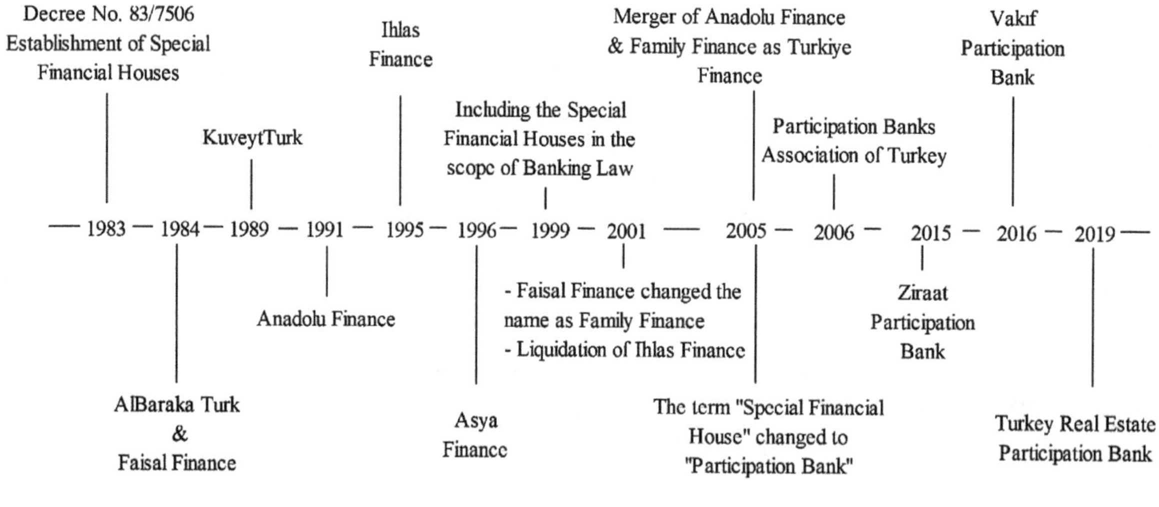

into the market. Interest-free banking, which started as special financial houses, has been strengthened by the legislative arrangements and new products offered to the financial markets. In fact, the special financial house model is unique for Turkey, there is no other country using this title. This definition has been controversial since it was inadequate in defining interest-free banking (Özcan and Hazıroğlu, 2000). Because of the 1980 military coup conditions, it was avoided using the Islam emphasis. Nevertheless, the interest of the community in Islamic finance has been increasing steadily. In spite of many local crises in the 1990s and the global financial crisis in 2008, this trend has continued. In a sense, this process has given a serious examination in terms of contribution of the system to the real sector and its resistance to the crisis. Subsequently, the legal basis of interest-free banking was partially strengthened during the banking reform and the title of Participation Banking, which emphasized the concepts of "interest-free" and "participation" were adopted (Özcan and Hazıroğlu, 2000).

The Transformation from Special Financial Houses to Participation Banking

The Turkish financial sector has met with interest-free banking system through the institutions named as special finance houses. With the legal regulations made in 2005, special financial houses have been subject to banking practices and their names have been changed to "participation banks". With the Banking Law No. 5411 dated November 1, 2005, Participation Banks have been defined as the institutions collecting funds and giving credits through current and participation accounts.

Participation Banking is a more coherent and meaningful definition of a banking model that offers banking and interest-free financial products according to Islamic principles. Thus, the system, which is defined as interest-free or Islamic Banking in the world, has gained a clearer understanding. Because the concept of participation refers to the "partnerships" that Islamic principles propose. The journey of Islamic banking in Turkey has been going on for nearly forty years. Currently, five participation banks (AlbarakaTurk Participation Bank, Türkiye Finance Participation Bank, KuveytTurk Participation Bank, Ziraat Participation Bank and Vakıf Participation Bank) operates in the Turkish financial system as of the beginning of 2019 after the liquidation (Ihlas Finance and Asya Participation Bank) and merger (Anadolu Finance and Family Finance) of the banks in this period. Participation banks serve their customers in the current system in accordance with the Islamic principles. In this way, they bring the ineffective funds that avoid interest in the economy.

The most important issue in the institutionalization of interest-free banking is the legal framework. If participation banking is to gain a strong momentum of development, it is necessary to prepare the permanent and legal framework of the system. There is a need for an independent law, including the basic principles, concepts, institutions, and rules. The most significant reason why Turkey falls behind in interest-free banking is the lack of specific legal framework although it started to operate interest-free banking on the same dates as Malaysia. The institutions in the sector had continued their activities by means of governmental decrees. They were included in the scope of law under the restructuring banking sector in 2005. Moreover, this law does not directly regulate interest-free banks, but it primarily supervises conventional banks. The strong legal framework is more important for capital markets and institutions than in other sectors. It is only possible for participation banks to carry out their activities easily and grow in such suitable market conditions. The importance of legal framework is obvious for the rapid growth of the sector and the increase of the market share as it can be seen in Malaysia and other countries (World Islamic Banking Competitiveness Report, 2013-214). It is inevitable to regulate this field with a special law so that Turkey can reach its goal of being a central country in interest-free finance and banking.

In addition, it is seen that actions are carried out to improve the sector both in terms of legislation and other issues. A significant change related to the account plan to be applied by participation banks was made by the Communiqué published in the Official Gazette on September 20, 2017. It was aimed to provide recognition and financial arrangement for Participation Banks. Thus, a uniform balance sheet and income statement will be obtained and a standard presentation, analysis, and interpretation will be provided to all stakeholders who need information for their supervision and monitoring. In the meantime, The Participation Banks Association of Turkey, which is a professional public organization providing services, consultancy, professional structures and functioning about the sector, was established. The association also aims to promote the rights and interests of participation banks within the framework of banking regulations and increase the competitiveness of the system as well as the growth of the system. Funds collected by participation banks are included in the scope of the Saving Deposit Insurance Fund. In addition, the Capital Markets Board gave the participation banks the right to purchase intermediary institutions or to provide agency services to intermediary institutions in order to intermediate the funds in the capital market. Thus, participation banks had the opportunity to offer securities.

Furthermore, the Interest-free Finance Coordination Board was established in order to be able to contribute the faster and healthier development of participation banking and insurance industry and to contribute to Turkey's international financial center vision. The activities of the Board are carried out by the Undersecretariat of Treasury. It is aimed to develop the interest-free finance system within the scope of the medium-term program for 2018-2020, which was announced by General Directorate of Budget and Fiscal Control in October 2017. In this respect, a draft law on interest-free finance was prepared by the Banking Regulation and Supervision Agency. It is aimed to establish the institution of interest-free finance standards and to determine the corporate governance principles in accordance with the principles of interest-free finance. It is also intended to implement the legislation to improve the participation insurance within the scope of the interest-free finance law in order to deepen the financial markets.

The Share of Participation Banks in the Sector

The banks constitute approximately 80% of the financial markets in Turkey (The Banks Association of Turkey, 2019). On the other hand, the participation banks, which are operating in accordance with Islamic principles, have a share of roughly 6 percent in total banking sector according to the data of Banking Regulation and Supervision Agency and Participation Banks Association of Turkey. Participation banks that operating banking services based on Islamic principles are able to implement many different banking facilities. In this respect, participation banks are alternatives for traditional banks.

As the beginning of 2019, five participation banks [AlbarakaTurk Participation Bank, Türkiye Finance Participation Bank, KuveytTurk Participation Bank, Ziraat Participation Bank, and Vakıf Participation Bank] have been operating in the sector. Participation banks collect funds by means of current accounts and profit-and-loss accounts, and also provide funds through financing support, profit-loss partnership, leasing, financing of securities and other interest-free financial services. According to the data of Participation Banks Association of Turkey, the participation banks in the total banking sector have shares

Table 1. The share of participation banks in the sector (%)

	2011	2012	2013	2014	2015	2016	2017	2018
Sum of funds collected	5.6	6.1	6.5	6.2	5.9	5.6	6.1	6.7
Sum of funds allocated	5.9	6.0	6.1	5.4	5.2	4.8	5.0	5.1
Asset size	4.6	5.1	5.5	5.2	5.1	4.9	4.9	5.3
Equity size	4.3	4.1	4.6	4.1	4.1	3.8	3.8	4.0
Net profit	2.5	3.9	4.3	2.5	1.6	2.9	3.2	4.0

Source: (Participation Banks Association of Turkey, 2019)

of 6.09 percent in funds collected, 5.44 percent in funds allocated, 5.08 percent in total asset size, 4.10 percentage in equity size and 3.11 percentage in net profit on average for the last eight years. The data obtained by the end of the years are shown in detail in Table 1.

In addition to economic necessities, the improvement of participation banks in Turkey has been affected by the discharge of under the mattress savings of individuals who wish to keep away from interest-bearing instruments. Interestingly, an average of 95% of the banking assets is in the interest rate system in a country where 99% of the population is Muslim. Even this is a worthwhile research topic to be investigated particularly.

According to the strategic plan prepared by the Participation Banks Association of Turkey, participation banks have set a target of obtaining a 15 percent share in the banking sector by 2025. Participation banks established by public capital (Ziraat Participation Bank-opened in 2015 and Vakıf Participation Bank-opened in 2016) are important steps taken to realize this goal. The Turkey Real Estate Participation Bank obtained permission from the Banking Regulation and Supervision Agency in February 2019 and became the sixth participation bank in the sector. It is unlikely that the share of participation banking in the sector could be increased without public support. The "negative perception problem" against the participation banks, which will be explained in detail in the further sections of the study, could only be overcome with the support of the state to the sector. In addition to the existing publicly-owned corporations, it is only a matter of time for Turkish Post (PTT) to operate in participation banking. PTT provides a wide range of services in the fields of mail, bank, and logistics, and is a corporation operating under the ownership of the Undersecretariat of Treasury. This will add more power to the sector.

DATA DESCRIPTION AND STUDY METHODOLOGY

Scope and Aim of the Study

The aim of this study is not to assess the significance of the FinTech firms for the country and the sector, which is now an indisputable fact. It is to explain what could be done in order to move the sector forward for the development of Islamic finance according to the meetings with the sector partners including participation banks, customers and FinTech firms.

The study examines the development of FinTech practices in Turkey and especially explores FinTech applications in Islamic finance. In this context, the paper assesses the viewpoints of the sector participants about Islamic finance and FinTech and discusses whether the share of Islamic finance in the sector can be increased by FinTech applications or not. In other words, the possible reinforcement of the financial technology to increase the share of Islamic finance in Turkish capital market will be discussed, demand and deficiencies for the industry will be tried to determine, and recommendations will put forward. In addition to these, we believe in that technological infrastructure and various advantages of Turkey will contribute positively to the development of Islamic finance in the world. In this regard, another goal of the study is to present a projection to market actors and decision-makers, as well as to contribute to the literature by providing a perspective to academicians and researchers.

Methodology and Sample Size

The quantitative data, which forms the basis of the study, is obtained by the survey method using the questionnaires through face-to-face, on the phone or online interviews[4]. Study participants are composed of participation banks, corporate customers, and FinTech companies. The data were collected in a period of approximately one year starting from the beginning of 2018 to the end of the year[5]. Before starting the research a pilot study comprising face to face interview was carried out with 15 academicians to raise engagement and awareness, and eliminate potential misunderstanding of survey questions.

The sample size for the participation banks is limited by the number of banks that is five only, operating in the sector as the end of 2018. These are AlbarakaTurk Participation Bank, Türkiye Finance Participation Bank, KuveytTurk Participation Bank, Ziraat Participation Bank, and Vakıf Participation Bank as stated previously.

In order to select the customer sample, we apply to the Interbank Card Center (BKM) periodical reports. BKM publishes the volume and the number of transactions with credit cards and debit cards by merchant category monthly. Among the 26 merchant categories 8 ones, which have the highest transaction number and volume, are selected[6]. These are Petrol Stations, Electric & Electronic Goods, Computers, Clothing and Accessory, Markets and Shopping Centers, Service, Insurance, Food, and Various Food. These eight categories account for approximately 80% of the number of transactions and roughly 65% - 70% of the transaction volume as of December 2018 (BKM, 2018). These merchant groups, which were traded with credit or debit cards, show us that these enterprises are naturally included in financial markets. The World Bank considers having an account as a sign of financial inclusion.

Lastly, to be able to determine FinTech companies, we ask for information from startups.watch platform. The platform is established to bring investors, business development experts, and many stakeholders of the entrepreneurship ecosystem together in the information and data-oriented environment. The platform creates a FinTech map and updates constantly. The map aims to give rough insights for potential domestic and foreign investors and acquirers. FinTech companies operating in Turkey are located on this map. To be able to take part in this map, firms should see themselves as an initiative to change the finance industry with technology.

Companies using FinTech solutions intensively does not mean they are FinTech companies. Also, government, municipality and bank initiatives are not included in the map. FinTech ecosystem composes of different categories. These are listed in 13 main groups: payment, banking, financing, corporate finance, insurance, crowdfunding, investment, personal finance management, wealth management, asset management, big data, hubs, and others, and crypto. Since the scope of our study is limited to the banking sector,

Table 2. Sub-groups and companies under the banking category

Subgroups of Banking	Companies
Digital Wallet	Beemo, BKM Express, GPay, Mobilexpress, papara, Paycell, peppara, Vodafone Cep Cüzdan
Card Schemes	American Express, Diners Club, Discover, Mastercard, VISA, TROY
Aggregator	BulutTahsilat, Kobaküs, manim, nakitex, Finstant
Conversation Banking / Chatbot	Chatbank, - dahi.ai
Unbanked	Multinet UP
Data	P1M1
Cyber-Security	SoolX, BVK Technology
Challenger Banks	-
Application Programming Interface (API) Banking Tech. Provider	-
Risk Management	Finecus
Infrastructure (Banking & Payment)	Asseco SEE, Banksoft, BIS Solutions, Cardtek, Cybersoft, Fineksus, Globit, Global Payment, innova, moneymo, Adam, C-Bilişim, Verisoft
Application Provider	Codevist, Enqura, Finartz, iPos, metamorfoz, Mobven, MOS Teknoloji, tmobtech, Commencis, Veripark, Verisun, PayBuy, RS Positive, Yaz, Architecht
Card Operational Service Provider	AUSTRIACARD, E-KART, Mastercard PTS, PlastKart

Source: Turkish FinTech Ecosystem Map, December 2018. Retrieved from https://startups.watch/reports

the sample was selected from the companies within this category. In this group, startups or ventures offer financial technology solutions to banks or perform banking services. As of the beginning of 2018, the sub-categories under the banking main group and the firms in these categories are presented in Table 2.

We could reach 10 firms out of approximately 60 firms in this group as listed in Table 2.

THE STUDY FINDINGS

Opinions of the Participation Banks

The development of technology affects many industries as well as the finance and banking sector intensively. The banking sector, which serves especially with its extensive branch network, has to compete with the thousands of technology companies that provide services in the financial area. Banks want to offer non-branch channel applications to reduce transaction, operation, and investment costs by utilizing technological advances. On the other hand, there is no clear data in the sector about whether financial services companies are a threat or an opportunity to the banks. In this context, how the participation banks perceived financial technologies and their applications are examined. Within the financial services sector, banks have retained their market share for years due to the difficulty of access to the sector such as entry barriers, and regulatory obligations and requirements. Thus, banks have used this advantage. The main reasons for this are the complexity of regulatory environments, high capital adequacy ratios, lack of favorable practices, and consumers and states' confidence in branded financial institutions. This protective shield is reinforced by the customers' stagnancy and the burden of opening a new account.

However, all these shields have now disappeared for banks and other traditional financial institutions. Rule-makers have begun working actively with new players in the market to offer more options to consumers, especially in an environment where the reputation of the banks has lost after the crisis. Some of the new FinTech services offer better, deeper or unique solutions than traditional financial products, and provide users a more intuitive experience. It is possible to complete the account opening in a few minutes through many FinTech applications.

Especially after the 2001 crisis, the banking sector in Turkey is forceful in terms of competition in the financial services industry and this makes Turkey different from other countries. Banks in Turkey are the industry leaders of the financial services with asset size, technological capabilities, and product diversity. Different perspectives emerge when the opinions of banks about financial technologies are considered. Some banks see FinTechs as business partners who support their digitalization process, while some banks consider FinTech as an adventure-loving actor who shows activities that could damage trust in the financial services sector.

Many people think of only financial technologies when they hear the word FinTech. Actually, it contains much more than financial technologies. FinTech describes companies that combine innovative business models and technology that will make the financial services industry more accessible and easier. Therefore, the use of existing technologies in banking activities or expression the importance of financial technologies by the banks does not adequately meet the scope of FinTech issue discussed in this study. In this context, when we look at the participation banks' perspectives to the FinTech companies, it is seen that some participation banks have already adopted, implemented and established FinTech subsidiaries and/or they have initiated project-based workouts. We observe that the attitudes of participation banks toward FinTech are consistent with the bankers' FinTech grief cycle approach presented by Nicols (2016). Nicols's 5-step approach is presented in Figure 2.

Figure 2. Bankers' fintech grief cycle
Source: http://jpnicols.com/2016/07/12/fintech-grief-cycle-bankers/

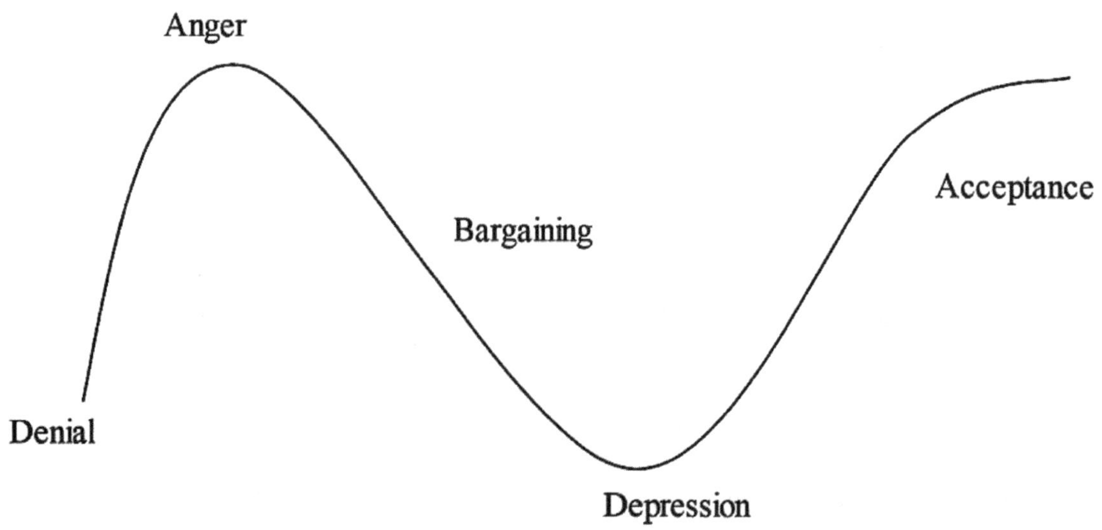

Nichols (2016) in his study states that the banks across FinTech companies have passed through a 5-stage grief process. First, the process starts by denying the existence of FinTechs and their contribution to the sector. Then it turns into anger and more aggressive measures are trying to be taken. In the bargaining phase, banks try to pass over the problems in resolving with temporary solutions. Afterward, banks start to think that the sector is not profitable and the struggle is meaningless in the depression process. And, eventually, banks inevitably accept the situation and make partnerships with the FinTechs which will be beneficial for both themselves and the sector. Similarly, first start-up firms are noticed in Turkey, then they are rejected and great anger is felt toward them, and lastly, they are accepted and treated with honor. FinTech companies are going through a similar process and in particular, FinTech executives think that their contribution to the financial sector in the future will be understood and held in high esteem.

All banks have digital banking applications such as telephone banking, mobile banking and internet banking. However, two prominent participation banks in FinTech are AlbarakaTurk and KuveytTurk participation banks. These two banks attract attention with their technological innovations among participation banks.

Participation banks have a wide range of applications, which are adapted to the financial technologies quickly and have a leading position in this area. For example, AlbarakaTurk continues its innovation journey with corporate culture and FinTech investments blended with entrepreneurship. Within the framework of this vision, Albaraka Fintech Venture Capital Investment Fund, a wholly-owned subsidiary of AlbarakaTurk, has been established. Albaraka Garaj, which is the first startup acceleration center in the world established within the participation bank and operates within the scope of this fund, was opened in June 2017. With this project, AlbarakaTurk aims to produce the products of the future with the innovative ideas in the field of technology for the banking sector and to support the entrepreneurs with the possibilities of incubation and acceleration. The bank aims to develop different cooperations with other institutions involved in the banking ecosystem, especially FinTech initiatives within the framework of open innovation and interoperability principle. In this regard, AlbarakaTurk leads the industry by way of the first FinTech venture capital investment fund of Turkey and reveals that FinTech will play an important role in the future of the banks.

Architecht, which is listed in the Application Provider subcategory, was established in 2015 as a 100% subsidiary of KuveytTurk Participation Bank Architecht operates in the information technology sector. Architecht aims to develop effective financial technological commodities in competitive market conditions, to contribute to the national economy by using innovative technologies, to expand the kinds of products and services through continuous research and development works and to become a brand that provides products and services at the global level. The company's main areas of expertise are financial technologies, security technologies, alternative channel solutions, software development, and support and consulting services. Architecht has quickly become an important technology exporter. It makes sales in million dollars at home and abroad. Architecht signed its largest agreement in December 2018 with ITS, a software firm that sells banking systems based in Kuwait. As a result of this agreement, Architecht could be able to export the technology of all transactions from branch automation system to a mobile branch, ATM to the operation center. The BOA Banking Platform, which was developed by Architecht, will be used in more than 60 banks in 20 countries, including Nigeria, Malaysia, Indonesia, and Egypt. Within three years, approximately 120 million TL worth of software exports are targeted (KuveytTurk Participation Bank, 2018). The world's first end-to-end integrated multi-channel participation banking package BOA is one of the most important products developed by considering the technologies and business needs of the next 10 years. The BOA banking platform, coded by the company's own engineers, was also sold to the PTT Participation Bank, which is in the foundation stage and newly established Real Estate Participation Bank of Turkey in 2019. Also, Kuwait Finance House, the main partner of KuveytTurk Participation Bank, uses the same software. In addition to BOA, it has been able to export innovative technologies such as BOAOne, XTM, Powerfactor, ViPOS, and Golden ATM- providing physical gold withdrawal- in a short time. Built on solid technology, justice, innovation, and trust values, Architecht continues to work with the mission of being a technology company seeking solutions in the areas of financial technologies and cybersecurity.

Within the scope and aim of this study, we ask the participation banks to measure the impact of technological innovations in the banking sector in the coming years and to measure their expectations on this issue. We apply the method of Efma-Infosys Finacle Digital Banking Report Survey 2018 (Marous, 2018). Participants rated the impact of technology on banking from 1 to 7 (1 is the smallest, 7 is the largest). The results are presented in Figure 3 below.

According to the graph results, P2P or New Payment Networks has rated 6.4, Open Banking has rated 6.2, Digital Currencies and Blockchain has rated 6.2, Artificial Intelligence/Robot/Smart/Autonomous applications has rated 5.8, Internet of Things 5.6, Automation/Digitalization has rated 5.2, Security/Authorization/Fraud has rated 5.0, Augmented Reality has rated 4.2, Mobile Banking has rated 3.4, Infrastructure has rated 2.4, Data Analysis has rated 2.2 and Chatbox has rated 1.6.

Participants state that data analysis, chatbox or mobile banking applications which are currently being used in the banking sector will remain in the background together with the progression of technology. Besides these, especially open-banking transactions, new payment methods and blockchain applications

Figure 3. Prospective technological application in banking

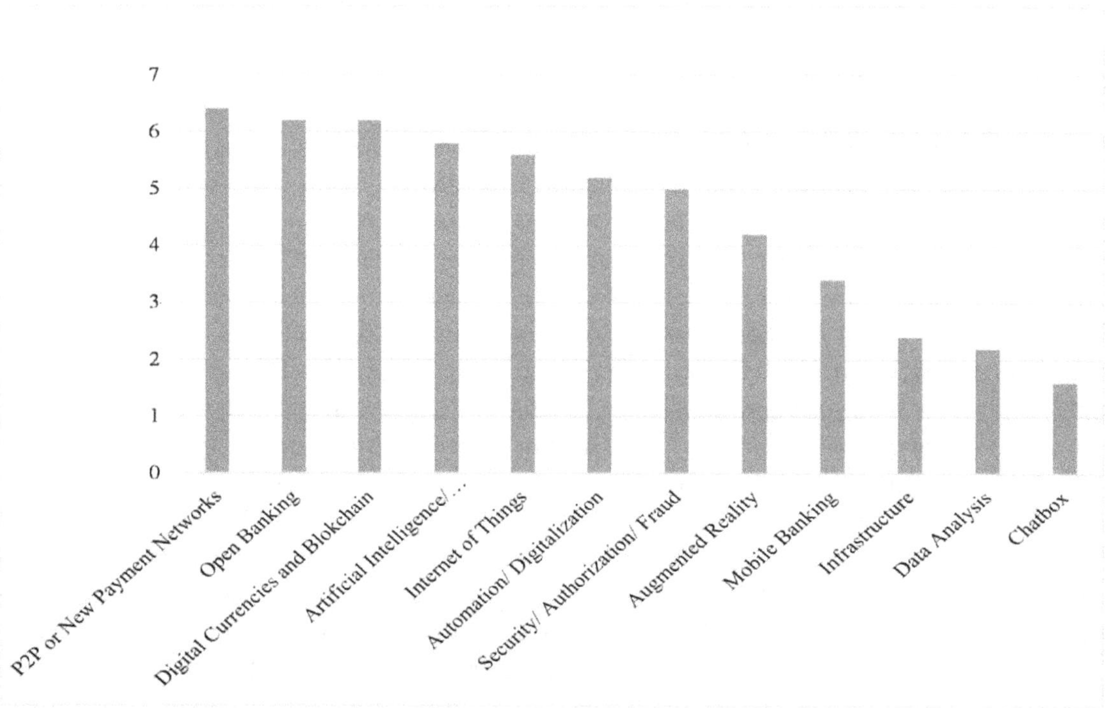

which are not widely used yet in the participation banking in Turkey will be in the forefront. They also mention that new payment methods such as peer to peer (P2P) and payment through fingerprint or eye scan are going to become more common. With the development of technology, banks have entered into a harmonization process. Banks have integrated technology into traditional methods in a number of ways. One of these is open banking. Open banking is sharing the data that banks hold within the framework of legal requirements. According to Payment Services Directive2 (PSD2) approved by the European Union, banks in Europe have to open the data that customers allow to the third parties and users. These channel-based data will be made public by the use of the Application Programming Interface (API) applications. These applications are also used for data sharing in the financial sector. Thus, banks, FinTechs, and other financial institutions could cooperate to provide the most suitable product and service to the customers.

The transition to open banking with PSD2 will offer tremendous opportunities to FinTechs, especially in the field of payment services. FinTechs, which can position themselves correctly in the market, will be able to manage the accounts of all customers in one place. In this way, while all payment transactions of the customers are provided by FinTechs, banks will have to focus more on their core businesses. As of December 2018, 428 banks have opened their APIs (ProgrammableWeb, 2018). These banks are mainly: BBVA, HSBC, Barclays, Danske Bank, Deutsche Bank, Capital One ve ASB Bank. In Turkey, Garanti, Yapi Kredi, KuveytTurk, and Intertech have opened a portion of their APIs. Banks have opened APIs of different products according to their strategies. As it is seen that only the KuveytTurk Participation Bank among the participation banks is included in this list. Within the scope of open banking and payment services directive, KuveytTurk opened applications of accounts, credit cards, loans, payments, money transfers, information services, derivatives, virtual pos, funds, donations, and digital payments (https://developer.kuveytturk.com.tr/#/).

Opinions of the Corporate Customers

This section of the study aims to reveal how customer expectations can affect the Islamic finance industry through the understanding of their needs that could be satisfied by financial technologies. Our main question is to determine whether businesses are involved in Islamic banking or in conventional banking and if they are outside Islamic banking, try to describe the reasons for this situation. Moreover, the purpose of this study is to identify whether or not the customers will change their banking preference when a condition suggested in which financial technologies can provide solutions to their problems. As a sample, we interviewed with 60 companies from 8 merchant categories which are stated in the sample size part of the study. First, we have determined whether these companies work with participation banks or not. The results are presented in Table 3.

We can categorize the companies under three different groups. The first group consists of the companies which do not have any commercial relations with participation banks. The second group worked with participation banks in the past but they are not currently working with. And the last group are the companies that work with the participation banks. The sample-set is selected from sectors where credit card and debit card transactions are heavily used according to BKM reports (BKM, 2018).

According to the results presented in Table 3, 18.3% of the companies (11 companies) had worked with participation banks in the past but they are not working with now and 77.3% of the companies (44 companies) have never worked with participation banks and these are not currently working with. Lastly, only 8.3% of the sample companies (5 companies) are working with participation banks. These results are consistent with the share of the participation banking sector in Turkey.

Table 3. Case situation of the businesses working with participation banks

Merchant Categories	Number of Interviewed Firms[7]	Not Working With	Working With	Worked in the past But Not Working With Now
Petrol Stations	4	3	-	1
Electric & Electronic Goods, Computers	8	7	-	1
Clothing and Accessory	7	5	1	1
Markets and Shopping Centers	10	6	2	2
Service	6	6	-	-
Insurance	5	4	-	1
Food	10	7	1	2
Various Food	10	6	1	3
Total	60	44	5	11

The first group, the companies that do not work with participation banks, do not prefer these banks because of the corporate culture of the companies. The individual preferences and perceptions of the owners of these companies are to keep away from Islamic banks. This is a very surprising result in a country where 99% of the population is Muslim. When the details of this situation are examined, it is understood that there is a wrong perception that the participation banks do not have any difference from other conventional banks. Another reason is that they do not have enough information about Islamic finance. In addition to these reasons, when we consider the opinions of the companies that had worked with the participation banks in the past but they are not currently working, we can list the reasons why the participation banks are not preferred as below;

- *Perception*: The perception that participation banks do not differ from other banks
- *Knowledge*: Lack of information about Islamic finance
- *Infrastructure*: Inadequacy of participation banks' infrastructure
- *Service network*: Lack of service networks such as branch, ATM and POS
- *Campaigns*: Lack of campaigns such as promotions in participation banks and inadequacy of installments in credit card purchases.

The percentage graph created for these findings is given in Figure 4.

The results obtained from 55 companies that are not currently working with participation banks are presented in Figure 4 above. According to these findings, the effect of insufficient service networks on the preference of participation banks is 30 percent. Secondly, 23 percent of companies assume that there is no difference between participation banks and other conventional banks. Another reason why participation banks are not preferred is that companies do not have sufficient knowledge about these banks and this factor constitutes the 21 percent of the companies.

On the other hand, when we analyze the firms that had worked with participation banks previously but which are not working with these banks now, they come up with the reasons such as the lack of infrastructure, insufficiency of the service network, and insufficient in various promotions, campaigns and installment processes. The percentage weights of these factors are 10%, 7%, and 5% respectively. For

Figure 4. Reasons why participation banks are not preferred

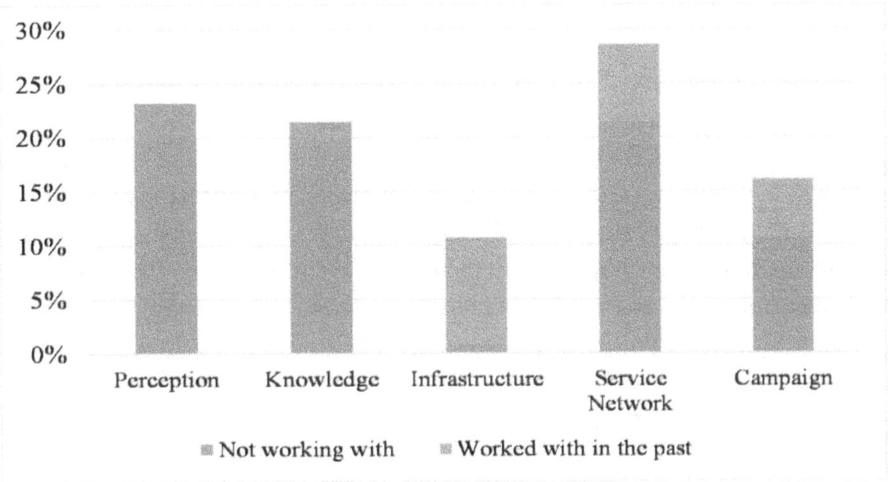

example, petrol stations often make campaigns such as free chip money on fuel purchases. However, there is no such free chip money application in Islamic principles. Therefore, petrol stations, unfortunately, do not want to work with participation banks. Also, petrol stations want to choose the banks with the highest number of credit cards in their sales campaigns to be able to increase fuel sales. According to BKM data, fuel purchases among total bank and credit card expenditures have an average share of 8% to 10% (BKM, 2018). This percentage corresponds to a transaction volume of approximately $ 1.2 billion in December 2018. Thus, the fuel station enterprises that want to get a share of this huge volume tend to prefer the banks that are able to offer widespread POS services and have a high number of card customers.

We can give another example from the retail sector. There is no facility of installment by credit card sales for basic food and consumer goods. BİM Stores Incorporation is one of the leading companies in the retail sector and it is the pioneer of the hard-discount model in Turkey. It carries out the operations with its shops scattered all over the country. By the end of 2018, the company has more than 6500 stores and serves 4.5 million customers daily. The company realizes 30% of sales by debit or credit card. The company may use the participation banks accounts in its commercial transactions with suppliers at the company headquarter. On the other hand, the company cannot intensively choose participation banks for POS services in its stores across the country. Although the corporate culture of the company is compatible with working with participation banks, the company cannot work with these banks for banking services at the stores due to the fact that participation banks cannot serve in every region and they also have infrastructure deficiencies. In addition to these reasons, the relatively high level of service and financing costs of participation banks and the insufficiency of Islamic product and service types are the main factors why participation banks are not preferred. Also, we remind you that the participation banks are not preferred because of an inadequate number of branches and ATMs.

Opinions of the FinTech Companies

The term FinTech indicate the enterprises which bring together the creative working styles and the innovation that support the financial services become more available and intelligible as well as changing it completely. Turkey is highly vulnerable to market innovations in financial technologies and is able to adapt to the changes easily and quickly. FinTech companies are capable of producing solutions to meet customer needs and requirements. However, it was quite difficult for FinTech companies to be able to establish a market presence at first. This case shows that the argument of Nicholas (2016)'s *bankers' fintech grief cycle* is also valid for the Turkish banking market.

In the beginning, starting with the denial process in this cycle, FinTech companies are rather forced to hold in the market. In this process, the excessive self-confidence of the banks and the perception that the competition and the power in the financial markets being on the banks' side are quite dominant. However, the rapid and radical developments in the field of technology together with the demands and expectations of the customers have forced the banks to accept the existence of FinTech, to do business with them or even to establish a partnership with them. Due to increased competition, increased costs and lower profit margins, banks have to work together with FinTech companies that offer alternative solutions in financial markets. In the beginning, this process started with the purchasing of outsourcing services from the FinTech companies which they are specialized in. Later, the cooperation between banks and FinTech companies have increased. These dynamic collaborations are a profitable situation for both banks and financial technology companies. In this respect, we try to determine the variables that will enable the development of the FinTech ecosystem in accordance with the opinions of FinTech companies in the market.

We ask the participants to score the following factors as a percentage. We asked them to give weight on the scale of hundred for the question of "What factors are important for the FinTech ecosystem?" We take the average results of the interviews conducted with 10 firms that could be reached from approximately 60 companies listed in Table 2 above in the banking group. As a result of open-ended questions, we try to group them into factors such as confidence, human resources, capital requirements, customer expectations, regulation and competition which may impact on the FinTech ecosystem. We make this grouping according to the challenges and solutions FinTech companies encounter in the sector.

In this context, the factors that FinTech firms predict for the development of the financial ecosystem and the percentage weights of these factors are given in Figure 5.

Figure 5. Factors affecting the FinTech ecosystem

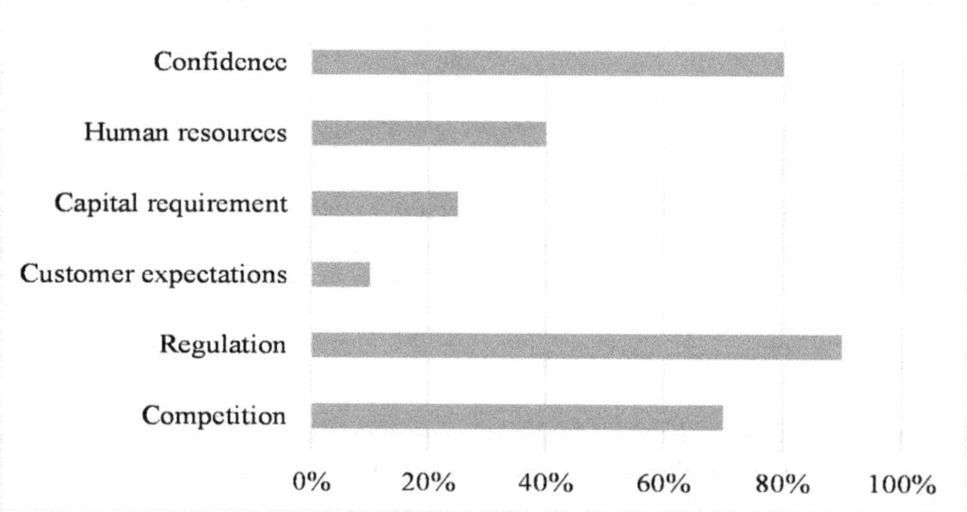

According to FinTech companies, the first factor that will contribute to the development of the financial ecosystem is the regulation variable with a degree of 90% importance. The regulation factor is followed by the confidence factor with 80% impact. The competition factor is ranked in third place with a rate of 70%.

Regulation seems to be the weakest area of FinTechs against banks (Milne, 2016; Carney, 2017; González-Páramo, 2017, Nicoletti, 2017, and Ojo, 2018). Unfortunately, there is no regulation which manages, regulates or supports the FinTech companies and their activities in Turkey. Only, the payment services, e-currency services, and system administration are regulated by "the Law on Payment and Securities Settlement Systems, Payment Services and Electronic Money Institutions" numbered 6493 and its sub-clauses. The law requires the payment and e-currency institutions, and system administration firms to get a permit for operation. This permit helps the FinTech institutions that provide these services become recognized in legal and regulatory aspects. At the same time, the requirement makes it obligatory to comply with certain financial, procedural and technological criteria.

In Turkey, the procedures and principles regarding payment and settlement systems, payment services and institutions, and electronic money institutions within the scope of European Union (EU) Payment Services Directive 1 (PSD1) are regulated by this law. The law imposes obligations on the issues relating to the equity structure, internal systems, information systems, and activities, in particular on obtaining operating permission for payment institutions and electronic money institutions. Also, new business models emerge in the payment services field and new players enter the market with the legislation of the EU Payment Services Directive2 (PSD2), which is mandatory at the end of 2018 (Romānova et al., 2018). It is foreseen that the PSD2 will open the way for "open banking" by enabling third parties to have access to the bank customers and infrastructure information. PSD2, which aims to encourage new players to enter into the payment market, fulfills this objective by enforcing the banks to allow third-party companies access to their bank accounts. These third-party companies are divided into two groups. The first group is the account information service providers (AISPs) and the second one is the payment initiation service providers (PISPs). PSD2 could provide access to the banks' systems through software developed by new players PISP and AISP. If new service providers are authorized, they will work in bank accounts of end-users and be able to mediate between banks and their customers. AISPs are the service providers that have access to the account information of bank customers. These services may use transaction data to analyze a customer's spending behavior or to collect a customer's account information from several banks. A typical example of AISP systems is an investment advisory service. This service is able to see how much money a customer can save on each month's income and so, it can make specific recommendations based on spending schemes. With PSD2, even if banks have to open client data and APIs out, they will be able to offer many innovative products and possibilities to their customers without any effort, through developers or FinTechs that develop products using these APIs.

On the other hand, while the changes introduced by Law No. 6493 increase confidence in the sector, the law creates a barrier for the relatively small organizations which want to operate in payment and e-money services in Turkey. Considering PSD2, it is expected that these obstacles will increase in time. It is evaluated by the stakeholders that the highest level of barriers created by the law is critical for the size and reliability of the sector. While the law no. 6493 and its subclauses have paved the way for the sector so far, the stakeholders underline that the regulations should continue without slowing down. In other respects, sharp measures such as the closure of all credit cards, if not approved by the cardholders, shopping on the internet will affect the confidence in the sector and the size of the sector negatively (Tsai et al., 2010 and Kamalul et al., 2018).

The second most important issue that FinTech companies care about with a rate of 80% is confidence. FinTechs review the confidence in two aspects: financial trust and information security. It is one of the views shared by all stakeholders that FinTechs should give confidence to banks, corporate companies, and consumers in order to be successful. First of all, the beneficiaries of FinTech services want to make sure that the FinTech companies, where they deliver their money or cooperate together, are financially safe. Thus, they believe that they can benefit from FinTech services more easily. Furthermore, customers especially attach great importance to the security of personal data that FinTech companies hold. These two issues; financial trust and information security, began to be regulated by the law no. 6493 and its sub-clauses. However, this area seems to be the weakest part of the FinTechs against banks. When we consider the opinions of FinTech companies, confidence is one of the most worrying areas. Especially, the constant inclusion of new firms in the FinTech ecosystem and their damage to the market is considered to be one of the biggest risks. The restrictions imposed by the legislation in this regard are considered as positive by the FinTech companies that have permission to operate in the market.

The third important factor in the FinTech market is competition. Competition can be considered as competition in the technology sector and the competition between FinTech companies and the banks (Nienaber, 2016, Romānova and Kudinska 2016). The strong banking sector, especially after the 2001 crisis, makes Turkey different from other countries in terms of competition in the financial services sector. Banks in Turkey are the industry leaders of the financial services with asset size, technological capabilities, and product diversity. The banking sector in Turkey constitutes the basis of the financial system. Therefore, the first competition arises between banks and FinTech companies. Apart from that, the main competition is the competition between the financial technology companies themselves. In the field of technology, many companies are entering the sector every year but most of these cannot keep up with the market.

Technological developments are happening faster than before. Almost all products and services could be imitated easily and instantly by other market participants. Thus, technological services and products could become obsolete in a short period of time. Companies investing in high amounts could be vanquished from the market in a flash. We are now able to see the companies that exist in the market, but make sure that there are two or three times more than the existing companies have gone bankrupt. For example, many businesses have invested in crypto-currency data mining along with the bitcoin prices being almost $ 20,000 at the end of 2017. However, the high volatility in prices and the sudden decrease in prices have resulted in a serious loss. Examples of this can be found in international markets. The Japanese internet giant GMO and DMM, one of Japan's largest e-commerce sites, have decided to end their crypto-currency mining activities since February 2018.

On the other hand, Block et al. (2018) suggest that FinTechs can be successful especially when they focus on markets and services which are not accessible by the banks or are not in their access plans and projects. One such example is the fact that banks have not been able to achieve success in prepaid card projects for many years, but FinTech companies have been successful in this field and they have provided prepaid card service to the banks. The importance of FinTech services that make life easier is better understood for the sector particularly in case of where the majority of the population is out of the banking sector and citizens need easily accessible financial tools and solutions. It is thought that appealing people who do not have access to the banking sector through FinTech products will create satisfaction in our country in terms of recording the transactions and so expanding the financial market.

One of the topics that differentiate FinTechs from other players in the financial services sector is their agility and thus they can quickly the changes in the sector. This agility also allows FinTechs to establish a partnership with other companies quickly. The different FinTech companies are expanding the financial services sector and increasing participation in the financial system by merging or supporting banks through innovative technological solutions. Through these partnerships, more comprehensive services can also be provided to customers. With the increasing participation of banks in this common structure, both FinTechs and banks will be able to benefit seriously. On the other side, one of the issues emphasized by the interview participants is that the FinTechs do not compete very much among themselves but the competition is most experienced with the banks. However, the most intense competition area among FinTechs is in the virtual POS services.

Human resources are another issue raised by the sample companies regarding the FinTech ecosystem. Finding qualified human resources is considered as a significant challenge for FinTech companies because the sector is relatively new and most of the companies in the sector are at the beginning level (Roy and Viswanathan, 2018 and Wonglimpiyarat, 2018). It is a common view that the human resources in the sector do not meet the need and therefore efforts are made to attract human capital from non-bank sectors. In addition, banks are sometimes more advanced than FinTech companies with career and salary opportunities. The search for human resources is more focused on universities, abroad and other FinTech companies. Human resources shortage in the FinTech sector is in the areas of sales, marketing and product development rather than technology. From the banks' point of view regarding human resource needs, the most important issue that banks are concerned about is to lose their trained and expert human resources to the FinTech companies. For this reason, there is still a competition between banks and FinTechs in raising high-quality human resources in the financial services sector. Many entrepreneurial ideas on FinTech also emerge from bank employees. Although banks in Turkey allocate time and give importance to the creative ideas of their employees as possible, the employees with entrepreneurial spirit, who have experience in the bank for a certain period of time and realize deficiencies or gaps in the services offered in the bank they work at, get a start in FinTech business by establishing their own companies.

Another common view stated by FinTech executives is that the universities have not yet provided adequate human resources to the FinTechs. The executives think that universities should invest in this area. Only in this way, in addition to the employees who have sector experience, school professionals will be included in the sector. At this point, it is desired that universities will lead students to entrepreneurship instead of working in a company, thus they could play an important role in the development of the FinTech sector. Although the technopolises of universities are an opportunity to attract young talents, it is stated that the location is a serious factor for human resources. In another saying, it is difficult to attract qualified human resources to the technopolises located away from the city center. Moreover, the sector has a high employee turnover rate which means that it is very difficult to maintain qualified employees. In addition to the intense business schedule of the sector, there are companies that offer higher wages, especially for highly qualified employees. Consequently, this high turnover rate causes the transfer of knowledge and experience to other companies.

Lastly, capital requirement and customer expectation issues are among the other important factors that will contribute to the development of the FinTech ecosystem. Turkish FinTech companies also receive investments from abroad. This illustrates the rapidly growing interest of foreign investors in this sector. The FinTech executives, whom we have interviewed with, point out that the companies which attract foreign investment could quickly institutionalize. The lack of sufficient data about the sector and the investors' cautions about Turkey's market conjuncture are the biggest determinants to attract especially foreign investments. Collecting the data about the sector in an independent and transparent manner and making the data available to the investors who are interested in the sector can encourage investments in the FinTech sector. Besides, we can assert that Turkey will be able to a place where international investors may choose as a FinTech hub in the future due to the geopolitical position of Turkey despite the banks are still dominant in the sector. It is stated that Turkey could be a center of attention for the international investors in the near future thanks to the necessary legislative arrangements, qualified and young population structure, technological infrastructure as well as Turkey's role as a bridge between Asia and Europe. Countries in nearby geography of Turkey such as the Middle East, the Balkans and Central Asia countries are the potential markets for the Turkish FinTech companies. Also, Turkish FinTech companies, which are successful in developing markets such as India, draw attention. In addition to geographic diversity, there are opportunities in front of FinTechs in terms of product variety. Examples of these opportunities include Blockchain, InsurTech, Robo Advisory, and personal health management. When we review the FinTech examples in an international word, new FinTech products, and services like credit scoring and peer to peer lending emerge as developments in the near future together with the arrangements in the regulations. When the results of FinTech Inclusion Index 2017 are examined, it is seen that the biggest increase will be in debt instruments as well as the growth will continue in the field of money transfer and payments.

When we look at customer expectation, we see that consumption habits show a difference in the payment services that FinTech companies operate intensively. Consumers tend to use electronic payment methods due to the difficulties to access cash and the risk to carry cash together with the cashless society vision. As a result of the interviews, we determine that the loyalty to a payment method is the most impressed by the campaigns and the customer experience. The financial strength behind banks in terms of their ability to organize campaigns makes them advantageous, nevertheless FinTechs could be able to compete with banks through their advantage of innovations in terms of customer experience. Apart from payment issues, customers are able to adapt the technological and innovative solutions very quickly in Turkey. These two factors form the FinTechs' market target. And they constitute a major advantage of space for the FinTechs operating in Turkey if the confidence is provided. FinTechs are able to offer end-to-end technologic solutions that the banks cannot provide to the consumers and SMEs. For example, FinTechs can provide services to the market from the payment infrastructure of a retailer or service company to analytical services and accounting system through integrated solutions. When the services offered directly to the customers such as Uber, BiTaksi, and AirBnB are taken into consideration FinTechs become prominent in these areas where the services and the solutions are integrated.

Almost all of the successful FinTech products make a world of difference in customer experience. FinTechs are expected to grow even faster, especially by means of technological developments and wearable technologies. Lastly, customer expectation affects the FinTech ecosystem at a rate of 10% according to the interview results. The importance of customer expectation factor is low because FinTechs are able to meet customer demands. FinTech companies report that customers are sometimes better than them at following the developments in technology. Thus, customers already demand new products and services instead of FinTechs' offer. Now we are in a market where the customers are inquiring, questioning and haggling.

CONCLUSION

The interest which constitutes the basis of the financial ecosystem in the world is prohibited in the Islamic religion. Thereby, Muslim societies created a separate financial ecosystem that is called Islamic finance. In the financial system, banks form the majority of the system. On the other hand, rapid developments in the field of technology have brought about great changes in every aspect of life as well as in the finance sector. The financial technology called FinTech is seen as a compelling technology that will enable companies to compete effectively in this century. In most countries around the world, Islamic banking is becoming widespread and these banks are adding new financial instruments in order to increase their share in the sector. Among the Muslim countries, Turkey is in a significant position in the banking sector in the world. For instance, according to the ING Survey (2015) results in the use of mobile banking in Turkey is at an advanced level compared to many European countries. Banks in Turkey follow the technology closely and offer innovative products and solutions to the customers in many different areas of financial services.

In this context, Turkey could contribute to the improvement of Islamic finance in the world although it has a limited share in Islamic banking. This research conducted with this motivation aims to examine the development of FinTech practices in Turkey and it especially explores FinTech application in Islamic finance. The paper assesses the viewpoints of the sector participants about Islamic finance and FinTech and discusses whether the share of Islamic finance in the sector can be increased by FinTech applications or not. The discussions presented in the study are the results obtained through interviewing the participants from influential stakeholders including participation banks, corporate customers, and FinTech companies.

The interview findings show that new technology products and services such as peer-to-peer or new payment networks, open banking applications, digital currencies, blockchain-based practices, and artificial intelligence/robot/smart/autonomous utilities will dominate the banking sector and these will change the way of doing business in the near future.

On the customer side, we tried to understand the customer expectations of Islamic finance and we found out that perception, knowledge, infrastructure, service network, and campaign factors affect the Islamic banking preferences.

And lastly, the interview results with FinTech companies prove that the challenges of legal acts, confidence, competition, and human resources primarily influence the development of the financial ecosystem.

SOLUTIONS AND RECOMMENDATIONS

The findings of this study that evaluates the participation banking, in other words, Islamic banking or interest-free banking, in Turkey in the lights of financial technologies give important clues for the development of the sector. In this context, we can list the suggestions and solutions for the development of the sector as follows:

The most important issue in the development and institutionalization of interest-free banking is the legal framework. There is a need for a specific law, including the basic principles, concepts, institutions, and rules. Additionally, the legal acts including developments and prospective technological applications, which specifically listed in Figure 3, such as peer-to-peer lending and open banking should be implemented as soon as possible in the field of financial technology. Also, the legislation should cover all parties involved in the Islamic Fintech practice, namely, the firms, customers, and investors.

To increase the share of participation banks in the sector and to decrease the negative opinions about participation banking could be overcome by the state's investments in this area.

Banks and FinTech should accept each other companies as a strategic business partner instead of a rival. Thus, they can develop cooperative models. Also, they should produce projects not only for the domestic market but also for especially the Middle East and Gulf countries in order to be a regional hub. Also, to be able to a financial center in the region and to support financial innovation, FinTech legislation and start-up projects should be given priority by the state.

Creation of a FinTech database is critical for the performance evaluation of FinTech start-ups and for providing accurate and objective data to the potential investors. This will increase the interest in FinTech area and also facilitate entrepreneurs' access to capital.

Regarding the human capital, we, unfortunately, have not adequate human resources who have substantial knowledge, skills, and experience at the desired level. Educational institutions especially universities play a significant role in providing essential human resources through appropriate education methods and technical complements. In this context, both universities and other educational institutions carry responsibility. The education system should be arranged accordingly by the related authorities.

Lastly, there is a need for extensive FinTech policies to able to become a FinTech hub in the region. In this respect, the legal and other arrangements should be started immediately. Also, joint platforms could be established to bring all the stakeholders together and to share opinions in order to improve the FinTech ecosystem.

FUTURE RESEARCH DIRECTIONS

Financial technologies are the most popular topics discussed recently. In the finance sector, banks are the leading actors. However, together with the technological developments, FinTechs are the new actors that could be able to change the traditional banking approaches.

When we analyze the Global Findex Database, we see that 73 percent of the adult population in the world who do not have access to bank services is concentrated in 25 countries. 22 percent of those who do not receive any financial services are located in Muslim countries and most of the people state religious reasons as one of the most important obstacles to accessing financial services. Therefore, we think that utilizing FinTech by Islamic finance can offer a solution for individuals and businesses to overcome existing financial access problems by taking advantage of FinTech developments. Thus, in line with this motivation framework, we try to assess the development of FinTech practices in Turkey. The study searches whether the FinTech can expand financial inclusion or not and also assesses the viewpoints of the sector participants about Islamic finance and FinTech. Additionally, it discusses whether the share of Islamic finance in the sector can be increased by FinTech applications or not.

The interview participants are composed of participation banks, corporate customers, and FinTech companies. However, the concept of FinTech could also be considered under Shariah headings. Furthermore, other stakeholders such as regulatory authorities, individual customers and educational institutions could be included in the scope.

ACKNOWLEDGMENT

I would like to thank the Research Fund of the Recep Tayyip Erdogan University that financed this project (Project no: 201653006107.04.03). And also, I would like to offer my sincere thanks to all the participants that I interviewed, who kindly agreed to share their rich experiences.

REFERENCES

Alaabed, A., & Mirakhor, A. (2017). Accelerating Risk Sharing Finance via FinTech: NextGen Islamic Finance. *The 1st International Colloquium on Islamic Banking and Islamic Finance*, 1–10.

Asutay, M. (2013). The development of Islamic banking in Turkey: regulation, performance and political economy. In V. Cattelan (Ed.), *Islamic finance in Europe: Towards a plural financial system* (pp. 213–226). Cheltenham, UK: Elward Elgar Publishing. doi:10.4337/9781781002513.00026

Bakar, N. A., & Rosbi, S. (2018). Robust Framework Diagnostics of Blockchain for Bitcoin Transaction System: A Technical Analysis from Islamic Financial Technology (i-FinTech) Perspective. *International Journal of Business and Management*, *2*(3), 22–29.

BKM. (2018). *General Statistical Reports.* Retrieved from https://bkm.com.tr/en/reports-and-publications/reports-2/

Block, J. H., Colombo, M. G., Cumming, D. J., & Vismara, S. (2018). New players in entrepreneurial finance and why they are there. *Small Business Economics*, *50*(2), 239–250. doi:10.100711187-016-9826-6

Carney, M. (2017, January). *The promise of Fintech–something new under the sun.* Speech at Deutsche Bundesbank G20 Conference, by Bank of England Governor Mark Carney.

Claessens, S., Frost, J., Turner, G., & Zhu, F. (2018). *Fintech credit markets around the world: size, drivers and policy issues. BIS Quarterly Review.*

Deloitte. (2016). *Islamic megabank. The redeemer? A Middle East Point of View.* Available at: https://www2.deloitte.com/content/dam/Deloitte/xe/Documents/AboutDeloitte/mepovdocuments/mepov21/islamic-megabank_mepov21.pdf

Demirguc-Kunt, A., Klapper, L., Singer, D., Ansar, S., & Hess, J. (2018). *The Global Findex Database 2017: measuring financial inclusion and the Fintech revolution.* The World Bank. doi:10.1596/978-1-4648-1259-0

Desai, F. (2015). *The Evolution of FinTech.* Retrieved from https://www.forbes.com/sites/falgunidesai/2015/12/13/the-evolution-of-fintech/#16ac4a847175

DESİYAB. (1981). *The Role and Future of Workers Companies in the Industrialization of Turkey*, State Industry and Worker's Bank (DESİYAB) 2nd Symposium, Ankara, Turkey.

Ernst & Young. (2017). *Luxembourg: the gateway for Islamic finance and the Middle East.* Retrieved from https://www.ey.com/Publication/vwLUAssets/Luxembourg:_the_gateway_for_Islamic_finance_and_the_Middle_East_-_May_2017/$FILE/Islamic%20Finance%20-%20May%202017-LR.pdf

Ferrari, R. (2016). FinTech Impact on Retail Banking–From a Universal Banking Model to Banking Verticalization. *The FinTech Book: The Financial Technology Handbook for Investors, Entrepreneurs and Visionaries*, 248-252.

Firmansyah, E. A., & Anwar, M. (2019). Islamic Financial Technology (Fintech): Its Challenges and Prospect. In *Achieving and Sustaining SDGs 2018 Conference: Harnessing the Power of Frontier Technology to Achieve the Sustainable Development Goals (ASSDG 2018)*. Atlantis Press.

Firmansyah, H. B., & Ramdani, A. L. (2018). The Role of Islamic Financial Technology (FinTech) Start-Up in Improving Financial Inclusion in Indonesia Case: Angsur. *3rd International Conference of Integrated Intellectual Community (ICONIC) 2018*. Available at SSRN: https://ssrn.com/abstract=3194546

González-Páramo, J. M. (2017). Financial innovation in the digital age: Challenges for regulation and supervision. *Revista de estabilidad financiera, 32*(9), 37.

Harrison, R., Jaumandreu, J., Mairesse, J., & Peters, B. (2014). Does innovation stimulate employment? A firm-level analysis using comparable micro-data from four European countries. *International Journal of Industrial Organization, 35*, 29–43. doi:10.1016/j.ijindorg.2014.06.001

ING Internationali. (2015). *Mobile Banking, New Technologies and Financial Behaviour*. ING International Survey.

Islamic Financial Services Board (IFSB). (2015). *Islamic Financial Services Industry Stability Report 2015*. Retrieved from http://www.ifsb.org/docs/IFSB%20Islamic%20Financial%20Services%20Industry%20Stability%20Report%202015_final.pdf

Kamalul Ariffin, S., Mohan, T., & Goh, Y. N. (2018). Influence of consumers' perceived risk on consumers' online purchase intention. *Journal of Research in Interactive Marketing, 12*(3), 309–327. doi:10.1108/JRIM-11-2017-0100

Kerényi, Á., & Molnár, J. (2017). The Impact of the Fintech Phenomenon–Radical Change Occurs in the Financial Sector? *Financial and Economic Review, 16*(3), 32–50.

Khalilov, M. C. K., & Gündebahar, M. (2012). XTM: An Alternative Delivery Channel in Turkish Banking Sector. *Procedia: Social and Behavioral Sciences, 57*, 373–380. doi:10.1016/j.sbspro.2012.09.1200

Khan, S. J. M., & Anuar, A. R. (2018). Access to Finance: Exploring Barriers to Entrepreneurship Development in SMEs. In Global Entrepreneurship and New Venture Creation in the Sharing Economy (pp. 92-111). IGI Global.

Kim, Y., Park, Y. J., Choi, J., & Yeon, J. (2016). The adoption of mobile payment services for "Fintech". *International Journal of Applied Engineering Research, 11*(2), 1058–1061.

KuveytTurk Participation Bank. (2018). *BOA Banking Plat*form. Retrieved from https://www.kuveytturk.com.tr/en/about-us/about-kuveyt-turk/news/boa-banking-platform-the-local-software-of-kuveyt-turk-is-to-be-used-in-20-countries

Lines, B. (2016). How FinTech Is Shaping Financial Services. *PwC Global Fin-Tech Report*.

Malaysia International Islamic Financial Centre. (2016). *Financial Technology (FinTech) in Islamic Finance*. Available at: https://www.islamicfinance.com/wpcontent/uploads/2016/05/Islamic-FinanceTechnology-and-Innovation.pdf

Marous, J. (2018). *Innovation in Retail Banking Digital Banking Report*. Retrieved from https://www.efma.com/assets/content/study/2018/Innovation_In_Retail_Banking_2018_preview.pdf

Milne, A. (2016). Competition policy and the financial technology revolution in banking. *DigiWorld Economic Journal*, *103*, 145–161.

Munch, J. (2015). *What is fintech and why does it matter to all entrepreneurs*. Retrieved from https://www.hottopics.ht/3182/what-is-fintech-and-why-it-matters/

National Digital Research Centre. (2014). *So what is FinTech? March 2014*. Available at: www.ndrc.ie/2014/03/fintech

Navaretti, G. B., Calzolari, G., Mansilla-Fernandez, J. M., & Pozzolo, A. F. (2018). *Fintech and Banking. Friends or Foes?* Available at SSRN: https://ssrn.com/abstract=3099337

Nicoletti, B. (2017). Regulations. In *The Future of FinTech* (pp. 195–209). Cham: Palgrave Macmillan.

Nicols, J. P. (2016). *The Fintech Grief Cycle for Bankers*. Retrieved from http://jpnicols.com/2016/07/12/fintech-grief-cycle-bankers/

Nienaber, R. (2016). Banks need to think collaboration rather than competition. *The FinTech Book: The Financial Technology Handbook for Investors, Entrepreneurs and Visionaries*, 20-21.

Ojo, O. (2018). Disruptive Technology and the Fintech Industry in Nigeria: Imperatives for Legal and Policy Responses. *Gravitas Review of Business and Property Law, 9*(3).

Özcan, M.E., & Hazıroğlu, T. (2000). *A new dimension in banking, participation banking, private financial institutions theory and practice in Turkey*. İstanbul: AlBaraka Turk Publications.

Pollari, I. (2016). The rise of Fintech opportunities and challenges. *Jassa*, (3), 15-21.

Romānova, I., Grima, S., Spiteri, J., & Kudinska, M. (2018). The Payment Services Directive 2 and competitiveness: The perspective of European FinTech Companies. *European Research Studies Journal*, *21*(2), 5–24.

Romānova, I., & Kudinska, M. (2016). Banking and Fintech: A Challenge or Opportunity? In Contemporary Issues in Finance: Current Challenges from Across Europe (pp. 21-35). Emerald Group Publishing Limited. doi:10.1108/S1569-375920160000098002

Roy, N. C., & Viswanathan, T. (2018). *Impact of Technological Disruption on Workforce Challenges of Indian Banks-Identification*. Assessment & Mitigation.

Rusydiana, A. S. (2018). Developing Islamic financial technology in Indonesia. *Hasanuddin Economics and Business Review*, *2*(2), 143–152. doi:10.26487/hebr.v2i2.1550

Saksonova, S., & Kuzmina-Merlino, I. (2017). Fintech as Financial Innovation–The Possibilities and Problems of Implementation. *European Research Studies*, *20*(3A), 961.

Sidlo, K. W. (2017). *Islamic Finance 2017: State of the Art and Outlook for the Future, K4D Helpdesk Report*. Brighton, UK: IDS.

Thakor, A. V. (2019). *Fintech and Banking*. Available at SSRN: https://ssrn.com/abstract=3332550

The Banks Association of Turkey. (2019). *Banks and Banking Sector Information, Statistical Reports*. Available at: https://www.tbb.org.tr/en/banks-and-banking-sector-information/statistical-reports/20

Tsai, W. H., Huang, B. Y., Liu, J. Y., Tsaur, T. S., & Lin, S. J. (2010). The application of Web ATMs in e-payment industry: A case study. *Expert Systems with Applications*, *37*(1), 587–597. doi:10.1016/j.eswa.2009.05.058

Ulya, N. U. (2018). Peer to Peer Lending on Financial Technology under Perspective Positive Law and Islamic Law. *Journal of Islamic Business Law*, *2*(1).

Vives, X. (2017). The impact of FinTech on banking. *European Economy*, (2), 97-105.

Wonglimpiyarat, J. (2017). FinTech banking industry: A systemic approach. *Foresight*, *19*(6), 590–603. doi:10.1108/FS-07-2017-0026

Wonglimpiyarat, J. (2018). Challenges and dynamics of FinTech crowd funding: An innovation system approach. *The Journal of High Technology Management Research*, *29*(1), 98–108. doi:10.1016/j.hitech.2018.04.009

World Islamic Banking Competitiveness Report 2013-2014. (n.d.). *The transition begins*. Available at: https://www.ey.com/Publication/vwLUAssets/EY_-_World_Islamic_Banking_Competitiveness_Report_2013%E2%80%9314/$FILE/EY-World-Islamic-Banking-Competitiveness-Report-2013-14.pdf

World Islamic Banking Competitiveness Report. (2016). *New realities, new opportunities*. Available at: https://www.ey.com/Publication/vwLUAssets/ey-world-islamic-banking-competitiveness-report-2016/%24FILE/ey-world-islamic-banking-competitiveness-report-2016.pdf

Yılmaz, C. (1993). Supporting the rural industry and the case of workers companies in Turkey. *Ondokuz Mayıs University Journal of Faculty of Education*, *8*(1), 305–334.

ADDITIONAL READING

Aldridge, I., & Krawciw, S. (2017). *Real-time risk: What investors should know about FinTech, high-frequency trading, and flash crashes*. John Wiley & Sons. doi:10.1002/9781119319030

Belli, M. (2016). *Banking and FinTech: Developing a FinTech Ecosystem in Istanbul, Learning Lessons from London. The Interbank Card Center (BKM)*. Publications.

Blakstad, S., & Allen, R. (2018). *FinTech Revolution: Universal Inclusion in the New Financial Ecosystem*. Cham: Springer. doi:10.1007/978-3-319-76014-8

Chishti, S., & Barberis, J. (2016). *The FinTech book: the financial technology handbook for investors, entrepreneurs and visionaries*. John Wiley & Sons. doi:10.1002/9781119218906

Duening, T. N., Hisrich, R. A., & Lechter, M. A. (2014). *Technology entrepreneurship: taking innovation to the marketplace*. Academic Press.

Goldstein, I., Jiang, W., & Karolyi, G. A. (2019). To FinTech and Beyond. *Available at SSRN:* https://ssrn.com/abstract=3328172 *or* doi:10.2139srn.3328172

Naifar, N. (2016). Do global risk factors and macroeconomic conditions affect global Islamic index dynamics? A quantile regression approach. *The Quarterly Review of Economics and Finance*, *61*, 29–39. doi:10.1016/j.qref.2015.10.004

KEY TERMS AND DEFINITIONS

Application Programming Interface (API): The interface covers a set of routines, protocols, and tools in order to run software applications. Chiefly, an API defines a specification for the interfaces used by software components and indicates how software parts should communicate with each other through allowing transfer of data between applications. The interface consists of items for routines, data structures, object classes, and variables. These specifications enable other programmers to use components of existing software, allowing for faster and more reliable software development.

Blockchain: Blockchain is the technology especially used by cryptocurrency transactions. It actuates like a distributed public ledger where information, once entered, cannot be changed. The straightforward interpretation is that blockchain is a decentralized digital ledger which transcribes all digital business activities as a string of data stored on a global network of computers. Blockchain technology has various non-cryptocurrency implementations, consisting of smart contracts and records of digital transactions. Blockchain is a data recording process including a digital ledger of transactions, agreements, contracts, and in short, anything that comes to your mind in a digital environment that needs to be independently recorded and verified as having happened. The blockchain operates across several, hundreds, or even thousands of data processing machines basically across computers. Each time a new batch of transactions is encrypted, it is added to the ledger "chain" as a "block."

Golden ATM: It is an automated teller machine (ATM) that provides dispense of physical gold. The machine contains a computer that tracks the market price of gold in real-time. Failsafes are built-in to prevent money laundering, including a maximum of three purchases in a single day, and a required identification number scan accompanying all purchases exceeding a specific amount.

Interbank Card Center (BKM): BKM is a legal entity established in 1990 for the purpose of finding a solution to common problems regarding card payments and developing rules and standards for the debit and credit cards in Turkey. The center provides clearing and settlement of domestic transactions between banks and other institutions arising from the use of credit, debit and prepaid cards. The main activities of BKM are; carrying out the authorization operation between the banks, developing the procedures applicable to the banks in the credit card and debit card sector, forming the domestic rules and regulations, making efforts in relation to provision of standardization and taking the relevant decisions, establishing relations with the international organizations and commissions and representing the members in these organizations when necessary and executing the ongoing bank operations from a single central operation site in a more secure, fast and cost-effective manner.

Open Banking: It is a system that supplies a user with a network of financial institutions' data through the use of application programming interfaces. The concept of open banking in financial services based on several principles such as the use of open application programming interfaces allowing third-party developers to build applications and services around financial institutions, increased financial transparency options for account holders, and the use of open source technology to achieve these principles.

Participation Banks: the banks which are situated in Turkey operate banking services based on Islamic principles. Participation banks are able to implement many different banking facilities according to Islamic rules. In this respect, participation banks are alternatives for traditional banks.

Peer-to-Peer (P2P) Lending: A way of debt financing that enables individuals to borrow and lend money without the use of a financial institution as an intermediary. It is also known as social lending or crowdlending.

Point of Sale (POS): It is a physical machine or a virtual (via a mobile device) application that sellers use to acquire payment credential information for buying or selling goods or services. POS devices which captures the payment transactions could be different tools such as cash registers, optical and bar code scanners, magnetic card readers, computers or any combination of these instruments. Also, POS is the district where a retail transaction takes place. A POS terminal means more generally to the hardware and software used at checkout stations.

Startup: That is a company which is in the first stage of its operations. Pioneering founders of startups roll them initially as they attempt to capitalize on developing a product or service for which they believe there is a demand. More specifically, startups are newly emerged business ventures and aim to develop a viable business model to meet a marketplace need. Due to limited revenue or high costs, most of these small-scale operations are not sustainable in the long term without additional funding from venture capitalists.

ENDNOTES

1 Detailed information about MenaPay is available at its web site https://www.menapay.io/

2 Customer Insight in Financial Services, Survey by Smart Money People, 2015. Available at https://smartmoneypeople.com/news/post/consumer-insight-december-2015

3 The legislation series on interest-free banking in Turkey can be accessed from the following web address. http://www.tkbb.org.tr/Documents/Yonetmelikler/KATILIM%20BANKALAR-MEVZUAT.pdf

4 The author has easily reached the participants thanks to the network created with his work experiences in the sector. The author has work experience at Deloitte Touche, an international audit and consultancy company. In addition, he cooperates with different companies in real and financial markets by means of the scientific research projects.

5 The data collection of the project is financed by research fund of the Recep Tayyip Erdogan University. Project no: 201653006107.04.03.

6 Detailed information about BKM reports can be accessed from the internet. https://bkm.com.tr/en/reports-and-publications/reports-2/

7 The companies' names are not stated in the study since the author do not have the permission to share. Only the names of companies that allow are clearly expressed.

Section 2

FinTech Risk Management and Regulation

Chapter 6
Risk Management in Emerging and Islamic Markets in Light of the Subprime Global Financial Crisis:
Optimization Algorithms for Strategic Decision Making Under Intricate Market Outlooks

Mazin A. M. Al Janabi
https://orcid.org/0000-0002-2249-932X
EGADE Business School, Tecnologico de Monterrey, Mexico

ABSTRACT

The 2007-2009 global financial crisis emphasized the need for rigorous integration of asset liquidity trading risk into value at risk (VaR) modeling algorithms. In this chapter, the author examines measures of certain kinds of liquidity risk that is useful for completing the definition of market risk and for forecasting liquidity-adjusted VaR (L-VaR) under illiquid and intricate market outlooks. This chapter proposes robust modeling algorithms for the quantification of liquidity risk for portfolios that consist of multiple-assets. The empirical testing is performed using data of emerging and Islamic Gulf Cooperation Council stock markets. To that end, the author simulates diverse portfolios and determines the risk-capital and risk-budgeting constraints. The optimization algorithms are interesting in terms of theory as well as practical applications, particularly in light of the 2007-2009 global financial meltdown. The optimization algorithms can have important uses and applications in expert systems, machine learning, and financial technology (FinTech) in big data environments.

DOI: 10.4018/978-1-7998-0039-2.ch006

INTRODUCTION AND OVERVIEW

The traditional Value at Risk (VaR) method for the computation of market risk for multiple-assets portfolios does not explicitly consider asset liquidity risk. Conventional VaR models assess the worst change in the mark-to-market multiple-assets portfolios value over a given time horizon but do not account for the actual trading risk of liquidation. Customary fine-tunings are made on an ad-hoc basis. At most, the holding period (it is routinely also known as the closeout, unwinding or liquidation period) over which the VaR number is calculated is adjusted to ensure the inclusion of asset liquidity risk (Al Janabi, 2010). As a result, asset liquidity risk can be imprecisely factored into VaR assessments by assuring that the liquidation horizon is as a minimum larger than an orderly liquidation interval. Moreover, the same liquidation horizon is employed to all trading asset classes, albeit some assets may be more liquid than others. Neglecting asset liquidity risk can lead to an underestimation of the overall market risk and misapplication of capital cushion for the safety and soundness of financial institutions. In emerging and Islamic financial markets, which are relatively well considered as illiquid, ignoring asset liquidity risk can result in significant underestimation of the VaR assessment, and especially under severe market conditions (Al Janabi, 2008 and 2009).

In its most general definitions, asset liquidity risk is depicted as the risk that the financial institution will not have sufficient funding at any period (i.e., has not enough cash at hand to meet its short-term obligations) or the risks associated with the market liquidity of financial assets—which can be considered as part of market risk and thus it is a function of the price impact of trades and the size of trading holdings. Comprehension of liquidity risk demands knowledge of several diverse fields, such as market microstructures. In general terms, market liquidity risk may arise due to the following circumstances (Al Janabi, 2011):

- When there is a mismatch between the contractual maturities (or more precisely: cash flows) of assets and liabilities; a large cash flow mismatch could for instance arise when treasury unit takes large interest rate trading positions.
- The inability of the financial entity to fund its assets, which is a function of its creditworthiness.
- Because of unexpected non-performance or late payments of debtors.
- When the market is illiquid and the financial entity unexpectedly cannot dispose assets (unwind or closeout trading positions) or attract new funds—due to credit crunch or event risk. This is related to the necessary time to closeout a position. Furthermore, the time to unwind a position may increase in event situations.

This chapter provides advanced quantitative risk management modeling techniques and simulation strategies that can be applied to equity trading portfolios in emerging and Islamic markets. The intent of this chapter is to examine a robust modeling technique for including of asset liquidation trading risk in typical VaR analysis. This chapter expands earlier techniques by explicitly modeling the liquidation of trading portfolios, over the holding period, with the aid of an appropriate scaling of the multiple-assets' liquidity-adjusted VaR (L-VaR) modeling algorithms. The key methodological contribution is a different and less conservative asset liquidity-scaling factor than the conventional root-t multiplier. The proposed add-on is a function of a predetermined liquidity threshold defined as the maximum position that can be unwound without disturbing market prices during one trading day.

In addition, the re-engineered modeling algorithms is quite robust to be applied even by very large financial institutions with multiple-assets and risk factors. In fact, the essence of the modeling algorithm relies on the assumption of a stochastic stationary process and some rules of thumb, which can be of crucial value for more accurate market risk modeling under illiquid and adverse market conditions[1]. In this chapter, the author attempts to incorporate and compute the impact of asset liquidity trading risk into L-VaR models by explicitly integrating the impact of the time-volatility dimension of asset liquidity risk instead of the movements in the bid-ask spread, as other authors have done heretofore. The modeling algorithm to computing L-VaR for distinctive equity portfolio has been illustrated with the help of a modified closed-form parametric modeling technique in which the author examines and tests a linearly distributed scheme for trading asset liquidation over the closeout period with the aid of an appropriate scaling multiplier. The author then demonstrates, by applying the asset liquidity risk measures to the Gulf-Cooperation-Council (GCC) financial markets, to what extent the quantified asset liquidity trading risk effects can impact traditional measurement of market risk under the assumption of unlike dependence measures (correlation parameters). The empirical testing, to determine the amount of risk-capital[2] and risk-budgeting, is performed for long-only trading positions (by imposing an operational constraint on short-selling) as well as for a combination of long and short-sales trading holdings.

In addition, the chapter demonstrates how L-VaR modeling techniques can be used by equity-trading units in a dynamic asset allocation framework for reporting potential risk exposures, assessing risk reduction alternatives, and maximizing risk-budgeting constraints. Using an extensive daily data of the GCC stock markets, the author examines different equity trading portfolios and determine the potential risk exposures and risk-budgeting allocations, with unlike correlation factors, under different illiquid and intricate market perspectives and with the imposition of operational constraints based on fundamental investment considerations. The results strongly confirm the importance of enforcing financially and operationally meaningful constraints, when they are available, on the L-VaR optimization process.

LITERATURE REVIEW AND OBJECTIVES OF CURRENT CHAPTER

The combination of the recent rapid expansion of emerging and Islamic markets trading activities and the recurring turbulence in those markets has propelled asset liquidity trading risk assessment and management to the forefront of market risk management research. Within the VaR framework, Jarrow and Subramanian (1997) provide a market impact model of liquidity by considering the optimum liquidation of an investment portfolio over a fixed horizon. They derive the optimum execution strategy by determining the sales schedule that will maximize the expected total sales values, assuming that the period until liquidation is given as an exogenous factor. The correction to the lognormal VaR they derive depends on the mean and standard deviation of both: an execution lag function and of a liquidation discount. Although the model is simple and intuitively appealing, it suffers from practical difficulties for its implementation. It requires the estimation of additional parameters such as the mean and the standard deviation of the discount factor and the period of execution—for which data are not readily available, none of which may be easy to estimate and may require subjective estimates such as a trader's intuition (Al Janabi, 2009 and 2010).

Bangia et al. (2002) approach the liquidity risk from another angle and provide a model of VaR adjusted for what they call exogenous liquidity—defined as common to all market players and unaffected by the actions of any one participant. It comprises such execution costs as order processing costs and adverse selection costs resulting in a given bid-ask spread faced by investors in the market. On the contrary, endogenous liquidity is specific to one's position in the market and depends on one's actions and varies across market participants. It is mainly driven by the size of the position: the larger the size, the greater the endogenous illiquidity. They propose splitting the uncertainty in market value of an asset into two parts: a pure market risk component arises from asset returns and uncertainty due to liquidity risk. Their model consists of measuring exogenous liquidity risk, computed using the distribution of observed bid-ask spreads and then integrating it into a standard VaR framework.

In a different vein, Almgren and Chriss (1999) present a concrete framework for deriving the optimum execution strategy using a mean-variance approach, and show a specific computational process. Their approach has a high potential for practical application. They assume that price changes are caused by three factors: drift, volatility, and market impact. Their analysis leads to general insights into optimum portfolio trading, relating risk aversion to optimal trading strategy, and to several practical implications including the definition of liquidity-adjusted VaR. Unlike Almgren and Chriss (1999), Hisata and Yamai (2000) turn the sales period into an endogenous variable. Their model incorporates the mechanism of the market impact caused by the investor's own dealings through adjusting VaR according to the level of market liquidity and the scale of the investor's position.

On the other hand, Berkowitz (2000) argues that unless the likely loss arising from liquidity risk is quantified, the models of VaR would lack the power to explicate the embedded risk. In practice, operational definitions vary from volume-related measures to bid-ask spreads and to the elasticity of demand. The author asserts that elasticity based measures are of most relevance since they incorporate the impact of the seller actions on prices. Moreover, under certain conditions the additional variance arising from seller impact can easily be quantified given observations on portfolio prices and net flows; and that it is possible to estimate the entire distribution of portfolio risk through standard numerical methods.

In their research paper, Madoroba and Kruger (2014) introduce a new VaR model that incorporates intraday price movements on high–low spreads and adjusts for a trade impact measure, a novel sensitivity measure of price movements due to trading volumes. Furthermore, the authors compare and contrast 10 worldwide-recognized liquidity risk management models including the "Al Janabi model," which is used in this chapter for liquidly risk modeling and for optimizing LVaR risk-budgeting constraints.

In a different modeling technique, Al Janabi et al. (2017) propose a portfolio optimization methodology based on the integration of DCC (dynamic conditional correlation) t-copula and LVaR models to enhance asset allocation decisions under illiquid market conditions. Their empirical findings prove the superiority of the DCC-copula-LVaR modeling technique over the traditional Markowitz (1959) optimization procedure for a portfolio composed of international stock market indices, gold, and crude oil across various trading scenarios. Likewise, within the copula technique, and particularly the vine copula approach, there were indeed very few studies in this respect and most of published research is still focused on the issue of transaction costs (i.e., bid-ask spreads). In particular, Weiß and Supper (2013) investigate the issue of forecasting liquidity-adjusted intraday VaR with vine copulas. In their paper, they propose to model the joint distribution of bid-ask spreads and log returns of a stock portfolio by implementing Autoregressive Conditional Double Poisson and GARCH processes for the marginals and vine copulas for the dependence structure. By estimating the joint multivariate distribution of both returns and bid-ask spreads from intraday data, they incorporate the measurement of commonalities in liquidity and co-movements of stocks and bid-ask spreads into the forecasting of three types of liquidity-adjusted intraday VaR[3].

In spite of the increasing importance of the GCC financial markets, there is very few published research in this respect, particularly within asset liquidity trading risk management context. Moreover, to the best of our knowledge, very little work has been published in the international literature, on modeling asset liquidity risk-capital structures and optimizing risk-budgeting upper-limits under adverse and crisis-simulated market outlooks, which takes into consideration the GCC zone as a concrete optimization case study. This chapter makes the following key contributions to the academic literatures in this specific quantitative risk management field. Firstly, it represents one of the limited number of academic and practitioner research papers that empirically examine risk-capital structures and risk-budgeting constraints using actual financial data of the six GCC stock markets. Secondly, the chapter in essence reviews and examines a variation on the root-*t* rule of augmenting standard one-day VaR by applying a less conservative asset liquidity scaling factor for including liquidation risk in ordinary VaR analysis. Thirdly, unlike most empirical studies in this field, this research study applies a no-nonsense and robust quantitative trading risk management modeling methodology, using the modeling algorithms and optimization techniques of the Al Janabi model (Al Janabi, 2008; Madoroba and Kruger, 2014), that considers risk analysis under normal (regular) and adverse (stressed) illiquid market viewpoints. The principal advantage of employing such a model is the ability to capture a full picture of possible loss scenarios of actual trading portfolios under different dependence measures (i.e., disparate correlation assumptions) and under the notion of different market scenarios and closeout periods.

This chapter aims to shed light on asset liquidity risk arising due to illiquid trading positions and to obtain an L-VaR estimation. In contrast to all existing published literature pertaining to the application of VaR method to emerging and Islamic markets, this chapter sets forth a robust modeling techniques and optimization algorithms for assessing a closed-form parametric VaR with unambiguous treatment of asset liquidity risk. The key methodological contribution of this work is to extend VaR calculation to allow for a steady liquidation of the portfolio over the holding period (closeout horizon) and by showing that asset liquidity risk can be straightforwardly and intuitively integrated into the proposed VaR modeling algorithm. Rather than modeling asset liquidity trading risk as such, the central focus of this chapter is to overhaul a wide-ranging and adaptable modeling framework for integrating asset liquidity risk in the overall assessment of trading risk. Its essence relies on the assumption of a stochastic stationary process and some rules of thumb, which can be of crucial value for more accurate market risk assessment during market stress periods when liquidity dries up. The asset liquidity framework presented in this chapter does not incorporate all the aspects of liquidity trading risk. However, it is effective as a modeling tool for evaluating trading risk, risk-capital and risk-budgeting when the impact of illiquidity of specified financial products is significant.

Asset liquidity risk-capital and risk-budgeting quantitative simulation models, which are put into practice in this chapter, are applied to the six GCC stock markets. Database of stock market indices are assembled, straightened-up and processed in such a manner so that to make meaningful quantitative testing and simulation of asset liquidity risk-capital and risk-budgeting measurements. Several simulation and optimization case studies are carried out with the objectives of assessing L-VaR under diverse illiquid and crisis-driven market situations. As such, L-VaR estimations have been obtained for varied long-only and long & short-sales equity portfolios in the GCC stock markets. The L-VaR has been obtained through a modified closed-form parametric VaR approach in which the author examines and tests a linearly distributed scheme for trading asset liquidation over the closeout period. As such, traders can liquidate on a daily basis small fractions of their illiquid assets throughout the holding period. The assumption of a given unwinding period for orderly liquidation inevitably implies that assets' liquidation occurs during the holding period. Accordingly, scaling the closeout period to account for orderly liquidation can be justified if one allows the assets to be liquidated throughout the holding period. Then, the author uses the empirical results to draw conclusions about the relative liquidity of the different stock markets and the importance of asset liquidity risk in L-VaR computation.

The modeling techniques, optimization algorithms, and empirical testing outcomes are interesting in terms of theory as well as practical applications, and can have many uses and application in financial markets, particularly in light of the 2007-2009 global financial meltdown. The implemented methodology and risk assessment algorithms can aid in advancing quantitative risk management practices in emerging and Islamic markets, particularly in the wake of the subprime credit crunch and the subsequent 2007-2009 financial turmoil. In addition, the proposed quantitative risk management techniques and optimization algorithms can have important uses and applications in expert systems, machine learning, smart financial functions, and financial technology (FinTech) in big data environments. Likewise, it can aid in the development of regulatory technology (RegTech) for the global financial services industry, and can be of interest to professionals, regulators, and researchers working in the field of finance and FinTech; and for those who want to improve their understanding of the impact of innovative quantitative risk management techniques and optimization algorithms on regulatory challenges for Islamic financial services industry and its effects on global financial stability.

The balance of the chapter is organized as follows. The next section two lays down the quantitative risk management framework of VaR, and its limitations. First, we show that liquidity-adjusted VaR can be derived for a single-asset portfolio assuming uniform liquidation over the holding period. We then derive a general and robust optimization technique that incorporates the effects of illiquid multiple-assets in daily market risk management by simply scaling the multi-assets' L-VaR modeling algorithm using Al Janabi model. Finally, we demonstrate, by applying L-VaR measures to the GCC stock markets, to what extent the quantified liquidity effects can affect conventional assessment of trading risk. The results and examination of the empirical and optimization tests are drawn in section three. The final section four provides concluding remarks and recommendations.

AL JANABI MODEL FOR THE INCORPORATION OF LIQUIDITY RISK INTO A CLOSE-FORM PARAMETRIC VALUE AT RISK MODELING ALGORITHM

One of the most significant advances in the past two decades in the field of measuring and managing financial risks is the development and the ever-growing use of VaR methodology. VaR has become the standard measure that financial analysts use to quantify financial risks including equity risk. VaR represents the potential loss in the market-value of multiple-assets portfolios of equities with a given probability over a certain time horizon. The main advantage of VaR over other risk measures is that it is theoretically simple. As such, VaR can be used to summarize the risk of an individual equity position or the risk of large portfolios of equity assets. Thus, VaR reduces the risk associated with any portfolio of equities (or other assets) to just one number—the expected loss associated with a given probability over a defined holding period (Al Janabi, 2011, 2010, 2009).

VaR is being embraced by financial and corporate risk managers as an important tool in the overall risk management process. In particular, upper level managers, that may or may not be well versed in statistical analysis, view VaR as an intuitive measure of risk since it concentrates only on adverse outcomes and is usually reported in dollars term. However, initial interest in VaR stemmed from its potential applications as a regulatory tool. Because of this, VaR is commonly used for internal risk management purposes (e.g. setting trading limits among traders) and is further being touted for use in risk management decision making by non-financial firms. In the case of a non-financial firm, such as an energy enterprise, a risk manager may examine the VaR associated with a portfolio of risky assets (e.g., cash positions) prior to and after risk management strategies (e.g. use of futures, options, forward contracts, or combination of the above) are implemented. This allows the risk manager to assess the potential large losses to the portfolio in the presence of various risk management strategies, thus allowing the risk manager to more efficiently implement these strategies (Al Janabi, 2011, 2010, and 2009).

In essence, VaR is intended to measure the largest amount of money a position or trading portfolio could lose, with a given degree of confidence, over a given time horizon and under normal market conditions. Assuming the return of a financial product follows a normal distribution, linear pay-off profile and a direct relationship between the underlying product and the income, the VaR is to measure the standard deviation of the trading income, which results from the volatility of the different markets, for a certain confidence level. This definition gives latitude in choosing both confidence level and time horizon. In practice, however, many financial and non-financial entities have chosen a confidence interval of 95% (or 97.5% if we only look at the loss side [one-tailed]) for their overall portfolio and a one-day time horizon to calculate VaR. This means that once every 40 trading days a loss larger than indicated is expected to occur. Some entities use a 99% (one-tailed) confidence interval, which would theoretically lead to larger loss once every 100 trading days. Due to fat tails of the probability distribution, such a loss will occur more often and can cause problems in calculating VaR at higher confidence levels. Some entities feel that the usage of a 99% confidence interval would place too much trust on the statistical model and, hence, some confidence level should be assigned to the "art–side" of the risk assessment process. Although the method relies on many assumptions and has its drawbacks, it has gained wide acceptance for the quantification and aggregation of trading risks. As a result of the generalization of this method, risk-capital allocations and risk-budgeting constraints for trading and active investment activities tend to be computed and adjusted with the VaR method (Al Janabi, 2011, 2010, 2009).

To compute VaR using a closed-form parametric (or customarily known also as the variance/covariance, analytical and delta-neutral) method, the volatility of each risk factor is extracted from a pre-defined historical observation period. The potential effect of each component of the portfolio on the overall portfolio value is then worked out. These effects are then aggregated across the whole portfolio using the correlations parameters between the risk factors (which are, again, extracted from the historical observation period) to give the overall VaR value of the portfolio with a given confidence level (Al Janabi, 2010 and 2008). As such, for a single trading asset the absolute value of VaR can be defined in monetary terms as follows:

$$VaR_i = \left|(\mu_i - \alpha * \sigma_i)\left[Asset_i * Fx_i\right]\right| \approx \left|\alpha * \sigma_i\left[Asset_i * Fx_i\right]\right| \tag{1}$$

where μ_i is the expected return of the asset, α is the confidence level (or in other words, the standard normal variant at confidence level α) and σ_i is the forecasted standard deviation (or conditional volatility) of the return of the security that constitutes the single position. The $Asset_i$ (henceforth, A_i) is the mark-to-market value of the trading asset and indicates the monetary amount of equity position in asset i and Fx_i denotes the unit foreign exchange rate of asset i. Without a loss of generality, we can assume that the expected value of daily returns μ_i is close to zero. As such, though equation (1) includes some simplifying assumptions, yet it is routinely used by researchers and practitioners in the financial markets for the computation of VaR for a single trading asset.

Asset trading risk in the presence of multiple risk factors is determined by the combined effect of individual risks. The extent of the total risk is determined not only by the magnitudes of the specific risks but also by their correlations parameters. Portfolio effects are crucial in risk management not only for large diversified multiple-assets portfolios but also for particular assets that depends on several risk factors. For multiple-assets or portfolio of assets, VaR is a function of each individual security's risk and the correlation factor [$\rho_{i,j}$] between the returns on the individual securities, detailed as follows:

$$VaR_P = \sqrt{\sum_{i=1}^{n}\sum_{j=1}^{n} VaR_i VaR_j \rho_{i,j}} = \sqrt{\left[VaR\right]^T \left[\rho\right]\left[VaR\right]} \quad (2)$$

In fact, the above formula is a general one for the computation of VaR for multiple-assets portfolios regardless of the number of securities. It should be noted that the second term of the above formula is rewritten in terms of matrix-algebra—a useful form to avoid mathematical complexity, as more and more securities are added. This tactic can simplify the modeling algorithms and programming/coding process and allows easy integration of short-sales positions into the market risk management process. This means, in order to compute VaR (of a portfolio of any number of assets), we need to generate first a transpose vector $\left[VaR\right]^T$ of the specific VaR positions—an $(1*n)$ vector, and hence the superscript "T" indicates transpose of the vector:

$$\left[VaR\right]^T = \left[VaR_1 \quad VaR_2 \quad \ldots \quad VaR_n\right] \quad (2a)$$

Second, a vector $\left[VaR\right]$ of individual VaR positions—explicitly n rows and one column $(n*1)$ vector, such as:

$$\left[VaR\right] = \begin{bmatrix} VaR_1 \\ VaR_2 \\ \ldots \\ VaR_n \end{bmatrix} \quad (2b)$$

Finally, a matrix $\left[\rho\right]$ of all correlation factors (ρ)—an $(n*n)$ matrix in the following form:

$$\left[\rho\right] = \begin{bmatrix} 1 & \rho_{1,2} & \rho_{1,3} & \cdots & \rho_{1,n} \\ \rho_{2,1} & 1 & \rho_{2,3} & \cdots & \rho_{2,n} \\ \rho_{3,1} & \rho_{3,2} & 1 & \cdots & \rho_{3,n} \\ \cdots & \cdots & \cdots & \cdots & \cdots \\ \rho_{n,1} & \rho_{n,2} & \rho_{n,3} & \cdots & 1 \end{bmatrix} \quad (2c)$$

Consequently, as one multiplies the two vectors and the correlation matrix and then takes the square root of the result, one ends up with the VaR_p of any portfolio with any n-number of assets. This simple number summarizes the portfolio's exposure to market risk. Investors and senior managers can then decide whether they feel easeful with this level of risk. If the answer is no, then the process that led to the computation of VaR can be used to decide where to reduce redundant risk. For instance, the riskiest equities can be sold, or one can use derivative securities such as futures and options contracts on equities to hedge the undesirable risk exposures (Al Janabi, 2010, 2009).

VaR method is only one approach of measuring market risk and is mainly concerned with maximum expected losses under normal market conditions. It is not an absolute measure, as the actual amount of loss may be greater than the given VaR amounts under intricate markets circumstances. In extreme situations, VaR models do not function very well and, hence, it is essential to augment VaR computational procedure with stress-testing and scenarios analysis. From a risk management perspective, however, it is desirable to have an estimate for what potential losses could be under severely adverse conditions where statistical tools do not apply. As such, Stress-testing estimates the impact of unusual and severe events on the entity's value and should be reported on a daily basis as part of the integrated risk management process (Al Janabi, 2011, 2010, 2009).

For emerging and Islamic economies with extreme volatility, the use of stress-testing and scenarios analysis should be highly emphasized and full description of the process is included in any trading risk policy manual. Stress-testing usually takes the form of subjectively specifying scenarios of interest to compute changes in the value of the multiple-assets portfolio and it can involve examining the effect of past large market moves on today's portfolio(Al Janabi, 2011 and 2010). In this chapter, quantitative risk management modeling algorithms are examined to assess potential exposure due to an event risk that is associated with large movements of the GCC stock markets indices, under the assumption that certain GCC markets have typical 3%-12% leap during periods of financial turmoil. The task here is to measure the potential trading risk exposure that is associated with a pre-defined leap and under the notion of several correlation parameters and liquidation horizons.

On another front, illiquid securities such as foreign exchange rates and equities are very common in emerging and Islamic markets. Customarily these securities are traded infrequently (at very low volume). Their quoted prices should not be regarded as a representative of the traders' consensus vis-à-vis their real value but rather as the transaction price that arrived at by two counterparties under special market outlooks. This of course represents a real dilemma to anybody who seeks to measure the market risk of these securities with a methodology that is based on volatilities and correlation matrices. The main problem arises when the historical price series are not available for some securities or, when they are available, they are not fully reliable due to the lack of liquidity (Al Janabi, 2011, and 2009).

Given that institutional investors usually have longer time horizons, the liquidity of their positions will be lower. The investment horizon of the investor as well as the liquidity characteristics of the mutual fund need to be integrated into the risk quantification process. For instance, portfolios with long investment horizons and/or low liquidity need distinct risk measures than those that have shorter horizons and are very liquid. The choice of the time horizon or number of days to liquidate (unwind) a position is very important factor and has big impact on VaR numbers, and it depends upon the objectives of the multiple-assets portfolio, the liquidity of its positions and the expected holding period. Typically, for a bank's trading portfolio invested in highly liquid currencies, a one-day horizon may be acceptable. For an investment manager with a monthly re-balancing and reporting focus, a 30–day period may be more appropriate. Ideally, the holding period should correspond to the longest period for orderly portfolio liquidation (Al Janabi, 2008, and 2009).

Liquidity is a key risk factor, which until lately, has not been appropriately dealt with by risk models. Illiquid trading positions can add considerably to losses and can give negative signals to traders due to the higher expected returns they entail. The concept of liquidity trading risk is immensely important for using VaR accurately and the 2007-2009 financial markets upheavals confirm the needs for laborious treatment and assimilation of liquidity trading risk into VaR models (Al Janabi, 2008, and 2009).

The simplest way to account for asset liquidity trading risk is to extend the holding period of illiquid positions to reflect a suitable liquidation period. An adjustment can be made by adding a multiplier to the VaR measure of each trading asset type, which at the end depends on the liquidity of each individual security. Nonetheless, the weakness of this method is that it allows for subjective estimation of the liquidation period. Furthermore, the typical assumption of a one-day horizon (or any inflexible time horizon) within VaR framework, neglects any calculation of trading risk related to liquidity effect (that is, when and whether a trading position can be sold and at what price). A broad VaR model should incorporate a liquidity premium (or asset liquidity risk factor). This can be worked out by formulating a method by which one can unwind assets holdings, not at some ad-hoc rate, but at the rate that market conditions is optimum, so that one can effectively set a risk value for the liquidity effects. In general, this will raise significantly the VaR, or the amount of risk-capital to support the trading position (Al Janabi, 2010).

In fact, if returns are independent and they can have any elliptical multivariate distribution, then it is possible to convert the VaR horizon parameter from daily to any *t*–day horizon. The variance of a *t*–day return should be *t* times the variance of a 1–day return, or in other words, $\sigma^2 = f(t)$. Thus, in terms of standard deviation (or volatility), $\sigma = f(\sqrt{t})$, and the daily or overnight VaR number [*VaR (1-day)*] can be adjusted for any *t-day* horizon as:

$$L - Var\left(t - day\right) = VaR\left(1 - day\right)\sqrt{t} \qquad (3)$$

The above L-VaR formula was proposed and used by *J.P. Morgan* in their earlier *RiskMetrics™* method (Morgan Guaranty Trust Company, 1994). This methodology implicitly assumes that liquidation occurs in one block sale at the end of the holding period and that there is one holding period for all assets, regardless of their inherent trading liquidity structure and ultimately leads to an overstatement of L-VaR. Unfortunately, the latter approach does not consider real-life-trading situations, where traders can liquidate (or re-balance) small portions of their long and short trading portfolios on a daily basis. The assumption of a given holding period for orderly liquidation inevitably implies that assets' liquidation occurs during the holding period. Accordingly, scaling the holding period to account for orderly liquidation can be justified if one allows the assets to be liquidated throughout the holding period[4]. Indeed, the square-root of time postulation has been disputed over the past two decades by several authors (see for example, Danielsson and Zigrand, 2006).

In another relevant study, Dowd et al. (2004) tackle the problem of estimating VaR for long-term horizon. In their paper they offer a different; however a rather straightforward, approach that avoids the inherited problems associated with the square-root of time rule, as well as those associated with attempting to extrapolate day-to-day volatility forecasts over long horizons. In addition, Al Janabi (2008) reveals that the square-root of time rule leads to a systematic overestimation of market risk. The author concludes that despite the widespread application and implementation of the square-root of time multiplier in Basel II regulatory accord, it nevertheless fails short to address the aim of Basel II and Basel III capital adequacy accords. It is clear that a comprehensive investigation into the nature of asset market/ liquidity risk and its effect on distinct portfolios of both long and short illiquid assets is necessary.

In this chapter, the author reviews and examines a clear-cut re-engineered modeling algorithm for the computation of a closed-form parametric VaR with explicit treatment of asset liquidity trading risk. The modeling algorithms and liquidity-scaling factor is more realistic and less conservative than the conventional root-*t* multiplier. In this research study, the robust modeling techniques and the non-linear quadratic optimization algorithms are based on Al Janabi model (Al Janabi, 2008; Madoroba and Kruger, 2014). In essence, the liquidity risk multiplier is a function of a predetermined liquidity threshold defined as the maximum position that can be unwound without disturbing market prices during one trading day. The essence of the modeling technique relies on the assumption of a stochastic stationary process and some rules of thumb, which can be of crucial value for more accurate overall trading risk assessment during market stress periods when liquidity dries up. To that end, a practical framework of a modeling methodology (within a robust mathematical approach) is examined below with the aim of incorporating and computing of illiquid multiple-assets' daily L-VaR, detailed as follows[5]:

The market risk of an illiquid long or short trading position is larger than the risk of an otherwise identical liquid position. This is because unwinding or closing out the illiquid position takes longer than unwinding the liquid position, and, as a result, the illiquid position is more exposed to the volatility of the market for a longer period of time. In this modeling approach, a trading position will be deemed illiquid if its size surpasses a certain liquidity threshold. The threshold (which is determined by each trader) and defined as the maximum position which can be unwound, without disrupting market prices, in normal market conditions and during one trading day. Consequently, the size of the trading position relative to the threshold plays an important role in determining the number of days that are required to close out the entire position. This effect can be translated into a liquidity increment (or an additional liquidity risk factor) that can be incorporated into VaR analysis. If for instance, the par value of a position is \$100,000,000 and the liquidity threshold is \$25,000,000 per day, then it will take four days to sell out the entire trading position. Therefore, the initial position will be exposed to market variation for one day, and the rest of the position (that is, \$75,000,000) is subject to market variation for additional 3-days. If it is assumed that daily changes of market values follow a stationary stochastic process, the risk exposure due to illiquidity effects is given by the following illustration, detailed along these lines:

$$\sigma_{adj}^2 = \left(\sigma_1^2 + \sigma_2^2 + \sigma_3^2 + \cdots \sigma_{t-2}^2 + \sigma_{t-1}^2 + \sigma_t^2\right) \tag{4}$$

In order to take into account the full illiquidity of multiple-assets (that is, the required unwinding period to liquidate an asset) we define the following:

$\sigma_{adj}{}^2$ = overnight conditional variance of the illiquid asset position;
σ_{adj} = asset liquidity risk factor or the overnight standard deviation (i.e., conditional volatility) of the illiquid asset position; and
t = number of liquidation days (that is, *t*–days to liquidate the entire asset fully).

The modeling technique assumes that the trading position is closed out linearly over t-days and hence it uses the logical assumption that the losses due to illiquid trading positions over t-days are the sum of losses over the specific trading days. Moreover, we can assume with reasonable accuracy that asset returns and losses due to illiquid trading holdings are independent and identically distributed (*iid*) and serially uncorrelated day-to-day along the liquidation horizon and that the variance of losses due to asset liquidity risk over t-days is the sum of the variance (σ_i^2, for all $i = 1, 2, \ldots, t$) of losses on the specific days, thus:

In fact, the square root-t approach (equation [3]) is a simplified special case of equation (4) under the assumption that the daily variances of losses throughout the holding period are all the same as the first day variance, (σ_1^2), thus, it is possible to show intuitively that:

$$\sigma_{adj}^{\ 2} = \left(\sigma_1^{\ 2} + \sigma_1^{\ 2} + \sigma_1^{\ 2} + \cdots + \sigma_1^{\ 2}\right) = t\sigma_1^{\ 2}.$$

As discussed above, the square root-t equation overestimates asset liquidity risk since it does not consider that traders can liquidate small portions of their trading portfolios on a daily basis and it implicitly assumes that the whole trading position can be sold completely on the last trading day. Indeed, in real financial markets operations, liquidation occurs during the holding period and thus scaling the holding period to account for orderly liquidation can be justified if one allows the assets to be liquidated throughout the holding period. As such, for this special linear liquidation case and under the assumption that the variance of losses of the first trading day decreases linearly each day (as a function of t) we can derive from equation (4) the following:

$$\sigma_{adj}^2 = \left(\left(\frac{t}{t}\right)^2 \sigma_1^2 + \left(\frac{t-1}{t}\right)^2 \sigma_1^2 + \left(\frac{t-2}{t}\right)^2 \sigma_1^2 + \cdots + \left(\frac{3}{t}\right)^2 \sigma_1^2 + \left(\frac{2}{t}\right)^2 \sigma_1^2 \left(\frac{1}{t}\right)^2 \sigma_1^2\right) \tag{5}$$

Evidently, the additional asset liquidity risk factor depends only on the number of days needed to sell an illiquid position linearly. In the general case of t-days, the variance of asset liquidity risk factor is given by the following mathematical structure of t:

$$\sigma_{adj}^2 = \sigma_1^2 \left(\left(\frac{t}{t}\right)^2 + \left(\frac{t-1}{t}\right)^2 + \left(\frac{t-2}{t}\right)^2 + \cdots + \left(\frac{3}{t}\right)^2 + \left(\frac{2}{t}\right)^2 \left(\frac{1}{t}\right)^2\right) \tag{6}$$

To calculate the sum of the squares, it is convenient to use a mathematical short-cut approach. From finite mathematical series the following relationship can be obtained:

$$(t)^2 + (t-1)^2 + (t-2)^2 + \ldots + (3)^2 + (2)^2 + (1)^2 = \frac{t(t+1)(2t+1)}{6} \tag{7}$$

Accordingly, after substituting equation (7) into equation (6) the asset liquidity risk factor can be expressed in terms of conditional volatility as:

$$\sigma_{adj} = \sigma_1^2 \left\{ \sqrt{\frac{1}{t^2}\left[(t)^2 + (t-1)^2 + (t-2)^2 + \ldots + (3)^2 + (2)^2 + (1)^2\right]} \right\}$$

or

$$\sigma_{adj} = \sigma_1^2 \left\{ \sqrt{\frac{(2t+1)(t+1)}{6t}} \right\} \tag{8}$$

The final results of equation (8) is of course a function of time and not the square root of time as employed by some financial market's participants based on the *RiskMetrics™* methodologies (Morgan Guaranty Trust Company, 1994). Furthermore, the above approach can be used to calculate the VaR for any time horizon. In order to perform the computation of VaR under illiquid market outlooks, the asset liquidity risk factor of equation (8) can be implemented in VaR calculation, hence, one can define the following:

$$L-VaR_{adj} = VaR\sqrt{\frac{(2t+1)(t+1)}{6t}} \tag{9}$$

where VaR = Value at Risk under liquid market environments and $L\text{-}VaR_{adj}$ = liquidity-adjusted VaR under illiquid market outlooks. The latter equation indicates that $L\text{-}VaR_{adj} > VaR$, and for the special case when the number of days to liquidate the entire assets is one trading day, then we can have the following equality: $L\text{-}VaR_{adj} = VaR$. Consequently, the difference between $L\text{-}VaR_{adj} - VaR$ should equal to the residual market risk due to the illiquidity of any asset under illiquid markets settings. Actually, the number of liquidation days (t) necessary to liquidate the entire assets fully is related to the choice of the liquidity threshold. However, the size of this threshold is likely to change under severe markets circumstances. Indeed, the choice of the liquidation horizon can be assessed from the total trading position size and the daily trading volume that can be unwound into the market without significantly disrupting market prices; and in actual practice it is generally estimated internally by dividing the trading position held in an asset by the average daily trading volume of that asset over recent days, so that:

t = *Total Trading Position Size of* $Asset_i$ / *Average Daily Trading Volume of* $Asset_i$ (10)

In real practice, the daily trading volume of any asset is estimated as the average volume over some period of time, generally a month of trading activities. In effect, the daily trading volume of assets can be regarded as the average daily volume or the volume that can be unwound under severe market periods. Thus, if trading volume is low because of a "one-way market," in that most people are seeking to sell rather than to buy, then *(t)* can rise substantially (Saunders and Cornett, 2008). The trading volume in an intricate market period can be roughly approximated as the average daily trading volume less a number of standard deviations. Albeit this alternative approach is quite simple, it is still relatively objective. Moreover, it is reasonably easy to gather the required data to perform the necessary liquidation scenarios.

Fundamentally, the above asset liquidity scaling factor (or liquidity multiplier) is more realistic and less conservative than the conventional root-*t* multiplier. Moreover, it can aid financial entities in allocating reasonable and liquidity-driven regulatory and internal risk-capital requirements. Furthermore, the above mathematical technique can be applied for the computation of L-VaR for each trading position and for the entire multiple-assets portfolio. In order to compute the L-VaR for the entire trading portfolio under illiquid market conditions ($L-VaR_{P_{adj}}$), the above mathematical algorithm can be extended, with the aid of equation (2), into a matrix-algebra form to yield the following:

$$L-VaR_{P_{adj}} = \sqrt{\left[L-Var_{adj}\right]^{T}\left[\rho\right]\left[L-Var_{adj}\right]} \tag{11}$$

It should be noted that when reporting individual $L\text{-}VaR_{adj}$ these figures are always taken as positive, even though they represent a loss (which conventionally has a negative sign). In assessing the portfolio $L-VaR_{P_{adj}}$ the sign of each trading asset "A_i" must be incorporated into the $\left[L-VaR_{adj}\right]^{T}$ and $\left[L-VaR_{adj}\right]$ vectors. That is, if the asset position is held long (i.e. you own it), then the $A_i > 0$, but if the asset has been sold short, then $A_i < 0$.

Worst-case $L-VaR_{P_{adj}}$ (or undiversified $L-VaR_{P_{adj}}$) can be deduced as a special case of equation (11) under the assumption that asset returns are perfectly positively correlated ($\rho = +1$) and that there are positive amounts of each asset. This indeed will give the worst-case scenario, since there are no benefits from diversification by holding multiple-assets. Thus, the maximum value that the $L-VaR_{P_{adj}}$ can take is given by setting $\rho = +1$ in equation (11), which gives:

$$Worst\text{-}case\, L-VaR_{adj_P} = L-VaR_{adj_1} + L-VaR_{adj_2} + \ldots + L-VaR_{adj_n} = \sum_{i=1}^{n} L-VaR_{adj_i} \tag{12}$$

Hence, in a worst-case scenario the $L-VaR_{P_{adj}}$ is simply the sum of the individual $L\text{-}VaR_{adj}$. In the real-world practices, it is unlikely that the correlation between the returns of the multiple-assets is one ($\rho = +1$). However, under critical periods, it is often the case that correlation factors increase, and the worst-case $L-VaR_{P_{adj}}$ provides a high figure that may be representative of these severe periods. Indeed, in actual risk management practices, risk managers usually look at and analyze different scenarios generated from both the diversified $L-VaR_{P_{adj}}$ [equation (11)] and the worst-case undiversified $L-VaR_{P_{adj}}$ [equation (12)]. This gives the risk managers a feel for what would happen if historical correlations parameters did not stay the same but rather increased due to an austere market period. Moreover, it is worth noting that if $\rho = +1$ and one or more of the trading assets is a short position (that is, $A_i < 0$), then there will be some risk offset and hence the worst-case scenario $L-VaR_{P_{adj}}$ of equation (12) cannot be held as a representative of the maximum loss of the trading portfolio.

Furthermore, the above mathematical structure of equation (11) (in the form of two vectors and a matrix, $\left[L-VaR_{adj}\right]^{T}$, $\left[L-VaR_{adj}\right]$ and $\left[\rho\right]$) can facilitate the modeling and programming/coding processes of the L-VaR's risk-engine so that the trading risk manager can specify different liquidation days for the whole portfolio and/or for each specific trading security according to the necessary number of days to liquidate the entire assets fully. The latter can be achieved by specifying an overall benchmark closeout period to liquidate the whole constituents of the portfolio completely. The number of days required to liquidate a position (of course, depending on the type of equity) can be obtained from the various publications of equity markets and can be compared with the assessments' of individual traders of each trading unit. As a result, it is possible to create simple statistics of the equity volume that can be liquidated and the necessary time horizon to unwind the whole volume. As a matter of fact, our re-engineered liquidity risk factor modeling technique, once compared with previously established liquidity risk models, could even lead to further reduction in the overall risk of the equity trading portfolio; and hence in the amount of regulatory capital and/or risk-capital, as specified by Basel II and Basel III capital adequacy requirements.

SIMULATION AND OPTIMIZATION PROCESS OF RISK-CAPITAL STRUCTURES AND RISK-BUDGETING CONSTRAINTS— AN OUTLOOK FROM THE GCC REGION

In this chapter, a database of daily returns of the six GCC stock markets main indicators (indices) are assembled and adequately adapted for the design of relevant inputs for the computation of all risk factors. The total numbers of indices that are considered in this work are nine indices; seven local indices for the six GCC stock markets (including two indices for the UAE markets) and two benchmark indices, detailed as follows: DFM General Index (United Arab Emirates, Dubai Financial Market General Index); ADX Index (United Arab Emirates, Abu Dhabi Stock Market Index); BA All Share Index (Bahrain, All Share Stock Market Index); KSE General Index (Kuwait, Stock Exchange General Index); MSM30 Index (Oman, Muscat Stock Market Index); DSM20 Index (Qatar, Doha Stock Market General Index); SE All Share Index (Saudi Arabia, All Share Stock Market Index); Shuaa GCC Index (Shuaa Capital, GCC Stock Markets Benchmark Index); and Shuaa Arab Index (Shuaa Capital, Arab Stock Markets Benchmark Index).

Moreover, in this work index returns are defined as $R_{i,t} = ln(P_{i,t}) - ln(P_{i,t-1})$, where $R_{i,t}$ is the daily return of index i, ln is the natural logarithm; $P_{i,t}$ is the current level of index i, and $P_{i,t-1}$ is the previous day index level. Furthermore, for this particular research study the author has chosen a confidence interval of 95% (or 97.5% with "one-tailed" loss side) and several liquidation time horizons to compute L-VaR. Historical database (of more than six years) of daily closing index levels, for the period 17/10/2004-22/05/2009, are assembled for the purpose of carrying out this research and further for the construction of market and liquidity risk management parameters[6]. In the process of analyzing the data, the daily returns of the nine indices have been calculated. These daily returns are essential items for the calculation of conditional volatilities (by means of GARCH-M (1,1) model), correlation matrices and systematic risk parameters (beta factors).

Analysis of the particular risk of each index (daily conditional volatility), the indices relationships—or the systematic beta factors—with respect to the benchmark index (that is, the Shuaa Arab Index) and finally a test of non-normality (asymmetry) are performed on the sample indices. To investigate the stochastic statistical properties of the data, we have computed the log returns of each series. Table (1) illustrates the daily conditional volatility of each of the sample indices under normal and intricate (severe) market conditions[7]. Conditional volatilities are estimated with the aid of a generalized autoregressive conditional heteroscedasticity in mean model [GARCH-M (1,1)][8]. Severe market volatilities are calculated by implementing an empirical distribution of past returns for all stock market indices' time series and, hence, the maximum negative returns (or downside losses), which are perceived in the historical time series, are selected for this end. This tactic can aid in overcoming some of the limitations of normality assumption and provide a better examination of L-VaR especially under critical and illiquid market settings. As such, Table (2) depicts the maximum daily positive (gains) and negative returns (losses) and their respective dates of occurrences. To that end, downside-risk under adverse market conditions is simulated as the conditional volatility of the maximum daily losses.

In another study, the computation of skewness, kurtosis and testing for non-normality are performed on the sample indices. The results of this study are depicted in Table (1) as well. It is seen, in general, that all indices show asymmetric behavior (both positive and negative values). Moreover, kurtosis studies show similar patterns of abnormality (i.e. peaked/flat distributions). As evidenced in Table (1), the departure from normality are also confirmed with the Jarque-Bera (JB) test. The JB test shows an obvious general deviation from normality and, thus, rejects the hypothesis that GCC stock markets' time series returns are normally distributed. The interesting outcome of this study suggests the necessity of combining L-VaR computations with other methods such as stress-testing and scenarios analysis to get an in depth view of other remaining risks (i.e., fat-tails in the probability distribution) that cannot be captured with the simple assumption of normality.

For the purpose of putting together a robust L-VaR and risk-capital engine, three matrices of correlation factors are generated in this research study, namely correlation (ρ) = +1, 0, and empirical. The objective here is to set the needed infrastructure for advanced quantitative risk management modeling that will follow shortly. The generated correlation matrix is depicted in Table (3), for the empirical correlation case, of all nine GCC indices. Contrary to general belief, our empirical results indicates that

Table 1. Risk analysis dataset: Conditional volatility, beta factor, expected return and test for non-normality

Stock Market Indices	Daily Volatility (Normal Market)*	Daily Volatility (Severe Market)*	Arithmetic Mean	Expected Return*	Sensitivity (Beta) Factor	Skewness	Kurtosis	Jarque-Bera (JB) Test
DFM General Index	1.81%	12.16%	0.12%	0.14%	0.58	0.01	7.86	955**
ADX Index	1.32%	7.08%	0.07%	0.07%	0.40	0.12	7.26	734**
BA All Share Index	0.58%	3.77%	0.05%	0.04%	0.06	0.43	10.24	2142**
KSE General Index	0.71%	3.74%	0.09%	0.08%	0.14	-0.18	8.38	1173**
MSM30 Index	0.79%	8.70%	0.12%	0.10%	0.10	-0.57	18.40	9617**
DSM20 Index	1.48%	8.07%	0.06%	0.07%	0.31	-0.11	5.59	273**
SE All Share Index	1.86%	11.03%	0.03%	0.01%	0.98	-0.97	8.47	1361**
Shuaa GCC Index	1.30%	8.10%	0.06%	0.08%	1.05	-0.66	14.00	4949**
Shuaa Arab Index	1.15%	7.57%	0.07%	0.10%	1.00	-0.61	13.79	4758**

Notes: 1) Asterisk * Denotes Estimation of Conditional Volatility and Expected Return Using GARCH-M Model
2) Asterisk ** Denotes Statistical Significance at the 0.01 Level

Source for Table (1): Designed by the author using in-house built algorithms and software.

Table 2. Risk analysis dataset: Maximum daily positive and negative returns and date of occurrence

Stock Market Indices	Maximum Daily Positive Return (Gain)	Date of Occurence	Maximum Daily Negative Return (Loss)	Date of Occurence
DFM General Index	9.94%	23/01/2008	-12.16%	14/03/2006
ADX Index	6.57%	9/05/2005	-7.08%	22/01/2008
BA All Share Index	3.61%	24/01/2006	-3.77%	13/08/2007
KSE General Index	5.05%	16/03/2006	-3.74%	14/03/2006
MSM30 Index	5.22%	16/10/2007	-8.70%	22/01/2008
DSM20 Index	6.22%	4/02/2008	-8.07%	22/01/2008
SE All Share Index	9.39%	13/05/2006	-11.03%	21/01/2008
Shuaa GCC Index	11.14%	13/05/2006	-8.10%	21/01/2008
Shuaa Arab Index	9.43%	13/05/2006	-7.57%	21/01/2008
Note: Downside Risk Under Severe Market Conditions is Simulated as the Conditional Volatility of the Maximum Daily Loss				

Source for Table (2): Designed by the author using in-house built algorithms and software.

there is a very small correlation (relationship) between the GCC stock markets in the long-run period. Nonetheless, in the short-run period (or on daily intricate market conditions), however, we found that correlations tend to increase in value (although not on a large scale) and it could even switch signs under certain extreme circumstances.

Computation of Risk-Capital Structures with L-VaR Modeling Algorithms

For the computation of risk-capital structures, a number of quantitative modeling case studies are carried out to emphasize the importance of equity trading risk management simulation reports for daily risk-taking practices. These simulation case studies can also help in understanding the methods used in determining the performance of alternative L-VaR estimation procedures in the context of equity trading risk management. To that end, Figure (1) illustrates a practical simulation report for modeling the risk-capital structures of a hypothetical multiple-assets equity portfolio consisting of some indices of the GCC stock markets region. Asset allocation and L-VaR examination (i.e., risk-capital assessment on a daily basis[9]) are performed under the assumption that local indices represent accurate replicas of diversified portfolios of domestic common stocks for each GCC stock market respectively. Furthermore, all risk modeling and testing are performed at the one-tailed 97.5% level of confidence over different closeout periods.

In this full simulation case study, the total multi-assets portfolio volume is AED70 millions (UAE Dirham), with the same asset allocation and one trading day asset liquidity horizon—that is, one day to unwind all equity trading holdings. Furthermore, Figure (1) illustrates the effects of stress-testing (that is, L-VaR under severe market conditions[10] calculated with the maximum negative returns (losses) of Table [2]) with different correlation factors on daily L-VaR assessments. In essence, this modeling tactic can aid in overcoming some of the limitations of the normality assumption and provide better examinations of L-VaR, especially under intricate and illiquid crisis-driven market outlooks.

As one might expect, the modeling case study in Figure (1) with $\rho = +1$ gives the highest L-VaR figures (i.e., AED1,712,470 [under normal market conditions] and AED10,908,688 [under severe market conditions]), owing to the fact that under these circumstances the total L-VaR of the actual portfolio

Table 3. Risk analysis dataset: Correlation matrix of stock market indices

	DFM General Index	ADX Index	BA All Share Index	KSE General Index	MSM30 Index	DSM20 Index	SE All Share Index	Shuaa GCC Index	Shuua Arab Index
DFM General Index	100%								
ADX Index	56%	100%							
BA All Share Index	12%	8%	100%						
KSE General Index	17%	16%	12%	100%					
MSM30 Index	12%	17%	11%	11%	100%				
DSM20 Index	18%	23%	12%	12%	20%	100%			
SE All Share Index	20%	20%	7%	16%	11%	10%	100%		
Shuaa GCC Index	37%	35%	13%	19%	13%	26%	62%	100%	
Shuua Arab Index	39%	36%	12%	24%	15%	26%	60%	93%	100%

Source for Table (3): Designed by the author using in-house built algorithms and software.

Figure 1. Simulation of liquidity-adjusted value at risk (LVaR) and asset allocation: full case study
Source for Figure (1): Designed by the author using in-house built algorithms and software.

Exhibit (1) Simulation of Liquidity-Adjusted Value at Risk (LVaR) and Asset Allocation: Full Case Study

Stock Market Indices	Market Value in AED	Asset Allocation	Liquidity Holding Horizon	Expected Return	Undiversified LVaR in AED (Normal)	Undiversified LVaR in AED (Severe)
DFM General Index	$ 10,000,000	14.3%	1	0.14%	181,364	1,215,727
ADX Index	$ 10,000,000	14.3%	1	0.07%	132,471	707,554
BA All Share Index	$ 10,000,000	14.3%	1	0.04%	58,084	376,816
KSE General Index	$ 10,000,000	14.3%	1	0.05%	71,249	373,646
MSM30 Index	$ 10,000,000	14.3%	1	0.10%	79,267	869,899
DSM20 Index	$ 10,000,000	14.3%	1	0.07%	148,033	807,413
SE All Share Index	$ 10,000,000	14.3%	1	0.01%	185,767	1,103,290
Shuaa GCC Index	$ -	0.0%	1	0.08%	-	-
Shuaa Arab Index	$ -	0.0%	1	0.10%	-	-
Total Portfolio Value in AED	$ 70,000,000	100%		0.07%		

Daily Liquidity-Adjusted Value at Risk (LVaR) in AED [Normal Market Conditions]		
ρ = *Empirical*	$\rho = 1$	$\rho = 0$
971,334	1,712,470	697,418
1.39%	2.45%	1.00%

Diversification Benefits	
$ 741,136	76.30%

Daily Liquidity-Adjusted Value at Risk (LVaR) in AED [Severe Market Conditions]		
ρ = *Empirical*	$\rho = 1$	$\rho = 0$
6,118,872	10,908,688	4,420,911
8.74%	15.58%	6.32%

Diversification Benefits	
$ 4,789,816	78.28%

Overall Sensitivity Factor: Portfolio of Stock Indices
0.366

is basically the weighted average of the individual L-VaRs of each GCC stock market. The degree of risk-capital diversification benefits, of this hypothetical simulation portfolio, can be shown as the difference in values of the two highest L-VaRs—that is, when L-VaR is computed with $\rho = +1$ versus the case at which L-VaR is simulated with ρ = empirical. For instance, the risk-capital diversification benefits, for the case of normal market conditions, is assessed as AED741,136 or 76.30%, and for severe market outlooks it is computed as AED4,789,816 or 78.28% of diversification advantage. The overall systematic risk sensitivity factor (beta parameter) of this multiple-assets portfolio is also indicated in this report as 0.366, or in other words, the total equity portfolio value, with the actual asset allocations, moves distantly from the benchmark index (Shuaa Arab Index). Furthermore, the L-VaR-engine's simulation report depicts the overnight conditional undiversified L-VaRs (or undiversified risk-capitals) for each GCC stock market. These undiversified risk-capitals (under normal and intricate market outlooks) are computed as well with the aid of conditional volatilities, estimated by the means of a GARCH-M (1,1) model.

Since the variations in daily L-VaR are mainly related to the ways in which the multiple-assets are allocated (that is, long-only or combinations of long and short-sales trading positions) in addition to the impact of the closeout periods, it is instructive to examine the way in which the L-VaR figures are influenced by changes in these parameters. All else being equal, and under the assumption of normal market conditions, Figure (2) illustrates the non-linear alterations to L-VaR figures when the closeout periods are incremented in intervals from one to ten trading days, for all long-only trading positions within the specified multiple-assets equity portfolio. Next, with the aim of demonstrating the effects of illiquidity of trading assets, under intricate market conditions, on daily L-VaR figures, Figure (3) illustrates the outcomes of increasing the unwinding periods from one to ten trading days for all trading holdings. In both simulation cases of Figures (2) and (3), the overall volume is kept at AED70 millions with identical asset allocation ratios of 14.3% in each of the seven GCC stock markets respectively (that is, long-only trading positions). Furthermore, the analysis of L-VaR under illiquid and crisis-simulated market conditions is performed with three different correlation parameters (ρ): empirical, zero and unity respectively and for long-only trading assets. Indeed, it is essential to include different correlation factors in any L-VaR and stress-testing exercises. This is because existing trends in correlation factors may break down (or change signs) under adverse and critical market movements, caused by unforeseen financial or political events and crises. As expected, the case with $\rho = +1$ provides the maximum L-VaR statistics owing to the fact that under these circumstances the total L-VaR is the weighted average of the specific L-VaRs of each equity trading asset. Furthermore, the degree of risk-diversification (or in other words the effects of diversified L-VaR) of this hypothetical simulated portfolio can be deduced simply as the difference in the values of the two greatest L-VaRs—that is, the L-VaR under $\rho = +1$ versus the L-VaR when ρ= empirical. Interestingly, the spread (or the degree of risk-diversification in risk-capital) between the two L-VaRs increases as the number of days to unwind the overall trading positions augments.

Finally, Figures (4) and (5) illustrate the impact of short-sales[11] on L-VaR figures with different liquidation horizons and for both normal and intricate market outlooks. In both case studies, the total volume of the multiple-assets portfolio is maintained at AED70 millions but with different long/short-sales asset allocation ratios as follows: 43% for Dubai, 29% for Abu Dhabi, 57% for Saudi Arabia, and 14% for Kuwait markets respectively. Likewise, a negative (-14%) asset allocation ratio is assigned equally across the board for each of Bahrain, Oman, and Qatar stock markets. Both Figures indicate the non-

Figure 2. L-VaR analysis is under liquid normal market conditions (pure long tradition positions constraint is imposed)
Source for Figure (2): Designed by the author using in-house built algorithms and software.

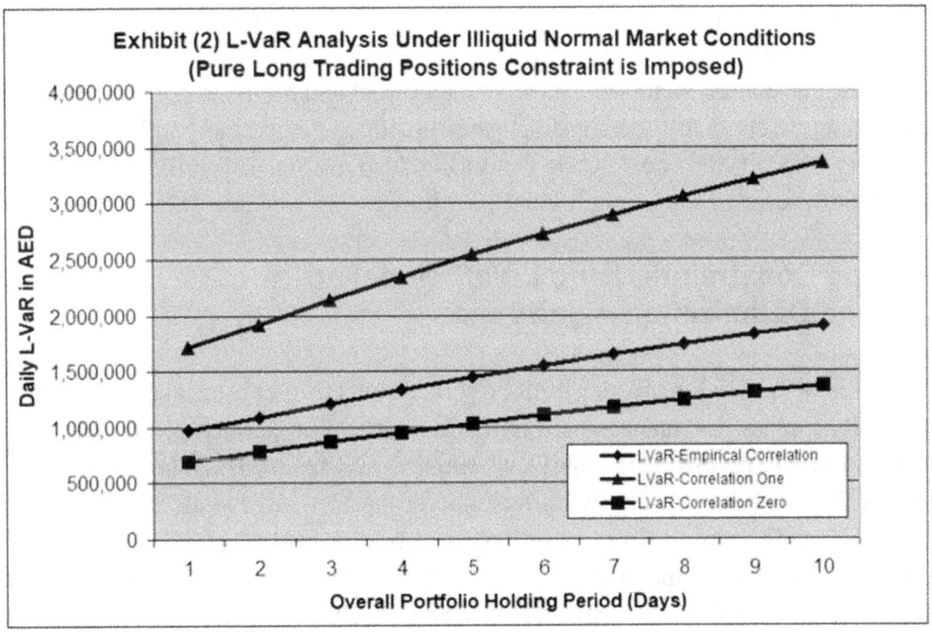

Figure 3. L-VaR analysis under liquid severe market conditions (pure long tradition positions constraint is imposed)
Source for Figure (3): Designed by the author using in-house built algorithms and software.

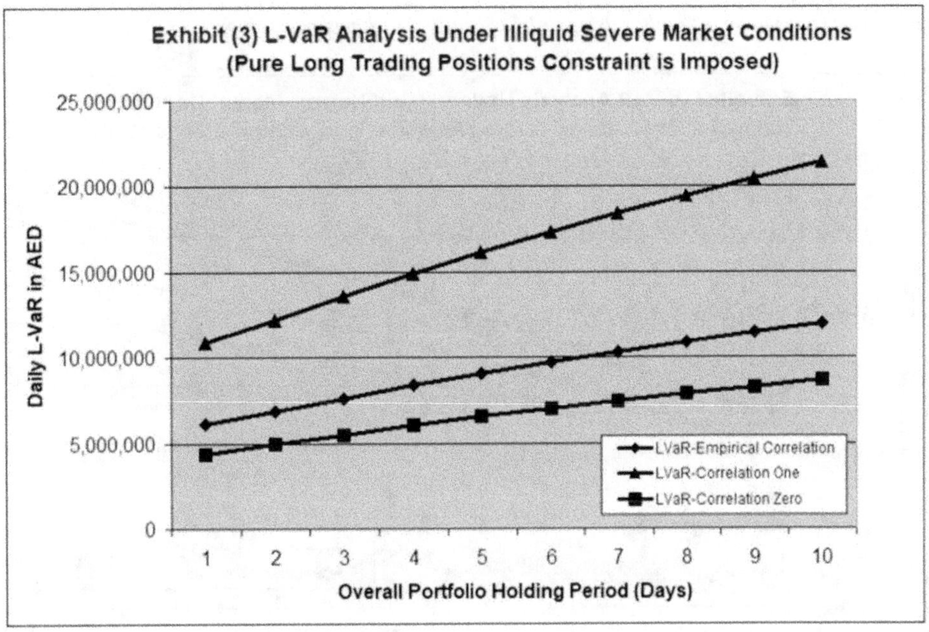

linear alterations to L-VaR figures when the liquidation period is increased from one to ten trading days, for all long/short-sales trading assets. Evidently, the spread or the degree of risk-diversification boosts up slightly as the number of days to unwind the overall trading positions increases but to a lesser extent than the case of long-only trading assets. The latter observed phenomena can be explained by the fact that the degree of correlation factors for the GCC stock markets is relatively low as shown in Table (3). Conspicuously, low correlation factors can have a rather direct and robust impact on risk-diversification for long-only trading assets than for long/short-sales positions. Thus, the combination of long/short-sales trading assets with very low correlation factors can lead to some diversification benefits, albeit to a lesser extent than the case of long-only trading positions.

Risk-Budgeting Constraints Using L-VaR Modeling Techniques and Optimization Algorithms

Optimization of maximum risk exposure limits (or risk-budgeting constraints) are an important element for any equity trading risk management unit and it should be defined clearly and used wisely to ensure control on the trading/investment unit's potential exposures to risk. The risk management unit, independently of the front office's equity traders, should perform all L-VaR upper limits setting and control, monitoring, and reporting. In most professional trading and asset management units (such as commercial banks, foreign exchange dealers, commodity traders, institutional investors, etc.), L-VaR optimum limit-setting is based on the concept of risk appetite. The risk appetite is defined as the maximum loss potential that management is willing to accept when an adverse move in equity prices occurs within a specified time horizon.

Figure 4. L-VaR analysis under liquid normal market conditions (long and short-sales trading positions and without a constraint)
Source for Figure (4): Designed by the author using in-house built algorithms and software.

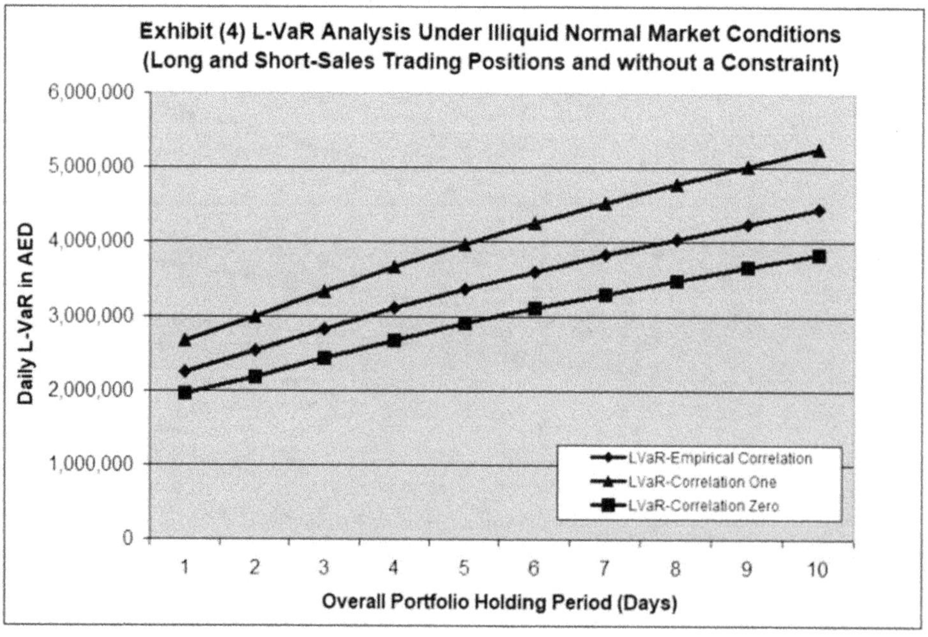

Figure 5. L-VaR analysis under liquid severe market conditions (long and short sales trading positions without a constraint)
Source for Figure (5): Designed by the author using in-house built algorithms and software.

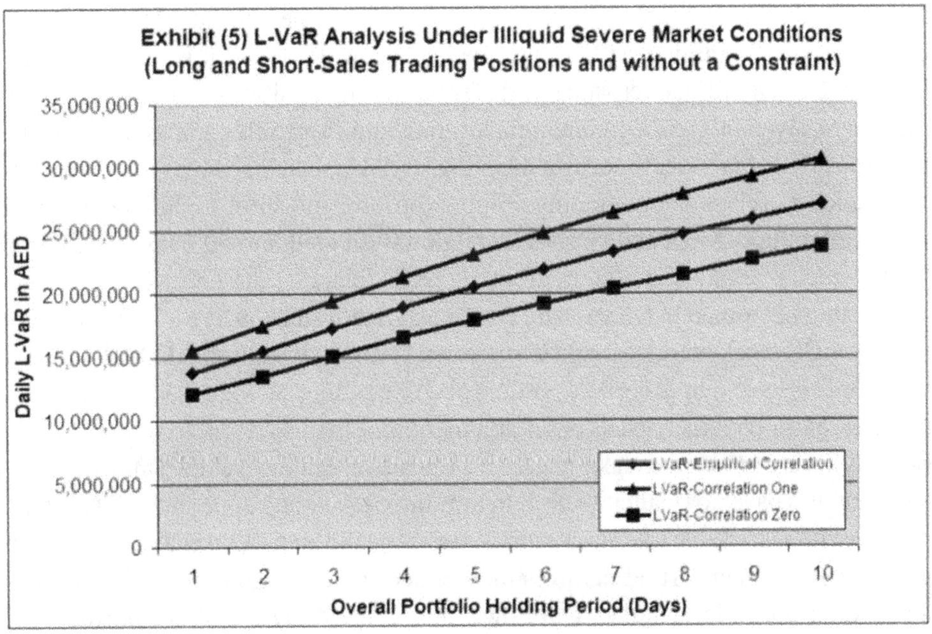

How should we set risk limits to safeguard against maximum loss amounts? These are some of the central questions risk managers must envisage. In this chapter, a robust and practical optimization technique is presented for the setting of maximum L-VaR constraints. To that end, an iterative optimization modeling technique, with different L-VaR boundaries, is examined in order to devise procedures for the computation of L-VaR upper limits. These maximum limits serve as a strict policy for handling situations in which the equity trading unit are above the authorized L-VaR risk-budgeting constraints.

In this research study, we look at the optimization problem from a more meaningful operational angle. In view of that, the optimization process is formulated in such a way to find the best combinations of multiple-assets portfolios that maximizes L-VaR, subject to the expected returns, trading volumes and closeout horizons are controlled according to the requirements of the trading risk manager. As such, the focus in this work is on the forecast of risk measure, rather than on expected returns for two reasons: first, several studies have analyzed the forecasts of expected returns in the context of the Markowitz (1959) mean-variance optimization (see for instance, Best and Grauer, 1991, for a discussion on this issue). The common opinion is that expected returns are not easy to foresee, and that the optimization process is very sensitive to these variations. Second, there exists a general notion that L-VaR, in a wide sense, is simpler to assess than expected returns from historical data (Al Janabi, 2013 and 2014).

In this chapter, the optimization process is based on the definition of L-VaR as the maximum possible loss over a specified time horizon, within a given confidence level. The optimization modeling technique solves the problem by finding the market positions that maximize the loss, subject to the fact that all constraints are satisfied within their boundary values. Furthermore, in all simulation cases the liquidation horizons are kept constant, throughout the optimization process, according to the following values for each stock market: DFM General Index (2 days); ADX Index (2 days); BA All Share Index (3 days); KSE General Index (3 days); MSM30 Index (4 days); DSM20 Index (4 days); SE All Share Index (2 days).

In addition, for the sake of simplifying the optimization routine and thereafter its interpretation, a volume trading limit of 100 million AED is assumed as a constraint—that is, the equity trading entity must keep a maximum overall market value of different trading positions of no more than 100 million AED between long-only assets and combinations of long and short selling positions. Furthermore, for optimization purposes, and in order to set up a meaningful risk management case study, other constraints are imposed, detailed as follows: total trading volume (of long and short trading positions) in all GCC stock markets is 100 million AED; equity asset allocation is divided into 50% investment in Dubai, Abu Dhabi and Saudi stock markets and 50% in all other GCC financial markets; total trading volume (of long and short trading positions) in Dubai, Abu Dhabi and Saudi stock markets is 50 million AED; trading volume in any GCC stock market should be between [-40, +40] million AED; all liquidity horizons for all equities are kept constant according to the specified values as indicated above; and the overall portfolio expected return on a daily basis is set at a margin of 0.13%.

While the weights are allowed to take negative or positive values, we determined, since arbitrarily high or low percentages have no financial sense, to introduce lower and upper boundaries for the weights and in accordance with reasonable trading practices. Based on the above optimization budget constraints, senior management of the financial trading/investment entity can set maximum daily L-VaR risk-budgeting for the equity trading portfolio, detailed as follows: 3,330,779 AED (3.33% of portfolio value) under normal (regular) market conditions and with the assumption of empirical correlations; 3,347,040 AED (3.35% of portfolio value) under normal market conditions and with the assumption of positive 100% correlations; 2,959,100 AED (2.96% of portfolio value) under normal market conditions and with the assumption of zero correlations; 20,903,484 AED (20.90% of portfolio value) under severe (intricate) or crisis market conditions and with the assumption of empirical correlations: 22,850,538 AED (22.85% of portfolio value) under severe or crisis market conditions and with the assumption of positive 100% correlations; and 18,603,366 AED (18.60% of portfolio value) under severe or crisis market conditions and with the assumption of zero correlations. The maximum approved trading volume limit for all equities in the six GCC stock markets between long and short selling positions is set at 100,000,000 AED, and that for total asset allocation limit for Dubai, Abu Dhabi and Saudi stock markets between long and short selling positions at 50,000,000 AED. Trading volume in any GCC stock market should be between [-40,000,000, +40,000,000] AED and with the possibility of short selling. And finally, with respect to the overall average portfolio, expected return on a daily basis is set at a margin of 0.13%, risk-adjusted expected return on a daily basis and under the notion of normal market conditions at a margin of 3.9%, risk-adjusted expected return on a daily basis and under the notion of severe market outlooks at a margin of 0.62%.

It should be noted here that the above optimum L-VaR risk-budgeting limits are in their converted (or equivalent) UAE dirham (AED) values at the current or prevailing foreign exchange rates of other GCC countries versus the UAE dirham.

CONCLUDING REMARKS AND SUMMARY

Recent years have witnessed the increasing role of investment funds in equity markets and with a particular emphasis on emerging and Islamic markets. Emerging and Islamic equity assets, in addition to offering high expected rates of return, also offer significant risk management benefits since these assets are customarily characterized by lower correlations between each other and with other financial assets. As such, investment funds, traditionally dealing with developed financial markets, are now diversifying into emerging and Islamic equity markets with the objective of achieving significant risk/return benefits. The focus on emerging and Islamic equity markets is motivated by the fact that many of these markets have progressively moved towards market-based systems, liberalized stocks, bonds and foreign exchange markets, and relaxed restrictions on foreign investor participation.

The last few years have witnessed a rapid expansion of emerging and Islamic markets trading activities—with several turmoil in capital markets—and an increasing interest in the computation and management of asset liquidity risk. During the last four decade, Value at Risk (VaR) became one of the most popular tools for assessing trading risk across financial institutions and markets. It is thus essential, at this stage, to be able to adapt the definition of traditional tools of quantifying trading risk to the needs and the requirements of this new environment in which the liquidity factor plays a central role. Asset liquidity is a key factor in formalizing and measuring overall trading risk and neglecting liquidity risk can lead to underestimation of overall trading risk and to undercapitalization of financial institutions, particularly if their portfolios are concentrated in emerging and Islamic markets. This has assumed special significance as more and more financial entities prepare themselves towards better internal modeling of trading risk within the context of Basel II and Basel III capital adequacy guidelines[12].

In essence, asset liquidity trading risk arises from the failure to recognize or address changes in market conditions that affect the ability to liquidate trading assets quickly with minimal loss in value. The 2007-2009 turmoil in financial markets endorses the needs for rigorous handling and integration of asset liquidity trading risk into VaR models. Yet despite this universal recognition of the phenomena, there exist no precise mathematical definition of asset liquidity risk and traditional VaR models fail to recognize the impact of asset liquidity trading risk. In this chapter we do not offer a definitive one either, but we examine and test measures of certain kinds of asset liquidity trading risk that is useful for completing the definition of market risk and for forecasting liquidity-adjusted VaR (L-VaR), risk-capital structure and risk-budgeting constraints under illiquid and intricate market outlooks, and within multivariate contexts.

Given the rising need for measuring, managing and controlling of financial risk, trading risk prediction under liquid and illiquid market conditions plays an increasing role in banking and finance sectors. Moreover, the ability to focus on additional moments in the return distribution with the possibility of allowing for skewed or leptokurtotic distributions enables additional risk factors (along with the use of conditional volatilities by mean of GARCH-M (1,1) modeling technique) to be included into the optimal portfolio selection problem and quantitative risk management processes. To that end, in this chapter the author examines a robust internal model of liquidity trading risk management for portfolios with multiple-assets. This is with the objective of forecasting L-VaR under illiquid market conditions and within a multivariate context. To that end, in this research study, the modeling techniques and the non-linear robust optimization algorithms are based on Al Janabi model (Al Janabi, 2008; Madoroba and Kruger, 2014).

Using an extensive dataset of emerging and Islamic Gulf Cooperation Council (GCC) markets, the author simulates different trading portfolios and determine potential risk-capital exposures and risk-budgeting constraints under different illiquid market outlooks and dependence measures. To investigate the stochastic statistical properties of the data, we have computed the log returns of each series. However, it is a stylized fact that the distributions of many financial return time series are non-normal, with skewness and kurtosis pervasive. As such, it would therefore be more desirable to focus on a measure for risk that is able to incorporate any non-normality in the return distributions of financial assets. For almost all the cases, the study of some preliminary statistics allows us to conclude that the considered time series are characterized by asymmetry and high leptokurtosis. Moreover, the normality hypothesis has been rejected for almost every time series through the Jarque-Bera test. As a result, the use of normal distribution, which is the case in a mean-variance approach (Markowitz, 1959), tends to give poor evidence of what is observed in our return time series. In fact, L-VaR computed under normality assumption can underestimate the actual risk exposure since the tails of the empirical distribution are fatter than those implied by the normal one. In order to overcome this shortcoming, in this chapter we implement the empirical distribution of past returns for all equity assets' time series. This approach has aid in providing a better analysis of L-VaR, especially under intricate and illiquid market settings.

Our empirical testing results for the GCC zone suggest that in almost all tests, there are clear asymmetric behaviors in the distribution of returns of the sample equity indices. The appealing outcome of this study suggests the inevitability of combining L-VaR computations with other methods such as stress-testing and scenarios analysis to grasp a thorough picture of other remaining risks (such as, fat-tails in the probability distribution) that cannot be revealed with the plain assumption of normality. In conclusion, the implications of the findings of this study on the GCC stock markets suggest that although there is a clear departure from normality in the distribution of equity indices returns, this issue can be tackled without the need of complex mathematical algorithms and analytical procedures. In fact, it is possible to justify and to handle these issues for cash equities with the simple use of a closed-form parametric VaR method; along with the incorporation of a credible stress-testing approach (under adverse and crisis-simulated market outlooks); as well as by supplementing the risk analysis with a realistic asset liquidity risk factor that takes into account real-world trading circumstances throughout the closeout period. Indeed, our suggested modeling technique is in-line with the recommendation of previous studies (see, for example, Neftci, 2000). In essence, a number of authors have argued that many asset distributions have "fat tails" and that *RiskMetrics* (Morgan Guaranty Trust Company, 1994), by assuming the normal distribution, underestimates the risk of extreme losses.

As such, this chapter has examined robust modeling algorithms for the computation of VaR by incorporating the liquidity of trading assets. In this chapter, we put forward a robust L-VaR modeling algorithm which, unlike the standard version (i.e., the square root-t multiplier) that assumes all trading positions can be sold instantaneously with no friction at the end of the holding period, takes into account different liquidation horizons with which the securities of a given portfolio could be liquidated. The key methodological contribution is the implementation of a different and less conservative asset liquidity scaling factor for including liquidation risk in standard VaR modeling. The examined asset liquidity multiplier is a function of a predetermined liquidity threshold, defined as the maximum position which can be unwound without disturbing market prices during one trading day, and is quite straightforward to implement even by very large financial institutions and institutional portfolio managers. As such, our modeling framework facilitates the relatively simple liquidity-adjusted VaR under certain assumptions and recognizes asset liquidity trading risk as a significant risk factor that should be integrated within the framework of VaR. Furthermore, the model is theoretically simple with moderate demands on additional computational power while capturing the essential aspects of asset liquidity risk-capital and risk-budgeting upper limits.

In essence, asset liquidity trading risk is found to be an important component of the aggregate risks absorbed by financial entities. Our results suggest that ignoring asset liquidity trading risk can produce substantial underestimates of the overall trading risk, particularly in emerging and Islamic markets securities. As such, asset liquidity trading risk should be included in any performance evaluation as part of returns adjusted for risk compensation. Likewise, it should be induced in the process of setting of maximum trading limits and risk-budgeting constraints.

As a final point, the asset liquidity framework presented in this chapter does not incorporate all aspects of liquidity trading risk and appraisal of risk-capital allocation and risk-budgeting constraints. However, it is effective as a tool for evaluating trading risk, risk-capital allocation and risk-budgeting constraints when the impact of illiquidity of specific financial products is significant. Indeed, future research on this topic can focus on generating other scenarios besides the "linear-liquidation-scheme" presented in this chapter. For instance, impending-crisis-inspired rush[13] to exit the market would call for selling as much as possible at once even when asset prices are starting to go down given that one will be trying to beat even lower prices. Further distribution permutations are possible and are not hard to imagine under other turmoil circumstances and adverse market outlooks.

The modeling techniques, optimization algorithms, and empirical testing outcomes are interesting in terms of theory as well as practical applications, and can have many uses and application in financial markets, particularly in light of the 2007-2009 global financial meltdown. The implemented methodology and risk assessment algorithms can aid in advancing quantitative risk management practices in emerging and Islamic markets, particularly in the wake of the subprime credit crunch and the subsequent 2007-2009 financial turmoil. In addition, the proposed quantitative risk management techniques and optimization algorithms can have important uses and applications in expert systems, machine learning, smart financial functions, and financial technology (FinTech) in big data environments. Likewise, it can aid in the development of regulatory technology (RegTech) for the global financial services industry, and can be of interest to professionals, regulators, and researchers working in the field of finance and FinTech; and for those who want to improve their understanding of the impact of innovative quantitative risk management techniques and optimization algorithms on regulatory challenges for Islamic financial services industry and its effects on global financial stability.

ACKNOWLEDGMENT

Recognition of the original source of previous publications: This chapter is partially based on previous research studies conducted by the author and published by De Gruyter, and World Scientific, namely:

1. Al Janabi M. A. M., (2010), "Incorporating Asset Liquidity Effects in Risk-Capital Modeling," *Review of Middle East Economics and Finance*, Vol. 6, No.1, pp. 60-89.
2. Al Janabi, M. A. M. (2009), "Market Liquidity and Strategic Asset Allocation: Applications to GCC Stock Exchanges", *Middle East Development Journal*, Vol. 1, No. 2, pp. 227-254.

REFERENCES

Al Janabi, M. A. M. (2008, Summer). Integrating Liquidity Risk Factor into a Parametric Value at Risk Method. *Journal of Trading*, 76-87.

Al Janabi, M. A. M. (2009). Market Liquidity and Strategic Asset Allocation: Applications to GCC Stock Exchanges. *Middle East Development Journal*, *1*(2), 227–254. doi:10.1142/S1793812009000115

Al Janabi, M. A. M. (2010). Incorporating Asset Liquidity Effects in Risk-Capital Modeling. *Review of Middle East Economics and Finance*, *6*(1), 60–89. doi:10.2202/1475-3693.1258

Al Janabi, M. A. M. (2011). Modeling coherent trading risk parameters under illiquid market perspective. *Studies in Economics and Finance*, *28*(4), 301–332. doi:10.1108/10867371111171555

Al Janabi, M. A. M. (2012). Optimal Commodity Asset Allocation with a Coherent Market Risk Modeling. *Review of Financial Economics*, *21*(3), 131–140. doi:10.1016/j.rfe.2012.06.007

Al Janabi, M. A. M. (2013). Optimal and Coherent Economic-Capital Structures: Evidence from Long and Short-Sales Trading Positions under Illiquid Market Perspectives. *Annals of Operations Research*, *205*(1), 109–139. doi:10.100710479-012-1096-3

Al Janabi, M. A. M. (2014). Optimal and Investable Portfolios: An Empirical Analysis with Scenario Optimization Algorithms under Crisis Market Prospects. *Economic Modelling*, *40*, 369–381. doi:10.1016/j.econmod.2013.11.021

Al Janabi, M. A. M., Arreola-Hernández, J. A., Berger, T., & Nguyen, D. K. (2017). Multivariate dependence and portfolio optimization algorithms under illiquid market scenarios. *European Journal of Operational Research*, *259*(3), 1121–1131. doi:10.1016/j.ejor.2016.11.019

Almgren, R., & Chriss, N. (1999). *Optimal Execution of Portfolio Transaction*. Working Paper. Department of Mathematics, The University of Chicago.

Amihud, Y., Mendelson, H., & Pedersen, L. H. (2005). Liquidity and Asset Prices. *Foundations and Trends in Finance*, *1*(4), 269–364. doi:10.1561/0500000003

Angelidis, T., & Benos, A. (2006). Liquidity adjusted value-at-risk based on the components of the bid-ask spread. *Applied Financial Economics*, *16*(11), 835–851. doi:10.1080/09603100500426440

Arreola-Hernández, J., Al Janabi, M. A. M., Hammoudeh, S., & Nguyen, D. K. (2015). Time lag dependence, cross-correlation and risk analysis of U.S. energy and non-energy stock portfolios. *Journal of Asset Management*, *16*(7), 467–483. doi:10.1057/jam.2015.33

Arreola-Hernandez, J., Hammoudeh, S., Khuong, N. D., Al Janabi, M. A. M., & Reboredo, J. C. (2016). Global financial crisis and dependence risk analysis of sector portfolios: A vine copula approach. *Applied Economics*, *49*(25), 2409–2427. doi:10.1080/00036846.2016.1240346

Bangia, A., Diebold, F.X., Schuermann, T., & Stroughair, J.D. (2002). *Modeling liquidity risk with implications for traditional market risk measurement and management*. Academic Press.

Berkowitz, J. (2000). *Incorporating Liquidity Risk into VaR Models.* Working Paper. Graduate School of Management, University of California, Irvine, CA.

Best, M. J., & Grauer, R. R. (1991). On the sensitivity of mean-variance-efficient portfolios to changes in asset means: Some analytical and computational results. *Review of Financial Studies, 4*(2), 315–342. doi:10.1093/rfs/4.2.315

Cain, B., & Zurbruegg, R. (2010). Can switching between risk measures lead to better portfolio optimization? *Journal of Asset Management, 10*(6), 358–369. doi:10.1057/jam.2009.20

Daka, V. R., & Basu, S. (2016). Assessing performance of liquidity adjusted Value at Risk models. *International Journal of Financial Research, 7*(5), 87–98. doi:10.5430/ijfr.v7n5p87

Danielsson, J., & Zigrand, J.-P. (2006). On time-scaling of risk and the square-root-of-time rule. *Journal of Banking & Finance, 30*(10), 2701–2713. doi:10.1016/j.jbankfin.2005.10.002

Dowd, K., Blake, D., & Cairns, A. (2004, Winter/Spring). Long-Term Value at Risk. *Journal of Risk Finance*, 52-57.

Hisata, Y., & Yamai, Y. (2000). *Research Toward the Practical Application of Liquidity Risk Evaluation Methods.* Discussion Paper, Institute for Monetary and Economic Studies, Bank of Japan.

Jarrow, R., & Subramanian, A. (1997). Mopping up Liquidity. *Risk (Concord, NH), 10*(12), 170–173.

Low, R. K. Y., Alcock, J., Faff, R., & Brailsford, T. (2013). Canonical vine copulas in the context of modern portfolio management: Are they worth it? *Journal of Banking & Finance, 37*(8), 3085–3099. doi:10.1016/j.jbankfin.2013.02.036

Madoroba, S. B. W., & Kruger, J. W. (2014). Liquidity effects on value-at-risk limits: Construction of a new VaR model. *Journal of Risk Model Validation, 8*(4), 19–46. doi:10.21314/JRMV.2014.127

Markowitz, H. (1959). *Portfolio Selection: Efficient Diversification of Investments.* New York: John Wiley.

Meucci, A. (2009). Managing Diversification. *Risk (Concord, NH), 22*(5), 74–79.

Morgan Guaranty Trust Company. (1994). *RiskMetrics-Technical Document.* New York: Morgan Guaranty Trust Company, Global Research.

Neftci, S. F. (2000). Value at Risk Calculations, Extreme Events and Tail Estimations. *Journal of Derivatives, 7*(Spring Issue), 23–37. doi:10.3905/jod.2000.319126

Roch, A., & Soner, H. M. (2013). Resilient price impact of trading and the cost of illiquidity. *International Journal of Theoretical and Applied Finance, 16*(6), 1–27. doi:10.1142/S0219024913500374

Ruozi, R., & Ferrari, P. (2013). *Liquidity Risk Management in Banks: Economic and Regulatory Issues.* Springer Briefs in Finance. doi:10.1007/978-3-642-29581-2

Saunders, A., & Cornett, M. (2008). *Financial Institutions Management* (6th ed.). Singapore: McGraw Hill.

Takahashi, D., & Alexander, S. (2002). Illiquid Alternative Asset Fund Modeling. *Journal of Portfolio Management*, *28*(2), 90–100. doi:10.3905/jpm.2002.319836

Weiß, G. N. F., & Supper, H. (2013). Forecasting liquidity-adjusted intraday Value-at-Risk with vine copulas. *Journal of Banking & Finance*, *37*(9), 3334–3350. doi:10.1016/j.jbankfin.2013.05.013

ENDNOTES

1 The robust modeling technique and non-linear quadratic optimization algorithms implemented in this chapter are based on Al Janabi model (Al Janabi, 2008; Madoroba and Kruger, 2014).

2 Risk-capital (or economic-capital) can be defined as the minimum amount of equity capital a financial entity needs to set aside to absorb worst losses over a certain time horizon with a certain confidence level. This is with the objectives of sustaining its trading operations activities and without subjecting itself to insolvency matters. Risk-capital can be assessed with an internal method and modeling techniques such as L-VaR. Risk-capital differs somehow from regulatory capital, which is necessary to comply with the requirements of Basel II and Basel III capital adequacy requirements. However, building an internal market risk modeling techniques to assess economic capital can significantly aid the financial entity in complying with Basel II and Basel III capital adequacy guidelines.

3 For other relevant literature on liquidity, asset pricing and portfolio choice and diversification one can refer as well to Arreola-Hernández, et al. (2017); Arreola-Hernández, et al. (2015); Daka and Basu (2016); Angelidis and Benos (2006); Amihud, et al. (2005); Ruozi and Ferrari (2013); Roch and Soner (2013); Low, et al. (2013); Cain and Zurbruegg (2010); Meucci (2009); Takahashi and Alexander (2002), among others.

4 A multiplier that is sometimes used by researchers and practitioners is the square root of time in which it is assumed that no autocorrelation exists between the rates of return on asset from one measurement period to another. The presumption of a lack of autocorrelation permits for simple addition of individual variances to produce the overall variance of the holding period. However, it overstates the overall impact of market risk since assets liquidation is not permitted during the closeout (unwinding) period.

5 For further details on the mathematical derivation and rational usefulness of Al Janabi model, refer to Al Janabi, 2014, 2013, and 2012, and Al Janabi et al. (2017) research papers.

6 The database is drawn from Reuters 3000 Xtra Hosted Terminal Platform and Thomson's Datastream dataset. In addition, the selected dataset falls within the most intricate period of the 2007-2009 global financial crisis.

7 In this chapter, severe (intricate) market conditions refer to unexpected extreme adverse market situations at which losses could be several-fold larger than losses under normal market situation. Stress-testing technique is usually used to estimate the impact of unusual and severe events.

8 In this chapter the following generalized autoregressive conditional heteroskedasticity in mean model [GARCH-M (1,1)], is used for the estimation of expected return and conditional volatility for each of the time series variables: $R_{it} = a_i + b_i\sigma_{it} + \varepsilon_{it}$, $\sigma_{it}^2 = c_i + \beta_{i1}\sigma_{it-1}^2 + \beta_{i2}\varepsilon_{it-1}^2$, where R_{it} is the continuous compounding return of time series i, σ_{it} is the conditional standard deviation as a measure of volatility, and ε_{it} is the error term return for time series i. The denotations a_i, b_i, c_i, β_{i1}, and β_{i2} represent parameters to be estimated. The parameters representing variance are assumed to undertake a positive value.

9 Effectively, it is possible to convert daily risk-capital requirement to an annual-basis benchmark specification. In this case, the time horizon is usually one year ahead, assuming 260 active business trading days in the year. For further details of the derivation of the mathematical algorithms for the computation of annual risk-capital, the author refers the readers to Al Janabi (2013) research paper.

10 In this research study, the analysis of severe market conditions is carried out by simulating the risk profile of a trading portfolio under extreme historical conditions. As such, stress-testing technique is employed to assess the impact of historical market upheavals by considering the maximum daily downside-risk (i.e. the maximum negative returns [losses] that are perceived in the historical time-series dataset of the GCC stock markets).

11 Albeit current operational platform in the GCC financial markets does not permit short-sales of financial assets, accordingly in this chapter we relax this restriction on short-sales as we strive to determine potential asset market liquidity risk exposures. As such, our asset liquidity risk modeling includes both long-only trading assets and a combination of long and short-sales positions. In fact, one of the principal advantages of computing L-VaR with matrix-algebra modeling framework is the ability in which one can incorporate the effects of short selling without tedious mathematical algorithms.

12 Indeed, despite the latest progress made by several emerging and Islamic markets to become Basel II & III-compliant countries, in light of the aftermath of the 2007-2009 sub-prime financial crisis it has become evident to the financial service industries that asset liquidity risk is an imperative risk factor and should be modeled as an integral part of any internal enterprise-wide risk management framework.

13 Under these conditions, market participants are tempted to be the first trader or dealer to exit the market with the minimum possible level of losses.

Chapter 7
Risk Management in the Era of Blockchain:
A Warning and Welcome for FinTech

Mohammed Fisal Abu Khaled
Al-Imam Muhammad Ibn Saud Islamic University, Saudi Arabia

ABSTRACT

This chapter intends to document the various ways that the nascent technology, blockchain, and other forms of distributed ledger technology (DLT) can provide both increased and decreased risk as well as offer FinTech industries a fertile environment to pursue key technological advancements that can help shape almost every facet of the financial world. Issues of trust, transparency, and privacy will be explored as it pertains to the execution of blockchain technology within financial sectors. Strengths and weakness will be explored within regulations, legal environments, risk management, and the environment. Based on the findings of a comprehensive literature review, possible solutions and recommendations will be provided for governmental agencies, regulators, and users of financial services with a special focus on Islamic FinTech. Future research directions will also be shared that can assist Islamic FinTech.

DOI: 10.4018/978-1-7998-0039-2.ch007

INTRODUCTION

In the ever-changing financial world, technology often plays a dichotomous role. In the analogy of a dog and its owner playing fetch, technology in finance (also known as FinTech), is both the dog and the tennis ball. As organizations create new technologies, those technologies fly out into the user-space like a ball. Other technologies are then created to chase the ball like a dog in order to prevent misuse or to alter the course of the ball into a more productive pattern. Rarely, new technologies come about that have the potential to alter the game irrevocably. This occurred when the computer became a ubiquitous object in the home and this is occurring again with the advent of blockchain. Blockchain is a ball that has been thrown too far but has the possibility to improve the vast majority of daily life as well as the financial world. As with many technologies, blockchain also comes with a hefty amount of risk. Risk tolerance is a well understood component of the financial world but, for now, blockchain's impact on risk is mysterious. When the computer revolutionized the financial world, there were growing pains that took many forms including fraud, theft, and difficulties both mundane and catastrophic.

Regardless of these pains, progress marches ever forward. According to DiNizo (2018, p. 3 – 4), in 2015 alone, "investments into the FinTech industry grew 75%, surpassing the $22 billion mark". Much of this money is spent on new technologies that could force over 20% of reinsurance, commercial/consumer banking, brokerage, fund transfer, payment, and wealth management services obsolete (DiNizo, 2018, p. 4). Blockchain has become the future cornerstone for ways to apply new technologies to improve financial services. FinTech applications of blockchain technologies are far reaching but include "capital raising, trading, clearing and settlement, global payments, deposits and lending, property and casualty claims processing, digital identity management and authentication, and 'regtech' solutions" (Zetzsche et al., 2018, p. 1364 – 5). Campenon (2016, p. 110) argues that FinTech currently already heavily rely on blockchain technology. NASDAQ is already using blockchain technology for issuance and share transfers for private companies (Campenon, 2016, p. 111).

In this chapter, a basic history of blockchain will be discussed and future implications for blockchain applications within FinTech will be demonstrated. These implications will take the form of both warnings against blockchain misuse and underestimation as well as welcoming rewards for those brave enough to establish trusted parameters within this cutting-edge technology.

BACKGROUND

Financial technology has always been a part of finance. Long ago, the 'technology' component of this pairing consisted of discovering new ways of securing funds and transactions such as coinage. As soon as money was invented as a means to facilitate bartering, technology has needed to keep up with counterfeiting. As such, those behind the economic purse strings needed ways to ensure that the overall institution was safe and secure because, above all else, the economy, financial institutions, and the processes between those individuals and organizations taking part, needed to be trustworthy. Trust is an implicit cornerstone of the financial world. Without trust, all components of the economy would crumble and become meaningless.

This is all the more true when the components turn digital. For example, a trader selling goods across the world would typically deal in either trading of goods for goods or accept payment for goods in the form of a universal currency. For many years, this universal currency took the form of precious metals such as gold or silver (Glass, 2017, p. 466). As time went on, gold and silver became too burdensome, both in weight and in size, to be useful. Governments also found a use for tying the economy to their own particular brand of currency such as the US dollar. For many years these governmental currencies were tied to an equivalent exchange in those precious metals but, over time, stable governmental currencies began to become valuable all on their own (Glass, 2017, p. 467 – 9). This began the inevitable process of decoupling physical materiality from the financial system concerning currency. Credit became a way for financial institutions and individuals to conduct transactions within a particular currency (Glass, 2017, p. 470). When those relationships faltered, the impacts were felt far and wide in the form of financial instability, job loss, and wealth deterioration. This highlights that the financial institution hinges on the concept of trust. An example of this trust can be seen from how various governments handled World War 1. At the time, most governmental currencies were tied to the gold standard but as hostilities increased and more money was needed, the countries printed vast amounts, paying no heed to the gold standard requirement to back up their printing of cash – instead promising to return to the gold standard values post-conflict (Glass, 2017, p. 479 – 80). Countries, institutions, and individual citizens were required to trust that this would be the case in order for the financial world to perpetuate during catastrophe.

One particular invention changed the landscape of the financial world – computers. Brummer and Yadav (2019, p. 254 – 5) attributed the ubiquitous nature of the computer gave rise to many of the technological innovations that are credited to creating the modern era of FinTech. ATM machines, store credit, and financial data creation, evaluation, and storage all originated from the expansion of financial technology from the computer era.

FinTech and the revolution surrounding it comes as a combination of venture capital and technological innovations from tech startup companies (Gomber et al. 2018, p. 223 – 4). At the core, FinTech concerns innovation. Gomber et al. (2018, p. 224) argue that "technology innovation is widely recognized as being the main engine behind economic growth and industrial transformation". These innovations often come in a disruptive manner.

In many ways, technology represents humanity's collective future goals. For example, a technology is created that leads to an invention. This invention promises an experience to the user that vastly improves over past experiences but the invention is perhaps clunky or opens up the user to privacy concerns. Over time, this invention either will fade away or be improved upon. Very rarely is a brand-new technology instantly simultaneously useful and safe. Typically, safety, usability, and simplifying daily life come later in time after several iterations of the technology. This iterative component of FinTech is of particular interest, given that trust comes from patterns formed over time. Gomber et al. (2018, p. 224) point out the way innovations beget new innovations at ever increasing speeds. But what happens when technology rushes ahead of trust? This is the conundrum that is Blockchain. According to DiNizo (2018, p. 4), "blockchain poses a threat to governments, international currency converters, attorneys, financial institutions, brokers, and a host of other business professionals."

Bacon et al. (2018, p. 5) simply describe blockchain as "a type of database". But from simplistic definition comes a much more complicated entity. Zetzsche et al. (2018, p. 1372) describe blockchain as the manner in which data is stored on a ledger – each block serving "as the container for multiple data points, and all blocks are stored in a specific order (the 'chain')." In order to fully appreciate how blockchain impacts and catalyzes FinTech, Bitcoin must be discussed since they are joined at the hip. After the financial crisis of 2007, banking trust was extremely fragile and an anonymous person or entity named Satoshi Nakamoto released a cryptocurrency named Bitcoin as both a banking entity as well as "a more transparent, equitable, and efficient payment system" (Ross, 2017, p. 355). It is important to note that for this chapter, digital currency and virtual currency will be referred to as cryptocurrency so as to highlight the cryptographic technology behind such currencies. As this area is currently developing, various authors will refer to cryptocurrency as digital or virtual currency within their writing. Cryptocurrency's, main selling point is the removal of intermediaries within the payment process (Surujnath, 2017, p. 263 – 4). Glass (2017, p. 485 – 6) argues that these intermediaries provided a necessary level of trust between transactional parties who do not know each other. For example, a person goes online to buy a shirt from a vendor. Neither the vendor nor the purchaser knows one another on any level so there is no inherent trust that the digital payment will be secure, hence the need for an intermediary such as Visa, Paypal, Apple, etc. to create trust for each party involved. When Bitcoin removed the intermediaries, trust was instead provided by the crypto component of cryptocurrency – blockchain.

Decentralization and anonymity are central to cryptocurrency's allure. Yin et al. (2019, p. 38 – 9) point out that these attributes also drew the attention of those with more nefarious intentions such as "terror financing, thefts, scams, and ransomware" as well as the drug market known as Silk Road. Blockchain provided these core concepts to cryptocurrencies. According to Surujnath (2017, p. 264), this stage in blockchain development is referred to as Blockchain 1.0. With the advent of the smart contract, Blockchain 2.0 arose (Surujnath, 2017, p. 270). Blockchain 3.0 is when the technology is used outside of finance and markets (Ross, 2017, p. 360). Each advancement in blockchain creates more unique opportunities for entities. For example, Ethereum, Bitcoin's top competitor, is a cryptocurrency that advanced blockchain technology by instituting smart contracts to provide more customization and optimization to the currency's usage (Surujnath, 2017, p. 264).

An outline of Bitcoin and blockchain is helpful to understand the evolution of blockchain technology in order to see its future impacts on FinTech in both positive and negative ways. Double spending of currency and trust are two core components of any currency system. For example, if a consumer gives a coin to a merchant, there is no way for that consumer to give that coin to another merchant as it is physical in the first merchant's hand. Similarly, the merchant can inspect the silver coin to determine if it is fraudulent, thus establishing trust within the transactional process. This process is similar with paper money but with the country's government acting as an intermediary providing trust that the paper money can be redeemed for value. When it comes to a check written against funds in a consumer's bank account, there are two intermediaries – the banking institution and the government to validate that the money has worth. A check, however, can be written twice and applied against the same value of the bank account, hence why fewer and fewer businesses accept check payment. Regardless, the bank insures that the check will be honored with the merchant and the merchant has trust regardless of the veracity of the consumer. With Bitcoin, there are no intermediaries. All security features for trust and double spending are inherent in the design surrounding the blockchain.

Bitcoin does this by providing a proof-of-work transaction and time-stamping the blockchain so as to verify that the blockchain has been updated and spread across a peer-to-peer network – thus ensuring that each transaction takes place only a single time, gets recorded among a peer-supported network, and occurs securely via cryptography (DiNizo, 2018, p. 8). Proof of work is when the other users connected to the peer-to-peer network add a 'block' of data to the blockchain regarding the current transaction in question (Ross, 2017, p. 364). This proof of work is computationally intensive which makes the mining "integral in the issuance of new bitcoins and is a necessary process for transactions to be added onto the blockchain and subsequently verified" (Ross, 2017, p. 364). The transactions are recorded and data is stored on computers spread out across the world so there is no centralized or decentralized hubs that can be vulnerable to attack. A transaction occurs between two people using Public-Key cryptography where each user has a public and a private key and they share the public keys when the transactions is processed so that it can be recorded across the blockchain (DiNizo, 2018, p. 8). Essentially everyone using the system simultaneously shouts their transactions and records them all together, thus preventing fraud as long as the user's private key is kept private. The currency itself is 'mined' from anyone with a computer by contributing processing power towards the maintenance, storage, and processing of the Bitcoin blockchain (DiNizo, 2018, p.8). There is only one way to defraud the system – bruteforce hacking. Bruteforce hacking is using a vast amount of computational power to randomly guess the decryption value. Seeing as each transaction is individualized and the more users that contribute to the blockchain adds additional security and processing power, it becomes more profitable for the hacker to convert their bruteforce computational power towards mining legitimate Bitcoins (DiNizo, 2018, p. 9).

In a centralized ledger, one node connects to all users or entities – imagine a bicycle wheel with the spokes all coming out of the center. The wheel continues to turn even if several spokes are removed unless the center is weakened. This creates a critical need for security in that central location. In a decentralized ledger, there are a number of nodes with each connecting to with their own individual spokes to users or entities. Similar to social media, in a decentralized ledger, the primary friends may know each other in a community but secondary and tertiary friends may have no connection to those primary friends. This spreads out risk by allowing the system to continue even in the presence of an attack on a number of key nodes. In a distributed ledger, however, all nodes are connected to every other single node. In this system, risk is spread equally throughout the network since no single node has any higher weight or value than any other node. A distributed ledger is the great equalizer of data but with this equalization comes at the cost of control from intermediaries and governmental agencies.

Blockchain technology that is applied outside of cryptocurrencies is also known as distributed ledger technology (DLT) as long as they are not centrally stored and instead distributed across peer-to-peer networks (Bacon et al., 2018, p. 6). Many FinTech ventures are looking at using distributed ledger technology but are still attempting to keep the database centrally secure. This bypasses the true benefit of blockchain which is full distribution. For many users of blockchain, trust in the system relies on the system remaining distributed. If not, the intermediary has a finger on the scale of trust and the whole system is opened to corruption, mismanagement, and being constrained by the decisions of the controlling entity. DLT can also be constructed as either permissioned where an entity or governmental agency has regulating control to permit those allowed to engage in the ledger or it can be permissionless, such as Bitcoin, are peer-to-peer and fully distributed with the code itself possibly being written by the public (Zetzsche et al., 2018, p. 1372). The issue of permissionless versus permissioned DLT will be discussed in further sections.

MAIN FOCUS OF THE CHAPTER

Trust is a necessary requirement within the financial world and "places a major role in any kind of transaction between a buyer and a seller on any marketplace platform" (Subramanian, 2018, p. 81). According to Ross (2017, p. 365), the direction of growth in financial institutions is "shaped by the relationship between varying levels of trust and differences in transaction costs". Blockchain threatens this relationship by disposing of the intermediary. If a merchant does not trust a bank, they will not deposit their funds. If a consumer does not trust their government, they will no longer use that government's printed money. If an investor does not trust the entrepreneur, they will not provide start-up funds. Trust must be implicit if a system is to survive. Blockchain technology has created a new definition of trust by providing trust solely within the technology of the database without reliance on any actor within it (Finck, 2018, p. 668 – 9).

Risk is also inherent in every financial system that has been used and in many ways is inextricably linked with trust. At any time, actors could perform any number of behaviors that could put the system in danger or attempt to take advantage of others within the system. Risk management has grown more complicated as the systems used become more complicated (Gejke, 2018, p. 149). Trust and risk are paired together, conceptually. The more trust that exists between individuals or entities, the less risk but risk never disappears completely. Even a trustworthy person can create risk through accidents, neglect, or ignorance. Blockchain seeks to alleviate issues of trust and risk by creating a ledger that cannot be altered after those within the network agree upon it (Waldo, 2019, p. 38). Blockchain creates a system where there is no need for trust since there is no one in control in which to place trust. Waldo (2019, p. 42) points out that trust always exists somewhere and in the case of blockchain, the trust is in the developers of the software. Seeing as blockchain is the root of the data in regards to verification, translation, transcription, and storage, risk permeates each area creating a merging of disciplines. Regulators, lawyers, computer scientists, government officials, CEOs, bank governance structures, consumers, law enforcement, lenders/borrowers, derivatives, stockholders, etc are all tied to the same framework of risk. As such it is difficult to talk about one sector of risk without the blending and melding of other sectors. In the next section, those concerns, along with others will be explored.

ISSUES, CONTROVERSIES, PROBLEMS

Regulations, Risk Management, and Legal Concerns

Governmental regulations can come up against the novel ways that blockchain can be utilized by FinTech. Researchers have pointed out that blockchain may by its very nature violate data privacy laws (Zetzsche et al., 2018, p. 1374 – 6). In May of 2018, the European Union pass the General Data Protection Regulation (GDPR) in order to provide a necessary layer of consumer data protection and privacy regarding centralized data storages (Munier and Kemball-Cook, 2019, p. 146). Due to the wording of the regulation, blockchain may or may not be in compliance due to its inherent design. Munier and Kemball-Cook (2019, p. 148) point out three main areas that conflict with GDPR – "the identification of the data control and the data processor", the right to be forgotten or to have your data erased, and the remit of pseudosymmetry and anonymity. Within blockchain, everyone is simultaneously a data controller and a data processor. Similarly, identities are, by nature, anonymous due to the hashing that the blockchain process performs on writing and updating data. This can be further complicated by some blockchain systems using *salting* to further obfuscate the individual hash by adding alphanumeric strings randomly thus requiring a literally impossible-to-break value (Munier and Kemball-Cook, 2019, p. 150).

At the core of many regulatory concerns is the decentralization that blockchain promotes. Smart contracts are a great example of this issue within regulation. Surujnath (2017, p. 271) describes smart contracts as ambiguous but generally consisting of a non-legally binding contract (in the traditional sense of the word) that the code within blockchain recognizes and self-enforces. Similar to how blockchain is threatening to remove the need for intermediaries such as banks and governmental monetary control systems, there is also a threat to completely change the way that contract law is executed. Surujnath (2017, p. 271) effectively demonstrates this by providing an example of a car debtor signing a smart contract that enforces payment provided there are funds available and, in the event of a lien, the debtor's car will no longer start. Ross (2017, p. 366) expands on smart contracts by arguing that they an extremely disruptive technological advancement within the practice of law since they can "facilitate the replacement of banking financial intermediaries". Yin et al. (2019, p. 42) mirror these findings by finding that "blockchain is a highly disruptive and innovative technology and argues for a more open-minded regulation without attempting to stop or slow its growth with suggestions to amend the existing legal provisions if necessary to create a workable regulatory model".

In the United States, a single regulatory choice avoided having to determine if Bitcoin was a private currency by treating it instead as a non-currency property (Glass, 2017, p. 502). If Bitcoin were labeled as a private currency, it would be subject to tax law and restrictions based on inflation caused by increasing the money supply (Glass, 2017, p. 500). It is possible that regulators chose this route because they did not see Bitcoin having the longevity or impact it currently does. Bitcoin is not helped by its unstable price (Glass, 2017, p. 503). Glass (2017, p. 506) equates the regulatory fear around Bitcoin and other blockchain-based economies by equating them to mortgage-backed securities around the time of the economic collapse of 2007 and 2008. Mortgage-backed securities were so trusted at the time that they were blindly being thrown around as a pseudo-currency in the vast majority of the US's financial transactions (Glass, 2017, p. 506). Fear around regulating blockchain technology is rooted in similar experiences in history such as the economic collapse of 2007 and 2008. There is an important note here that it was not mortgage-backed securities themselves that led to the collapse but rather the misplaced trust in those in control of the *value* of those securities. In the example of cryptocurrencies in a distributed system, the trust results from the fact that the blockchain cannot experience greed, malfeasance, or hubris. Instead, the blockchain performs as it has been instructed.

Risk management has often relied on behavioral models with certain parameters in order to determine possible outcomes so as to mitigate their effects (Gejke, 2018, p. 149). According to Yang and Li (2018, p. 3256 – 7), FinTech in China has done little to lessen financial risks over the past several years, instead overlaying and collecting "technical risk, operational risk, and systemic risk" and allowing it to grow rapidly. As such, China is now in a position to provide more effective regulations in order to curb FinTech risk (Yang and Li, 2018, p. 3257). Trust within risk management is complicated as the whole goal is to preemptively assume a breakdown in trust at some point in order to provide damage control or to avoid the incident all together. For example, if I have a behavioral model that demonstrates that newly graduated students rarely pay off student loan debt, instead of risking faulty loans, lenders would instead perhaps choose not to offer as many student loans. While reality is much more complicated than this, risk management presents a way to deal with a known quantity in an unknown world – certain amount of risk is required in certain industries. Blockchain adds additional layers of protection as well as potential sources of risk.

Gejke (2018, p. 153) points out how liquidity risk management can use blockchain technologies to provide "real-time and efficient one clicks services with increased granularity, offering more transparency for identifying and moving cash and collateral around". However, Gejke (2018, p. 154) also points out that the Bank for International Settlements is concerned that DLT technology could lead to longer settlement times and provide more liquidity risks. Within smart contracts, risk is reduced due to their "autonomous, self-sufficient, and decentralized" nature (Ross, 2017, p. 366).

Research has also been performed that demonstrates that the confusing nature of blockchain also provides a block in practicing law as well as regulatory environments (Walch, 2017). Interlinked with trust, legal concerns regarding DLT have been pointed out by researchers (Walch, 2017; Zetzsche et al., 2018). Zetzsche et al. (2018, p. 1367) argues that many who brandish DLT and, specifically blockchain, may be overzealous in their assessment that legal liability vanishes when trust goes to the code rather than the institution. This is particularly of importance given the global demand for ever increasing cybersecurity solutions which DLT has been hailed as a savior. These systems are still vulnerable to attack, albeit across a wider spectrum. Instead of having a centralized ledger or database, the risk and liability are spread across all the nodes of the distributed DLT (Zetzsche et al., 2018, p. 1369).

Another area of risk with using blockchain concerns storage of data. According to Zetsche et al. (2018, p. 1373), the ledger's data storage needs are only resolved when there is participation from the community nodes. Essentially, if the community picks up and walks away from a particular DLT, the data can become inaccessible. DLT such as Bitcoin account for this possible risk by incentivizing their individual nodes with cryptocurrency rewards for maintaining and perpetuating the blockchain's functions (Zetzsche et al., 2018, p. 1373).

Derivatives is another area that is susceptible to disruption from blockchain's implementation. The derivatives market has long existed and is a sector that could be drastically shaped by integrating DLT. According to Surujnath (2017, p. 279 – 80), if the derivatives market implements blockchain technology and loses much of its centralized process, Goldman Sachs estimates the banking industry will save between \$11 and \$12 billion annually. This is an enormous amount simply from removing intermediaries. Surujnath (2017, p. 280) argues that the best way of implementing blockchain within the derivatives market would be to "involve a system of several interoperable ledgers that use multi-sig smart contracts for effectuating transfers and oracles for asset monitoring and collateral management". It is important to note that this kind of implementation of DLT would include the anonymity similar to Bitcoin. Essentially, the bidders would upload their asks anonymously and smart contracts would select the highest bid and establish an agreement that is every bit as binding as the current method except with less need for dealers (Surujnath, 2018, p. 280). These are the ways that DLT can affect numerous systems without a cryptocurrency yet still disrupt large sections of the financial world.

Environmental Concerns

Many researchers have pointed out one particular drawback from cryptocurrencies as well as peer-to-peer DLT technology and that is the power consumption required to process all the calculations (Waldo, 2019; Weber, 2018). Waldo (2019, p. 42) points out that DLT is not the only system that uses such 'crowd-sourced' computational power via the internet such as SETI. Organizations such as SETI allow outside participants to offload computations onto their own computers. This results in a large power consumption increase for these individuals. Weber (2018, p. 52) points out that the servers running Bitcoin consume almost as much energy as the entire country of Ireland. He also points out that Bitcoin miners' power consumption increase five fold over last year and several "orders of magnitude" higher than years before. Compared to a centralized ledger system such as a typical data server cluster hub, DLT cryptocurrency mining is like burning down an entire forest to cook your family's dinner. According to Eyal (2017, p. 45), "the rate of energy consumption for Bitcoin . . . will become equal to Denmark's". This level of power consumption does not coincide with the recent societal focus on 'green energy' and conservation.

Centralized, Decentralized, or Distributed Ledgers

As mentioned previously, the ability for blockchain to create trust just by the technology alone is a core component that appeals to many. This is, however, not a requirement of blockchain. Waldo (2019, p. 42) argues that decoupling the issue of trust from the issue of intermediaries can also create new advances without having to hassle with the issue of trustlessness. For example, banks or other entities can adopt blockchain technology to create ledgers that are actually controlled by those entities, thus creating a system of trust based off of existing layers of trust built through the past history of the financial world. Waldo (2019, p. 42) points out that this centralized system of blockchain ledger transactions could still be monitored by government agencies and watchdog groups. He also points out that in such a centralized system, the 'leader' could hash the group immediately instead of requiring vast amounts of computational power in order to link the last ledger with the new one as is currently done in cryptocurrencies like Bitcoin (Waldo, 2019, p. 42). This would also decouple the need for the blockchain transactional system to create an incentivized digital currency to operate as many of the necessary maintenance tasks such as checking hashed ledgers can occur easier and faster, thus negating the need for these vast sources of computational power (Waldo, 2019, p. 42).

Decentralized systems may or may not have an intermediary or a controlling entity. Within permissioned DLT, these decentralized systems could have several controlling entities who share in order to increase security within the blockchain environment or increase security by providing additional oversight to provide additional trust. For example, a decentralized DLT may have overlook and a permissioned system that is ultimately controlled by an existing banking entity but oversight by either governmental agencies or community members could be provided to increase transparency. Similar to centralized systems, there still exists a relatively high degree of risk given that an entity or entities retains control of the DLT parameters. In cases of permissioned DLT this could open the database up to cybersecurity vulnerabilities

Distributed systems, however, have a much wider presentation than the other two due to the complete lack of intermediaries and oversight. They are also vastly more open and transparent than centralized or even decentralized ledgers – so much so that they open themselves up to further risk. Being an open and public storage, DLT opens up a vast array of market abuse such as "insider trading, tipping, and market manipulation" (Zetzsche et al., 2018, p. 1376). It is important to note that these manipulations are nothing new to financial institutions and existing regulations appropriately control for and penalize those behaving in such fashions.

Privacy Concerns

Yin et al. (2019, p. 43 – 4) point out that one allure to Bitcoin and blockchain technology is the privacy it affords while simultaneously pointing out that this increases illicit activities in the system. Anonymity is another core component of blockchain but it does not have to be so. There are ways of creating DLT systems without anonymity or pseudonymity but this will most likely require using a centralized entity or intermediary that has absolute control over the users in the blockchain. Anonymity can lead to "an environment for hate speech and defamatory remarks by individuals who behave irresponsibly with impunity" (Yin et al., 2019, p. 45) but it can also lead to "enhanced societies and flourishing human communications" that help protect from profiling (p. 47).

The data storage method of blockchain, itself, is a privacy concern. Zetzsche et al. (2018, p. 1375 – 6) argue that the transparent nature of blockchain creates the possibility to re-personalize the user based on transaction logs and metadata or even assist criminals in stealing another user's identity. Essentially, with enough metadata it can be possible to rework transactional characteristics for individual users thus granting them possible personal information. Due to the legal concerns listed above, this can cause an issue with existing regulations. Yin et al. (2019, p. 67) have preliminarily shown methods to de-anonymize Bitcoin blockchain, stating that "the assumed level of anonymity of the Bitcoin Blockchain is not as high as commonly believed, and the number of potential owners of a Bitcoin address can be narrowed down to a certain degree". Such findings raise questions regarding one of the core features of blockchain – anonymity. Another privacy concern exists within DLT due to the longevity of the data. In theory, the data will exist as long as the ledger is being maintained by active users – individual blocks cannot be extricated once connected to the chain. For example, a user on a DLT determines another user's hashed identity. They position inaccurate data regarding this individual's past history such as credit worthiness, incurred debt, or other such ill comments. Due to the nature of the blockchain, once that data is secured and in place, it is immutable and cannot be erased unless the whole chain is dropped (Zetzsche et al., 2018, p. 1376).

FinTech

Fintech is always interested in using new technologies to benefit the financial world. As such, blockchain offers up some real solutions in additional areas such as "insurance, supply-chain monitoring, and Internet of Things" (Eyal, 2017, p. 41). Daj (2018, p. 212) agrees that blockchain and more specifically smart contracts can offer a unique solution for machine to machine communication within an Internet of Things system. This kind of advantage should not be overlooked by the FinTech community.

Another area that FinTech has seen a focus is within the securities industry. According to Workie and Jain (2017, p. 348), DLT adoption represents "the potential to create a fundamental change for several traditional processes in the securities industry through the development of new business models and new practices". The industry will not just shift or mold around a new technology. Instead, it will be completely reworked into new models. Blockchain will offer those in the securities industry increased efficiency and decreased risk while adding necessary levels of transparency for all involved in the industry (Workie and Jain, 2017, p. 348).

SOLUTIONS AND RECOMMENDATIONS

Out of the conflicting environment between FinTech and regulatory bodies, a new domain has been created in the UK called 'RegTech' which specializes in "the adoption and use of technology to help financial services firms to understand and comply with regulatory requirements more efficiently and effectively" (Yang and Li, 2018, p. 3257). A recommendation can be made in developing FinTech countries to pair RegTech growth with regulatory changes so as to create a more stable environment for financial service firms to operate within the bounds of the new legal environment. Creating a regulatory environment conducive to RegTech cannot only decrease friction between regulating bodies and firms but the primary goal is to decrease risk. According to Yang and Li (2018, p. 3258), RegTech benefits both the firms and the regulators by helping firms "to control costs and risks more effectively, liberate surplus regulatory capital, and present new opportunities for FinTech startups, consulting firms, and tech companies" while helping regulators in "the development of continuous-monitoring tools to identify problems as they develop and reduce the time it takes to investigate compliance breaches". Zetzsche et al. (2018, p. 1365) also points out the benefits of RegTech, stating that it can benefit by providing "automated compliance, administration and risk management, and anti-money laundering and client suitability checks".

In the Islamic FinTech environment, pairing RegTech solutions while controlled regulations are being introduced allows for both parties to move a measured pace and add stability to a very unstable process. Regulators should use financial technology such as "AI, the blockchain, cloud computing, and big data . . . to assess the risk level, capital flow, and capital use of financial institutions and even individuals (Yang and Li, 2018, p. 3263). Regulatory oversight should not be overlooked as a solution. Blockchain complicates this endeavor since it operates outside of an intermediary. While the data is open for all to see, oversight is difficult given the anonymity of ownership. Yang and Li (2018, p. 3263) and the author recommends blockchain transactions should be visible for all parties so as to promote oversight by both the regulators and the financial entities. In this example, regulators could make use of the 'clean' and immediately accessible data provided from blockchain technology to regulate firms while those firms will have access to the same data. Technology can assist financial regulators also by accurately providing information that leads to a sizeable decrease in information asymmetry (Yang and Li, 2018, p. 3264). This reduction in information asymmetry allows for a much greater control over financial outcomes and a huge decrease in risk. It also allows for all to benefit, not just regulators or profiteering firms. Finck (2018, p. 689) advises regulators to "focus on specific use cases of blockchains rather than the technology itself". Similar to the disruptiveness caused by the advent of the Internet, blockchain technology is inherently a "neutral technology" and many existing regulations cover the vast majority of crimes committed through blockchain use (Finck, 2018, p. 689). In many ways, blockchain is out of the box and cannot be put back in. Finck (2018, p. 689) points out that "there is no realistic option of preventing the spread of blockchains except for disconnecting citizens from the Internet, or intervening at a protocol level.

Transparency issues abound within DLT such as identity theft, market abuse, insider trading, immutable data, and discovering identities of users. Zetzsche et al. (2018, p. 1405) argue that the real issue of DLT systems will not be how they can best assist and grow FinTech but that it opens more users to potential risk than centralized systems. In spite of this, researchers are pushing the boundaries of areas that blockchain can be applied. Susskind (2017) finds that blockchain technology can be extremely beneficial in providing secure online elections due to the immutability of blockchain data and security features inherent in the technology.

As for power consumption from the required proof-of-work transactions in most popular cryptocurrencies, there are possible solutions in future technology. According to Eyal (2017, p. 45), Intel is working on a new way of greatly reducing power consumption by changing the proof-of-work concept into a "Proof of Elapsed Time (PoET)". PoET would, in theory, allow the miner to run a trustworthy application that idles for a random amount of time and "the miner that is first to awaken is the leader of the consensus round and receives a reward" (Eyal, 2017, p. 45). Unfortunately, this only incentivizes miners to run hundreds of idling low-end computers instead of several high-powered computers. The net power consumption could be the same given enough time (Eyal, 2017, p. 45 – 6). Eyal (2017, p. 46) recommends an alternative that allows miners to use their stronger computers for mining but in a more practical manner while including time-based analysis. Such novel solutions provide an easy alternative to the power waste that is currently occurring while still maintaining a decentralized system.

There are massive benefits from integrating DLT into FinTech as well as existing financial institutions. The application and innovations surrounding smart contracts are worth noting. Many researchers have explored the positive applications of using smart contracts in a blockchain manner (Daj, 2018; Eyal, 2017; Glass, 2017; Halaburda, 2018; Henly et al., 2018; Subramanian, 2018; Surujnath, 2017; Workie and Jain, 2017; Zetzsche et al., 2018). Risk is never a zero sum game. It will not be eliminated and blockchain is not going to be a miracle remover of risk. Smart contracts, however, do remove the intermediary requirement and provide much stronger and more binding agreements as they are tied into the blockchain and, potentially, tied to usable funds or even the physical world by using the Internet of Things. According to Zetzsche et al. (2018, p. 1386), smart contracts already have legal status in many jurisdictions including certain US states such as Arizona. In this manner they are already legally binding and can be upheld in court. In this case, regulating bodies actually approve and condone the use of smart contracts to create new ways to improve the legal environment.

Another benefit has been discovered in research on how blockchain can more easily bring financial services to billions of people in developing countries through entrepreneurship (Larios-Hernandez, 2017). Across the world there are billions of individuals who are unconnected to financial institutions. Entrepreneurs could, in theory, utilize blockchain technology to help incorporate these individuals into financial institutions. Larios-Hernandez (2017) points out the need for expanding entrepreneurial growth towards semi-formal financial services for those who have not bought in to the current system. This kind of focus could bring access to advanced services such as lending and other transactional advantages to a user base that has never accepted traditional financial services. Such research points at an area of focus that could be very beneficial for Islamic FinTech entrepreneurs to pursue given the amount of individuals living in rural environments.

Subramanian (2018, p. 82) argues that decentralized markets will have a whole host of positive effects. In traditional buyer and seller marketplaces, Subramanian (2018, p. 82) points out that both the buyer and seller will have an easier time finding products and listing them as well as a reduction in listing errors due to the formation of the blockchain. Transactional costs will also be greatly minimized since there are no intermediaries (Subramanian, 2018, p. 82).

Governmental regulations should aid and buffer blockchain growth in ways that benefit FinTech and the general consumer base. Gejke (2018, p. 153) argues that the growth of blockchain technology will require the support of government and central banks in order for success in the long run. Regulators should also take into account the environmental cost of cryptocurrency and future DLT applications. Given the global environmental concerns that are being discovered, creating and fostering an industry that consumes such a vast amount of power for something as simple as database management is surprising at the very least and possibly irresponsible. As mentioned above, there are innovators and researchers currently working on solutions to this problem but, in the present moment, none exist. Until appropriate solutions are presented, this should be a top priority for blockchain developers.

A final solution for regulation may be key – specifically for Islamic FinTech. Seeing as blockchain offers a new set of systems that need to be regulated, other research has pointed out the benefit of providing a 'regulatory sandbox' for both FinTech developers and regulators (Brummer and Yadav, 2019, p. 291). In a regulatory sandbox, regulators provide a real-world equivalent scenario for FinTech innovators to explore and experiment while the regulator maintains a relaxed position to observe what happens (Brummer and Yadav, 2019, p. 291). The benefit with a sandbox is that both the regulators and the innovators get to benefit from new technology. The regulators get to see the decision-making process from the innovators along with how they can 'break' systems and the innovator gets a chance to create new products in a relaxed environment free of stiff regulations. Islamic FinTech can benefit greatly by creating a regulatory sandbox to explore potential solutions in controlled environments.

FUTURE RESEARCH DIRECTIONS

One particular area for future research that specifically will help guide Islamic FinTech is within the formation of DLT. There needs to be more research performed on permissioned and permissionless DLT to determine which of these two types of DLT best suit Islamic FinTech needs. This research will determine which scenarios benefit a permissioned DLT and which ones benefit from a permissionless DLT. Each configuration has with it a long list of pros and cons that should be explored in order to determine the best course of action. This future research, in conjunction with other topics, will be integral in establishing a list of 'best practices' for blockchain development and implementation.

Future research can also be performed on how best to navigate privacy concerns within DLT. The immutability of data once added to the chain is an alarming trait for new adoption of DLT as well as regulatory bodies. Privacy obligations will need to be considered if DLT is to progress beyond niche markets and uses. Research can and should be performed to determine if and how privacy concerns can be addressed. There are two particular areas of focus. The first is how readily available transactional metadata, in a large enough quantity, can lead to depersonalization of individual users or at the very least build a composite list of characteristics or traits regarding their identity. In centralized ledgers, this would not be an issue because the metadata would be locked beyond a wall that, in optimal conditions, only the organization with control over the ledger can access. With DLT, that metadata is out in the form of blocks being ever added to the chain. The second privacy area that should be researched regards how to treat how difficult it is to erase data. This issue must be solved in several jurisdictions such as the European Union due to the recently passed GDPR which calls for the 'right to be forgotten'. Zetzsche et al. (2018, p. 1376) argue that "immutability and the requirements of law will clash". Future research should be focused on how to address this issue through innovative avenues of data rewriting, specifically for cases of fraudulent transfers (Zetzsche et al., 2018, p. 1376). Even staunch proponents of net neutrality and freedom of access to data can see the inherent flaw in a system where inappropriate images, hate speech, fraud, inaccurate data, and illicit actions are veritably written in stone.

Another area that needs further research is how blockchain and smart contracts can be utilized specifically within the Islamic Banking institution. Contract law can be difficult within this area and smart contracts offer a novel solution to many problems experienced within Islamic Banking. In particular, research is need to determine the exact manner in which smart contracts function with top efficiency while ensuring that they still stay within the letter of the law and do not run up against any current or future regulations or governmental agencies. In this area, Islamic FinTech has a truly unique problem ahead and future research could offer a way to link FinTech adoption with a safer version of blockchain technology.

Blockchain regulations should find a natural balance between security and flexibility so as to allow for future technological growth. One way this can be secured is to approach blockchain cases individually and attempt to limit the amount of reactionary regulating. Future research similar to Walch (2017) could look at how behavioral patterns can affect both the adoption of DLT as well as provide recommendations for regulators so as to avoid a panic.

One advantage of blockchain is that, contrary to its name and popular opinion, it is modular and flexible in nature. While the blockchain itself is very rigidly constructed, there are many combinations of technologies and structures that allow blockchain to be customized to the environment at hand. DLT coders and creators can focus on either a permissionless or a permissioned architecture. Permissionless could be a benefit in a buyer and seller environment while a permissioned architecture could be better for securities trading so as to ensure identity and transparency in transactions. DLT could include smart contracts to provide additional security that transactions go according to plan. Smart contracts in general provide a degree of modularity simply by enabling their use, particularly within Internet of Things applications. While it is an incredibly unpopular idea currently, blockchain can still be centralized within an intermediary. This allows the owner control over the use of the technology while still taking advantage of the power of blockchain, especially within supply chain management. Decentralized and fully distributed options can also provide a large degree of control or lack of control if that is helpful for the environment at hand. In general, blockchain is a neutral tool to be used in similarly crafted ways as the early versions of the Internet. Imagination, innovation, creativity, and usability will determine the path blockchain takes – along with necessary regulation.

Everyone about blockchain is not perfect, however. The power consumption costs of current blockchain use such as Bitcoin need to be addressed. Decentralized and distributed ledger system power consumption rates could be a fruitful ground for future research. There is also the problematic nature of balancing incentive systems that promote continual power drain by providing cryptocurrency. Potential future research could investigate other avenues for incentivizing consumer to buy-in to the DLT process. For example, sociology or psychology could be shed light on behavioral patterns that can help to discover unique ways that people can buy into a system without the need to continually mine at the cost of the environment. As mentioned above, there are novel solutions to create an incentive system that does not require the power expenditure that current systems use. This is an area that FinTech research should be focused on.

Research should also focus on risk management needs. Gejke (2018, p. 154) points out the need for risk managers to focus on the data side of the equation in order to provide a better understanding of future risk within new trends. Seeing as blockchain is a complicated piece of coding at heart, risk managers will need to begin learning more about data and how computer science and information systems specialties can assist in risk management. Risk management will be an important sector as blockchain develops.

CONCLUSION

This chapter has discovered a particular need for many answers to many questions regarding the implementation and experimentation with blockchain. When adding in specific Islamic FinTech needs such as legal requirements and culturally specific values and considerations, there is a true need for an assembly of best practices that fit Islamic FinTech parameters. Most professional systems have an established set of ‘best practices. These are a set of flexible but established rules and ‘go-to’ solutions for tackling problems that occur spontaneously. Blockchain development and Bitcoin osculating price shifts denote a need for the establishment of a set of best practices. Seeing as Islamic FinTech functions similar yet different than other FinTech networks around the world, there is a real drive to establish parameters before this nascent technology races ahead and cannot be curbed. A preliminary ‘best practice’ might be securing DLT through permissioned ledgers only when the transparency issues warrant concern. For example, creating a permissioned DLT where the personal identity for each user is known by an intermediary that enables or disables permissions based on activity could be a first step towards a best practice. While this certainly limits the possibilities on the DLT by creating an intermediary where none could exist, it does decrease risk and has been argued to reduce liability (Zetzsche et al., 2018, p. 1406). Other research recommends similar actions by

Regulation hurdles will be painful surrounding blockchain innovations. There is no easy way around this and the growing pains will be pervasive regardless of jurisdiction given the digital nature of the technology. Walch (2017, p. 762) cautions for regulators to have patience and to resist ‘herd behavior’ as it can create the “potential for misunderstandings about the technology to drive adoption, rather than actual capabilities”. Before regulators create new decrees, they should pause to reflect if they are acting in a reactionary way to fears of risk or greed for rewards. Blockchain is not a technology that creates or generates wealth directly. Instead it streamlines, simplifies, and connects in a more seamless way than previous databases. There should be caution in both quick adoption and quick restriction of blockchain technology.

Throughout this chapter, blockchain has been referenced as both representing trustlessness and trust. This mirrors the actuality of blockchain as it is simultaneously, by definition, both a source of trust and inherently trustless. This dichotomy represents the truly unique world that blockchain opens up within FinTech.

There seems to be two different avenues for future FinTech growth within blockchain. First is the lawless, decentralized, trustlessness of a peer-to-peer network writing transactions and incentivizing buy-in from adopters by including a linked currency. This path takes the financial world for a huge spin by negating vast sections of systems the world has relied on for over a century such as banks and paper money. The second path is one where DLT technologies are integrated into the established intermediaries that are currently in place such as banks and governmental agencies. The trust stays where it has – in those entities with control. In many ways, the path chosen by FinTech represents more of a philosophical or ideological one.

The chapter has also argued that DLT is both anonymous in nature yet open to vulnerability given enough metadata to determine a user's identification. This type of dichotomy is a sure sign that DLT is in its infancy and requires further maturing before definitive statements can be made regarding security features and characteristics. As more researchers pick away at the shiny exterior of DLT, the true nature will develop. There is no doubt that DLT will pave the way for vast shifts in FinTech innovation and development but the exact manner and, more importantly, the amount of risk required to do so is still to be determined.

In many ways, this chapter demonstrates many advantages to keeping blockchain and other DLT transactional growth within a centralized system. Canaday (2017, p. 20 – 1) echoes this argument by recommending that future blockchain use should include better visibility of cash transactions to deter fraudulent activity, a full written record of all activity on the ledger, and some measure of personal identification by an authentication process such as a permissioned DLT. Across regulating, privacy, and power concerns, there is a natural stepping stone afforded by allowing blockchain to act as an intermediary itself between a completely deregulated, completely private, and completely rampant consumptive model of decentralized DLT systems and allowing already trusted entities to manipulate blockchain so all can gain the affordances offered by such powerful technology. The issue is complicated when an alternative model is attempted to be created that pushes the financial world completely into decentralized and unregulated transactions. No one knows what that model would look like – the technology as well as the philosophical and ideological frameworks are too unknown. The Islamic FinTech industry needs to consider risk versus reward when it looks at how profitable and powerful blockchain technology can be. In one hand, Islamic FinTech will hold an innovative and unique tool that can shape existing networks and systems to optimize an already established pattern of use. In the other hand, Islamic FinTech holds an unknown quantity with equal parts risk and reward.

There is also a need to allow for a balance between innovation, regulation, and research. If any one sector has too much influence or focus, the growth potential from FinTech will wither away. If entrepreneurs simply focus on ways to integrate DLT into as many avenues as possible, regulators will not be able to keep up the pace. Security concerns will rise and there could be a large threat to the overall financial world. If regulators respond to possible disruptive change with strict regulations, innovation will suffer and FinTech will not reach the peak possibilities for incorporating such strong technology into financial institutions. If both regulators and innovators wait for academic research to provide all the answers, novel solutions born out of innovation and creativity will not occur nearly as often. Within blockchain, there resides a need for a balance for all three of these groups to function interconnected. Researchers can provide data analysis that can point to areas of potential growth or risk that could not be discovered without trial and error on the part of the entrepreneurs. Innovators can explore unique new possibilities without fear of running up against regulations that completely void their technological inventions once conceived. Regulators can gauge appropriate response while working in conjunction with those who know the most about the technology at hand as well as avoid knee-jerk reactions that can kick a nascent technology down before it has a chance to grow.

Future regulations need to allow blockchain freedom to grow yet protect against the more nefarious aspects such as crime due to blockchain's inherent anonymity. Islamic FinTech and regulatory bodies could utilize a regulatory sandbox as demonstrated above to assist in determine best practices and initial regulations. Blockchain only works if the trust in the system is based on the technology, not in a controlling body that curbs blockchain use. It must stay as distributed as possible for the full benefits to be felt – especially in regards to the Internet of Things and other FinTech future solutions.

REFERENCES

Bacon, J., Michels, J. D., Millard, C., & Singh, J. (2018). Blockchain Demystified: A Technical and Legal Introduction to Distributed and Centralised Ledgers. *Richmond Journal of Law and Technology*, *25*(1), 1–106.

Brummer, C., & Yadav, Y. (2019). Fintech and the Innovation Trilemma. *The Georgetown Law Journal*, *107*, 235–307.

Campenon, B. (2016). Fintech and the Future of Securities Services. *Journal of Securities Operations and Custody*, *8*(2), 107–112.

Canaday, T. (2017). Evolving a Payments Business to Meet the Demands of a Distributed Economy. *Journal of Payments Strategy and Systems*, *11*(1), 15–22.

Daj, A. (2018). Beyond Cryptocurrencies: Economic and Legal Facets of the Disruptive Potential of Blockchain Technology. *Bulletin of the Transilvania University of Brasov. Series V, Economic Sciences*, *11*(2), 207–216.

DiNizo, A. M. Jr. (2018). From Alice to Bob: The Patent Eligibility of Blockchain in a Post-CLS Bank World. *Journal of Law. Technology and the Internet*, *9*, 1–28.

Eyal, I. (2017). Blockchain Tecnology: Transforming Libertarian Cryptocurrency Dreams to Finance and Banking Realities. *Computer*, *50*(9), 38–49. doi:10.1109/MC.2017.3571042

Finck, M. (2018). Blockchains: Regulating the Unknown. *German Law Journal*, *19*(4), 665–692. doi:10.1017/S2071832200022847

Gejke, C. (2018). A New Season in the Risk Landscape: Connecting the Advancement in Technology with Changes in Customer Behaviour to Enhance the Way Risk is Measured and Managed. *Journal of Risk Management in Financial Institutions*, *11*(2), 148–155.

Glass, J. (2017). What is a Digital Currency. *IDEA – The Journal of the Franklin Pierce Center for Intellectual Property, 57*(3), 455 – 517.

Gomber, P., Kauffman, R. J., Parker, C., & Weber, B. W. (2018). On the Fintech Revolution: Interpreting the Forces of Innovation, Disruption, and Transformation in Financial Services. *Journal of Management Information Systems, 35*(1), 220–265. doi:10.1080/07421222.2018.1440766

Halaburda, H. (2018). Economic and Business Dimensions: Blockchain Revolution Without the Blockchain? *Communications of the ACM, 61*(7), 27–29. doi:10.1145/3225619

Henly, C., Hartnett, S., Endemann, B., Tejblum, B., & Cohen, D. S. (2018). Energizing the Future with Blockchain. *Energy Law Journal, 39*, 197–232.

Larios-Hernandez, G. J. (2017). Blockchain Entrepreneurship Opportunities in the Practices of the Unbanked. *Business Horizons, 60*(6), 865–874. doi:10.1016/j.bushor.2017.07.012

Munier, L., & Kemball-Cook, A. (2019). *Blockchain and the General Data Protection Regulation: Reconciling Protection and Innovation*. Academic Press.

Ross, E. S. (2017). Nobody Puts Blockchain in a Corner: The Disruptive Role of Blockchain Technology in the Financial Services Industry and Current Regulatory Issues. *The Catholic University Journal of Law and Technology, 25*(2), 353–386.

Subramanian, H. (2018). Decentralized Blockchain Based Electronic Marketplaces. *Communications of the ACM, 61*(1), 78–84. doi:10.1145/3158333

Surujnath, R. (2017). Off the Chain! A Guide to Blockchain Derivatives Markets and the Implications on Systemic Risk. *Fordham Journal of Corporate and Financial Law, 23*, 257–304.

Susskind, J. (2017). Decrypting Democracy: Incentivizing Blockchain Voting Technology for an Improved Election System. *The San Diego Law Review, 54*, 785–827.

Walch, A. (2017). The Path of the Blockchain Lexicon (and the Law). *Review of Banking and Financial Law, 36*, 713–765.

Waldo, J. (2019). A Hitchhiker's Guide to the Blockchain Universe. *Communications of the ACM, 62*(3), 38–42. doi:10.1145/3303868

Weber, R. (2018). An Advisor's Introduction to Blockchain. *Journal of Financial Service Professionals, 72*(6), 49–53.

Workie, H., & Jain, K. (2017). Distributed Ledger Technology: Implications of Blockchain for the Securities Industry. *Journal of Securities Operations and Custody, 9*(4), 347–355.

Yang, D., & Li, M. (2018). Evolutionary Approaches and the Construction of Technology-Driven Regulations. *Emerging Markets Finance & Trade, 54*(14), 3256–3271. doi:10.1080/1540496X.2018.1496422

Yin, H. H. S., Langenheldt, K., Harlev, M., Mukkamala, R. R., & Vatrapu, R. (2019). Regulating Cryptocurrencies: A Supervised Machine Learning Approach to De-Anonymizing the Bitcoin Blockchain. *Journal of Management Information Systems*, *36*(1), 37–73. doi:10.1080/07421222.2018.1550550

Zetzsche, D. A., Buckly, R. P., & Arner, D. W. (2018). The Distributed Liability of Distributed Legers: Legal Risks of Blockchain. *University of Illinois Law Review*, *4*, 1361–1406.

APPENDIX

Figure 1. A description of a blockchain and a blockchain transaction
(Du et al., 2019, p. 52)

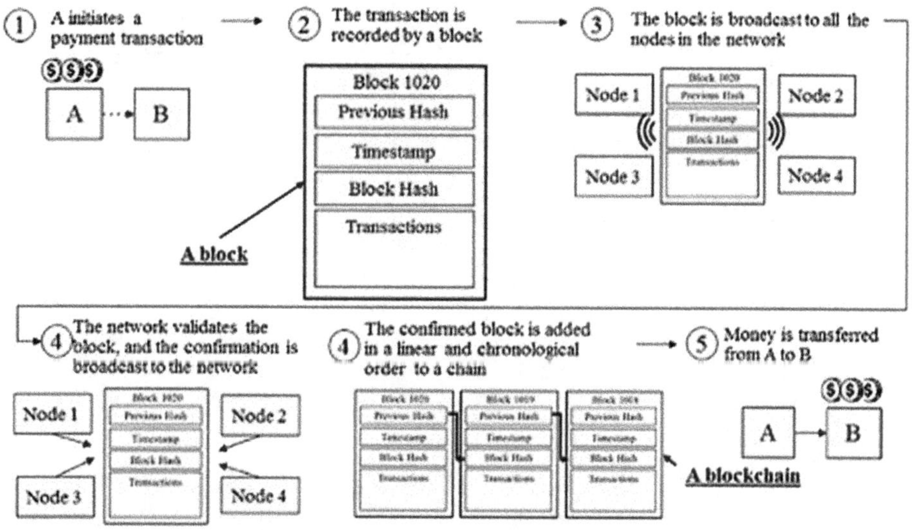

Figure 2. Description of database nodes in different possible configurations. A fully distributed and permissionless DLT will look like Diagram C above with the addition of each individual node being connected to every other node as well
(Zetzsche, 2018, p. 1371)

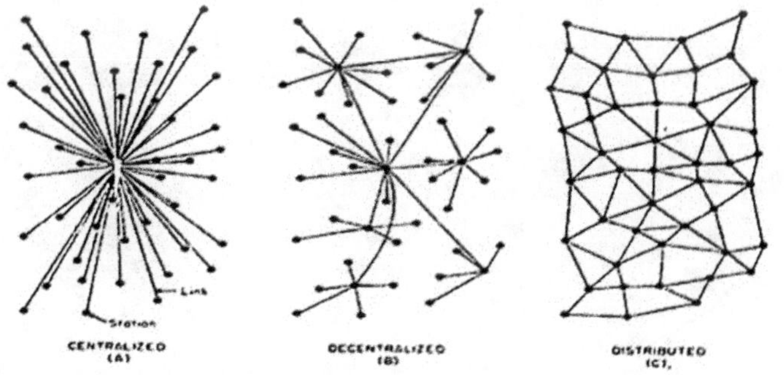

Figure 3. A decision tree to assist in determining when to use blockchain and what type to use
(Munier and Kemball-Cook, 2019, p. 153)

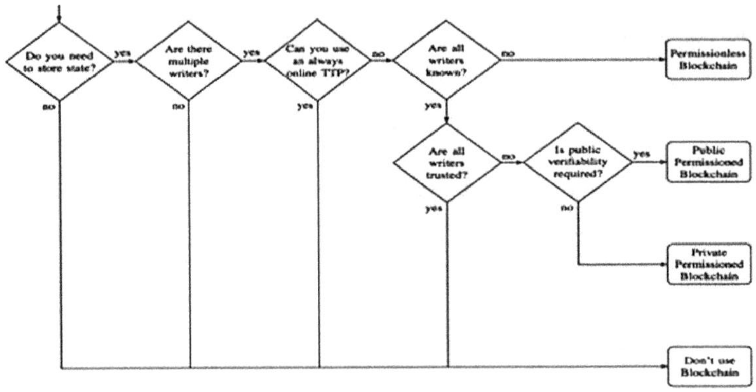

Chapter 8
Regulating FinTech Businesses: The Malaysian Experience

Sherin Kunhibava
University of Malaya, Malaysia

Aishath Muneeza
International Centre for Education in Islamic Finance (INCEIF), Malaysia

ABSTRACT

The Malaysian finance industry is governed by Bank Negara Malaysia (BNM) and Securities Commission Malaysia (SC). BNM governs the banking and insurance industries and the SC regulates and develops its capital market. Both authorities have issued regulations to cater for the proliferation of fintech businesses. For example, BNM issued regulations on digital currency exchanges, electronic-know your customer requirements for fintech companies facilitating remittances, and a regulatory sandbox framework for fintech businesses. Similarly, the SC issued a digital investment management framework, another to facilitate equity crowdfunding, peer-to-peer lending, and digital asset exchanges, and the instrumental digital currency and digital token order. All were issued to encourage innovation in the industry, manage disruption, mitigate risks, and ensure consumer protection. This chapter will explain the steps taken by Malaysia's financial regulatory authorities in dealing with fintech-based companies, critically review the regulations, and recommend some ways forward.

DOI: 10.4018/978-1-7998-0039-2.ch008

INTRODUCTION

Research has shown that regulation and in particular macroprudential regulation, is one way to deal with systemic risks and ensure financial stability of a financial system (Allen & Gu, 2018). While regulation alone cannot ensure financial stability it is one of the tools available that is effective (Allen & Gu, 2018). Research also shows that markets and institutions that fell outside the regulatory perimeter of governance during the financial crisis in 2008-2009 was a cause for financial instability (Lipsky, 2012). Following this it is only relevant to the topic of this book that regulatory steps taken to mitigate against risks associated with fintech should be reviewed as a tool to ensure financial stability of the Islamic financial system. In this chapter regulations that Malaysia has recently issued to include fintech within the purview of its regulators will be reviewed. This introduction will proceed with explaining the benefits and risks associated with fintechs and the layout of this chapter.

The use of technologies in financial services, known as fintech, holds many benefits for business, whether small, medium, or large. In particular, fintechs offer more efficient and cost-effective solutions for businesses seeking financing through equity crowdfunding (ECF) or peer-to-peer lending (P2P) platforms. For example, Nusa Kapital claims to be the world's first fully Shariah compliant P2P platform operating in Malaysia. Regulated by the Securities Commission Malaysia (SC), it performs the role of an intermediary between businesses and investors seeking alternative means of financing and investment (Nusa Kapital, 2017). Other solutions fintechs can offer are online trade finance, online supply chain finance, and invoice finance (Australian Government Treasury, n.d).

The global rise in fintech start-ups, thus, comes as no surprise (KPMG, 2018). Indeed, KPMG reported that investment in fintech companies in the first 6 months of 2018 alone surpassed the total number of fintech investments in 2017 (KPMG, 2018). However, with the proliferation of fintechs comes the need to ensure adequate regulation. As such, an appropriate legal framework is necessary to protect and safeguard the interests of the public and businesses alike as a number of risks arise with its introduction, many of which may not be easily identifiable due to the technology's newness (Kovas, n.d). The creators and providers of fintech must therefore include proper risk identification and management systems.

The risks that have been identified thus far can be categorized into three broad categories: speed, safety, and illegal activity. Ideally, the improved speed of transactions must be commensurate with the speed at which fraud or other malpractice is identified and reported necessitating fintech's creators to include efficient systems for the specific purpose of identifying and reporting wrongdoings (Kovas, n.d). Safety from cyberattacks and hacking is another concern that needs addressing, an example of which can be seen in the 2018 theft, through cyberattacks, of USD500 million from the Japanese digital currency exchange, Coincheck Inc (Star Online, 2018). Also a survey in 2018 by PricewaterhouseCoopers on Malaysian companies, 48% stated that they had been targeted by cyberattacks in the past two years (PwC, 2018). Moreover, the array of customer data and information as stored by fintechs is similarly at risk of misuse. Finally, the risks of money laundering and terrorist financing must also not be ignored as fintech may be exploited for illegal activities (Griffin, 2018, Kovas, n.d).

Accordingly, regulation and a conducive legal environment are necessary to mitigate the particular risks relating to fintechs.

At the same time, over-regulation can stifle innovation and the benefits associated with such technology; thus, a careful balance must be struck between the two. Consequently, Malaysia has introduced regulations or provisions expressly to mitigate such risks while simultaneously encouraging innovation in the field of fintech related services.

The objective of this chapter is to explain the steps taken by Malaysia's financial regulators to deal with fintech based companies, critically review the regulations, and lastly, to offer recommendations and suggest some specific ways forward.

BACKGROUND

The Malaysian financial industry is governed by two regulators: the Central Bank or Bank Negara Malaysia (BNM) which governs *inter alia* banks, Islamic banks, insurance companies, takaful operators, and money service businesses; and the SC which regulates and develops Malaysia's capital markets. Also falling under the jurisdiction of BNM are fintech activities dealing with traditional and investment banking (both Islamic and conventional), insurance/takaful, money changing, remittances, the operation of payment systems, and the issuance of payment instruments.

Both organizations have actively issued regulations to cater for the proliferation of fintech businesses. For example, BNM introduced a provision to deal with digital currency exchanges and another enabling electronic-know your customer requirements (e-KYC) for fintech companies facilitating remittances. Another step taken by BNM was to initiate a regulatory sandbox for fintech businesses. Likewise, the SC issued a digital investment management framework to allow licensed portfolio management companies to provide digital investment management services following fulfilment of the requirements listed therein. Furthermore, the SC also introduced a comprehensive regulatory framework to facilitate ECF, P2P, and digital asset exchanges (DAX) to regulate the offering and trading of digital assets, and the Digital Currency and Digital Token Order.

All these regulations were issued to encourage innovation in the industry, manage disruptions, mitigate risks, and facilitate consumer protection (see Table 1).

Table 1. Provisions issued by the regulators in Malaysia

Regulations Issued by BNM	Regulations Issued by SC
Anti-Money Laundering and Counter Financing of Terrorism (AML/CFT) – Digital Currencies (Sector 6) ('Policy Document on Digital Currencies')	Guidelines on Compliance Function for Fund Management Companies SC-GL/CGL-2005 (R3-2018) ('Digital Investment Management Framework')
Anti-Money Laundering and Counter Financing of Terrorism (AML/CFT) – Money Services Business (Sector 3) (Supplementary Document No 1) ('Policy Document on e-KYC')	Capital Markets and Services (Prescription of Securities) (Digital Currency and Digital Token) Order 2019 PU(A) 12/2019 ('Digital Currency and Digital Token Order')
Financial Technology Regulatory Sandbox Framework ('Regulatory Sandbox Framework')	Guidelines on Recognized Markets SC-GL/6-2015(R2-2019) ('Guidelines on Recognized Markets' covering ECF, P2P, and DAX)

Source: (Bank Negara Malaysia, 2019; Securities Commission Malaysia, 2019a)

REGULATIONS ISSUED BY BANK NEGARA MALAYSIA

Policy Document on Digital Currencies

The Anti-Money Laundering and Counter Financing of Terrorism (AML/CFT) – Digital Currencies policy (Sector 6) or the Policy Document on Digital Currencies was issued in late February 2018 by BNM. In summary, it is directed at businesses involved in converting digital currencies to money and *vice versa* (digital currency exchanges) which although not licensed or regulated by BNM, are "reporting institutions" under the Anti-Money Laundering, Anti-Terrorism Financing and Proceeds of Unlawful Activities Act 2001 (AMLA). This means digital currency exchanges are required to provide detailed information on the buyers and sellers of such currencies.

To expand, the policy document defines digital currencies as a digital representation of value that:

- Functions as a medium of exchange; and
- Is interchangeable with any money but is not electronic money

Electronic money refers to the digital representation of fiat money (Financial Action Task Force, 2014). The policy document is applicable to any persons providing the following services:

- The exchange of digital currency for money;
- The exchange of money for digital currency; or
- The exchange of one digital currency for another, whilst carrying on a digital currency exchange business or otherwise.

Thus, reporting institutions are digital currency exchanges doing business in a digital currency (i.e. a medium of exchange that is convertible to fiat money). These digital currency exchangers are not licensed or regulated by BNM, neither are they recognized as legal tender under the policy document. However, such exchanges must be incorporated and comply with the provisions of the Companies Act 2016 of Malaysia.

Under the policy document, reporting institutions must ensure that they:

- Send a declaration of their details to BNM;
- Assess risks relating to anti-money laundering (AML) and terrorist financing (TF);
- Verify the identity of clients through customer due diligence;
- Identify and assess the AML and TF risks that may arise in relation to the development of new digital currencies, products, services, and business practices;
- Put in place management information systems;
- Keep records which must be maintained and stored for at least 6 years;
- Appoint a "fit and proper" compliance officer who is based in Malaysia; and
- Submit suspicious transaction reports when certain suspicious circumstances arise.

Enforcement measures can be taken against the reporting institution, its directors, officers, and employees for non-compliance in accordance with ss 22, 66E, 86A, 87, 88, 92, and 93 of the AMLA.

Comments on the Policy Document on Digital Currencies

The purpose of the policy document is clear – it ensures that the risks associated with AML and TF are mitigated at digital currency exchanges by the identification and collection of customer data and transactions. Also, an adequate management information system must be installed by the reporting institution. The authors reiterate the importance of such a system and recommend that the improved speed of currency exchange transactions must be commensurate with the speed at which fraud or other malpractice is identified and reported.

Risk mitigation is furthered by the fact that the policy document applies to digital currency exchanges whether they have a physical presence in Malaysia or not. Digital currency exchanges need only send a declaration of their details to BNM which means it may not be the responsibility of the regulatory body to determine whether reporting institutions are offering services to Malaysian citizens. However, as seen below, if digital currency exchanges are deemed digital asset exchange platforms, SC registration will be required. As such, BNM's role would only entail monitoring AML and TF risk. Therefore, digital currency exchanges may have the dual obligation of reporting to two regulators, the SC and BNM.

A major plus point of the policy document lies in its enforcement powers against reporting institutions and their staff in the event of non-compliance with its provisions.

Policy Document on Electronic-Know Your Customer

On 30 November 2017, BNM issued its Anti-Money Laundering and Counter Financing of Terrorism (AML/CFT) – Money Services Business (Sector 3) policy document (or its Policy Document on e-KYC) outlining the minimum requirements that must be observed to implement e-KYC as applicable to remittance businesses using online and mobile channels. E-KYC refers to the identification of customers via electronic means without the need for physical or face-to-face identification.

Unlike digital currency exchanges, online and mobile remittance providers are regulated by BNM under Malaysia's Money Services Business Act 2011 so long as they transfer legal tender. According to the policy document, a licensed remittance provider under the Money Services Business Act 2011 is a "reporting institution" and as such will be required to obtain prior written approval from BNM to implement e-KYC for online or mobile remittances. Thereafter, the following requirements must be fulfilled:

- The board of the reporting institution must ensure proper policies and procedures are in place to address any specific risks associated with implementation of the e-KYC;
- A reporting institution should, on a continued basis, demonstrate that the e-KYC identification and verification methods are at least as good as face-to-face customer verification processes; and
- The systems and technologies developed by reporting institutions should be capable of supporting processes and procedures required for AML or TF compliance programmes.

A reporting institution should also ensure:

- Remittance transactions can only be performed by a person with a valid bank account;
- Individuals can only remit up to a total of MYR30,000 a day;
- Remittance by foreign workers is limited to a maximum total per day of MYR5000; and

- The existence of robust IT security controls including ensuring a customer's remittance account is tied to only one mobile phone device.

Comments on the Electronic-Know Your Customer Policy Document

With this policy document, fintechs can now provide e-KYC which, in turn, allows customers to remit funds faster and at a lower cost, thereby enabling remittance providers to work more efficiently since all verifications and procedures may now be done online in a matter of minutes. Accordingly, it is no longer necessary for customers to be physically present at financial institutions to remit funds. At the same time, this permission is coupled with safety features to prevent money laundering or terrorist financing risks by the tracking of remittances. An example of a fintech utilizing e-KYC is MoneyMatch Sdn Bhd which provides remittance and money exchange services. Beginning operations in May 2017, the company describes itself as a fully digital peer-to-peer currency exchange platform that reduces costs for remittance and money exchange services (Moneymatch, 2018).

Further advancements in this area could include requiring e-KYC for other financial services beyond money service businesses (McKenzie, 2017), for example, takaful related services. Also, to further strengthen the e-KYC framework, it is imperative to enact a legal framework for national digital identification and its use by third parties in Malaysia. This area requires further research and will be discussed below.

Regulatory Sandbox Framework

The Financial Technology Regulatory Sandbox Framework was introduced on 18 October 2016 to enable innovation of fintech to be deployed and tested in a live environment within specified parameters and timeframes (Bank Negara Malaysia [BNM], 2016). The framework allows companies to launch their services without having to comply with the full spectrum of regulations and determines how participants will be considered for placement under the sandbox (Risen, 2017). BNM also created a unit called the Financial Technology Enabler Group (FTEG) to oversee the entry of technological innovations in financial services. According to FTEG, seven participants have been approved to operate within the sandbox although one has since ceased participation (Financial Technology Enabler Group, 2017). According to paragraph 1.5, the considerations are:

- The potential benefits of the proposed product, service, or solution;
- The potential risks and mitigating measures; and
- The integrity, capability, and track record of the financial institutions or fintech companies.

As regards eligibility, participants must demonstrate the following according to paragraph 5.1 of the framework:

- That the product, service, or solution is genuinely **innovative** with a clear potential to:
  - Improve accessibility, efficiency, security, and quality in the provision of financial services,
  - Enhance the efficiency and effectiveness of Malaysian financial institutions' management of risks, or

  - Address gaps in or open new opportunities for financing or investments in the Malaysian economy;
- That the applicant has conducted an adequate and **appropriate assessment** to demonstrate the usefulness and functionality of the product, service, or solution and has identified the associated risks;
- That the applicant has the **necessary resources** to support testing in the sandbox;
- That the applicant has a **realistic business plan** to deploy the product, service, or solution on a commercial scale in Malaysia after exiting the sandbox;
- That the provision of the product, service, or solution is either wholly or **partly incompatible with laws,** regulations, or standards administered by the bank; and
- That the applicant is led and **managed by persons with credibility** and integrity.

The above highlighted words summarise the framework's purpose to promote innovation in the financial industry while simultaneously mitigating its risks. Under the framework, BNM also provides that participants must assess the potential risks to financial institutions and consumers that may arise from the testing of the product, service, or solution and propose appropriate safeguards to address said risks. BNM may also require participants to furnish reports during the 12 month test period which can be extended upon application.

Upon completion of the testing, BNM will decide whether to allow the product, service, or solution to be introduced to the market on a wider scale. If approved, the participant will be required to comply with the relevant licensing, approval, and registration criteria under the relevant banking laws.

Alternatively, BNM may revoke an applicant's approval to participate in the sandbox at any time before the end of the testing period or it may prohibit deployment of the product, service, or solution at the end of the testing period. In any event, if the participant is prohibited from introducing its product or its participation is revoked, the participant must provide the following safeguards under paragraph 10.4. It must:

- Immediately implement its exit plan to cease provision of the product, service, or solution to new and existing customers;
- Provide notification to customers informing them of the cessation and their rights to redress where relevant;
- Comply with obligations imposed by the bank to dispose of all confidential information;
- Compensate any customers who have suffered financial loss arising from the test; and
- Submit a report to the bank on the actions taken under paragraphs 10.4(a)-(d) within 30 days of the revocation.

Comments on the Regulatory Sandbox Framework

The authors contend it is necessary to further clarify consumer protection in the event a participant in a sandbox ceases operations because it has been revoked or because it failed to gain BNM approval. Such details include avenues for redress in the event participants fail to comply with the framework safeguards. For example, certain questions arise including would a customer of a participant in a sandbox be entitled to dispute resolution under alternative avenues? Additionally, while the benchmark to be used for such compensation must be provided in the framework, will other remedies also be available to consumers? All these issues must be addressed appropriately by the framework.

REGULATIONS ISSUED BY THE SECURITIES COMMISSION MALAYSIA

Digital Investment Management Framework

The Guidelines on Compliance Function for Fund Management Companies SC-GL/CGL-2005 (R3-2018) or the Digital Investment Management Framework were first issued by the SC on 15 March 2005 and were last revised on 17 December 2018 (6th revision). Including thirteen chapters, the framework was issued pursuant to s 377 of the Capital Markets and Services Act 2007 (CMSA) and outlines the requirements to be complied with by any person intending to establish or carry out portfolio fund management activities in Malaysia. The framework replaces both the Guidelines on Compliance Function for Fund Managers and the Guidelines on Reporting Requirements for Fund Managers. Accordingly, it aims to establish adequate controls and compliance mechanisms to safeguard investor protection and market confidence, whilst also ensuring fund management activities are carried out in compliance with regulatory requirements.

Chapter 13 introduces additional requirements relating to digital investment management companies. According to the SC, these lay out licensing and conduct requirements for companies offering automated discretionary portfolio management services to investors (Securities Commission [SC], 2017). **Digital investment management** refers to fund management businesses incorporating innovative technologies into their portfolio management services (SC, 2017). In addition to the duties stipulated by the framework, the board of directors must ensure the company has the technological capability and support to undertake such a business. It must also:

- Have sufficient understanding of the rationale, risks, and rules behind the algorithm underpinning the digital investment management business;
- At all times, ensure the outcomes produced by the algorithm are consistent with the company's investment strategies;
- Be commensurate with the risk profile of the investor and comply with securities laws and relevant guidelines;
- Have the system to support the digital investment management business including maintaining a secure environment pursuant to the Guidelines on Management of Cyber Risk and other relevant guidelines; and
- Conduct at least an annual review of the effectiveness of its governance and supervision of the technology and algorithm underpinning its business.

In addition to the responsibilities outlined in the framework, the compliance officer's responsibility includes establishing a compliance programme taking into consideration the unique and specific aspects of the digital investment management's business model. Further, a digital investment management company's risk management framework must include any other risks related to the business.

Such companies must also disclose and display prominently on their platforms:

- Any relevant information relating to the company including that an algorithm is being used;
- Its function;
- The assumptions and limitations of the algorithm;
- The risks inherent in the use of such technology;
- The direct and indirect fees, charges, and other remunerations related to the services provided;
- The investment strategies used and any future changes to the strategy; and
- Information about complaints handling or dispute resolution and its procedures.

Moreover, a digital investment management company must provide in writing to the client complete and accurate information of all investments including any unique features, characteristics of investments, and the nature of underlying assets (if any) to enable customers to make informed investment decisions. Furthermore, the company must obtain the client's prior approval, explain general and specific investment risks including but not limited to pricing, liquidity, and any rights, obligations and attribution of ownership under investment policies or recommendations, prior to the first transaction undertaken on the client's behalf. Subsequent changes to the information specified must be reflected in its reporting to its clients at least on a quarterly basis and the company must also report the performance of each client's portfolio against appropriate benchmarks, any changes in risk (if any) which may affect the client's investments, and any impact on the client's capital and earning of the investment arising from the change in risk.

On top of that, a digital investment management company must establish, implement, and maintain written policies and procedures which include ensuring the algorithm is monitored and tested to confirm it is fit for purpose at all times. Additionally, it must ensure that access to and the ability to make changes to the algorithm is limited to authorised personnel only. Similarly, ongoing due diligence towards any third party developing, owning or managing the technology and algorithm utilised by the company is necessary.

Where the trust account is maintained under an omnibus structure, a digital investment management company must ensure that co-mingling of assets at the custodian or issuer of assets level is confined to clients of the same company. In terms of naming conventions, 'clients' accounts' or 'clients' trust accounts' are maintained in substitution of unique client identifiers. Further, clients must agree to have their assets held under an omnibus structure, be notified of the risks of having their assets held under such a structure, and be notified that they may not be subject to the same protection conferred to assets held on a segregated basis. Likewise, clients must also be made aware of information relating to the custodial arrangement, that the custodian conducts reconciliation of the trust account on a daily basis against third-party records, maintains records to enable identification of assets to the digital investment management company, and immediately credits into the trust account all proceeds and revenue generated from client investments in the company.

Comments on the Digital Investment Management Framework

The Digital Investment Management Framework is comprehensive, even including additional requirements relating to digital investment companies. It is essential to note that under this framework robo-advisory firms may obtain a licence. Although the phrase 'robo advisory' is not specifically used, clearly such firms are covered by the framework because, according to s 2.05(3) of the Licensing Handbook (SC,

2018), anyone carrying on the business of fund management and incorporating innovative technologies into automated discretionary portfolio management services, will be granted a licence for fund management in relation to portfolio management as a digital investment manager. It also states that holders of a capital markets service licence (CMSL) as regards portfolio management including digital investment management companies and boutique portfolio management companies, may provide investment advisory services to clients, pursuant to an advisory mandate (SC, 2018).

DIGITAL CURRENCY AND DIGITAL TOKEN ORDER

The Capital Markets and Services (Prescription of Securities) (Digital Currency and Digital Token) Order 2019 PU(A) 12/2019 or the Digital Currency and Digital Token Order was published on 8 January 2019 and came into effect on 15 January 2019 under the powers conferred by s 5 of the Capital Markets and Services Act 2007 to Malaysia's Minister of Finance. Under this order, digital currency refers to:

- A digital representation of value which is recorded on a distributed digital ledger whether cryptographically-secured or otherwise;
- That functions as a medium of exchange; and
- Is interchangeable with any money, including through the crediting or debiting of an account.

A digital token refers to a digital representation which is recorded on a distributed digital ledger whether cryptographically-secured or otherwise.

It would appear the order's definition of digital currency is similar to the one offered by BNM's Policy Document on Digital Currencies (see above) except it includes the term "which is recorded on a distributed digital ledger whether cryptographically-secured or otherwise." This effectively means all blockchain-based digital currencies will fall within the definition. Digital tokens are differentiated from currency only in that they are not exchangeable for money, i.e. they are not mediums of exchange.

The order contains a total of 5 parts including when digital currencies and tokens are to be prescribed as securities and the application of requirements under securities laws.

Digital currencies and tokens will be prescribed as securities: if traded in a place or on a facility where offers to sell, purchase, or exchange such currencies are regularly made or accepted; a person expects a return in any form from the trading, conversion, or redemption of the digital currency or an appreciation in its value; and where they are not issued or guaranteed by any government body or central banks as may be specified by the Commission.

A digital token that represents a right or interest of a person in any arrangement made for the purpose of, or having the effect of, providing facilities for the person: where the person receives the digital token in exchange for a consideration; the consideration or contribution from the person, and the income or returns, are pooled; the income or returns of the arrangement are generated from the acquisition, holding, management or disposal of any property or assets or business activities; the person expects a return in any form from the trading, conversion, or redemption of the digital token, or an appreciation in the value of the digital token; the person does not have day-to-day control over the management of the property, assets, or business of the arrangement; and the digital token is not issued or guaranteed by any government body or central banks as may be specified by the Commission, **is prescribed as a security** for the purpose of the securities laws.

Thus, the provisions of securities laws shall apply to such digital currencies and tokens with the exception of Division 3 of Part VI (prospectus) of the Act. Finally, for the purpose of securities laws, digital currency and tokens prescribed as securities that are offered or traded on or through a recognized market cannot be shares in or debenture of, a body corporate or an unincorporated body, or units in a unit trust scheme, or a prescribed investment scheme.

Comments on the Digital Currency and Digital Token Order

Issuance of this order simply indicates that the primary regulatory authority for digital currencies and tokens is the SC. In the first week of March, the SC also issued a separate consultation paper on the offering of digital assets via initial coin offerings (ICO) (discussed below). In addition, the guidelines on recognized markets have been amended to accommodate a digital asset exchange or DAX. The effect of this order is that anyone intending to make available digital currencies and tokens must seek the prior approval of the SC, then register a disclosure document with it. Further, anyone dealing in digital currencies and tokens as a business must be licenced by the SC.

However, it is essential to note that a crypto asset is only a security if used in the specific ways detailed (Pikri, 2019). This was clearly stated by Chin Wei Min, the Executive Director of the SC, when he was asked whether all types of digital assets were to be considered securities. He stated crypto assets would only become securities if they met, fulfilled, or displayed the characteristics listed in the order (Pikri, 2019). Only then would tokens be considered as securities (Pikri, 2019). Accordingly, Pikri (2019) noted that a digital asset's status in this regard would be based on how it is used. For example, if Bitcoin is traded, it falls under the purview of securities law. However, if that same Bitcoin is used to pay for a packet of nasi lemak, it will not be captured under the order and will therefore not be considered a security (Pikri, 2019). Chin Wei Min also affirmed that a person expecting returns in any form from trading, converting, or redeeming a token, or from an appreciation in its value will be regulated by the SC (essentially making it a DAX as discussed below) (Pikri, 2019).

GUIDELINES ON RECOGNIZED MARKETS

The Guidelines on Recognized Markets SC-GL/6-2015(R2-2019) were first issued on 11 December 2005 and revised on 31 January 2019 (2nd revision). Issued by the SC pursuant to s 377 of the Capital Markets and Services Act 2007 (CMSA), they must be read together with subdivision 4, division 2 of Part II of the CMSA. Part F encompasses equity crowdfunding and peer-to-peer lending platforms while Part G deals with additional requirements relating to DAX.

The term 'recognized market' covers alternative trading venues, marketplaces, or facilities bringing together purchasers and sellers of capital market products. The guidelines set out the registration requirements of **recognized market operators** (RMO) and any ongoing requirements applicable to them. A RMO must be structured as a body corporate unless specified otherwise by the SC. Although the guidelines do not specifically define a RMO, it can be understood that any body corporate operating an alternative trading venue, marketplace, or facility bringing together purchasers and sellers of capital market products such as equity crowdfunding platforms, peer-to-peer lending platforms, or DAX will constitute RMOs.

Significantly, the level of regulation for recognized markets is less stringent than those applying to approved markets. However, terms and conditions may be imposed on the RMO commensurate with the risk profile, nature, and scope of proposed recognized market operations.

Malaysia is the first country in Asia to regulate digital fundraising mechanisms, in particular equity crowdfunding and peer-to-peer lending (Goh, 2016). The guidelines below are specific to the digital fundraising mechanisms of equity crowdfunding, peer-to-peer lending, and digital asset exchanges, and are in addition to the requirements stated above. It should be noted that where an Islamic capital market product is offered on or through the recognized market, the RMO must also appoint a Shariah adviser.

Equity Crowdfunding Platforms

Covered by Chapter 13, Part F of the Guidelines on Recognized Markets, equity crowdfunding platforms or ECF enable individuals to invest in early stage companies and small and medium enterprises (SMEs) in exchange for a share in the company. ECF platforms are fintechs which provide an alternative venue for SME and early stage company fundraising with paid-up capital of not more than MYR5 million. RMOs operating an ECF platform must ensure due diligence is carried out on companies submitting their online profiles and funding campaigns as the risks involved are higher than investment in established companies listed on stock markets.

The following are some of the conditions that must be adhered to under Chapter 13:

- **Investment Limits**
    - Retail investors can invest a maximum amount of MYR5,000 for each company and MYR50,000 a year in total crowdfunding investment
    - 'Sophisticated' investors face no restrictions on investment amounts
        - Refers to persons falling within any of the categories of investors set out in Part 1, Schedules 6 and 7 of the CMSA and includes venture capital corporations, venture capital management corporations, private equity corporations, and private equity management corporations registered with the SC
    - 'Angel' investors may invest a maximum of MYR500,000 a year
        - Refers to individuals who are tax residents in Malaysia, whose total net personal assets exceed MYR3 million or its equivalent in foreign currencies, whose gross total annual income is not less than MYR180,000 or its equivalent in foreign currencies, or who, jointly with his or her spouse, has a gross total annual income exceeding MYR250,000 or its equivalent in foreign currencies
- An **ECF operator** is defined as a RMO who operates an **ECF platform**
    - An ECF platform is defined as an equity crowdfunding platform registered by the SC
    - All ECF operators must be locally incorporated
- An **Issuer** is defined as a person who is hosted on an ECF platform to offer its shares
    - The **amount of capital** an issuer can collect through crowdfunding is limited to MYR5 million while SMEs can crowdfund any amount up to MYR3 million in a year
- Any fraud committed in crowdfunding activities will fall under s 179 of the Capital Markets and Services Act 2007 carrying a jail term of not more than 10 years and a minimum fine of MYR1 million

- **Obligations of ECF Operators**
    - In addition to the obligations specified in Chapter 6, ECF operators must carry out due diligence on prospective issuers planning to use its platforms
    - Operators must ensure the issuer's disclosure document is verified for accuracy and made accessible to investors through the ECF platform
    - Operators must inform investors of any material adverse change to the issuer's proposal including any of the following matters:
        - the discovery of a false or misleading statement in the disclosure document in relation to the offer;
        - the discovery of a material omission of information required to be included in the disclosure document;
        - a material change or development in the circumstances relating to the offering or the issuer;
        - that fundraising limits imposed on the issuer are not breached; and
        - that investment limits imposed on the investor are not breached.
    - The scope of the due diligence exercise by an ECF operator shall include taking reasonable steps to conduct background checks on the issuer to ensure the fit and properness of the issuer, its directors, senior management and controller, and verifying the issuer's business proposition

Peer-to-Peer Financing Platforms

P2P financing platforms are digital platforms connecting SMEs and early stage companies needing investor financing. Unlike ECF, investors in a P2P platform do not receive a share or ownership in the business but rather act as its creditors. Their advantage lies in the fact that companies and SMEs get funding from a source other than banks at lower rates with no need of collateral (Malay Mail, 2017).

Chapter 14 under Part F of the Guidelines on Recognized Markets covers P2P financing platforms. The main points are listed below:

- **Investment Limit**
    - Sophisticated and angel investors (defined above) face no limits on investment
    - Retail investors are limited to MYR50,000 in any period of time
- **Islamic Investment**
    - While P2P financing involves investors lending money and receiving an interest, Shariah compliant P2P financing platforms utilize different mechanisms known as Islamic investment notes
    - An Islamic investment is defined as any contract, agreement, note, or other document evidencing undivided ownership or investment in any assets complying with Shariah principles and concepts endorsed by the Shariah Advisory Council, and that is executed or offered, on or through an electronic platform where an investor expects a financial return, but does not include any right, option or interest in respect thereof: a cheque, banker's draft or any other bill of exchange or a letter of credit; a banknote, guarantee or a takaful policy; or a statement, passbook or other document showing any balance in a current, deposit or savings account.

- **Issuer**
  - Defined as a person seeking funding on or through a P2P platform
- **P2P Operator**
  - Defined as a RMO who operates a P2P platform which is an electronic platform that facilitates directly or indirectly the issuance, execution, or offering of investment notes or Islamic investment notes
  - Must apply for registration under these guidelines
  - Must be locally incorporated and have a minimum paid-up capital of MYR5 million

Digital Asset Exchanges

Digital asset exchanges or DAX are covered under Chapter 15, Part G of the Guidelines on Recognized Markets. The main points are as follows:

- **DAX**
  - Refers to an electronic platform facilitating the trading of a digital asset
- **Digital Asset**
  - Refers collectively to a digital currency or token which has the same meaning assigned to it as in the Digital Currency and Digital Token Order
- **DAX Operator**
  - Refers to a RMO operating a DAX
  - All DAX operators must be locally incorporated and have a minimum paid-up capital of MYR5 million
  - The SC may at any time impose additional financial requirements or other terms and conditions on the DAX operator commensurate with the nature, operations, and risks posed by said operator
  - If a DAX operator is a public company, at least one member of the board must be an independent director
- **Conflict of Interest**
  - The DAX operator's framework on conflicts of interest must include policies and procedures relating to, amongst other issues:
    - proprietary trading by the DAX operator on its platform;
    - trading in digital assets by its officers and employees on its own or other platforms;
    - the management of non-public material information; and
    - the offering of any digital asset to be traded on its platforms.
  - DAX operators are prohibited from providing direct or indirect financial assistance to investors, including its officers and employees, to invest or trade in digital assets on its platform
  - DAX operators should identify possible sources of operational risk, both internal and external, and mitigate their impact through the use of appropriate systems, policies, procedures, and controls
    - Such systems should be designed to ensure a high degree of security and operational reliability including having adequate capacity

- **Operational Risk Management**
    - In this regard, a DAX operator must:
        - establish a robust operational risk management framework with appropriate systems, policies, procedures, and controls to identify, monitor, mitigate, and manage operational risks;
        - have in place clearly defined roles and responsibilities for addressing operational risk;
        - have in place clearly defined operational reliability objectives and policies designed to achieve such objectives;
        - ensure it has adequate capacity proportionate to stress volumes to achieve its service-level objectives; and
        - have comprehensive physical and information security policies that address all potential vulnerabilities and threats.

Comments on the Guidelines on Recognized Markets

The Guidelines on Recognized Markets provide a framework for the operation of ECF and P2P financing platforms, and DAX to safeguard investors and operators of digital assets. The amended guidelines followed the coming into force of the Digital Currency and Digital Token Order on 15 January 2019 and applies to any person interested in operating a digital asset platform (Rosli, 2019). A digital currency exchange that is a reporting institution under the Policy Document on Digital Currencies is deemed a DAX and will therefore have to be registered as a RMO with the SC.

According to the SC's official website, currently there are three general RMOs: Bay Supply Chain Technology Sdn Bhd, Bursa Malaysia Bonds Sdn Bhd, and Citibank Berhad (SC, 2019b).

Presently, the following companies are registered as RMOs of ECF platforms: Ata Plus Sdn Bhd, Crowdo Malaysia Sdn Bhd, Eureeca SEA Sdn Bhd, FBM Crowdtech Sdn Bhd, Funnel Technologies Sdn Bhd, Pitch Platforms Sdn Bhd, and Crowdplus Sdn Bhd (SC, 2019b). Registered RMOs of P2P financing platforms include: B2B Finpal Sdn Bhd, Ethis Kapital Sdn Bhd, FBM Crowdtech Sdn Bhd, Modalku Ventures Sdn Bhd, Peoplender Sdn Bhd, and QuicKash Malaysia Sdn Bhd (SC, 2019b).

As regards DAX, 22 companies have been registered as such. These are: AES Signatum Berhad, Arbor Digital Sdn Bhd, B4U EXC (M) Sdn Bhd, Belfrics Malaysia Sdn Bhd, Bitpoint Malaysia Sdn Bhd, BLOKMY Sdn Bhd, Chako Global Sdn Bhd, EZYTRONICS Sdn Bhd (World Cloud Ventures Sdn Bhd), FINX Blockchain Sdn Bhd (FINX Capital Sdn Bhd), GetCoinApp Sdn Bhd, GiGaex Sdn Bhd, Luno Malaysia Sdn Bhd, MCP International Sdn Bhd, MX Global Sdn Bhd, PinkExc (M) Sdn Bhd, Sinegy Technologies (M) Sdn Bhd, MBAEX Online Pte Limited (Tezatech Sdn Bhd), Tokenize Technology (M) Sdn Bhd, UDAX International Sdn Bhd, Upbit Malaysia Sdn Bhd, Vardiz Commerce Sdn Bhd, and Xbit Asia Sdn Bhd (SC, 2019c).

Paragraph 1.03 makes it clear that all RMOs must be a body corporate or a limited liability partnership meaning RMOs should be registered either under the Companies Act 2016 or the Limited Liability Partnerships Act 2012. Accordingly, Hong (2018) concludes that unlike other jurisdictions, societies or non-profit organisations *per se*, such as many promoted on Kickstart, will not be eligible to become RMOs in Malaysia. Another point to note is that since RMOs are not public companies, they are not obliged to publicly disclose their financial reports. Hong (2018) believes that at the moment the law does not allow societies or non-profit organisations to operate ECFs. As such, he states there is need to enact a framework to govern non-equity crowdfunding.

As regards digital assets, a joint statement was issued by the SC and BNM to provide clarity on the regulatory approach for the offering and trading of digital assets in Malaysia (BNM and SC, 2018). It stated that the SC will regulate issuances of digital assets via ICOs and the trading of digital assets at DAX in Malaysia. At the same time, ICO issuers and DAX involved in the issuance or dealing of digital assets with a payment function must comply with relevant BNM laws and regulations relating to payments and currency matters. In addition, ICO issuers and DAX are subject to the SC's Guidelines on Prevention of Money Laundering and Terrorism Financing.

Thereafter, on 6 March 2019, the SC issued a public consultation paper (No 1/2019) on the proposed regulatory framework for the issuance of digital assets through an ICO inviting written comments from the public (SC, 2019d). Excluding the overview, the consultation paper consists of five parts:

1. Introduction;
2. Definition of an ICO;
3. The risks associated with ICOs;
4. The need for regulation; and
5. A proposed regulatory framework (SC, 2019d).

Paragraph 4.1 states that the current lack of an ICO regulatory framework exposes investors to a number of risks such as those associated with an ICO issuer not having a physical presence in Malaysia, fraud, manipulation, money laundering and terrorist financing, the general risks associated with start-ups, and cyber security risks. ICO issuers are therefore required to mitigate the risks posed to safeguard investor protection and promote confidence in the ICO market.

Paragraph 5.2 declares that to mitigate incidences of fraud whilst protecting market integrity, the SC will adopt a two-pronged approach entailing, first, an authorisation for the offering or issuance of the ICO, and second, registration of a disclosure document (or whitepaper) necessitating compliance with SC prescribed minimum requirements. The whitepaper should encompass brief information on the ICO issuer including, where applicable:

- The group structure and details of material entities within the group;
- The details and profiles of the board of directors/senior management team/promoters;
- A brief description of the shares and/or digital tokens held by the board of directors/senior management team/promoters;
- The objective or purpose and timeline of the ICO, including detailed information on the underlying business/project to be managed and operated by the ICO issuer;
- A business plan, including a detailed description of the sustainability and scalability of the underlying business/project;
- The targeted date for each major phase in the business/project;
- The targeted amounts to be raised through the ICO;
- A scheduled timeline for the utilisation of the proceeds including the details of each utilisation;
- Any rights, conditions, or functions attached to digital tokens issued from the ICO including any specific rights/privileges/benefits attributed to a digital token holder;
- Details of the independent custodian, escrow agents, or entity acting in the capacity of a trustee;
- Discussions on the determination of the price per digital token including the valuation methodology and reasonable assumptions adopted in such calculations;

- Financial information including audited financial statements or management accounts (where applicable);
- A detailed technical description of the protocol, platform and, or application, as the case may be; and
- The associated benefits of the technology and details of the associated challenges and risks including any conflict of interest and related party transactions.

According to the consultation paper, an ICO issuer may raise funds calculated as a multiple of 10 times the amount of shareholder funds and subject to a ceiling of MYR100 million. Proceeds should be subject to BNM's exchange controls meaning at least 50% must be utilised in Malaysia and if the ICO is asset-backed, at least 50% of the assets must be based in Malaysia. Further, an ICO issuer should only be able to withdraw monies based on the milestones disclosed in their whitepaper.

Moreover, an ICO issuer must be a locally incorporated company and carry out its main business in Malaysia with a minimum paid up capital of MYR500,000, and it must not be publicly listed. However, public listed companies are allowed to establish a separate entity to carry out an ICO to prevent potential impact on the company's price, valuation, and shareholder rights. In addition, the board of directors and senior management must collectively hold 50% equity in the ICO issuer and retain it for 18 months to ensure their commitment to its success.

Drawing from its experience in regulating ECF and P2P financing, the SC also proposed formation of a third party platform to host and assess ICOs, similar to SMEs hosting their notes on platforms such as pitchIN and Funding Societies. Additionally, it proposed the host be regulated as a RMO. Finally, the framework explores the possibility of permitting certain SC recognised individuals to conduct assessments.

Having discussed the SC and BNM regulations, this chapter will now critically review the regulations discussed above.

CRITICAL REVIEW OF THE REGULATIONS

The introduction to this chapter raised unique concerns from the literature in relation to the use of fintechs. These concerns apply to all fintechs whether offering Shariah compliant solutions or otherwise. The following section will review the regulations issued by BNM and the SC to assess whether those concerns have been addressed.

As mentioned previously, the concerns are speed, safety, and illegal activity. Transactions carried out through fintech occur quickly, thus, the speed at which malpractice and fraud by external parties is reported should occur just as swiftly. Further, fintech systems must be safe from cyberattacks while simultaneously protecting customer user data. Finally, risks from money laundering and terrorist financing must also be mitigated. While the authors acknowledge other vulnerabilities or concerns may arise with the introduction of fintechs, this research will focus on the above mentioned issues and analyse whether they have been adequately addressed by the regulations, the results of which are illustrated in Table 2.

Table 2. Examining BNM and SC issued regulations

	Policy Document on Digital Currencies	Policy Document on e-KYC	Regulatory Sandbox Framework	Digital Investment Management Framework	Digital Currency and Digital Token Order	Guidelines on Recognized Markets
Reporting malpractice	Must report √	X	√	X	X	The SC may issue a direction regarding the requirement to submit periodic reports to the SC
Timely identification of malpractice	System must give timely information √	X	X	X	X	X
Cyber security system in place	X	X	Applicant to identify potential risks and propose safeguards	Maintain a secure environment pursuant to the Guidelines on the Management of Cyber Risk and other relevant guidelines	X	Maintain secured environment pursuant to the Guidelines on the Management of Cyber Risk and other relevant guidelines
Protection of consumer personal data	X	X	Applicant to identify potential risks and propose safeguards	X	X	Establish and maintain policies and procedures to ensure compliance with all relevant laws, regulations, and guidelines including the Personal Data Protection Act 2010
System in place to detect risks of money laundering and terrorist financing	√	√	Applicant to identify potential risks and propose safeguards	Company's risk management framework must also include any other risks	X	Establish and maintain policies and procedures to ensure compliance with all relevant laws, regulations, and guidelines

Source: (Bank Negara Malaysia, 2019; Securities Commission, 2019a)

Thus the table above summarises whether the various regulations addressed the following factors:

- The need for service providers to report malpractice;
- The need to report malpractice or whether systems are required to give timely reports on malpractice or irregularities;
- The need for service providers to have in place adequate cyber security systems to prevent hacking and other cyber threats; and
- The risks of money laundering and terrorist financing and whether such risks have been addressed through the detection and reporting of suspicious activities.

BNM's policy document on digital currencies contains extensive provisions on the risks associated with money laundering and terrorist financing. In addition, it requires service providers to report malpractice and irregularities whilst having in place a management information system to report irregularities within a timely manner. However, the policy document neglects to mention the need for cyber security systems or arrangements to protect customer data.

While the policy document on e-KYC enabled the prompt identification of customers and the mitigation of risks associated with money laundering and terrorist financing, provisions requiring customer data protection, cyber security, and the timely reporting of malpractice were not similarly included.

The Regulatory Sandbox Framework requires applicants to provide an interim report on any fraud and for applicants and the BNM to decide on the frequency and specific details of said report. Further, the applicant must identify potential risks including money laundering and terrorist financing, protect the confidentiality of customer information, and promote the safety, reliability, and efficiency of payment systems and payment instruments. The applicant may also propose appropriate safeguards to address the identified risks.

While the Digital Investment Management Framework provides no definite provisions on timely malpractice reporting or the need to protect customer data, it does contain provisions to ensure systems are in place to counteract cyber security threats, money laundering, terrorist financing, and other risks.

The Digital Currency and Digital Token Order does not provide for any of the issues highlighted in the table above; however, securities laws will apply to digital currencies and tokens prescribed as securities leaving them subject to other SC regulations.

The Guidelines on Recognized Markets encompass provisions on all the concerns raised except the timely reporting of external malpractice to the SC. Broad provisions require RMOs to comply with all SC regulations and parliamentary legislation, thus ensuring risks are mitigated and concerns are raised.

Significantly, the SC has issued separate provisions on cyber risks (the Guidelines on Management of Cyber Risk 2016) which are applicable to all capital market entities. As such, the guidelines lay out the roles and responsibilities of the board of directors and management as regards cyber risk, require capital market entities to have cyber risk policies and procedures, require entities to have comprehensive strategies and measures to manage cyber risk including its prevention, detection and recovery, and require reports of breaches to occur on the day of the cyber incident to the SC. Hence, it can be seen the guidelines are comprehensive and help to cover the risk posed by cyber threats even if individual regulations do not.

BNM also issued an Exposure Draft on Risk Management in Technology (RMiT) to provide guidelines and standards to BNM licensed financial institutions on risks relating to technology including cyber threats. Therefore, similar to the aforementioned provisions, even though individual BNM regulations may not require the use of cyber security systems, the exposure draft will cover such incidences.

In other words, both the SC and BNM have introduced provisions requiring adequate cyber security systems be put in place to counteract such threats.

SOLUTIONS AND RECOMMENDATIONS

Resulting from the critical review above, the authors make the following comments and recommendations.

- Aside from the Policy Document on Digital Currency, the Regulatory Sandbox Framework, and the Guidelines on Recognized Markets, other regulations do not specifically provide that malpractice and fraud from external sources should be reported to regulators. It is, therefore, recommended by the authors that all such regulations should include this provision.
- Time periods within which to report fraud and malpractice are not specified by the majority of regulations. Accordingly, it is recommended a time frame be provided considering the nature of the fintech business.
- The protection of personal data has not been provided for by the regulations. While Malaysia does have legislation to protect personal data (Personal Data Protection Act 2010), such provisions may not be suitable to cover the unique features of fintechs. Because it is beyond the scope of this chapter for the authors to examine this Act, it is recommended that further research be conducted to analyse the need for other special provisions as regards the personal data of consumers.
- To further strengthen the e-KYC framework, it is imperative to enact a legal framework to enable the use of national digital IDs and their usage by third parties in Malaysia. Avoiding potential disputes in this regard will entail a framework of trust at the national level.
- All fintechs, whether conventional or Islamic, must comply with the regulations discussed above. The Guidelines on Recognized Markets also require Islamic fintech RMOs to have a Shariah advisor but it has yet to be determined whether other special provisions may be necessary to ensure complete Shariah compliance of fintech. While the authors contend that further provisions appear unnecessary, additional research may be conducted in this regard.
- The Policy Document on Digital Currencies does not specifically state that digital currency exchanges are DAX under the Guidelines on Recognized Markets. It is therefore recommended that the former should contain this provision. Such DAX would then require registration with the SC.
- The Policy Document on e-KYC currently only applies to remittance fintech companies. Consequently, it is recommended the provision be expanded to other types of business such as certain takaful products.
- It is also recommended the Regulatory Sandbox Framework include details on avenues for redress in the event participants fail to comply with framework safeguards. Moreover, a benchmark for compensation should be suggested.
- Not all digital assets listed in DAX will be Shariah compliant. That being so, to inform investors, it is imperative to introduce a Shariah screening methodology specific to digital assets which is cognizant of the Shariah compliance of digital assets.

FUTURE RESEARCH DIRECTIONS

This research recommends four types of future research be conducted in this area of study. First, future research needs to focus on whether the Personal Data Protection Act 2010 is sufficient to address issues relating to the risk of abuse of personal data by fintechs, and if not, what provisions should be inserted to protect said data.

Second, further research must be conducted to determine the need for other special provisions, aside from requiring a Shariah advisor to instruct the RMO, to ensure Shariah compliance of fintechs.

Third, extra research needs to be carried out to enact a framework for national digital IDs and their use by third parties in Malaysia. With the dawn of the fourth industrial revolution and swift developments in technology-based financial transactions, it is becoming ever more crucial to switch to a national digital ID system. In addition, the scope of such a system's use by third parties requires specification.

Finally, because digital assets are a new concept, it is essential Muslim investors be confident of Shariah compliance to enable informed investment. Therefore, it is necessary to conduct additional research to establish a Shariah screening methodology for digital assets to inform investors about the Shariah compliance of DAX-listed digital assets.

CONCLUSION

Malaysian financial regulators have taken the bold step of issuing regulations to ensure risks are mitigated in this digital era. This chapter has examined six pieces of regulation issued over the past three years in Malaysia with the BNM covering the banking sector and the SC overseeing capital markets. All regulations apply to fintechs whether offering conventional or Islamic solutions.

BNM issued regulations on digital currencies, e-KYC systems for remittance companies, and a regulatory sandbox framework for fintech start-ups. Each ensured innovation in the following ways. First, regulating digital currencies allowed for their trading even though such currencies are not recognized as legal tender. Next, the e-KYC as regards remittance companies permitted the use of online boarding and verification thus allowing the companies to offer faster and cheaper services. Finally, the regulatory sandbox framework allows fintech start-ups to test their products in a controlled yet less regulated environment. All these innovations were encouraged under the watchful gaze of BNM to ensure the mitigation of risks associated with money laundering and terrorist financing.

Similarly, the SC issued regulations on digital investment management companies incorporating innovative technologies into portfolio management services, recognized market operators operating alternative trading venues, and marketplaces or facilities bringing together purchasers and sellers of capital market products, in particular ECF, P2P, and DAX platforms, and digital assets comprising of digital currency and digital tokens. Significantly, the SC is the first regulator in Asia to form and issue regulations on ECF and P2P platforms and one of the earliest to issue directives on the classification of digital assets. Digital assets—digital currencies and tokens meeting the characteristics of the Digital Currency and Digital Token Order—are now considered securities and must abide by the laws and regulations applying to securities. Moreover, the SC regulations take into account the need for innovation – for example, less stringent levels of regulation apply to recognized markets than approved markets. At the same time, guidelines to ensure transparency and investor protection are also provided for.

Having reviewed the regulations issued by BNM and the SC, further improvements to the guidelines are recommended below. Overall, the regulations demonstrate the following points.

- Risks associated with money laundering and terrorist financing have been addressed by the regulations.
- Risks associated with cyber security and the personal data of consumers have not been addressed. However, it would appear that separate regulations issued by BNM and the SC may cover cyber security risks while personal data in Malaysia is covered by the Personal Data Protection Act 2010. Nevertheless, further research is required to investigate the extent to which said legislation is sufficient to protect customer data.
- Timely malpractice reporting from external sources to regulators seems omitted by most, if not all, the regulations. It is recommended provisions be inserted to address this omission.
- All fintechs, whether conventional or Islamic, must comply with the regulations discussed above. The Guidelines on Recognized Markets require Islamic fintech RMOs to have a Shariah advisor. Questions arise as to whether there is a need for other special provisions to ensure complete Shariah compliance of fintech. The authors contend not but recommend additional research be conducted in this regard.
- Not all the digital assets listed in DAX will be Shariah compliant. As such, to inform investors about Shariah compliance of digital assets, introduction of a Shariah screening methodology specific to digital assets is imperative. Further, this methodology must be formulated taking into account the nature of digital assets.

REFERENCES

Allen, F., & Gu, X. (2018). The Interplay between regulations and financial stability. *Journal of Financial Services Research*, *53*(2-3), 233–248. doi:10.100710693-018-0296-7

Australian Government Treasury. (n.d.). *Economic benefits of fintech.* Retrieved from https://treasury.gov.au/publication/backing-australian-fintech/economic-benefits-of-fintech/

Bank Negara Malaysia. (2016). *Financial technology regulatory sandbox.* Retrieved from http://www.bnm.gov.my/index.php?ch=57&pg=137&ac=533&bb=file

Bank Negara Malaysia. (2019*). Laws and guidelines.* Retrieved from www.bnm.gov.my

Bank Negara Malaysia and Securities Commission. (2018). *Press release: Joint statement on the regulation of digital assets in Malaysia.* Retrieved from http://www.bnm.gov.my/index.php?ch=en_press&pg=en_press&ac=4783

Federal Government Gazette. (2019). *Capital Markets and Services (Prescription of Securities) (Digital Currency and Digital Token) 2019.* Retrieved from http://www.federalgazette.agc.gov.my/outputp/pua_20190114_PUA12.pdf?fbclid=IwAR3RG1vaiM3MSd_lONZl4jyuVeAUt_anYTJmI08GhVB0k-b8IAWKhhTaV1rQ

Financial Action Task Force. (2014). *Virtual currencies – Key definitions and potential AML/CFT risks.* Retrieved from http://www.fatf-gafi.org/media/fatf/documents/reports/Virtual-currency-key-definitions-and-potential-aml-cft-risks.pdf

Financial Technology Enabler Group. (2017). *Approved Participants in Sandbox.* Retrieved from https://www.myfteg.com/?page_id=1131

Goh Thean Eu. (2016). *Malaysia first to regulate P2P financing, after SC introduced six P2P operators.* Retrieved from https://www.sc.com.my/api/documentms/download.ashx?id=cb6aedad-aa7b-43fc-8a34-a1061f0554f5

Griffin, A. (2018). *Tackling the risks of the FinTech boom - AML considerations.* Retrieved from https://www.lexology.com/library/detail.aspx?g=5f081a53-caf3-46f6-9d57-e1958dca977d

Hong, L. C. (2018). Crowdfunding: Issues pertaining to financial reporting and assurance in Malaysia. *Journal of Wealth Management and Financial Planning*, *5*, 17–24.

Kovas, A. (n.d.). *Understanding the risks of fintech.* Retrieved from https://legal.thomsonreuters.com/en/insights/articles/understanding-the-risks-of-fintech

KPMG. (2018). *The pulse of fintech 2018.* Retrieved from https://assets.kpmg/content/dam/kpmg/xx/pdf/2018/07/h1-2018-pulse-of-fintech.pdf

Lipsky, J. (2012). Session III: Introductory remarks. BIS Papers No 62 Financial sector regulation for growth, equity and stability. *Proceedings of a conference organised by the BIS and CAFRAL in Mumbai.* Retrieved from https://www.bis.org/publ/bppdf/bispap62.pdf

Malay Mail. (2017). *Funding societies eyes institutional investors in 3 years.* Retrieved from http://epaper.mmail.com.my/2017/09/05/funding-societies-eyes-institutional-investors-in-3-years/

McKenzie, B. (2017). *Malaysia welcomes two new participants to fintech regulatory sandbox.* Retrieved from https://www.lexology.com/library/detail.aspx?g=8f3948d0-e82a-4d1f-8af2-ef2aac7214af

Moneymatch. (2018). *Rethinking finance.* Retrieved from https://moneymatch.co/#WhatWeDo

Nusa Kapital. (2017). *About us.* Retrieved from https://www.nusakapital.com/about-us/

Pikri, E. (2019). *SC Malaysia clarifies: A crypto-asset is only a security if used in specific ways.* Retrieved from https://fintechnews.my/19737/blockchain/securities-commission-malaysia-status-tokens-coins-utility-bitcoin/

PwC. (2018). The fight against economic crime and corruption: Aligning people, processes and technology to emerge stronger. *Global Economic Crime and Fraud Survey 2018 (Malaysia Report).* Retrieved from https://www.pwc.com/my/en/assets/publications/2018/gecfs-2018-pwc-malaysia-2.pdf

Risen, J. (2017). *Bank Negara kicks off fintech sandbox.* Retrieved from https://www.thestar.com.my/business/business-news/2017/05/29/bank-negara-kicks-off-fintech-with-licences-issued/#aajmZoCBJdbgOkaB.99

Rosli, L. (2019). *Securities Commission amends guidelines for digital assets trading*. Retrieved from https://www.nst.com.my/business/2019/01/456233/securities-commission-amends-guidelines-digital-assets-trading

Securities Commission. (2017). *Media release: The SC initiates aFINity Innovation Lab for alternative trading*. Retrieved from https://issuance.sc.com.my/digital/ats/

Securities Commission. (2018). *Licensing handbook*. Retrieved from https://www.sc.com.my/api/documentms/download.ashx?id=1f230c0d-988e-4b34-b497-71d8372a3998

Securities Commission. (2019a). *Regulations*. Retrieved from www.sc.com.my

Securities Commission. (2019b). *List of market operators*. Retrieved from https://www.sc.com.my/development/digital/list-of-registered-recognized-market-operators

Securities Commission. (2019c). *List of digital asset exchanges in transitional period*. Retrieved from https://www.sc.com.my/regulation/guidelines/recognizedmarkets/list-of-digital-asset-exchanges-in-transitional-period

Securities Commission. (2019d). *Consultation paper (No 1/2019) on proposed regulatory framework for the issuance of digital assets through ICO*. Retrieved from https://www.sc.com.my/api/documentms/download.ashx?id=d3067bf4-ba39-4bce-8dc4-1b660ff37977

The Star Online. (2018). *Coincheck begins allowing yen withdrawals ahead of FSA deadline*. Retrieved from https://www.thestar.com.my/business/business-news/2018/02/13/coincheck-begins-allowing-yen-withdrawals-ahead-of-fsa-deadline/#vkDQydOdk3yBPDAu.99

ADDITIONAL READING

Abu-Bakar, M. (2018). *Shariah analysis of bitcoin, cryptocurrency and blockchain*. Retrieved from https://blossomfinance.com/bitcoin-working-paper

Bailey, J. B. (2016). *Future of fintech in capital markets*. Retrieved from https://caia.org/aiar/access/article-1021

Carstens, A. (2018). *Money in the digital age: What role for central banks?* Retrieved from https://www.bis.org/speeches/sp180206.pdf

Financial Action Task Force. (2014). *Virtual currencies - Key definitions and potential AML/CFT risks*. Retrieved from http://www.fatf-gafi.org/media/fatf/documents/reports/virtual-currency-key-definitions-and-potential-aml-cft-risks.pdf

Finder. (2017, September 7). *Cut out the middle man with peer-to-peer money transfers*. Retrieved from https://www.finder.com/international-money-transfers/peer-to-peer

Khalid, M., & Kunhibava, S. (2018). Regulatory sandbox: Malaysia's response in regulating fintech. *The Law Review*, 377-388.

University Malaya. (2018). *University Malaya blockchain regulatory report.* Retrieved from http://ibs.edu.sg/repos/UM-MalaysianBlockchainRegulatoryResearchReport.pdf

Vizcaino, B. (2018). *Malaysian firm adds Islamic certification to cryptocurrency.* Retrieved from https://www.zawya.com/mena/en/story/Malaysian_firm_adds_Islamic_certification_to_cryptocurrency/

Yap, A. (2017). Currency exchange: What does the future hold for the industry. Proceedings of the Money Services Business Asia Pacific Conference, BNM Sasana Kijal, Kuala Lumpur.

KEY TERMS AND DEFINITIONS

Bank Negara Malaysia (BNM): The Central Bank of Malaysia which governs banks, Islamic banks, insurance companies, takaful operators, money payment systems, and money service businesses.

Digital Asset: Collectively refers to a digital currency or digital token.

Digital Asset Exchange: An electronic platform which facilitates the trading of a digital asset.

Digital Currency: A digital representation of value that functions as a medium of exchange and is interchangeable with any money but is not electronic money.

Digital Investment Management: A fund management business which incorporates innovative technologies into portfolio management services.

Digital Token: A digital representation which is recorded on a distributed digital ledger whether cryptographically-secured or otherwise.

Electronic Know Your Customer (e-KYC): Identification of the customer through electronic means without the need for physical or face-to-face identification.

Equity Crowd Funding Platform (ECF): FinTechs which provide an alternative venue for the raising of funds for SMEs and early stage companies with a paid-up capital of not more than MYR5 million.

Recognized Market Operator (RMO): A body corporate that operates an alternative trading venue, marketplace, or facility that brings together purchasers and sellers of capital market products.

Peer-to-Peer Financing Platforms (P2P): Digital platforms that connect SMEs and early stage companies requiring financing with investors.

Securities Commission (SC): Regulator that regulates and develops Malaysia's capital market.

Chapter 9
Does Shariah Recognize Cryptocurrencies as Valid Currencies?

Abdulazeem Abozaid
Qatar Foundation, Qatar

ABSTRACT

Undoubtedly, the emergence of cryptocurrencies has imposed the challenge of addressing their Shariah issues. These issues include the very permissibility of their issuance in view of the fact that they are not backed by real valuable assets or supervised by financial authorities, which makes their holders vulnerable to possible fraud and manipulative fluctuations in their values. Other issues include trading in them and whether or not they are considered as commodities subject to the injunctions pertaining to Riba as they apply to conventional currencies. In addition, they have potentially negative implications for the market, such as their use in money laundering, drugs trafficking, and other illegal dealings. This paper treats these Shariah aspects of cryptocurrencies.

DOI: 10.4018/978-1-7998-0039-2.ch009

INTRODUCTION

The term cryptocurrency is a term used to describe a digital asset designed principally to function similarly to a regular currency - as a medium of exchange, unit of account and store of value - using encryption techniques to secure the transactions and to control the creation of additional units of the currency. Cryptocurrency generally operates independently of a central bank, central authority or government. There are hundreds types of cryptocurrencies although the most famous of which is Bitcoin, which came into existence in 2009.

Currencies are treated with the upmost importance in the Shariah. This is evident by the strict rules pertaining to their transactions, more so than any other asset. This is because Islam deems currency as the most important component of the economy, and the preservation and development of economy is one of the primary objectives of the Shariah.[1]

Similar to any economic system, Islamic economics recognises the following three economic functions of currencies:

- **Means of Exchange:** With currency one may exchange asset and services.
- **Store of Value:** The currency holds its value for future purchases of assets and services.

Unit of account: the currency measures the value of any economic item; i.e. goods, services, assets, liabilities, income and expenses.

To maintain and protect these three functions of currencies, the Shariah governs them by several rules so that they remain safe from the manipulation of human greed. One of the most dangerous factors that may affect currencies is excessive trading, especially by means of derivatives when used for speculation. Excessive trading inevitably impacts their value and purchasing power, thereby impairing the first two functions of a currency, namely being a means of exchange and a store of value. When currencies are traded through options contracts, which simply require owning the margin to enter the options market, the enormous number of contracts executed on a currency will inevitably impact its purchasing power and possibly cause huge depreciation or appreciation of its market value. The 1997 Asian financial crisis provides a stark example, as the value of the currencies of certain Asian countries drastically depreciated after they were subject to excessive speculation. To prevent speculation on currencies, the Shariah commands that when a currency is sold against the same or another currency the transaction has to be effected on the spot, without any delay. This rule aims to prevent speculation since speculation involves future contracts, and future contracts on currencies are forbidden in Islam. The same rule applies to all assets that are basic and vital to the economy and human use and consumption, such as staple grains, oil and metals. No rule would protect these basic and necessary commodities from price manipulation like invalidating their future sales, especially when used for speculative purposes. Shariah text that pertains to this rule, such as: "[Sell] gold for gold, silver for silver, wheat for wheat, barley for barley, dates for dates, salt for salt hand to hand equal to equal" (Muslim, 1990, p 1211), may have been perplexing fourteen centuries ago, since no one would sell such assets on future basis since such a sale would serve no purpose at that time. However, reading them in the present time enables us to appreciate the wisdom behind this Shariah rule, as if this rule and its likes were in fact meant for our time; a time when people attempt to create enrichment opportunities for themselves out of the thin air in order to make profit, even if they come at the expense of the economy or the public interests.

In addition to impairing the first two economic functions of currencies, excessive trading causes high volatility in their values. A currency whose value is highly volatile will never be suitable as a unit of account to measure against which the value of other assets. Thus, excessive trading impairs the third function of money. Again, the Shariah protects this economic function of money by simply forbidding future sales of currencies. Interest also causes currency value volatility and depreciation, yet ironically, economists often quote interest as a tool to control the value of the currency, thereby making interest a cure to the very disease that it contributes to creating.

Are Gold and Silver the Only Valid Forms of Money in Islam?

In the past, gold and silver were the primary if not the only currencies in the world. This subsequently changed when other currencies emerged alongside gold and silver, and when eventually gold and silver were taken out of circulation for a variety of reasons. The primary reason for their replacement was to introduce a currency that would reflect the diverse resources and assets of the issuing country without limiting them to gold or silver. Economic strength of a country would not be measured by how large its reserves of gold or silver are, but by other economic resources, such as its industrial and agricultural output (Evans, 2015). Thus, a country's currency would embody the various economic resources of that country from which it derives its value and strength from these resources. The question, however, is whether the Shariah accepts such a departure from gold and silver in currency?

In fact, from its inception, Islam recognized the then existing currencies and allowed people to deal in them (Muedinai, 2018). The dominant currencies in Arabia at the time were either Persian or Roman and were gold and silver (Abozaid, 2004). At a later stage the Muslim state began to issue its own gold (dinar) and silver (dirham) currencies (Abozaid, 2016). The Shariah rules of currencies were then formulated on the assumption that currencies were gold and silver, and some Shariah texts came to state that the exchange of gold and silver should be subject to certain rules in order to avoid *riba*. The most famous text in this regard is the aforementioned Hadith narrated by Ubada Bin Al-Samit in which the Prophet, peace be upon him, is reported to have said "Gold for gold, silver for silver … hand to hand, equal to equal…". This Hadith states clearly that when gold is sold for gold, or sliver is sold for silver, it is necessary to observe two rules in order to avoid *riba*: i) equality in amount and ii) spot delivery of the two counter values. The Hadith goes on to mention that if gold is sold for silver, then equality in amount will no longer be required, while spot delivery remains a must.

When Muslim jurists attempted to rationalize and understand the effective cause (*'illa*) for gold and silver in particular being subject to these rules, they concluded that gold and silver are simply currencies, as if they were suggesting that currencies in general, regardless of their nature, would have to be subject to these rules. However, at that time they could not envisage any other commodity would replace gold and silver as currency, and they noticed that the cooper/iron currency (*fulūs*), which were used as complementary to gold and silver, were excluded from the *Riba* rules due to their trivial value. They also observed that gold and silver could take forms other than currencies, like being jewelry, but yet they would fall under the generality of the Hadith (Abozaid, 2004). Therefore, when the *Fiqh* schools attempted to define the effective cause (*'illa*) for the occurrence of *riba* in gold and silver, some of them rationalised in a way that would seem to suggest that the *'illa* is because of their nature as metals, not because they were the currency in circulation, such that any currency that could be in circulation would share the same rules. However, in the actual fact, they rationalised in this way only in order to include in these *riba* rules all the possible forms of gold and silver, due to the generality of the Hadith, and to exclude *fulūs*. Hence, they said the *'illa* for gold or silver is because they are "*'asl al-athmān*", which literarily means 'the origin' or 'the essence of prices', and includes any forms of gold and silver, since their metal is still the essence of prices, and excludes *fulūs* since such currencies do not constitute the essence of prices, but rather are complimentary prices (Abozaid, 2016). The intention of the jurists was not to exclude other possible currencies from the *riba* rules but only to include all forms of gold and silver and exclude complementary trivial currencies, such as *fulūs*. This is evident from the numerous *fiqh* texts that allude to the applicability of *riba* rules to all currencies, as will be discussed in the next section.

Thus, the classical Muslim jurists did not envisage that new currencies would come and replace gold and silver, and therefore some of them, such as the *Mālikis* and *Shāfi'īs*, expressed the *'illa* for *riba* in gold and silver in a way that would exclude *riba* from anything that was not gold or silver. However, interestingly enough, some scholars from both schools clarified that this position was held based on the prevalent circumstances at the time, that if in the future circumstances would change, and other currencies would assume the status of gold and silver as the primary currencies, then the same *riba* rules would be applicable to them (i.e. gold and silver would continue to bear these rules and the new currencies would assume the same rules). Al-Nawawı, the renowned Shāfi'ī scholar from the seventh century (A.H.), states: "This 'illa (asl al-athmān) is useable, not static, because something could exist and share the meaning that exists [in gold and silver] and would therefore have the same rules applied to it" (Al-Nawawi, 1995, p. 491).

From the Māliki school Imam Malik says: "Even if people started making currencies from animals' hide I would deem selling them on a deferred basis as prohibited, and subject them to riba rules" (Malik, 1996, p. 396). On the other hand, while the Hanafis do not relate the *'illa* in gold and silver to prices or currencies they believe that their use as currencies is fundamental in this regard. This is evident in their discussion of *fulūs* as they ruled it as a currency subject to *riba* based on analogy to gold and silver (Abozaid, 2004). However, Muslim scholars of the past had always believed that gold and silver, given their unique features and relative scarcity, would always remain the best embodiment of money. Al-Maqrizi from the fifteenth century enthusiastically and rather subjectively says: "The money that is considered by the Shariah is gold and silver only, and what is beyond that is not worth being money" (Al-Maqrizi, 2011, p. 71).

Therefore, we can conclude by saying that the Shariah does not limit the concept of money (currency) to gold and silver, but rather recognizes as currency whatever people use as currency, and the Shariah then governs this currency with certain rules - notably the *riba* rules - in order to protect its economic functions and ensure fairness in dealings and transactions (Abozaid, 2004). Thus, in principle the Shariah does not object to issuing and dealing in new currencies regardless of their nature, including digital and cryptocurrencies.

Cryptocurrencies and Shariah Policy

It is no secret that since the introduction of fiat paper money, the countries with strong economic, political and military powers have found ways, using the power of their currencies, to somehow control the economies of the so-called 'developing' countries. The United States nowadays has a powerful control on the world economies and politics by different means including its dollar, which originates from its political power before anything else.

A wide spectrum of Muslims believes that using the fiat money, especially when pegging it to other currencies like the dollar or the euro, is just another manifestation of the western hegemony over the economies of the Muslim countries, and therefore seek to reinstate gold and silver as money like they used to be during the golden era of the Muslim state. Hence, there have been some attempts recently by some Muslim countries, like Malaysia and Libya, to introduce gold or silver-based currency to ultimately substitute and replace the paper money.

Due to the aforementioned and the other known shortcomings of fiat money, such as being exposed to excessive fluctuation in their purchasing power, it is expected that the people of these affected counties will welcome introducing a new currency that would help to liberate the affected counties from the political and economic hegemony of the world super powers. In this context, if reinstating gold and silver as currency is not feasible in our present time, then even a digital currency backed by precious metal and given an Islamic character will receive acceptance by both Muslim economists and Shariah scholars.

However, when it comes to digital currency or cryptocurrency, the challenge is whether it can gain people's trust, and this may not be feasible if it is not controlled and regulated by a trustworthy authority. This is because people justifiably are suspicious of any currency introduced digitally or electronically given the possibility of fraud. In fact, the relative success of a cryptocurrency such as Bitcoin does not challenge this argument since its relative success relates to speculative trading rather than being used as real currency, as will be discussed later in the paper.

CHARACTERISTICS OF A VALID CRYPTOCURRENCY

From the Holders' Perspective

What matters to holders of a currency is its wide acceptability and preservation of its value and purchasing power. This naturally requires that the currency should be backed by some real assets, be recognised by law as legal tender, and controlled by a trustworthy authority. It is noteworthy in this regard to distinguish between people who accept a currency for its perceived economic functions and those who accept it as a trading instrument. If the latter, people do not care much for the aforementioned features of currency, just like they do not care in stock trading about the market value of the stock being equal or close to its book value. This is because they do not hold the stock for long-term investment but for speculative and quick trading. And in this regard it can be said that most of stocks are traded far beyond their book value and without consideration for their average return. Therefore, acceptance of a cryptocurrency as a trading tool is completely different to accepting it as currency. The more volatile a currency, the more desirable it is for speculators but less desirable for normal users, due to its incapability to properly perform its economic functions.

From the Shariah Perspective

From Shariah perspective, there are general conditions for a valid currency, such that whatever currency meets these conditions can be deemed as valid currency and thus, acquires the known Shariah characteristics pertaining to currencies. The following conditions are intended to preserve the established economic functions that money is supposed to perform, and comply with the general Shariah norms of fairness and removal of harm.[2]

CONDITIONS OF A VALID CURRENCY

Protection of Its Value

If the currency does not have intrinsic value, i.e. it does not have a value of its own in isolation from the value legally assigned to it by the issuing authorities, then its technical value has to be safeguarded by virtue of certain rules and regulations. As discussed earlier, the Shariah does not object to people departing from the intrinsically valuable money to a new form of money whose value is only technical, like a legal tender, as long as the issuing party is capable of safeguarding its value or has the authority to do so. Understandably, this condition is meant to protect the economy as well as the individual rights of the people dealing with fiat currency from the impacts of a possible manipulation, fraud or unexpected loss of value. In fact, protection of wealth is one of the major Shariah objectives and therefore, measures have to be taken to protect wealth, especially the most important constituent of wealth, namely money (Abozaid, 2016).

Wide Acceptability

Wide acceptability ensures that the currency will effectively play its perceived role as a means of exchange, a value-storing unit and a unit of account (Meera, 2018).

The acceptability of a currency does not necessarily need to exceed the boundaries of the territory where it is in circulation, as it is enough to be accepted within its territory in order to be deemed as a valid currency within this territory. Hence, all local currencies of countries are valid currencies, since they are widely accepted therein even if they are not commonly accepted outside.

Relative Stability of Its Value

The economic functions of a currency will not be sufficiently performed if the currency value is highly volatile. If the currency unit I hold today buys me one loaf of bread today but half a loaf tomorrow and two loafs the day after, then it would no longer function as store of value and unit of account; it loses its capacity to measure the values of other assets and it also loses its preference amongst people as a store of value. If this happens, then people may desist from accepting it or be reluctant to deal in it, causing the primary function of currency as being a means of exchange to cease (Meera, 2018). However, if the described economic functions of a currency are only temporarily or exceptionally impaired or suspended due to war or some natural calamity then this does not disqualify the currency from being basically valid. But if the exception becomes the norm, and the currency changes drastically in value, then this could disqualify the currency from being a valid currency from a Shariah perspective. This does not apply to a currency that is backed by valuable assets or is recognised by the authorities of the country of its circulation as a legal tender. This submission is based again on the Shariah notion of a valid currency as one that discharges its economic functions, while a highly volatile currency, which is typically technical and not real, fails to properly discharge these functions. Ibn Al-Qayyim beautifully expresses this fact in the fourteenth century by saying: “Dirhams and dinars are the price of commodities, and the price is the standard unit of account for measuring the value of assets, so it has to be stable in terms of its value, for if its value is volatile then it will not function as a standard unit of account" (Ibn Al-Qayyim,, 1991, p. 2/394). Al-Maqrizi also refers to this fact says by saying: "there will be no variation in prices if commodities' values are measured against Dinar and Dirham" (Al-Maqrizi, 2011, p. 71).

Shariah Rules for Dealing in Cryptocurrency

If the aforementioned conditions for the valid currency are fulfilled, then dealing in a new currency, regardless of its nature being digital or otherwise, is subject to the same Shariah rules of a regular currency. While *fiqh* books mention these rules in the context of gold and silver, these rules have been outlined by the Shariah for currencies in general, as discussed earlier, the Shariah never limits the concept of money to particular assets. The rules are:

1. When exchanged with another currency, the transaction must be on a spot basis without delay in payment of one or both counter values. This Shariah rule is meant to prevent speculation.
2. Based on the previous rule, no forward or future contracts are allowed on digital currencies when sold against other digital currencies or against regular currencies.
3. If lent, it must be with no increment. Similarly, if sold for the same digital currency there must be equality in the amounts exchanged, in addition to spot payment of both values.

These rules are still applicable to a digital currency backed by gold or silver, or by other valid currencies even if the aforementioned conditions - protection of value, wide acceptability and relative stability of value - are not fulfilled. This is because the digital currency would then represent these underlying assets and as such, be subject to the same Shariah rules of these assets, as only the exchange of gold, silver and money in general are subject to the above Shariah rules. Accordingly, the above rules are applicable to cryptocurrency upon the fulfilment of one of the following two conditions:

- The digital currency meets the Shariah criteria of valid currency so it can be deemed as money.
- The digital currency is backed specifically by gold, silver, other currencies or a combination of those.

Does Bitcoin Fit the Shariah Standards of a Valid Currency?

Despite the existence of numerous cryptocurrencies, Bitcoin, which emerged in 2009, has dominated the market and become the most popular and the most well-known cryptocurrency. According to the Economist, Bitcoins have three useful qualities of a currency: they are hard to earn, limited in supply and easy to verify (Anonymous, 2015). The table below shows the popularity of Bitcoin compared to other cryptocurrencies.

Like other cryptocurrencies, Bitcoin has been created to assume the same functions of a regular currency. However, in order to determine whether or not Bitcoin is acceptable and can be recognized as a valid currency from a Shariah perspective, Bitcoin should fulfil the aforementioned three Shariah conditions, which function as Shariah standards of a valid currency. The following discussion will explore the applicability of these standards to Bitcoin in order to determine its validity as currency from a Shariah perspective.

Figure 1. Popularity of Bitcoin compared to other cryptocurrencies (investing.com)

All ▾ Coins ▾ Tokens ▾ USD ▾ Next 100 → View All

#	Name	Market Cap	Price	Volume (24h)	Circulating Supply	Change (24h)	Price Graph (7d)
1	Bitcoin	$168,154,093,718	$9,968.97	$8,730,850,000	16,867,750 BTC	1.59%	
2	Ethereum	$90,192,327,234	$923.67	$2,820,220,000	97,645,829 ETH	-1.96%	
3	Ripple	$43,746,495,009	$1.12	$953,742,000	39,009,215,838 XRP *	-2.66%	
4	Bitcoin Cash	$25,298,478,708	$1,490.77	$806,826,000	16,970,075 BCH	8.72%	
5	Litecoin	$11,846,564,674	$214.46	$1,461,520,000	55,238,783 LTC	-8.46%	
6	Cardano	$10,292,528,462	$0.396980	$247,800,000	25,927,070,538 ADA *	-2.59%	
7	Stellar	$8,282,089,669	$0.449197	$82,134,000	18,437,544,483 XLM *	-2.30%	

Wide Acceptability

The legal status of Bitcoin and other cryptocurrencies varies substantially from one country to another and is still undefined or is subject to change. While some countries have explicitly allowed its use and trade, others have banned or restricted it. Qatar, for example, is among the countries that have categorically banned all sorts of dealing in Bitcoin. The list includes Algeria, Morocco, Russian, Taiwan, Thailand, Bolivia and India. Other countries, like China and Australia, have imposed restrictions on its use, such as accepting Bitcoin as a private virtual currency but not as a public currency. Australian banks have also been reported to have closed down bank accounts of operators of businesses trading in Bitcoin (Lam, 2017). Furthermore, some countries do not recognize Bitcoin as a currency although they do recognize it as a taxable asset. For example, to the Australian taxation office "Bitcoin is neither money nor Australian or foreign currency. Rather, it is property and is an asset for capital gains tax (CGT) purposes. Other cryptocurrencies that have the same characteristics as Bitcoin will also be assets for CGT purposes and will be treated similarly for tax purposes" (Australian Taxation Office, 2018).

However, Bitcoin is legal in many countries including the United States, Canada and the United Kingdom. The European Union has not passed any legislation regarding the status of Bitcoin as a currency. However, the legal status of Bitcoin is changing, and most governments are concerned about their lack of control over Bitcoin and how to tax it (Chohan, 2017).

On the individual level, Bitcoin is gaining intermittent popularity. According to a research by Cambridge University, the number of cryptocurrencies users in 2013 was between 300,000 and 1.3 million users, and have significantly increased since then. As of 2017, the estimated number of cryptocurrency users is between 2.9 million and 5.8 million, most of whom use Bitcoin (Hileman & Rauchs 2017). To facilitate the use of Bitcoin, exchange houses exist to exchange Bitcoin with any other conventional currencies, in addition to thousands of ATM machines that exchange Bitcoin and cash in many countries around the world. However, the relatively large number of Bitcoin users does not necessarily constitute its acceptability as currency as it is not demanded to be used like a conventional currency, i.e. as a means of exchange, store of value or unit of account. Rather, Bitcoin has been mostly demanded for speculative investment purposes as people aim to make money through trading Bitcoins and have very minimal interest in using it to perform the functions of a currency.

This view has been confirmed by a number of leading practitioners. For example, the Bank of Japan chief, Haruhiko Kuroda, commented on Bitcoin in December 2017, saying: "if it's a question of whether it's functioning like currencies as a form of payment or means of settlement, I don't think it is. [Bitcoin] is being traded for investing or for speculation" (Lam, 2017). Australia's central bank governor, Philip Lowe, said: "The current fascination with these currencies feels more like a speculative mania than it has to do with their use as an efficient and convenient form of electronic payment" (Lam, 2017). Similarly, the Bank of France Governor, Francois Villeroy de Galhau, described Bitcoin in January 2018 as a "purely speculative asset…we need to be clear: Bitcoin is in no way a currency" (Lam, 2017).

Moreover, despite being useable for making online payments, Bitcoin is still not a favoured means of payment among online retailers. In 2017 Bitcoin's acceptance among major online retailers dropped from five out of the top 500 online merchants in 2016 to three in 2017. Reasons for this drop include high transaction fees,[3] long transaction time and a rise in value making consumers unwilling to spend it (Katz, 2017). Therefore, due to the limited acceptability of Bitcoin as a direct means of exchange, it can be said that it has functioned as store of value asset more than as a means of exchange, and this is conditioned on its ability to hold its value, which in turn depends on market participants sharing a demand for it. The diagram below shows the median confirmation time needed to complete one transaction online since inception.

Figure 2. Median confirmation time

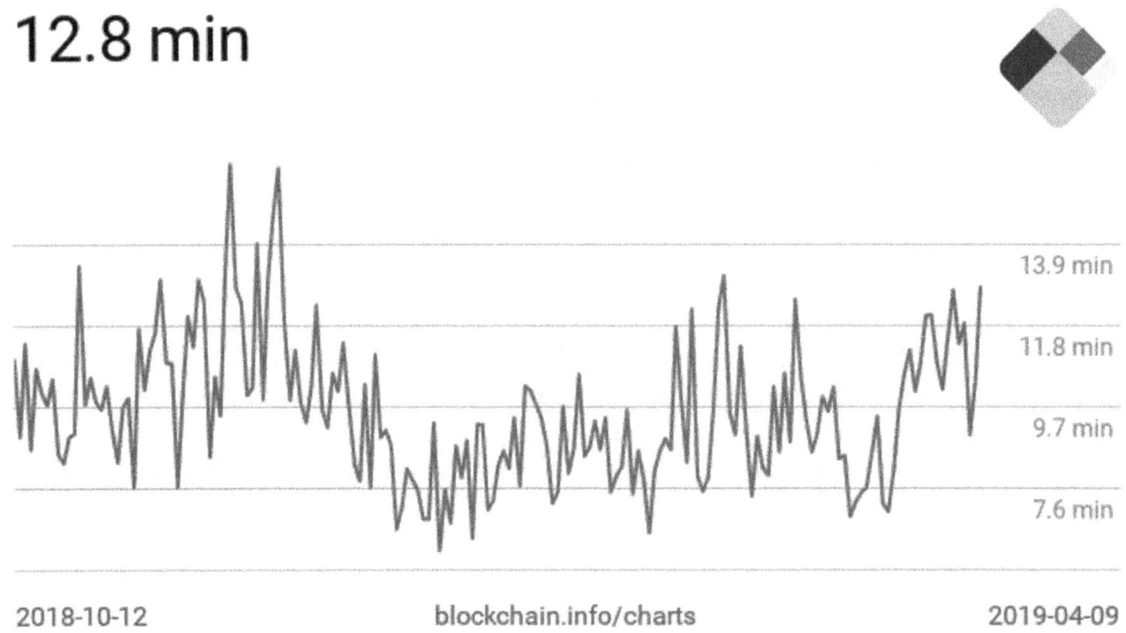

The chart below shows the number of Bitcoin transactions per day. The sharp volatility of transactions indicates that Bitcoin is used as a trading instrument and for reasons other than as a real currency, because if it is used as a real currency the number of daily transactions would not be that volatile, especially in the last couple of years.

Prior to 2015, Bitcoin's popularity depended on its ability to be used to purchase illegal goods rather than for investment. Researchers at the University of Kentucky in 2014 found "robust evidence that computer programming enthusiasts and illegal activity drive interest in Bitcoin, and find limited or no support for investment motives" (Wilson & Yelowitz, 2014, p.13).

In fact, the acceptability and the potential illegal use of Bitcoin on the one hand, and its volatile value on the other, have been interrelated. *Business Insider,* an American financial and business news website, reported in January 2015 that drug dealers were losing profits due to being unable to convert Bitcoin revenue to cash after the price declined, and it also reported that if drug dealers decided to sell reserves to stay in business this could bring down the Bitcoin price even further (Business Insider, 2015, January 16).

The potential of Bitcoin for illegal use is also one of the contributors to its popularity. Several reports describe Bitcoin as a haven for criminals and drug dealers. According to a report by *Business Insider*, "Even small-time dealers are embracing currencies like Bitcoin, Litecoin and Ethereum as a way of banking drug money without getting caught … the warning given by officers shows that the increased public profile of cryptocurrency — particularly Bitcoin — means that even relatively unsophisticated criminals are embracing it" (Business Insider, 2017, Dec 13). According to the same report "Brothels were using currency exchanges to bank profits … while organised gangs are spending cryptocurrency on the dark web to purchase guns. The inherent privacy of Bitcoin — which is anonymous and very

Figure 3. Number of Bitcoin transaction per day

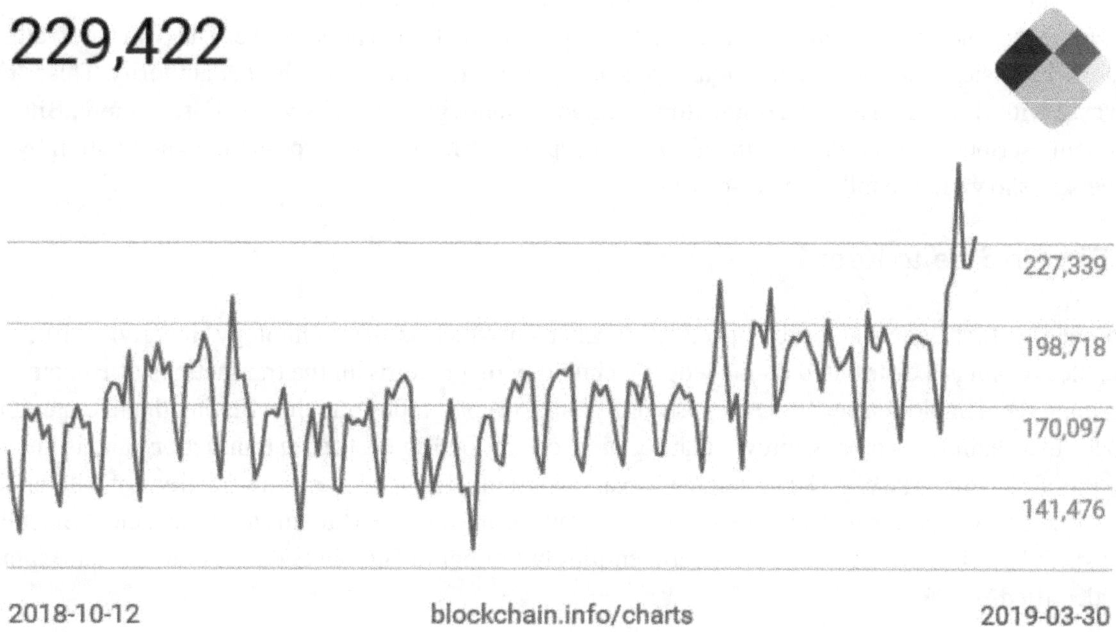

difficult to trace — means that it is "open to exploitation" by criminals" (Business Insider, 2017, Dec 13). Hence, Australia's central bank governor, Philip Lowe, criticised cryptocurrencies as more likely to appeal to criminals than consumers (Lam, 2017).

Moreover, people may resort to purchasing Bitcoins, or some other cryptocurrencies, for other reasons. According to Timothy (2013), some Argentinians bought Bitcoins to protect their savings deposits against high inflation or against the possibility that the government could confiscate their savings accounts (Timothy, 2013). In Cyprus, and during the 2012–2013 Cypriot financial crisis, purchases of Bitcoins rose due to fears that savings accounts would be confiscated or taxed (Salyer, 2013).

In conclusion, it can be said that dealing in Bitcoin has been driven by reasons other than the use of a regular currency and hence, it is not within the boundaries of the acceptability needed to obtain the necessary Shariah recognition.

Protection of Value

Since Bitcoin does not have intrinsic value nor is it backed by any assets or has value guaranteed by authorities, it involves high risk such that its holders have no sort of protection whatsoever with regard to its value. Bitcoin's value stems from its recognition as a valuable asset. However, there is no guarantee that it will hold its value since Bitcoin's acceptability is limited and restricted and its value has been subject to excessive fluctuations, as discussed earlier.

The very realism of Bitcoin has been questioned as some economists have voiced concerns that Bitcoin could be a Ponzi scheme, but reports by official institutions excluded this possibility. A report by the World Bank in 2014 concluded that Bitcoin was not a deliberate Ponzi scheme (Kaushik, 2014). The Swiss Federal Council, after examining some concerns that Bitcoin might be a pyramid scheme, concluded that "Since in the case of Bitcoin the typical promises of profits are lacking, it cannot be assumed that Bitcoin is a pyramid scheme." (Federal Council of Switzerland, 2014).

Being real and not a pyramid scheme is not enough from a Shariah perspective. The coin has to either possess intrinsic value, be backed by real assets or has value guaranteed by a higher authority. This is not the case with Bitcoin, as even its originators or miners cannot guarantee its value. Furthermore, Bitcoin has some serious issues related to the ability to keep it safe from theft or possible manipulation by its miners as shown in the following discussion.

Is Bitcoin Safe to Keep?

We need to first understand the concept of blockchain which is the technology underlying Bitcoin. The blockchain is a distributed public ledger technology that records all the transactions of Bitcoins by grouping them in blocks, verifying them securely using cryptography and then linking them to previous blocks in a chain. This process proves that certain work is done against those transactions and is known as "Proof of Work" (PoW). The first one who validates a block is rewarded with fractions of Bitcoin for the work that was performed and this is what is known as mining. As Bitcoins are mined electronically, and since Bitcoins are not tied to real-world entities but rather to Bitcoin addresses, the owners cannot be identified.

The blockchain records Bitcoin transactions without any trusted central authority but rather through a consensus of all "nodes" or computer entities connected to the blockchain validating that transactions of a block.[4] In the blockchain, Bitcoins are registered to Bitcoin addresses which are created through picking a random valid private key to be assigned to the Bitcoin address. Disclosing this address will not compromise the safety of the Bitcoin, but disclosing or losing the private key is the real problem. To spend the Bitcoin, the owner must know the corresponding private key and digitally sign the transaction. The network verifies the signature using the public key (Antonopoulos, 2014). If the private key is lost, the Bitcoin network will not recognise any other evidence of ownership, and the coins are effectively lost. In 2013 one user claimed to have lost 7,500 Bitcoins, worth $7.5 million at the time, when he unintentionally discarded the hard drive in which his private key was saved (CBS, 2013).

Besides losing the private key, Bitcoin can be subject to hacking and manipulation. In January 2018 someone in Tokyo hacked into the digital wallet of Japanese cryptocurrency exchange and pulled off one of the biggest heists in history.[5] Some reports describe what has become known as the possible 51% attack, which means having more than 51% of network resources dominating the blockchain network. This enables fake transactions or double spending to be validated (Dawkins, 2018). According to Investopedia, the online resource for financial terminology, the 51% attack would allow attackers to prevent new transactions from gaining confirmations by halting payments between some or all users. Attackers would also be able to reverse transactions that were completed, which means they could spend a coin twice. This would potentially undermine the entire cryptocurrency system, giving bad agents control over Bitcoin and other cryptocurrencies globally (Investopedia.com).

Although experts believe that controlling more than 50% of Bitcoin network resources is unlikely they acknowledge that it is not an impossible scenario (Dawkins, 2018).

Who Issues the Bitcoin, and how it can be Subject to Manipulation?

In order to acquire transparency and maintain transparency, the issuance process of Bitcoin was designed to be decentralized, so that no central authority can monopolise its mining. (Muedinai, 2018). Furthermore, when Bitcoin's inventor Satoshi Nakamoto (the name used by the unknown person(s) who invented Bitcoin) invented Bitcoin, he set a monetary policy system that there would be a limit of only 21 million Bitcoins in circulation (Meera, 2018). The policy also set the rate at which the Bitcoins can be generated, which is to have the rate drop by half every four years until all are in circulation, and the Bitcoins latest number is released approximately every ten minutes. The chart below shows the number of Bitcoins in circulation since inception.

Despite the above, research indicates that there exists a trend towards centralisation of Bitcoin mining by miners joining large mining pools in order to minimise variation in their earnings (Gervais, Arthur; et al, 2016). It was found that only six mining pools controlled 75% of overall Bitcoin hashing power. Besides, one mining pool (Ghash.io) could in 2014 obtain 51% of the hashing power, which raised significant controversies about the very safety of the network (Wilhelm, 2017).

Generating Bitcoin is open to anyone who has the necessary technical capability and resources. It is not theoretically centralised, but it is practically so to some extent. Either way, neither miners nor authorities have the capacity to control the monetary value of the Bitcoin. While some may consider this an advantage, it is in fact a matter of concern from a Shariah perspective, because since Bitcoin has no intrinsic value, it should be supervised and controlled by some monetary authorities to ensure security as well as relative stability of its value. If no one can guarantee that, or if Bitcoin is not designed to be in

Figure 4. Bitcoin in circulation

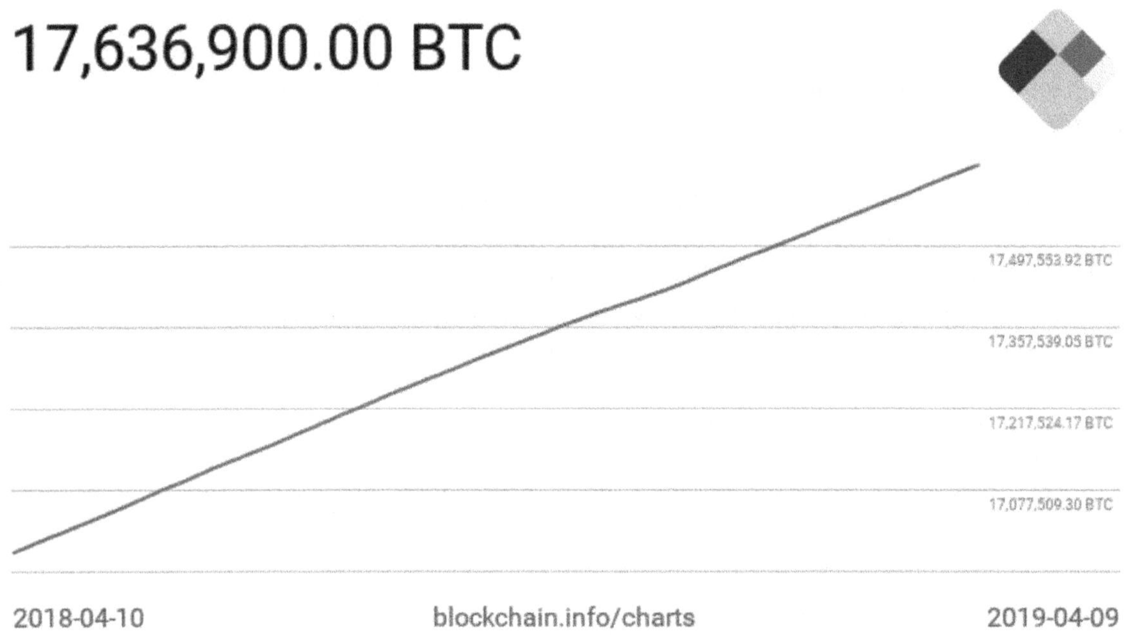

principle supervised or controlled by any authority, then Bitcoin lacks a basic feature of a valid currency from a Shariah perspective. Technically, it can be also said that Bitcoin has the potential to totally lose its value causing tremendous loss to its holders.

If Bitcoin value so far has mainly been derived from excessive speculative trading rather than from its use or recognition as a currency, then quick-wealth seekers may desist from trading in within a single day and turn to more novel trading instruments to capitalise on the opportunity of quick wealth making, especially given that modern technology has lifted all boundaries for engineering gambling-like investments, and Bitcoin would be considered then as nothing but a trigger. Mark T. Williams, an economist and finance expert, raised some concerns in his testimony about Bitcoin, including a lack of consumer protection, being a high-risk virtual commodity, having an artificially inflated price, being subject to extreme hoarding, and with high potential for market manipulation and fraud (Williams, 2014).

Stability of Value

Bitcoin's value has been very volatile, especially in 2017, ranging from about $1000 to $20000, and in December 2017 when it doubled in value and subsequently lost around 50% of its value.

Prior to this, and according to articles quoted by Wikipedia, "the price of Bitcoins has gone through various cycles of appreciation and depreciation referred to by some as bubbles and busts. In 2011, the value of one Bitcoin rapidly rose from about US$0.30 to US$32 before returning to US$2. In the latter half of 2012 and during the 2012–13 Cypriot financial crisis, the Bitcoin price began to rise, reaching a high of US$266 on 10 April 2013, before crashing to around US$50. On 29 November 2013, the cost of one Bitcoin rose to a peak of US$1,242. In 2014, the price fell sharply, and as of April remained depressed at little more than half 2013 prices. As of August 2014 it was under US $600" (Investopedia.com).

Nobel Memorial Prize laureate Robert Shiller said that Bitcoin "exhibited many of the characteristics of a speculative bubble" (Shiller, 2014, P. 2). In fact, speculation in Bitcoin has been compared to the tulip mania of seventeenth-century Holland. Nout Wellink, a former president of the Dutch Central Bank, remarked "This is worse than the tulip mania, At least then you got a tulip, now you get nothing" (The Guardian, 2013). According to Mark T. Williams, as of 2014, Bitcoin's volatility was seven times greater than gold, eight times greater than the S&P 500, and 18 times greater than the US dollar (Williams, 2014). According to Bloomberg, "The European Central Bank has repeatedly warned about the dangers of investing in digital currencies. ECB President Mario Draghi said in February the blockchain was 'quite promising' and the bank is 'very interested' in the technology. Draghi does not consider Bitcoin a currency however as it is too volatile. Vice President Vitor Constancio said in September that Bitcoin isn't a currency, but a 'tulip' -- alluding to the 17th-century bubble in the Netherlands" (Lam, 2017, p. 9).

Figure 5 depicts the sharp volatility of Bitcoin market value since inception to date - especially from 2017 onward.

In conclusion, given the facts above, it can be said that Bitcoin, since its inception, has not enjoined the necessary stability of value in a currency that is valid from a Shariah perspective. Stability of value is required by the Shariah in order for the currency to properly perform its perceived economic functions as discussed earlier, but Bitcoin fails to satisfy this particular Shariah requirement.

All in all, despite the relative success of Bitcoin on some levels its journey has been full of controversies, and due to its fragility as a currency, its value and popularity have been severely affected by several external events as shown in the table below. This in general should disqualify it from acquiring the status of a true currency.[6]

Figure 5. Bitcoin market price

CONCLUSION

In conclusion, this paper has shown that both Islamic and conventional economics share the same view with regard to the criteria of a valid currency and its three economic functions. From both perspectives, despite cryptocurrencies being an innovative mode of payment and a trading instrument it does not amount to or qualify as being a currency, simply because it fails to possess the features of a currency - being a means of exchange, a unit of account and a store of value. Although these three features exist in cryptocurrencies to some extent, they are not evident or entrenched therein to the extent that it would qualify these cryptocurrencies becoming valid currencies. It is possible that cryptocurrencies may evolve in the future to successfully attain full status of currencies or even replace the conventional currencies, but this may take some time and require appropriate governance to regulate cryptocurrencies and subject them to scrutiny and control to avoid the high risks currently associated with them. According to Bank of International Settlements, which is considered the central bank for all central banks, "while digital currencies are a revolutionary tool, they remain far too risky to be used as legal tender any time soon" (Lam, 2017, p. 9). With regards to Bitcoin specifically, it has excelled and superseded other cryptocurrencies but most likely as a speculative trading tool more than anything else. However, Bitcoin is still lacking the necessary characteristics of a valid currency in view of the points discussed in this paper. Nevertheless, Bitcoin may have the potential to evolve and acquire the features of a valid global currency if the world authorities recognise it unconditionally and subject it to the necessary regulations and controls.

The results of this paper can be summarised as following:

- There is no Shariah objection, in principle, to the creation of a new currency, such as a digital currency, as long as it meets the Shariah conditions of a valid currency, and its trading and dealing are subjected to the same Shariah rules as the regular currency.
- From a Shariah perspective, a currency whose value is technical and not intrinsic has to be properly backed by real valuable assets or be supervised by a trustworthy financial authority in order to protect people from fraud.
- A careful study of Bitcoin reveals that it fails to satisfy the Shariah standards of a valid currency, due to instability in its value, limited acceptability and a lack of sufficient protection.
- The recent popularity and success of Bitcoin is due to speculative trading rather than its genuine use as a currency. Most of those who buy it are speculators aiming to make a quick profit from quick trading without taking the risk of holding it for long time. To them Bitcoin is an investment chance that availed itself rather than a currency to be treated and used as such.
- The vulnerability of the cryptocurrencies to possible hacking and digital monopoly is a significant concern from a Shariah perspective, especially given that the average user has limited knowledge about hacking and cyber-attacks. Indeed, we know little about the safety of our data on our computers, and the trend has been that hackers will hack or create a bug and then computer scientists come up with some solutions. However, from the time of hacking until the emergence of the counter procedure many cryptocurrencies can be stolen or lost.
- Despite the Shariah objection to the dominance of certain fiat-money currencies over the world economies, this fiat money remains in final analysis better than a cryptocurrency such as Bitcoin, due to the possible economic harms caused by the latter.

- Finally, efforts should be made to break the hegemony of the US Dollar, not through introducing more controversial currencies like Bitcoin, but rather through reinstating the currencies that have intrinsic value like gold and silver, so that no super power can impose its fiat money on others.

REFERENCES

Abozaid, A. (2004). *Fiqh Al-Riba*. Beirut: Al-Risalah.

Abozaid, A. (2016). Critical Review of the Tools of Ijtihad Used in Islamic Finance. *Journal of Islamic Economic Studies, The Islamic Research and Training Institute*, *24*, 31.

Abozaid, A. (2016). The Impact of Currencies Value Depreciation on Debt Repayment, (Arabic) *Al-Tajdid Journal. International Islamic University Malaysia*, *20*, 40.

Al-Maqrizi, T. (2011). *Ighathat al-Umma bi Kashf al-Ghumma*. Cairo: Al-Manarah Al-Azhariyah Publilsher.

Al-Nawawi, Y. (1995). *Al-Majmouh, Jaddah*. Irshad Publisher.

Anonymous. (2013, December 4). *Bitcoin hype worse than 'tulip mania' says dutch central banker.* https://www.theguardian.com/technology/2013/dec/04/bitcoin-bubble-tulip-dutch-banker

Anonymous. (2013, November 29). Man Throws Away 7,500 Bitcoins, Now Worth $7.5 Million. *CBS DC*. Retrieved from https://washington.cbslocal.com/2013/11/29/man-throws-away-7500-bitcoins-now-worth-7-5-million/

Anonymous. (2015 January 13). The magic of mining. *The Economist.* Retrieved from https://www.economist.com/business/2015/01/08/the-magic-of-mining

Anonymous. (2015 October 31). The great chain of being sure about things. *The Economist.* Retrieved from https://www.economist.com/briefing/2015/10/31/the-great-chain-of-being-sure-about-things

Anonymous. (2015, January16). Deep Web Drug Dealers Are Freaking Out About the Bitcoin Crash. *Business Insider.* Retrieved from https://www.businessinsider.com/bitcoin-crash-drug-dealers-2015-1

Antonopoulos, A. M. (2014). *Mastering Bitcoin. Unlocking Digital Crypto-Currencies*. O'Reilly Media.

Chohan, U. (2017). Assessing the Differences in Bitcoin & Other Cryptocurrency Legality Across National Jurisdictions. *Information Systems & Economics eJournal, Social Science Research Network*, *6*, 4.

Dawkins, D. (2018, Feb 9). The HACK that could break bitcoin - '51% attack' concerns mainstream 'banking bunnies'. *Sunday Express*.

Evans, C. W. (2015). Bitcoin in Islamic Banking and Finance. *Journal of Islamic Banking and Finance.*, *3*(1), 5. doi:10.15640/jibf.v3n1a1

Federal Council of Switzerland. (2014, June 25). *Swiss Confederation*.

Gervais, A. (2016). Is Bitcoin a Decentralized Currency? *InfoQ & IEEE Computer Society.*

Gervais, A. (2016, October 10). Is Bitcoin a Decentralized Currency? *InfoQ & IEEE Computer Society.*

Hileman, G., & Rauchs, M. (2017). *Global Cryptocurrency Benchmarking Study*. Cambridge University Press.

Ibn Al-Qayyem, J. (1991). *I'lam al-Muwaqe'*. Beirut: Dar al-Kutub al-Elmiyya.

Katz L. (2017). *Bitcoin Acceptance Among Retailers Is Low and Getting Lower.* Bloomberg.com.

Kaushik B. (2014). *Ponzis: The Science and Mystique of a Class of Financial Frauds.* Worldbank.org.

Lam, E. (2017). *What the World's Central Banks Are Saying About Bitcoin.* Bloomberg.com.

Lee, T. (2013, August 21). Five surprising facts about Bitcoin. *The Washington Post.*

Ma'lum, M. (2016, February 11). ACCC investigating why banks are closing bitcoin companies' accounts. *Financial Review*.

Meera, A. K. (2018). Cryptocurrencies from Islamic Perspective: The Case of Bitcoin. *Bulletin of Monetary Economics and Banking, 20,* 475–491.

Muedinai, F. (2018). The Compatibility of Cryptocurrencies and Islamic Finance. *EJIF – European Journal of Islamic Finance, 10,* 12-19.

Muslim, H. (1990). Sahih Muslim. Beirut: Dar Ehia' al-Turath al-'Arabi.

Salyer, K. (2013, March 20). *Fleeing the Euro for Bitcoins.* Bloomberg L.P.

Shiller, R. (2014, March 1). In Search of a Stable Electronic Currency. *New York Times.*

Tole, F. (2017, Dec. 12). Drug Dealers Laundering their Money at Bitcoin ATMs. *Business Insider*.

Wilhelm, A. (2017). *Popular Bitcoin Mining Pool Promises to Restrict its Compute Power to Prevent Feared '51%' Fiasco.* TechCrunch.com.

Williams, M. T. (2014). Virtual Currencies – Bitcoin Risk. In *World Bank Conference*. Boston University.

Williams, M. T. (2014). *The New York State Department of Financial Services: Hearing on Virtual Currencies.* Academic Press.

Wilson, M. G., & Yelowitz, A. (2014). *Characteristics of Bitcoin Users: An Analysis of Google Search Data.* Social Science Research Network. Working Papers Series.

ENDNOTES

1. The primary objectives of the Shariah are five: preservation and promotion of the religion, life, lineage, intellect and wealth.
2. Removal of harm is one of the primary Shariah principles, and it is considered one of the major Fiqh maxims.

3 This excludes the interchange fee, because, while merchants accepting credit cards are typically charged 2–3% as interchange fees, merchants accepting bitcoins often pay fees from 0% to 2%. Wingfield, Nick, (30 October 2013). "Bitcoin Pursues the Mainstream", The New York Times.

4 For more information on the way bitcoins are recorded in the blockchain see "The great chain of being sure about things". The Economist. 31 October 2015.

5 It worth noting that experts are attempting to combat hacking using a technique called 'hard fork', which is based on splitting the blockchain to complicate the hacking process. For example, Bitcoin has been split and as a result new Bitcoin emerged, which meant free money to holders: Bitcoin Private on 28 Feb 2018, Bitcoin Gold 24 October 2017, and Bitcoin Cash on 1st August 2017. Although, this did not stop the recent hacking in Japan. See report on Reuters.com issued on January 28, 2018. See also: Alyssa Hertig; Blockchain Forks Are All the Rage, But Can They Ever Be Safe? Oct 19, 2017, published on www.coindesk.com.

6 It is worth noting that Grant Spencer, the former acting governor of the Reserve Bank of New Zealand, said: "I think they [cryptocurrencies] are part of the future, but not the sort that we see in Bitcoin." Eric Lam, (15 Dec 2017). "What the World's Central Banks Are Saying About Bitcoin", Bloomberg.com.

Section 3

Financial Inclusion and Financial Stability in the Era of FinTech

Chapter 10
The Nexus Between FinTech Adoption and Financial Inclusion

Marouane Moufakkir
University Ibn Tofail, Kenitra, Morocco

Qmichchou Mohammed
University Ibn Tofail, Kenitra, Morocco

ABSTRACT

Notwithstanding the increase of using and adopting FinTech all over the world by users who prefer managing their lives through digital channels, including financial and banking services, a large number of customers are still using the classic financial services, or even ignore the existence of such financial technologies. The aim of this chapter is to underline the concept of FinTech, a technological innovation in the financial field. Indeed, several theories and models has tried to explained the factors of adopting an innovation. Besides the theoretical framework of innovation, FinTech has to pass through different business models to attain the maturity as a successful pure player actor. Accordingly, the overall purpose of this paper is to provide an overview of the financial technologies use evolution, as a business model, and to highlight how FinTech contribute to enhance the financial and social inclusion, by providing convenient and accurate digital financial services (DFS) to the excluded population.

DOI: 10.4018/978-1-7998-0039-2.ch010

INTRODUCTION

"The new does not come out of the old, but appears next to the old, competes with it until he ruins it" (Schumpeter, 1951, p. 40). The current use of the Internet and information and communication technologies (ICT), especially with the fast-paced expansion of technological innovations, makes us realize that we are only at the beginning of the digital transformation journey. Indeed, every aspect of human's life has been radically changed, thanks to the information technologies (IT) revolution and web 2.0 tools: from transportation and education, to travelling and communication. Technology has transformed Business-to-Business, Business-to-Customer and within-business interactions enabling a widespread reconfiguration in all business side from marketing, supply chain, and manufacturing, to financial and banking industry, contract warehousing and delivery (International Finance Corporation, IFC, 2017).

While these upheavals are facilitated by new players, online marketplaces and distributors, Fintech, IT companies and innovating start-ups, are becoming a serious threat for the traditional financial providers such as banks, finance companies, microfinance institutions, and insurance companies (IFC, 2017). As a result of their innovative financial services and potentially disrupting impacts on the financial and banking industry (Ferreira et al, 2015), it is predicted that Fintech players will have a lasting and enduring effects on the financial sector (Heap & Pollari, 2015). Besides the fact that Fintech has covered many financial needs (money transfer, digital payment, insurance, borrowing, etc), it leading to the merge of new, innovative and agile solutions to data, security, easy access to financial and banking services, reliability and convenience (Deloitte, 2016).

In fact, Fintech is not the only channel whereby financial inclusion can be enhanced. Indeed, there is alternative delivery channel (ADC) that can be any channel providing numerous financial and banking services apart from brick-and-mortar bank branch. Conforming to Alternate Delivery Channels for Financial Inclusion report (2016), "ADCs include Automated Teller Machines, agents, mobile phone banking, online banking, call centers, limited service branches, and roving staff such as susu collectors or mobile vans" (Abrams, Carraro & Ahmed, 2016, p.2). Still, mobile money in emerging markets, especially Sub-Saharan Africa is widely used by poor population enabling them to have access to financial transactions, since there are 122 million active accounts on the Sub-Saharan Africa region (The Mobile Economy Sub-Saharan Africa report, 2018).

Still, Fintech deservers more attention while some researches consider Fintech as a phenomenon with an essential shift. For example, Kauffman & Ma, have discussed the ongoing "global Fintech revolution" (Kauffman and Ma, 2015, p.261) as well as Mackenzie who wrote an article on innovators in financial service "The Fintech revolution" (Mackenzie, 2015, p.50). According to IFC (2017), by adjusting a single link of the financial industry value chain, Fintech players can provide a bank-beating solution that can connect to the rest of the financial ecosystem. In other words, delivering financial services directly to users' mobile or related devices instead of using the traditional banking system through bank branches. Those services are delivered via proprietary communication lines by utilizing encoded Internet transmissions, or using cloud computing over data centers (IFC, 2017).

Nowadays, the relevance of digital financial services (DFS) and Fintech is increasing all around the world as a bridge that can help to enhance the financial inclusion and reduce the poverty. In fact, "Countries are demanding deeper access to financial markets, and the World Bank Group will focus on delivering Fintech solutions that enhance financial services, mitigate risks, and achieve stable, inclusive economic growth" (World Bank Group President Jim Yong Kim, The Bali Fintech Agenda, 2018).

Many studies have discussed the Fintech evolution and their impact on financial traditional system. Whereas significant researches have been published in academic journals about Fintech and the new opportunities provided, the interlink review between Fintech and financial inclusion remains missing and insufficient. Reviewing existing literature affords an opportunity for a better understanding of the existing state of the research, as well as outlines the research area evolution. In one hand, the overall purpose of this chapter is to understand, analyze and summarize findings related to Fintech and financial inclusion. On the other hand, the increase of Fintech adoption, as a financial technological innovation, can be an opportunity for a better financial inclusion and financial system stability. Firstly, a theoretical framework linked to innovation adoption seems to be necessary to place the concept of Fintech within the appropriate literature. This will help us to have a better understanding of using, adopting and mostly trusting the digital channels for financial transactions. Secondly, this analysis is then used to shed light on the impact of Fintech adoption on the enhancement of financial inclusion and thus the financial system stability and a better social inclusion. It also summarizes the main conclusions, determined relevant gaps needing more emphasizing, and requires further research.

The Theoretical Framework of Technological Innovation Adoption

We have found several articles in the literature related to the topic of technological innovation, while researchers and scholars find difficulty to agree on a universal definition of this concept. This disagreement is led by the confusion between innovation and other concepts such as invention, new product or new process. According to Perrin (2001), this multitude of visions is due partly to a confusion between innovation, invention, scientific development and technological progress. In addition, the concept of innovation refers, at the same time, to the process, its result or both. Thus, the definition given by the Organization for Economic Cooperation and Development (OECD) is generally the most detailed definition since it gives more details about technological innovation. Indeed, it encompasses a wide range of possible innovations as well as for new products as for new processes, while specifying the managerial fields that this innovation could be involved in. "Technological Innovations cover products and technologically new processes as well as significant technological improvements in products and processes that have been accomplished. A technological innovation has been accomplished once it has been introduced on the market (product innovation) or used in a production process (process innovation). It involves all kinds of scientific, technological, organizational, financial and commercial activities" (OECD, EC & Eurostat, 1996, p. 36). This definition

Since the adoption of "Online Banking" is considered in the literature as a field of Innovation Management (Ratten, 2008), we will be interested first in the concept of innovation in order to undertake more efficiently the Fintech concept as long as it is a technological financial innovation. Despite the existence of numerous theories related to innovation's adoption, we can cite Innovation Diffusion Theory (IDT), Technology Acceptance Model (TAM), United Theory of Acceptance and Use of Technology (UTUAT), TAM 2, Technology Readiness (TR), Theory of Planned Behavior (TPB) or Theory of Interpersonal Behaviour (TIB), we have chosen to focus on the three first models. This choice does not mean that the other theories are not as relevant as the chosen ones. We focused on those theories because they provide pertinent constructs that enable us to undertake more efficiently the Fintech adoption as a technological financial innovation. In addition, those theories provide explaining details such as utility, usability, trialability and relative advantage of Fintech as well as cognitive determinants related to Fintech adoption.

Innovation Diffusion Theory (IDT)

Founded by Rogers (1962), the aim of this theory is to understand and explain how individuals can adopt a new idea, technology, service or product. Rogers has established five constructs in order to give a scientific explanation to innovation's adoption, which are relative advantage, compatibility, complexity, trialability and observability. Thus, a voluntary use of a specific innovation with a low level of complexity involves an easier adoption of this innovation.

Accordingly, in order to offer a better innovation adoption experience, companies, including the banking and financial institutions, must rethink their business model by bringing accurate innovations. On one hand, employees can use and adopt them effortlessly without showing a big change resistance. On the other hand, the customer can also use this innovation easily without difficulty. In addition, innovations must have a significant advantage and results that are perceptible and palpable (Moore and Benbasat, 1991).

However, forcing individuals to adopt a particular innovation increase the risk of rejecting it. The study done by Agarwal and Prasad (1997) confirmed that voluntarism was directly associated with the successful adoption of information technology. In addition, the innovative system must also allow the customer to have a better experience. Indeed, Fintech has changed the face-to-face banking experience. Customers are enjoying the fact of having several banking/financial services, with low cost, available 24/7 online just from their smart phones and therefore, the increase of Fintech adoption rate. The Ernest & Young Fintech Adoption Index Report 2017 has revealed that the average of Fintech adoption is 33% globally, compared with 16% in 2015.

To give a better understanding of the constructs and their impact on Fintech adoption, we reviewed through the table below (see table 1), the factors given by Rogers in his theory that explains the innovation adoption. Those factors are the perceived attributes of innovation, which are the five constructs cited above, type of innovation's decision, innovation communication channel, nature of social system and change agent. All those factors have an impact on innovation adoption rate. The aim of this table is to give a clear explanation of each point supported by an example.

By applying those constructs into Fintech as a financial technological innovation, we could understand why Fintech has been easily adopted and continue to attract people all over the world. Indeed, Fintech providers present several advantages (low cost, online services 24/7, etc), those financial services are very compatible with the user values especially the digital natives. The use of Fintech services is very easy, with the opportunity to try the services for free without any risk and we can notice the results very quickly almost instantly. Moreover, people are using Fintech on voluntary basis without being forced to do it, using interpersonal networks and web 2.0 tools. Those persons belong to a community (generation Y and Z mostly) that foster the use of innovation and ICT.

Fintech respects most of the attributes that explains an innovation adoption established by Rogers. Another theoretical model gives different constructs for such adoption.

Technology Acceptance Model (TAM)

In order to predict the acceptability level of a new technology, Davis (1989) has developed the TAM model based on the Theory of Reasoned Action of Fishbein and Ajzen (1975). The TAM model aims to identify the modifications that must be done to the process in order to make this new technology suitable for users and be adopted in a final stage.

Table 1. Diffusion of innovation theory of Rogers revisited

Factors Related to the Innovation Adoption	Explanations
Perceived attributes of Innovation	- Relative Advantage: The perceived advantage by the user after adopting an innovation. More the innovation presents an advantage for the user, more the willingness of adopting it is big. - Compatibility: How the innovation is perceived for being compatible with the user's values. As far as the innovation is compatible with the existing user's values, he will be easily tented to adopt it. - Complexity: The perception of using easily an innovation. The user adopts an innovation, presenting less complexity, more easily. - Trialability: The possibility to try an innovation without a perceived risk. The innovation is more likely to be adopted if the customer can try it without risk (Darpy & Volle, 2007). - Observability: The level and the speed to which the user notices the results of using an innovation. The user will be more motivated to adopt an innovation if he observes concrete results of his use.
Type of innovation's decision	Forced by the top management, collective, optional An innovation used on a voluntary basis will be adopted much more easily than if imposed by the organization.
Innovation communication channels	Individual, mass communication, interpersonal networks The use of interpersonal channels increases strongly the possibility of adopting an innovation.
Nature of social system	Social norms, user community The fact that the user belongs to a community that shares positive social norms toward innovation, increases the chance of adoption it.
Change Agents	Persons who directly or indirectly causes a changing in organization, community (leader, Manager…). "Change agent is somebody who influences clients' innovation decisions in a direction deemed desirable by a change agency" (Rogers 2005, p. 37). The more the change agent promotes innovation, the more it will be adopted easily.

Source: Diffusion of innovation, Rogers (1962)

Even though the innovative system is uncomplicated, users must first perceive its usefulness and its ease of use in order to adopt it. Thus, when we have two systems offering the same functionalities, the user will find more useful the one he found easier to use (Dillon and Morris, 1996). In addition, according to Bandura's theory (1982), more the system is easy to use, more the user will have a feeling of self-efficacy. This will make the adoption of this new system or technology more flexible and easier. Nielsen's model (1993) explains that the acceptability of a new technology is based on a combination of "social acceptability" and "practical acceptability" factors.

The social acceptability refers to the use of a new technology, what this use is allowing to do and how it meets the social standards adopted by a group of people, a company or an Organization. For example, it is socially unacceptable to set up an innovative technological system aiming the improvement of traffic arms management.

The practical acceptability deserves to be more emphasized because of the key factors which determinate and explain the actual usefulness of the innovation, namely: the technological compatibility, he cost of the product/service, the reliability of the product/service and the usefulness of the technological innovation. According to Neilson, the concept of "Usefulness" can be divided on two categories: utility, summarized to the functional side of the product/service, and usability, defined as the simplicity of using the product/service.

Senach (1990) provides a very complete definition of utility: "Utility determines whether the system allows the user to perform his task, if he is able to achieve what is needed by the user. Utility covers functional capacity, system performance and support qualities" (Senach 1990, p. 3). As far as usability is concerned, the definition from the International Organization for Standardization (ISO 9241-11) is becoming the main reference of usability (Jokela et al., 2004). The ISO standard states that usability can be defined as the extent to which, a product can be used by specified users to achieve specified goals with effectiveness, efficiency and satisfaction in a specified context of use (ISO 9241-11, 1998)

Indeed, Fintech, as a financial technological innovation, concords strongly with the constructs above which allows customers of new generation to accept it and adopt it. Fintech provides reliable banking/financial services, 24/7 with a low cost, which have a great usefulness for people, especially the rural one who lives far from banks branches. For instance, managing our accounts from our smart phone anytime, anywhere was a big gab for individuals providing lot of utility. Besides, the use of digital platforms allowing customer to do so, is very simple via application programming interface (API) on their mobile.

Unified Theory of Acceptance and Use of Technology (UTAUT)

Venkatesh et al. (2003) have established this theory for the sake of evaluating the impact of various factors on user's intention and the new technology acceptance. In order to do that, the UTAUT model was founded on eight theories: Theory of Reasoned Action (TRA), Technology Acceptance Model (TAM), Motivational Model (MM), Theory of Planned Behavior (TPB), Model of Personal Computer Utilization (MPCU), the Social Cognitive Theory (SCT), Innovation Diffusion Theory (IDT) and the combination of TAM and TPB models.

This model highlights four constructs to explain the behavioral intention and use behavior towards a technological innovation.

- **Performance Expectancy:** How a user believes that using the technological innovation will help him to achieve a better performance. This can refer to the perceived usefulness of the technological innovation.
- **Effort Expectancy:** How it is easy to use the technology. This may also be viewed as complexity of use.
- **Social Factors:** How environmental factors such as friends, parents, and managers affect the behavior of users. This is referring to social acceptability, social factors and change agents.
- **Facilitating Conditions:** How a user believes that, an organizational and technical infrastructure exist in order to support the use of technologies.

In addition, the UTUAT model includes four moderating variables: age, gender, education and voluntariness of use. This model explains that performance expectancy, effort expectancy, social factors and facilitating conditions affect directly the behavior intention of using a technological innovation. There are also lot of interactions between the moderating variables (age, gender, education and voluntariness) of use with the four constructs in different levels (Venkatesh et al. 2003).

Fintech actors are respecting mostly the four constructs of the UTUAT model as they are providing financial services helping users to achieve performance and usefulness. In addition, using those services is effortless while facilitating conditions if using the technology is increasing globally.

Throughout those three models, we can set a clear idea about why people are more and more interested in Fintech, as a financial technological innovation, doing research about it in order to understand and discover what kind of banking/financial services these disruptive actors are providing. Indeed, as reported by Google, the term "Fintech" has been searched on average about 201,000,000.00 times a month worldwide (Google, 2016a).

Additionally, we can notice that Fintech services are progressively used and adopted widely by customers. This increase of use embraces several sectors from banking services, insurance, saving to borrowing and peer to peer lending. The figure bellow shows the current use and the increase of use intention of Fintech category in the future. Which is very relevant and significant especially related to the category of money transfer and payment. That means that those services present lot of reliable advantage, simple, low coast and easy to use with no constraints such as opening time and parking. A real usefulness compared to the traditional retail banking services.

Besides, another fact contributes to the Fintech use rise is that all the Digital Financial Services (DFS) are provided via digital channels only. As reported by The Ernest & Young Fintech Adoption Index Report 2017, 68% of Fintech users prefer using digital channels to manage all aspects of their life. The report states that consumer sentiment toward Fintech is incredibly positive, with all markets and categories reporting future increases in Fintech adoption. Hence, this adoption can be a support for a enhancing financial inclusion while enabling deprived people to have financial transactions.

FINTECH: FOR A BETTER FINANCIAL AND SOCIAL INCLUSION

"Banking is essential, Banks are not" (Bill Gates, 1994)[1]. These last years, we are witnessing the incarnation of what Bill Gates said 25 years ago in the wake of the advent of Digital Financial Services (DFS) and Fintech players. Indeed, digital transformation and ICT have radically changed the banking and financial industry. Cooper and De Brentani (1991) had stated that the banking sector is considered one of the most exposed sectors to technological and computer disruptions.

Fintech: Definition and Typology

We have found in the literature several articles about Fintech, DFS and the connection between them since Fintech is offering financial services throughout digital channels. So, what does the concept of DFS means? We can define Digital Financial Services as the broad range of financial services accessed and delivered through digital channels, including payments, credit, savings, remittances, insurance and financial information. The term "digital channels" refers to the internet, mobile phones (both smartphones and digital feature phones), Automatic Teller Machines (ATM), POS terminals, NFC-enabled devices, chips, electronically enabled cards, biometric devices, tablets, phablets and any other digital system (AFI, 2016).

Thus, the DFS include a wide range of financial/banking services delivered to the final consumer throughout digital channels and under different names according to each author: Electronic banking, Internet banking, Mobile banking, Online banking, Cashless banking, Branchless banking, Service technology, Digital banking and Internet/self-service. In fact, according to Arner, Barberis and Buckley (2015), the ATM is still the only palpable way for most consumers to see the transition from a pure digital experience to financial operation involving a physical tool. Besides, Paul Volcker, who was the former president of the US Federal Reserve (1979-1987), said in 2009: "The most important financial innovation that I have seen in the last twenty years is the ATM, which really helps people and prevents visits to the bank, which is very convenient" (Paul Volcker, The wall street journal, 2009)[2]. That was as a comment describing the role of financial innovation in the 2008 financial crisis.

Moreover, another relevant point, which is not the least, stirred us about this new way of delivering those DFS. Apart the usefulness and the benefits of these services, but also, who delivers them: Start-ups instead of large multinational financial firms who impose their laws as it has always has been. Indeed, recent advances in ICT have led to the rapid expansion of innovative new financial services development, often called Fintech (Jun & Yeo, 2016).

Therefore, we have to set a clear definition of Fintech concept. Several definitions can be found in the literature. For instance, "Fintech is a service sector which uses mobile-centered IT technology to enhance the efficiency of the financial system. As a term, it is compound of 'finance' and 'technology' and collectively refers to industrial changes forged from the convergence of financial services and IT" (Kim Park, & Choi, 2016, p.1058). Another definition provides more details: "Fintech refers to the application of technology within the financial industry. The sector covers a wide range of activities from payments (e.g. contactless) to financial data and analysis (e.g. Credit scoring), financial software (e.g. risk management), digitized process (e.g. authentication) and perhaps most well-known to the wider public, payment platforms (e.g. peer to peer lending)." (Barberis, 2014). Even the Oxford Dictionary has set a definition to the concept of Fintech suggesting that Fintech are computer programs and other technology used to support or enable banking and financial services: Fintech is one of the fastest-growing areas for venture capitalists (Oxford English Dictionary, 2016).

Nevertheless, the use of the Fintech concept to describe the fusion between finance and technology is not as recent as it seems. Indeed, the Vice-President of the Manufacturers Hanover Trust, Mr. Abraham Leon Bettinger, had given his definition of the Fintech concept as follows: "FINTECH is an acronym that stands for financial technology, associating the bank's expertise with modern techniques of Management Science and computer" (Bettinger, 1972). A recent research by Arner et al. (2015) about the origins of the Fintech concept, highlighted the emergence of the concept in the 90s through the 'Financial Services Technology Consortium' project. Which did Citigroup initiate with the intention of supporting technological cooperation efforts.

Nowadays, most of IT players, new economy investors, banking and financial actors are aware of the growing relevance of Fintech. According to Schueffel (2016), investments in Fintech have increase by 75% in 2015 to 22.3 billion USD compared to 2014 (Skan et al., 2016). In wider scale, more than 50 billion USD have been invested worldwide in Fintech firms since 2010 (Skan et al., 2016). Indeed, Arner et al. (2015) support that Fintech expansion can be considered as a continuing process whereby finance and technology have grown together. This development led to more than a few incremental (API, E-signature…) and disruptive (chatbot, AI, blockchain…) innovations. Indeed, Fintech have disrupting effects on the financial and banking industry (Ferreira et al., 2015) covering five main areas:

Finance and Investment

This category includes a wide range of alternative financing mechanisms especially crowdfunding and peer to peer lending. This digitalization of financing and placement can be extended to several other financial services such as venture capital, private equity, private placements, public offerings, listings, robo-advisory services etc. According to Horn, Geerts & Coolen (2014), crowdfunding and all comparable peer-to-peer platforms have shown an increase over the last few years, hereby competing with and partly disrupting the lending banks monopole.

Financial Operations and Risk Management

After the 2008 financial crisis, the banking and financial industry has been through a lot of regulations and changes related to risk management especially in banking sector. In fact, risk-operational processes such as credit administration today account for some 50% of the function's staff (Härle, Havas & Samandari, 2016). Therefore, the financial industry has spent a lot on IT investment in order to find a better compliance system to deal with the massive volume of post-crisis regulatory changes (Arner, Barberis, & Buckley, 2015).

Today, Fintech companies are using additional intelligence for instance, social media behavioral analysis or spending history in order to evaluate and measure the risk related to a specific loan. Which helps Fintech actors to manage credit risks while reducing the fact that money could not be repaid or repaid lately.

Payments and Infrastructure

This is by far the most famous and well know category among people since it has been a driving force particularly in developing countries toward internet, digital and mobile banking. Indeed, numerous Fintech players are focusing more and more on this category by optimizing and simplifying the payment experience for customers. Hence, start-ups and IT companies are seeking and creating opportunities to disintermediate the traditional financial institutions, namely banks. In fact, people now can operate E-payment without having a bank account, they just have to own a mobile phone instead. According to the E&Y Fintech adoption report, 50% are using Fintech for money transfer and payment on 2017, with a rate of anticipated future use up to 65%. Thus, poor individuals can receive/send money from family and friends, helping them to leverate their life standards, simply via their mobiles.

Data Security and Monetization

During this last decade, the monetary value of Data is being more and more exploited by numerous players: Google, Amazon, Facebook and Apple (GAFA), IT companies, Fintech, etc. Accordingly, several institutions admitted that data cyber-attacks have sapped the customer trust. Indeed, according to the PwC's 20th Annual CEO Survey 2017, 68% of respondents said soaring volumes of digital data in this new digital economy, had made it harder for companies to gain and retain customer trust. In fact, those personal data can be used for monetization in different ways to predict consumer behavior and trend analysis (Thenuan & Raina, 2016). According to the same authors, Data monetization has emerged due to increase in digital penetration, which is 3.17 billion of internet user consisting of 2.08 billion of smartphone users that produce huge volume of data.

Consumer Interface

Since Fintech is using the online and mobile banking to deliver their financial services, it will be always a matter of the traditional financial services delivery versus non-traditional DFS developments throughout Fintech actors. As said earlier, the payments and infrastructure category is a way for the start-ups to compete directly with traditional financial system. Curiously, it is more supported in developing countries where it is likely facilitating factors to support the Fintech growth. Always according to the EY Fintech adoption report, the rate of adoption in China is 69% (first Fintech adopting country in the world), India 52%, Brazil 42%, Mexico 36%, and South Africa 35% with a global average of 33%.

To conclude, we can assume clearly that all financial transactions gaps have been fulfilled by Fintech and more precisely, Fintech 3.5. According to the industry foretells, no area of business will be spared (Grebe et al., 2016; Gulamhuseinwala et al., 2015). From mobile peer-to-peer payment platforms, to personal financial management, crowdfunding, robo-advisors as well as digital currencies and distributed ledger technologies. It democratizes, through smart contracts and Blockchain technology, lending and investments by simplifying processes, lowering costs and increasing capital efficacy.

Some experts predict changes in the competitive structure and ecosystem of financial services caused by Fintech (Deloitte, 2016). This change concerns all types of banks, financial institutions, asset and wealth managers, fund and payment providers, brokers, exchanges, insurers alike (PricewaterhouseCoopers, 2016). This "global Fintech revolution" (Kauffman and Ma, 2015) will allow poor and discriminated people from the financial system to have an easy access to banking and financial services and thus, a better financial and social inclusion.

The Relationship Between Financial Inclusion and FINTECH

According to Gomber, Koch, and Siering (2017), digital finance covers an extent number of new financial and banking services, financial businesses, finance-related software, and novel forms of customer communication and interaction, delivered by Fintech companies and innovative financial service providers (Ozili, 2018). Those DFS are delivered mostly by Fintech via the internet (online) without the necessity of visiting a bank branch or even having a bank account. This is somehow a revolution since we were used to operate financial and banking transactions via bank account in banking institutions through bank branches. We are going toward the disintermediation in the banking and financial industry and "the death of distance" (Cairncross, 1997). In Europe, for example, the banking industry is widely using the online channel by traditional banks as well as new players (Fintech and other digital financial service providers), since they are discovering its effectiveness compared with other channels (Barbesino, Camerani, & Gaudino, 2005). According to Ozili (2018), the goal of financial services made available via digital platforms is to contribute to reduce poverty level and enhancing financial inclusion in developing economies (United Nations, 2016).

However, what financial inclusion means and how it is different from digital financial inclusion? The Consultative Group to Assist the Poor (CGAP) defines digital financial inclusion as "digital access to, and the use of, formal financial services by the excluded and underserved population" (CGAP, 2015). As far as financial inclusion is concerned, it can be defined as stated by the United Nations Report, as the sustainable provision of affordable financial services that bring the poor into the formal economy (United Nations, 2016). Financial inclusion involves increasing the use of formal financial services by the poor (Beck et al., 2007; Bruhn & Love, 2014), which contributes to poverty reduction and economic growth. According to Ozili (2018), improving the financial inclusion rate can help individuals, who were previously financially excluded, to invest in education, save and launch businesses, which contributes to decrease poverty and improving economic growth (Beck et al., 2007; Bruhn & Love, 2014). An inclusive financial system is required as it will provide opportunities mostly for all the people to access and move funds, grow capital, and reduce risk (Ozili, 2018).

According to Asli et al. (2015), having an easy access to financial services can help as a support to reduce the poverty level. In 2014, two billion people lacked access to transaction account (Global Findex, IMF Financial Access survey, 2014). Karlan et al. (2016) reported that 2.5 billion people in the word are living with less than two USD a day and struggling very hard every single day to get out from this poverty. Classically, this escape can be done by finding an employment or launch businesses through entrepreneurship. However, finding a job or being an entrepreneur is not the easiest thing to do in these last years (financial crisis, joblessness rate, the increase of jobseekers…). Hence, people resort to financial tools e.g. personal saving, insurance, credit and especially cash transfer from friends and relatives to help them finding a way out from misery. Nevertheless, high transactions costs, constraints of having a bank account and lack of competition create obstacles that inhibit the delivery of traditional financial services (Karlan et al.,2016). Indeed, as reported by the Global Findex Database report (2017), 1.7 billion adults do not have a bank account. 66% of them, however, have a mobile phone that could allow them to access to financial services. Still, the number of people worldwide having an account grew by 700 million between 2011 and 2014. In addition, the report explains that technology could promote financial inclusion by replacing cash transactions with digital transactions.

Enhancing financial inclusion through DFS have been discussed many times these last decades. Indeed, since 2010, the G-20 and the World Bank have led initiatives in order to reduce poverty levels in developing and emerging economies (Global Partnership for Financial Inclusion, 2010) by increasing financial inclusion in those countries. Practically, those initiatives aim to promote national or regional financial inclusion strategies, which include regulatory reforms facilitating access to innovative financial services and measures strengthening financial education and consumer protection (Guérineau & Jacolin, 2014). Additionally, Fintech providers can endorse economic growth during good economic times by increasing the volume of financial transactions in the financial system (Ozili, 2018) and thus promoting financial inclusion.

Since we are focusing on improving financial inclusion using the digital channels whereby Fintech are offering their financial services, we are no more talking about facilitating access to formal financial services mainly through having formal bank accounts. Currently, innovative digital financial services via mobile phones and similar devices have been launched in at least 80 countries (GSMA, 2014), to encourage millions of poor customers to exclusively use digital financial services rather than cash-based transactions (Ozili, 2018). While the use of Fintech is based on having a smart phone to operate all kind of financial operations easily, the average of world mobile subscription penetration in 2017 is 103% (Ericsson mobility report, 2017). This increase use of smart phones facilitates, seamlessly, the adoption of Fintech services and therefore contribute to enhance the financial inclusion. Indeed, according to the annual Measuring the Information Society (ITU's) Report at the end of 2016, 95% of the global population lives in an area that is covered by a mobile cellular signal and most people can access the Internet through a 3G or higher-quality network. In addition, at the end of 2018, 51.2% of individuals, or 3.9 billion people, were using the Internet (ITU's Report 2018). The ITU's predict online access in 2020 will reach 60% of the world's population.

There is no doubt that Fintech has, seamlessly, enlarged the delivery of traditional banking and financial to the customers widely using technological innovation such as digital banking, mobile-phone-enabled solutions, electronic money models and digital payment platforms. Deloitte

The Centre for financial services (2016) reported that Digital and mobile-based payments are likely to overtake traditional card-based payments in the next several years, particularly via APIs and micro payments. In addition, those ICT and digital tools are offering fast and disruptive channels not just for delivering the traditional banking services but also opened the path for new products and services as well. Indeed, PayKey, for instance, provides a secure environment for banks' customers to make payments within any social network (Deloitte Centre for financial services, 2016). In fact, the scope of 3G, 4G and now 5G mobile technology in conjunction with the extended smartphone use has been the major way whereby the demand for DFS has increased. Therefore, they have to provide access to the unbanked population who are excluded from the banking and financial system and the new economy, and thus, increasing the financial inclusion.

Table 2 summarizes the main benefits engendered by Fintech and DFS toward financial inclusion and the banking and financial system (see table 2).

Fintech companies are playing a crucial role in the digital new economy since they are evolving in the financial and banking industry to compete with banks. In addition, they provide services that match the unsatisfied needs linked to undelivered financial services or being delivered with difficulty by banks to their customers. In one hand, Fintech players do not handle cash deposits like traditional banks, which implies that they will be confronted to less regulation or even no regulations at all in some countries. Therefore, Fintech are more likely to focus on improving their financial technology, providing reliable and suitable financial services with a better intermediation function while reducing costs in order to serve poor population. On the other hand, Fintech have the opportunity to work and team with traditional lending and financial institutions. This partnership can contribute to the decrease of operational costs and thus, improve the intermediation activities quality. Furthermore, associating with traditional lending institutions can lead Fintech players to become sustainable while they can add real value to the traditional lending institutions with whom they collaborate.

The potential for technological innovation, ICT and digital transformation to provide convenience, security and easy access to financial services for poor population, in the banking and financial industry via DFS and Fintech players is more and more demonstrated through several researchers (Karlan et al., 2016). Indeed, Fintech is using digital platforms to provide electronically an increased appropriateness to users by simplifying access to such services and making it available 24/7 remotely from anywhere to each individual. This accessibility of DFS enables Fintech companies to help deprived population, especially the poor individuals in emerging and developing countries, to be part of the financial system with the ability to undertake financial and banking transactions, receiving and sending money, loans, etc. Therefore, a tremendous contribution to improve the financial and social inclusion and human wellbeing.

FUTURE TRENDS AND CONCLUSION

In this chapter, we reviewed the concept of Fintech from the theoretical side as long as we are talking about financial technological innovation, and the practical side by giving some clarifications and explanatory components of Fintech since there is no common definition has yet been derived leading to a consensus about what the term Fintech means (Schueffel, 2016). Indeed, Fintech can be linked to IT companies, Neo-banks, business segment or just an innovative technology providing financial services. Moreover, the definition of Fintech can be as different as languages available in Wikipedia related to Fintech definition especially English, French, German and Italian, which is normal, as Fintech is a global phenomenon (Mackenzie, 2015).

Table 2. Main benefits of Fintech and DFS toward financial inclusion

Digital Financial Tools	Impact on Financial Inclusion	Endorsement	Impact on Financial/Banking System and the Economy
- Mobile - Smartphone - Fintech - API - Digital transactional platform - DFS - Digital Finance tools	- Better financial inclusion as the extension of basic financial services to individuals via mobile phone and via non-financial companies is easier and cheaper. - Simple and easy access to financial services for rural and poor communities who are unable to access traditional banks located in the formal sector due to poor transportation and traditional transactions high cost.	- Global penetration rate of mobiles is 103% (2017). - 51,2% of individuals are using Internet (2018) targeting 70% Internet penetration by 2023, and 75% by 2025.	- Offering appropriate access to numerous financial and banking services and loans facilities for people as well as small, medium and large businesses can lead to improve the Gross Domestic Product (GDP) of the Economy. - Fostering the economic stability while increasing financial intermediation, both for individuals and for the Economy (Ozili, 2018). - Improving government's benefits by providing a platform to simplify increase in collective spending which subsequently engenders more tax returns arising from the growth of financial transactions volume (Manyika et al., 2016). - Enhancing uptake, global savings and investment levels in global scale - Helping formal financial sector development, which fortifies the use of interest rate as a key policy instrument for financial stability, which has positive effects for economic growth (Cecchetti & Kharroubi, 2012).
	Providing reasonably priced, appropriate and secure banking/financial services to poor and unbanked individuals especially in developing countries (CGAP).	The average of Fintech adoption in emerging markets namely: Brazil, China, India, Mexico and South Africa is 46%, which is higher than the global average adoption (33%).	
	Upgrading the availability and affordability of DFS around the world can help poor population to move from cash-based transactions to formal digital financial transactions through secured digital platforms (CGAP).		
	- Better personal finance management, quick financial decision-making, and the ability to make and receive money transfer and payments promptly, almost. - A convenient access and use of DFS can provide more suitable digital platforms for individuals to realize basic financial transactions including water supply, payments, money transfer to and from family and friends.	50% are using Fintech for money transfer and payment on 2017 with an anticipated intention of future use up to 65%.	
	The convenient delivery of financial services via digital channels is making the daily financial transactions management easier, cheaper for low-income population.	64% of Fintech users prefer using digital channels to manage their life aspects.	
	Fintech are able to provide instantaneous funds or loans in small amounts to poor individuals with low incomes compared to traditional banks and financial institutions.	The actual use of Fintech borrowing activity is 10% (2017) with a future intention of use up to 20%.	

Furthermore, Fintech as pure player model is mostly respecting the three key factors established Tecee (2010) for a successful business model:

- Value Proposition: Fintech provides convenience and easy access to financial and banking services to underbanked Customers and omitted population worldwide.
- Revenue Model: Fintech has no branches or stores made from bricks and mortar to be maintained. Instead, they are using digital channels, which enables them to focus more on the services value, delivered with low cost.
- Cost Model: Compared to traditional banks that are trying to be perfect at everything, which have some drawbacks, Fintech players have chosen to focus on their core activities: delivering convenient financial and banking services through digital channels with cheaper cost.

The endorsement for the relationship between digital finance, Fintech, DFS and financial inclusion is the clear evidence that numerous of the excluded individuals own a mobile phone. Thus, the delivery of financial and banking services through digital channels namely, mobile phones and related devices can enhance access to the financial and banking transactions for the omitted population (World Bank, 2014).

Despite the raising of Fintech adoption in emerging markets, some challenges for emerging markets are still constraining this digital transformation of traditional financial system and thus, the digital finance and Fintech services adoption. Indeed, at the end of 2018, 51.2% of individuals, or 3.9 billion people, were using the Internet (ITU's Report 2018), which is for sure a progress, but also means that more than 49% of the world's population is not, especially in the least-developed countries when four out of five individuals (80%) are not yet using the Internet. According to the IFC report, World Bank Group (2017), there are four relevant challenges:

- Low penetration of formal financial services: The emerging countries are known for using cash to manage most of the financial transactions. Which is fair since the banking rate remains low, in the range of 10% to 20% in low-income countries (Guérineau & Jacolin, 2014).
- Low income and financial literacy levels: Individuals in the developing countries earn low income (2 USD per day). Consequently, there is low value transactions with smaller fees. In addition, the huge lack on education is a big constraint especially toward IT tools and APIs.
- Underdeveloped technology ecosystems: Besides the dominance in cash transactions, people living in emerging markets are using informal loans and savings in order to coverage of current consumption needs, therefore, limited revenue potential. Moreover, the lack of skilled financial entrepreneurs in IT remains a real obstacle for the ecosystem growth.
- Relative Weak infrastructure: Indeed, emerging countries are suffering from payment underdevelopment payment systems, the weak density of the banking infrastructure (branches, ATMs, etc.) and the quality of transportations. For example, the banking infrastructure density is very low with an average of 3.8 bank branches per 100,000 adults (Guérineau & Jacolin, 2014).

After all, financial inclusion depends on limited access to the traditional financial system, the relevance of the informal financial system enabling poor people to manage their daily basis needs and macro-level elements such as telecommunication, transportations, education, network coverage, etc. Fintech players cannot resolve all those problems by themselves. Hence, Fintech players, banks, financial institutions, government and international institutions must work together to bring a global solution for the stability of financial system reaching the overall purpose: A universal financial inclusion. Nevertheless, we noticed a lack of indicators for measuring the impact of Fintech and DFS on the Bank's performance and Finance in general, which can be an interesting direction for future research.

REFERENCES

Abrams, J., Carraro, M., & Ahmed, W. (2016). *Alternate Delivery Channels for Financial Inclusion: Opportunities and Challenges in African Banks and Microfinance Institutions*. The MasterCard Foundation and Bankable Frontier Associates.

Arner, D. W., Barberis, J. N., & Buckley, R. P. (2015). *The Evolution of Fintech: A New Post-Crisis Paradigm? Academic Press.*

Barberis, J. (2014). *The rise of Fintech: Getting Hong Kong to lead the digital financial transition in APAC*. Academic Press.

Cairnscross, F. (1997). *The death of distance*. Harvard Business Review Press.

Commission Européenne, Eurostat. (1996). La mesure des activités scientifiques et technologiques: Principes directeurs proposés pour le recueil et l'interprétation des données sur l'innovation technologique. In *Manuel d'Oslo*. OCDE.

Contreras, G. (2008). *Internet transactions and business models*. Investigación Review.

Davis, F. D. (1989). Perceived usefulness, perceived ease of use, and user acceptance of information technology. *Management Information Systems Quarterly*, *13*(3), 319–340. doi:10.2307/249008

Davis, F. D., Bagozzi, R. P., & Warshaw, P. R. (1989). User acceptance of computer technology: A comparison of two theoretical models. *Management Science*, *35*(8), 982–1003. doi:10.1287/mnsc.35.8.982

Delmond, M.H., Coelho, F., Keravel, A., & Mahl, R. (2016). *How Information Systems Enable Digital Transformation: A focus on Business Models and Value Co-production*. CIGREF foundation (the French association of CIOs), hal-01369141v2.

Deloitte. (2016). *Disaggregating Fintech: Brighter shades of disruption.* Deloitte Centre for Financial Services.

Dillon, A.P., & Morris, M. G. (1996). User Acceptance of Information Technology: Theories and Models. *Annual Review of Information Science and Technology, 31*, 3-32.

Flanagan, K. (2017). *TimeTrade 2017 State of Retail survey report*. Retrieved from https://www.timetrade.com/blog/state-of-retail-2017-infographic/

Flavián, C., Guinalíu, M., & Torres, E. (2006). How bricks-and-mortar attributes affect online banking adoption. *International Journal of Bank Marketing*, *24*(6), 406–423. doi:10.1108/02652320610701735

Google. (2016a). *Google Adwords-Keywords*. Retrieved from https:/www.google.com/adwords

Google. (2016b). *Google Trends - fintech search term*. Retrieved from https://www.google.com/trends/

Guérineau, S., & Jacolin, L. (2014). L'inclusion financière en Afrique subsaharienne: faits stylisés et déterminants. In *Revue d'économie financière, N° 116* (pp. 57–80). Cairn. doi:10.3917/ecofi.116.0057

Gulamhuseinwala, I., Hatch, M., Lloyd, J., Bull, T., & Chen, S. (2017). *EY FinTech Adoption Index 2017: The rapid emergence of Fintech*. Ernst & Young Global Limited.

Härle, P., Havas, A., & Samandari, H. (2006). *The Future of Bank Risk Management*. Retrieved from https://www.fintech.finance/featured/the-future-of-bank-risk-management/

IMF Communication Department. (2018). The Bali Fintech Agenda: A Blueprint for Successfully Harnessing Fintech's Opportunities. *International Monetary Fund*. Retrieved from https://www.imf.org/en/News/Articles/2018/10/11/pr18388-the-bali-fintech-agenda

Jun, J., & Yeo, E. (2016). Entry of FinTech Firms and Competition in the Retail Payments Market. *Asia-Pacific Journal of Financial Studies*, *45*(2), 159–184. doi:10.1111/ajfs.12126

Karlan, D., Kendall, J., Mann, R., Pande, R., Suri, T., & Zinman, J. (2016). *Research and impacts of Digital Financial Services*. HKS Faculty Research Working paper series, RWP14-037.

Kim, Y., Park, Y.-J., & Choi, J. (2016). The Adoption of Mobile Payment Services for Fintech. *International Journal of Applied Engineering Research*, *11*(2), 1058–1061.

Kunt, D. A., Klapper, L., Singer, D., Ansar, S., & Hess, J. (2018). The Global Findex Database 2017: Measuring Financial Inclusion and the Fintech Revolution. Washington, DC: World Bank. doi:10.1596/978-1-4648-1259-0

Kunt, D. A., Klapper, L., Singer, D., & Oudheusden, P. V. (2015). *E-global findex database 2014 measuring financial inclusion around the world*. World Bank Policy Research Working Paper, (7255).

Mackenzie, A. (2015). The Fintech Revolution. *London Business School Review*, *26*(3), 50–53. doi:10.1111/2057-1615.12059

Moore, G.C. & Benbasat. (1991). Development of an Instrument to Measure the Perceptions of Adopting an Information Technology Innovation. *Information Systems Research, 2*(3), 192-222.

Ozili, P. K. (2018). *Impact of digital finance on financial inclusion and stability*. Borsa Istanbul Review.

Perrin, J. (2001). *Innovation et analyse fonctionnelle*. Congrès AFAV.

Ratten, V. (2008). Technological innovations in the m-commerce industry: Aconceptual model of WAP banking intentions. *Journal of High Technology Management Research, 18*, 111–117.

Rogers, E. M. (1962). *Diffusion of innovations*. New York: Free Press of Glencoe.

Schueffel, P. (2016). Taming the Beast: A Scientific Definition of Fintech. *Journal of Innovation Management, JIM*, *4*, 32–54.

Schumpeter, J. (1951). *Capitalism, Socialism and Democracy*. Payot Edition.

Senach, B. (1990). *Evaluation ergonomique des interfaces homme-machine: une revue de la littérature*. Rapport de recherche, RR-1180, INRIA.

Teece, D. J. (2010). Business Models, Business Strategy and Innovation. *Long Range Planning, Elsevier*, *43*(2–3), 172–194. doi:10.1016/j.lrp.2009.07.003

Thenuan, P., & Raina, A. (2016). Data privacy congress for big data monetization in mobile application. *Researchgate*. Retrieved from https://www.researchgate.net/publication/309012928_DATA_PRIVACY_CONCERNS_FOR_BIG_DATA_MONETIZATION_IN_MOBILE_APPLICATION

Venkatesh, V., Morris, M.G., Davis, G.B., & Davis, F.D. (2003). User Acceptance of Information Technology: Toward a Unified View. *MIS Quarterly, 27*(3), 425-478.

Wilcocks, L., & Plant, R. (2001). Getting from bricks to clicks. *Sloan Management Review*, 50 59.

ENDNOTES

1 See Falk Rieker, "Does the future need banks?" (2 April 2013) SAP, available at http://blogs.sap.com/banking/2013/04/02/does-the-future-need-banks/

2 See Paul Volcker, "The Only thing useful banks have invented in 20 years in the ATM" (13 December 2009) The New York Post, available at: http://nypost.com/2009/12/13/the-only-thing-useful-banks-have-invented-in-20-years-is-the-atm/

Chapter 11
Impact of Crypto-Asset Trade on Financial Stability

Nader Trabelsi
Al-Imam Mohammad Ibn Saud Islamic University, Saudi Arabia

ABSTRACT

The chapter attempts to test the hypothesis that cryptocurrencies are real independent financial instruments that pose no danger to global financial system stability. For the empirical analysis, the authors use data related to bitcoin and widely traded asset classes. They also utilize the copula approach as well as the CoVaR model. The results show a significant role of crypto-asset market in the stability of global markets. Precisely, they find a dependence between bitcoin and oil prices defined by a normal copula model. The empirical results regarding the systemic risk show that extreme changes in bitcoin prices may have an adverse effect on equity and gold markets. There are positive and significant effects of EUR, JPY, and WTI markets when bitcoin goes down. The authors have also shown that after 2016 the virtual market sudden changes are more likely to raise the whole regular financial system losses, except the energy market. These results are important for policymakers and investors.

DOI: 10.4018/978-1-7998-0039-2.ch011

INTRODUCTION

Since its creation in 2009, the usage of Bitcoin has dramatically increased much higher than expected. This dramatic increase has served to embolden the launch of other crypto-assets and brand-new derivative products (e.g. Bitcoin futures and options contracts introduced by CBOE and MSE).[1] The Blockchain technology has led to the development of these markets by capturing the trust of huge users. The crypto ecosystem has thus changed to a big concurrent to mainstream financial system.

As the economic system is becoming more and more digital, the exposition of traders to risk will also increase. The cryptocurrency traders worldwide can face risks associated generally with a combination of factors such as: liquidity conditions, volatile market price swings or flash crashes, leverage of users, and market manipulation. In addition, crypto markets are not regulated by the same controls or customer protections available with regular markets. It is worth to note that these are not all risks of cryptocurrency traders. We should certainly need more experimental and analytical observation studies to document all crypto market risks.

In this chapter, we will first look at the key factors to be taken into account to better understand the risks related to digital markets. We will then discuss the contagion risk from these markets which may be spread to mainstream financial system and highlight the diverse transmission mechanisms and tools that related them to other global markets. This is the main motivation of our study since there is now a growing fear among policymakers and analysts that these digital markets could cause the next global crisis. This is similar to fears, on the role of derivatives markets in financial meltdowns.[2] In this context, a mature body of literature (Stein (1987), Conrad (1989), Bessembinder et al. (1992), among others) has often shown that the phenomenal growth of derivative markets is broadly conducive to global financial crisis, which may raise the question as to whether a similar conclusion can be held for crypto markets.

In line with the Financial Stability Board (FSB) report submitted to the G20 Finance Ministers and Central Bank Governors ahead of their meeting in Buenos Aires on 19-20 March, 2018, the present chapter attempts to test empirically the following hypothesis:

Hypothesis: "Crypto-assets are real independent financial instruments that pose nowadays no material risk to global financial system stability."

It is important to note that there is now an outstanding growth in papers that analyse cryptocurrencies as investment assets (e.g. Cheah and Fry (2015)) or as hedging and safe haven assets (e.g. Bouri et al., 2017b), and as speculative assets instead of functioning as money (e.g., Urquhart (2016), Bariviera (2017)). There are also other papers that focus on the technical aspects and stylized facts of cryptocurrency markets (e.g. Dwyer (2015), Bariviera et al. (2017)) and their risk/return profile (e.g. Liu and Tsyvinski (2018)). The relationship between the digital asset and other global assets are also achieved by Trabelsi (2017) and Corbet et al. (2018). This study seeks to contribute to this small but fast growing economic literature on cryptocurrencies. Precisely, we will take a different approach from previous research, which investigated the contagion risks and captured distress dependence, to assess the systemic risk of cryptocurrencies in the whole economic system. To the best of our knowledge this is the first study that mixed the copula approach and the systemic risk measures of Adrian and Brunnermeier (2016), to investigate the relation between the nascent market of crypto-assets and the regular market defined by selected traded assets such as fiat money, equity markets, and commodities. The time span for this study is from February 02, 2012 to March 08, 2019. Unlike previous studies (e.g. Trabelsi (2017) and Bouri et al. (2018)), our empirical framework takes into account the linear and the non-linear dependence features between series, as well as the relationship among the centre and tails of distributions. We believe that the findings of this chapter will hopefully fill a significant gap in the empirical studies seeking to avoid the fears of crypto markets' systemic risk.

We have shown from the copula approach that there is a significant dependence between Bitcoin and WTI daily changes defined by a normal copula model. We also find the presence of a significant loss of equity and gold markets and a significant gain of EUR, JPY and WTI markets when cryptos were going into distress. As is the case with other results, we have also shown that after 2016 the crypto market sudden changes are more likely to increase the whole regular financial system losses, except for the energy market that exhibits positive spillover effects from the digital system. The debt market appears, however, without reaction in the face to crypto price losses.

The chapter is organized as follows: section 2 explores the broader crypto markets and how they are evolving. It also outlines the sorts of risks related to them and how they can influence the financial stability. Section 3 provides an overview of the financial stability concepts and the measures used in section 4 for the empirical analysis. Section 5 concludes and puts forward a number of recommendations.

CRYPTO TRADING: EVOLUTION AND RISKS

Evolution of Crypto Markets

There are approximately 1500 crypto-assets introduced, about 600 of which are actively traded today.[3] For instance, the market capitalization of Bitcoins has surpassed $800 billion in January 2018, accompanied by a significant jump of trading volumes per day. The daily activate wallet users have to go on rising day by day via the growing interest of new private and institutional users. There are now approximately between 20 and 25 Million users on the crypto-asset trading platforms. Figure 1 shows the exponential growth of the number of users from 2014 to early 2018 in traditional crypto exchanges (i.e., platforms) such as Binance, Coinbase, and Poloniex. It is easy to see that the Coinbase (San Francisco based company) is the most trusted company in the space with about 20 Million costumers actively exchanging tokens and running the various transaction networks.

Bitcoin currently dominates the digital market. Since last December 2018, Bitcoin's price has fallen from $19,000 to $4,000, and the total market value of all digital currencies has contracted by 70% to roughly $200 billion. Despite this dramatic turndown, the Bitcoin market capitalization is more than ten times its value compared to 2015. As can be seen in figure 2, after a period of relative tranquillity the Bitcoin price was going through a super bearish band from 2015 to 2017. After that, the bitcoin is traded within a bullish band since 2018 until Q1-2019.

To characterize the crypto market dynamics better, table 1 resumes the main historical events that have to affect (have affected?) the Bitcoin price significantly.

Figure 1.

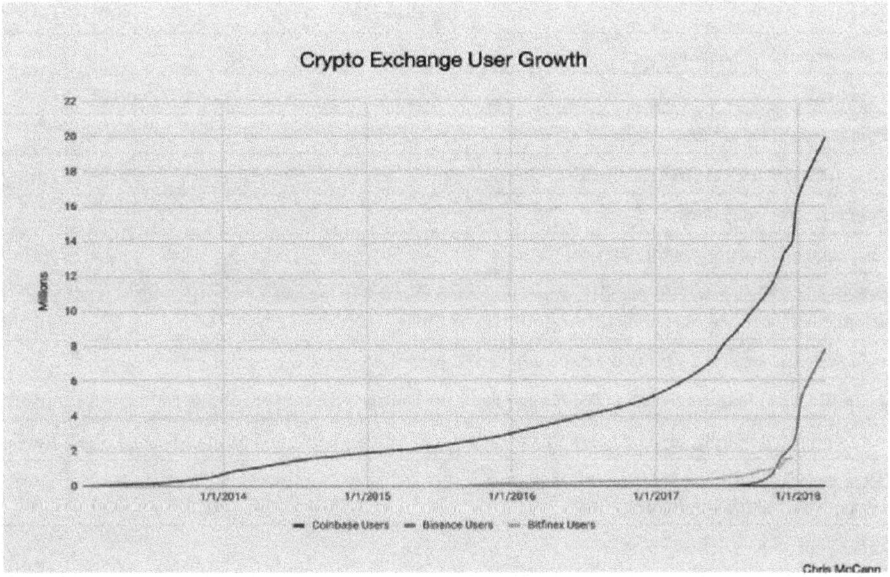

Figure 2.

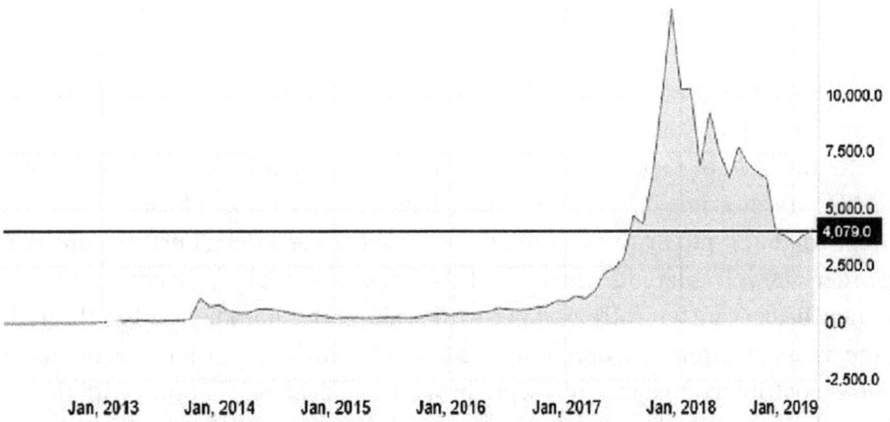

How Do Crypto Markets Alter the Global Financial Stability?

The crypto market has grown rapidly since its emergence. This will certainly boost the economic growth by introducing new opportunities for businesses and consumers. Despite this general acceptance, the crypto market proprieties and promises have not yet been tested (e.g., enhance efficiency, foster new economic value; enable decentralized competition to gatekeepers of the Internet, etc.). In addition to that, this rapid growth of crypto markets can carry several risks (i.e., market liquidity risks, volatility risks, leverage risks, and technological and operational risks) that policymakers, regulators, supervisors, and overseers should consider. This needs also the focus on the transmission channels that may give rise to global financial stability risk. In this sub-section, we are looking mainly at these risks associated with crypto markets and how they potentially affect the regular financial system stability.

Table 1. Bitcoin historical events

Date	Events
2008	The Mysterious Mr. Nakamoto.
2009	Bitcoin begins.
2010	Bitcoin is valued for the first time
2011	Rival cryptocurrencies emerge (NameCoin, Litecoin, etc.)
2013	Bitcoin price was gone down.
2014	Scams and theft (the story of Mt.Gox)
2016	Ethereum and ICOs. (In the US the SEC warned investors that due to the lack of oversight ICOs could easily be scams or Ponzi schemes disguised as legitimate investments. The Chinese government went one further, by banning them outright).
2017	Bitcoin price has reached $10,000 and has continued to grow.
2017	The CBOE Global Markets Inc. and CME Group Inc. have launched their crypto option and futures contracts.
2018	Bitcoin's price fell sharply, dipping below $8,000 as news of tougher regulation from China and South Korea surfaced
Q1 2019	• CBOE suspended Bitcoin Futures. • Nasdaq launched Bitcoin futures.

Source: www.forbes.com

A. Market Liquidity Risks

The 2008 global financial crisis has highlighted the risks related to liquidity. All major financial institutions and governments are acutely aware of the risk that liquidity withdrawal can be a nasty accomplice in transmitting shocks through the system. By definition, the liquidity risk is divided into two types: funding liquidity risk and market liquidity risk. In crypto markets, the latter type seems more accentuated, while due to the limit of their interface compared to other markets, users can be unable to liquid their positions (i.e., transferring, buying or selling). This limited number of users can also contribute to reducing the depth of the crypto markets for relatively large market orders. Furthermore, the situations of large pending orders, as well as large order size in these markets, may also exacerbate risks from volatility.

The brokers and dealers are typically assumed to provide market liquidity. Unlike the traditional financial markets, the trading platforms in crypto markets are globally not registered as regulated exchanges. This situation has contributed to a lack of crypto brokers and dealers. Working with these intermediaries can facilitate the interaction between buyers and sellers; eliminate the need to split a trade up into multiple legs; and help traders to show price differences and take advantage of them by routing orders to the best buy and sell prices for execution. Furthermore, the broker and dealers can enable their retail customers to take advantage of arbitrage opportunities, which are currently accessible to hedge funds using sophisticated automated trading systems. Often because crypto market trading platforms are either not registrable or fail to register. Unlike traditional financial institutions or infrastructures, their activity, in most jurisdictions, is not supervised in any capacity.

In addition to that, crypto derivative markets were first launched in December 2017. For some analysts, these markets will increase the depth and liquidity of the spot crypto market by increasing the demand and by facilitating short-selling. Likewise, others suggest that the presence of derivative markets helps contain speculative dynamics by providing financial instruments to shorten the market. However, trading volumes and open interest on the US-based bitcoin futures exchanges remain relatively small and exchanges have tight position limits and substantial margin requirements for investors.

Lastly, illiquidity, concentrated ownership, fragmented market structure, and other issues also make crypto markets potentially susceptible to price manipulation and other misconduct.

B. Volatility Risks

Crypto-assets are nowadays used both as a way of payments and for speculation. Bohme et al. (2015) argue that crypto asset's exchange rate volatility is of concern to users who are transacting in virtual markets, as well those who are using crypto as a store of value. According to Yermack (2013) and White (2015), the self-organization of different usages both within single crypto and as an element of differentiation between crypto-assets makes the crypto market unique, and their price extremely volatile. This can give rise to several concerns. Precisely, investors may not be prepared to bear exposures to rapid boom/bust cycles. Some crypto-assets, including bitcoin, have been susceptible to fast, deep price fall.

On the other hand, unlike regulated stock and derivatives exchanges, many crypto-asset trading platforms do not have measures such as Market-Wide circuit breakers to stabilize the market when prices are trigged by high up-down moves (e.g., if the SP500 index falls to 7% below its previous close, this is known as Level 1; Level 2 is a 13% drop; Level 3 a 20% drop), even if such measures are required by existing regulations.

Finally, since wallet users are dominated in bitcoin and liabilities are dominated in USD Yermak (2013) argues that the volatility of Bitcoin exchange rate against the USD is particularly problematic to users by creating volatility in the net worth via the volatility of their tax liabilities.

C. Leverage Risks

According to recent statistics by FSB, nearly 20% of the wallet owners used leveraged capital. Furthermore, the margin trading is currently available to crypto-assets investors in some jurisdictions, which may also help wallet owners to improve their act of borrowing funds. As is the case with ordinary market, this higher degree of leverage in crypto markets may magnify volatility and spread risks across financial entities, as losses may exceed investor's initial outlay. On the other hand, the information about the role of leverage in crypto-asset markets is incomplete. Since the available platforms offer online trade for anyone anywhere, and given that transaction information is not stored, this will lose some useful information behind the volume of trade based debt. Therefore, the use of leverage, the margining for crypto-asset derivatives, and financial institution exposures to crypto-asset markets are important metrics of transmission of crypto-asset risks to the broader financial system.

D. Technological and Operational Risks Including Cyber-Security Risks

The Distributed ledger Technology (DLT) that underlies most crypto-assets offers four keys elements: the decentralization of control, the cryptography, the programmability, and the automation. Using this technology has the potential to enhance system resilience; improve the efficiency of end-to-end settlement processes and reporting, auditing and oversight; and enable greater automation. Despite a broad range of use cases, DLT is still a relatively young technology and there are several challenges which must be overcome before it can be deployed at scale in financial services.

E. Transmission Channels Affecting Financial Stability

The primary risks present in the crypto-asset markets could have financial stability implications through a variety of transmission channels. These include:

1. Confidence effects. There's an interesting paradigm related to confidence shift in the digital and convenient systems that are really enhancing the systemic risk. Indeed, the growing range of acceptance on the cryptocurrencies could damage the confidence in financial institutions and regulators. This may shift users from the convenient system to the digital one. At the same time, the confidence in crypto-asset markets themselves can be affected by the presence of a number of risks and costs that come from the errors, fraud and cybercrime related to trading platforms and the application of DLT technology. These conditions may certainly shift users from the digital system to the regular one.

In sum, the confidence reactions that enable users to move from one system to another create perturbations in the whole system.

2. Financial institutions' exposures to crypto-assets. The virtual markets is an attractive prospect for any bank looking to grow its revenues through holding crypto-assets or by creating new banking services or products to wallet owners and firms accepting crypto-assets as a mean of payment. Nevertheless, as the reliance between digital and traditional funding deepens, it may spread financial stress and contribute to the amplification of systemic risk.
3. Level of the market capitalization of crypto-assets. If the crypto market capitalisation grew significantly, this could have an impact on the real economy via wealth effects. For instance, crypto-assets could be used as collateral to get secured personnel loans that can be liquidated to pay any shortfall left by the defaulting borrower. As is the case with any asset, a decline in value of such collateral, may lead to defaults of borrowers and lenders, which in-turn affect the economic activity. On the other hand, a large market capitalisation of crypto-assets and its easy convertibility with fiat currencies could involve new risks to the financial system, mainly if funds were suddenly shifted from deposits into crypto-asset holdings.
4. The extent of their use for payments and settlements. Given their high volatility, less credibility and illiquidity, it will be difficult to use crypto-assets in payments. Moreover, jurisdictions' and monitoring approaches to crypto-assets may further restrain their use in payments. For instance, implementing international AML/CFT standards may limit the anonymity of crypto-asset transactions and reduce their appeal, insofar as anonymity features may drive such use. In addition, approaches directed at, for example, anti-fraud, consumer protection, and/or cyber security safeguards may also affect the business case for certain uses of crypto-assets. These conditions will add to the potential tensions of the digital system for the stability of the whole financial system.

Prior Concepts of Financial Stability

Before developing our empirical analysis on the impact of crypto market trading on financial stability, it would be useful to consider the following definitions. As certain authors argue, financial stability is a broad concept that encompasses the absence of turbulence, low volatility, and the soundness of the institutions or firms in a system. Such a situation is prone to lead to an increase in financial benefits, as it allows participants (i.e., investors, policy makers, etc.) to implement their decision-making process without troubles.

Looking at the nature of the recent crisis (e.g. 2008 global financial crisis, European debt crisis, etc.), several studies have linked their analysis to the financial instability or financial weaknesses hypothesis that central banks and financial regulators should not ignore. The main arguable causes for financial instability are (i) high volatility, (ii) contagion risk, and (iii) systemic risk. According to Adrian and Brunnemeir (2016), the systemic risk increases when the risk associated with the failure of an individual institution propagates through the system and triggers the failure of the system on the whole. This can be also defined as a measure of the increase in tail comovement that can increase due to the spreading of financial distress across related institutions. In this case, contagion is the factor generating fat tails in the distribution.

As the recent turbulence in the global financial system following the failure of Lehman Brothers in September 2008 vividly showed, the contagion risk is extended from the national level to the international one. Looking at their size and complexity, the financial institutions of industrial countries have generated a link between the financial systems of different countries and have fostered an international financial integration. According to Agenor (2003), financial integration will further raise the financial system stability and efficiency, which are required to achieve a faster global economic growth. From the literature on crises in the context of financial globalization, financial integration may also drive costs through contagion, volatility, and loss of macro-economic stability. In fact, several types of research have underlined that markets tend to peak at the same time during a crisis. This situation is usually referred to as spatial contagion. The definition proposed in this study of financial stability is in this direction. In other terms, due to the international integration, any crisis of one of the key markets around the world can propagate to crypto markets and can have more severe negative externalities on the global financial system around the world. These externalities may arise from direct exposures, or from asymmetric information about them or from large failures causing liquidity dry-ups in key markets.

Finally, it is important to note that in parallel to the above segments in the literature that related the financial stability or instability only to the absence of crisis, low volatility or the soundness of institutions, there is another recent segment that attributes the stability of the financial system to its aptitude to (i) facilitate the efficient allocation of economic resources, geographically and over time, as well as other financial and economic processes (such as saving and investment, lending and borrowing, liquidity creation and distribution, pricing and ultimately wealth accumulation and output growth), (ii) assess, prices, allocates, and manages financial risks; and (iii) maintain its ability to perform these key functions even when faced with external shocks or a build-up of imbalances.

The background to this chapter is shaped by the first strand of the literature review that related the financial stability only to the absence of a crisis.

METHODOLOGICAL FRAMEWORK

Studies about systemic risk can be divided into two major groups. One approach consists of using network analysis and works directly on the structure and the nature of relationships between financial institutions in the market. The other approach investigates the impact of one institution on the market and its contribution to the global system risk. In this sub-section, we will only discuss some measures related to the second approach, that will be applied in our empirical analysis.

Classical Dependence Measures

Numerous dependence measures exist in the literature (see Joe, 1997 and Nelson, 2006). The Kolmogorov-Smirnov (K-S) test is one of the most useful statistics and general non-parametric measure for comparing two variables. In this test, we attempt to determine the largest vertical distance between the empirical distribution functions of two samples: $F_1(x)$ and $F_2(x)$. The statistic is

$$D_n = Sup\left|F_1(x) - F_2(x)\right| \tag{1}$$

If the value of the K-S statistic is greater than a critical point, the null hypothesis is rejected.

As an alternative to the K-S test, there is also the Gramér-von Mises (CVM) criterion, which is a criterion used for judging and comparing two empirical distributions. Thus, the statistic is:

$$\omega^2 = \int_{-\infty}^{\infty} \left[F_1(x) - F_2(x)\right]^2 dF(x) \tag{2}$$

The hypothesis of independence is rejected if the approximate p-value is small.

Finally, we can simply use correlation measures which contain (i) Pearson's product moment coefficient, which indicates the strength and direction of a linear relationship between two random variables. (ii) Two well-known nonparametric measures of dependence (based on ranks), related to copula: Spearman's Rho, ρ and Kendall's tau, τ which are described as non-linear correlation measures. The main advantages of these rank correlation measures over ordinary correlation are the invariance under monotonic transformations and the sensible handling of perfect dependence.

Tail Dependence: Copula Approach

According to Bradley and Taqqu (2004), there is contagion from market X to market Y if there is more dependence between X and Y when X is going down than when X exhibits typical performance. That is, if there is more dependence at the loss distribution of X than at its centre. For this reason, the strength of the dependence between X and Y is measured in different regions of the domain of their joint distribution. Durante and Jaworski (2008) have followed the ideas and the motivations by Bradley and Taqqu (2004) to investigate the contagion between two financial markets X and Y, by describing their dependence not by means of the local correlation coefficient, but by using the copula approach. In fact, as well known among people working in applied probability and finance, copulas are functions that enable us to find both the tail dependence and the asymmetric dependence. In addition, the marginal behavior and the dependence structure are separated by the framework of copulas. With this separation, one can find worthy facilities for model specifications and estimation results. Finally, copulas are invariant to increasing and continuous transformations, such as the scaling of logarithm returns, which is commonly used in economic and finance studies. Formally, let H denotes the joint distribution function, and F(x) and G(x) the univariate marginal functions. Notice that the quantile function associated with F is given by

$$F^{[-1]}(\alpha) = \inf\{x : F(x) \geq \alpha\}.$$

In view of Sklar's Theorem, there is a function C, called copula, such that

$$H(x,y) = C(F(x),G(x))\, for\, all(x,y) \in \bar{\mathbb{R}}^2 \tag{3}$$

Despite their usefulness in modelling the average dependence and tail dependence, copula cannot rank the system components according to their contribution and reception of shocks.

Systemic Risk Measures: VaR, CoVaR, and ΔCoVaR

The unusual depth, breadth, and length of the crisis occurred in the past decades (e.g. the 2007-2009 global financial crisis sparked by US subprime market failures, the 2009–2013 European sovereign-debt crises, etc.), has drastically changed the sense of risk exposition from static measures (such as beta and standard deviation) to dynamic measures related to tail distribution with catastrophic losses. Many systemic risk measures have been proposed in the academic literature over the past years (see Benoit et al. 2015 for a survey), the most well-known being the Marginal Expected Shortfall (MES) and the Systemic Expected Shortfall (SES) of Acharya et al. (2010), the Systemic Risk Measure (SRISK) of Acharya et al. (2012) and Brownlees and Engle (2015), and the Delta Conditional Value-at-Risk (ΔCoVaR) of Adrian and Brunnermeier (2016). In our empirical analysis, we will focus only on the latest measure.

As Adrian and Brunnermeier (2016) argue, the CoVaR measure detects the possible risk of spillover between two markets by giving information on the VaR of a market 'j', conditional on the other market 'k' being under extreme events (Reboredo & Ugolini, 2015). This can be expressed as:

$$P\left(X^j \leq CoVaR_{q,t}^{j/k} \mid X^k = VaR_{q,t}^k\right) = q, \tag{4}$$

While CoVaR estimates the size of the tail distribution of the j's market and how it changes, $\Delta CoVar_{q,t}^{j/k}$ can be used to capture particular market returns (denoted by j) when the j market 'k' experiences a return equal to the q-quantile of its unconditional return distribution. By definition, $\Delta CoVaR$ is the difference between its CoVaR when the market 'k' is, or is not, in distress:

$$CoVar_{q,t}^{j/k} = CoVar_{q,t}^{j/k} - CoVar_{50\%,t}^{j/k} \tag{5}$$

Another approach that has been used to illustrate the contagion is the spillover index approach. This is a network-inspired concept that was already developed by Diebold and Yilmaz (2009). The basic spillover index idea is simple but often effective in ranking assets by their systemic importance. The weak connectedness can allow a lower forecasting error variance. Furthermore, an increase in the total spillover index means that there is a rise in the number of links across markets, and hence a higher level of systemic interconnectedness.

In addition to that, the spillover index allows identifying the market that plays a dominant role in information transmission between two markets. To determine how all markets jointly contribute to a single market, we partially aggregate "total directional connectedness."

Introduced by Acharya et al. (2010), the MES of market 'j' is defined as its short-run expected equity loss conditional on another market 'k' incurring a loss greater than its Value-at-Risk(q). This can be also defined as the average return of market 'j' on the α% worse days when the other market 'k' is on the tail of its distribution. Formally, this can be formulated as:

$$MES\left(X_i, q\right) = E\left(X_i \mid X_{oil} \leq VaR\left(X_k, q\right)\right) \quad (6)$$

Accordingly, the MES of market 'j' corresponds to the conditional mean of its return X_j based on the other market return X_k being at or less than the sample q-quantile.

The MES is simple to compute and therefore easy for regulators to consider. This measure has been used by several authors to rank the financial institutions according to their systemic risk since the firms with the highest MES are the largest contributors to the undercapitalization of the financial system in times of distress.

On the other hand, the MES constitutes one of the key elements (with the leverage and the market value) of two popular systemic risk measures, i.e., the SRISK and the SES. The latter is equal to the expected amount by which a financial institution or a market is undercapitalized in a future systemic event in which the overall financial system is undercapitalized (Acharya et al. 2010). Thus, SES tends to increase during the crisis. According to Brownlees and Engle (2015), the SRISK corresponds to the expected capital shortfall of a given financial firm or market j, conditional on a crisis affecting the whole financial system or a market 'k'.

EMPIRICAL ANALYSIS

Literature Review

There are still few empirical works on the general relation between crypto prices and other financial instrument prices. Witold and Srokosz (2015) make an analysis of the dependence of Bitcoin rates on the traditional currencies and other financial instruments (such as S&P index, EUR/USD, as well as gold rates (XAU/USD) or oil prices (CL.F/USD). Using statistical measures (i.e., correlations), they show that there is a very low, or actually no dependency between the BTC rates and the changes in the rates of return for other financial instruments. Furthermore, the correlation between the currency pairs which take into account BTC is very high. These results prove that the financial market does not currently recognize cryptocurrencies as independent instruments, but rather a common basket of currencies which are linked with one another.

The copula approach has been largely utilized by authors to modelling the joint distribution in different markets (equity, bonds, foreign exchanges, commodities, etc.) and among different spatial regions (e.g. European countries, G7, BRICS, GCC, etc.). Bouri et al. (2018) have recently utilized the same approach but with the view to examine the dependence between Bitcoin returns and the global financial stress index (GFSI) introduced by the Bank of America Merill Lynch that can better capture global stress than

VIX[4]. Data used in this study are daily and cover the period between 2010-2017. According to the copula log likelihood, the Gumbel copula allows the best fit for data. Through this type of copula, dependence is mainly defined in the right tail. All other copulas utilized in the study (i.e., Normal, Clayton, Rotated Clayton, Plackett, Frank, Gumbel, Rotated Gumbel, Student's t and symmetrized Joe-Clayton copulas) indicate no tail dependence. The other results showed that global financial stress strongly Granger-causes Bitcoin returns at the left tail (deficient performance) and the right tail (superior performance) but not at the middle (average performance) of the joint distribution. Finally, according to the quantile-to-quantile analysis and revealed evidence of directional predictability from the GFSI to Bitcoin returns, the results suggest that Bitcoin can act as a safe-haven against global financial stress for approximately 60 days.

Trabelsi (2018) has used the spillover index approach to investigate the internality and the externality dependence within the virtual financial system as well as across the Bitcoin index and a widely of traded asset classes (i.e., foreign currencies, equity indices, and commodities). This study shows a low index, which reflects no evidence of spillover effects across the virtual currency market and other markets. The digital markets are thus not perfectly integrated to the real economy and they cannot pose any danger to the instability of the financial system. Concerning the connectedness within the cryptocurrency market, the study reported the presence of a time-frequency-dynamics connectedness nature. Cryptos are so heavily exposed to each other's risks. Using similar models, Corbet et al. (2018a) examine also the relation between three major cryptocurrencies (i.e., Bitcoin, Ripple and Litecoin) and other assets (i.e., the MSC GSCI Total Returns Index, the US$ Broad Exchange Rate, the SP500 Index and the COMEX closing gold price, VIX and the Markit ITTR110 index). Authors find evidence of a relative isolation of the virtual assets from regular ones. They also show that cryptocurrencies may offer diversification benefits for investors with short investment horizons. Finally, time variation in the linkages reflects external economic and financial shocks. More recently, Kumar and Suvvari (2019) study the dynamics of volatility spillover across four major cryptocurrency returns. Using an IGARCH (1,1)-DCC (1,1) multivariate GARCH model to estimate the nature of volatility spillover, they find that there is statistically significant volatility spillover among the crypto-currency returns mainly after 2017. Using Wavelet coherence measures, they also provide evidence that correlation among the cryptocurrencies is persistent across the short-run. Concerning the volatility of virtual market, Baek and Elbeck (2015) conclude that the Bitcoin market is highly speculative. However, Blau (2018) finds that this speculative trading did not have any relationship with the 2013 Bitcoin price increases or the dramatic increases in its volatility.

Studying the tail behavior of the returns of five major cryptocurrencies by using VaR and ES, Gkillas and Katsiampa (2018) find that Bitcoin Cash is the riskiest cryptocurrency, while Bitcoin and Litecoin are the least risky. Peng et al. (2018) provide an evaluation of the predictive performances of the volatility of crypto-currencies. Using daily and hourly-frequency data, they found that the Support Vector Regression (SVR)-GARCH methodology managed to outperform that of GARCH, EGARCH and GJR-GARCH models with Normal, Student's t and Skewed Student's t distributions. On the other hand, Phillip et al. (2018) used a cross-section analysis of 224 different cryptocurrencies to identify several unique properties including leverage effects and Student-t error distributions. Jang and Lee (2017) use Bayesian Neural Networks (BNN) while incorporating the underlying fundamentals of Bitcoin to present evidence of a well-performed predictor of Bitcoin price time series while explaining the high volatility of Bitcoin in recent times.

Data and Descriptive Analysis

For the crypto market, we use BTC daily change data. For other markets, our data cover the daily changes for three stock indexes (i.e., SP500, DOW30 and Shanghai indexes) and the 10 years of US Treasury notes. For the currencies, we retain EUR/USD, GBP/USD and USD/JPY daily change data. We limit also our attention to the daily changes of Gold and crude oil WTI futures contracts launched by COMEX and NYMEX, respectively. The data span is from February 02, 2012 to March 08, 2019, with a total of 1662 daily observations. The summary statistics of this data can be found in Table 2.

Following Table 2, it is observed that the average return varies within the examined markets. The SP500 and BTC give the greatest couple mean/variance to the other series, respectively. The skewness is mixed, with some asset classes having a skewness that is positive, implying that there is a greater chance that the series go up rather than down during our period sample (e.g., Shanghai index and WTI). Compared with the normal density, kurtosis of all series is higher than 3, which can reflect the presence of fat tails.

Results and Interpretation

In order to examine dependence and discuss how systemic and non-systemic factors drove the relation between the famous crypto-assets and several other asset classes, we utilize the correlation measures then we implement the quantile measure analysis.

Following Table 3, results of combining Pearson's correlation coefficient, Spearman's rank correlation coefficient and Kendall tau rank correlation coefficients show the presence of a weaker dependence between BTC daily changes and the selection traded assets. These findings are interesting, but they may not be the most suitable measure of joint failures since they focus on the centrality of distributions, which is appropriate if the true dependence structure is linear.

Table 2. Summary statistics of daily returns related to BTI and several asset classes.

	BTI	SP500	Dow30	Sh	EUR	JPY	GBP	US TN10Y	WTI	GOLD
Mean	0.41	0.6	0.04	0.01	3.0 e-4	0.023	2.44e-3	-1.31e-3	0.02	-8.67e-4
Median	0.22	0.09	0.06	0.60	0.00	0.020	0.00	0.00	0.08	0.01
Maximum	36.15	6.16	4.98	5.76	3.07	2.86	3.03	1.23	11.22	4.66
Minimum	-100	-4.50	-4.60	-8.49	-2.38	-3.70	-8.06	-2.16	-8.67	-9.35
Std. Dev.	5.52	1.00	0.80	1.40	0.51	0.57	0.54	0.28	2.06	1.05
Skewness	-3.315	-28.6	-0.36	-0.90	0.23	-0.31	-1.80	-0.36	0.20	-0.42
Kurtosis	70.35	6.15	6.67	9.41	5.27	6.54	32.58	6.23	5.73	8.98
J-B	54.0544	711	968.33	3072	372.66	898.72	61482	761.55	530.49	2526.1
Prob.	0.00	0.00	0.00	0.00	0.00	0.00	0.00	0.00	0.00	0.00
ADF Obs.	-39.12* 1663	41.2* 1663	-41.12* 1663	-39.34* 1663	-3.53* 1663	-0.93 1662	-17.71* 1662	-17.37* 1662	-0.35 1662	-18.40* 1662

Data concern daily returns of BTC - equity indices – Exchange rate – Gold - WTI- Bonds for the period of 02/02/2012 to 08/03/2019. Dow Jones 30 industrial index (DW30), Standard & Poor's 500 (SP500), EUR (EUR/USD), JPY (USD/JPY), GBP (GBP/USD), West Texas Intermediate crude oil (WTI), Shanghai index (Sh) and US Treasury notes 10 Years (US TN10Y).

Table 3. Pearson's product-moment, Spearman's rank correlation, and Kendall's Rank correlation tau

BTC	Pearson's Product-Moment Correlation (%)	Spearman's Rank Correlations RHO (%)	Kendall's Rank Correlation Tau (%)
DW30	-0.69	-1.26	-0.80
SP500	-0.19	-1.35	-1.87
Sh	3.19	-3.56	-0.24
Nikkei225	1.10	-1.77	-1.17
EUR	-0.98	-3.13	-2.06
JPY	-1.05	1.87	1.31
GBP	0.31	0.12	0.10
Gold	1.74	1.87	1.28
WTI	-5.02	-3.47	-2.27
US TN10Y.	1.00	0.18	0.20

Note: Data concern daily returns of BTC - equity indices – Exchange rate – Gold - WTI- Bonds for the period of 02/02/2012 to 08/03/2019. Dow Jones 30 industrial index (DW30), Standard & Poor's 500 (SP500), EUR (EUR/USD), JPY (USD/JPY), GBP (GBP/USD), West Texas Intermediate crude oil (WTI), Shanghai index (Sh) and US Treasury notes 10 Years (US TN10Y).

Extreme quantile dependence functions can better describe tail dependence than correlation measures. For that reason, we start by fitting univariate ARMA (1, 1) - GARCH (1, 1) model for each return series, assuming normal innovations[5]. In this case, conditional mean and variance equations of daily changes of BTC and different examined markets can be expressed as

$$r_t = \mu + \varnothing r_{t-1} + \varepsilon_t + \theta\varepsilon_{t-1}, \varepsilon_t = \sigma_t z_t \tag{7}$$

$$\sigma_t^2 = \omega + \alpha\varepsilon_{t-1}^2 + \beta\sigma_{t-1}^2 \tag{8}$$

with $z_t \rightsquigarrow$ normal distribution. Where r_i denotes return at t, μ_t is the conditional mean (7), σ_t^2 is the conditional variance (8). ω, α and β are non-negative.

After that, we generate standardized residuals from the estimation (i.e., the residual divided by the standard deviation of the residual). The obtained series will be used in the estimation of left and right tails.

Figure 3 provides a preliminary idea of the extreme relation between BTC returns and several traded assets. The plots are closely similar where they exhibit the same visual trend at the lower and upper tails, suggesting the presence of a strong long-term relationship at the right (i.e., extreme positive returns) and independence otherwise, except WTI and Sh which present a weak left dependency. The Bitcoin market daily changes move asymmetrically to the main market changes with a positive response to increases rather than decreases in their prices. This finding indicates that the crypto market is prosperous when other asset classes are strongly positive. We can so think here of the copula model as having these relations.

Table 4 resumes the selected copula for each pair.

The results of table 4 are related to the copula function selecting from a range of methods. The corresponding parameter estimates are obtained by maximum likelihood estimation using pseudo-observations defined as normalized ranks. The finding shows that there are relative traded relations between bitcoins and some traded assets. Nonetheless, once we perform the independence test several relation pairs become compatible with the independent copula, except the Gaussian copula of the pair BTC-WTI is significant.

Figure 3.

1) BTC vs. DW

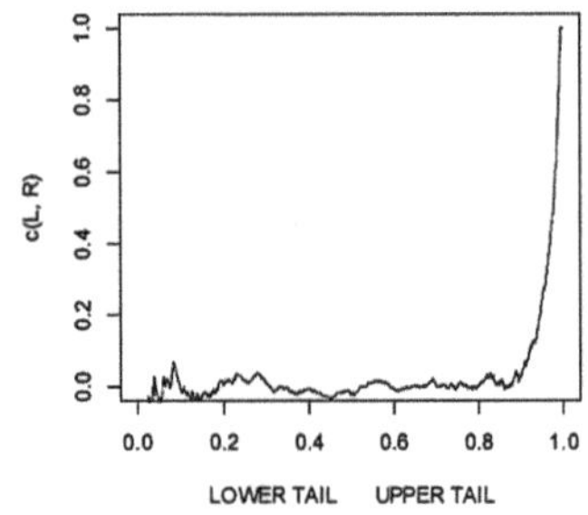

BTC vs. SP500

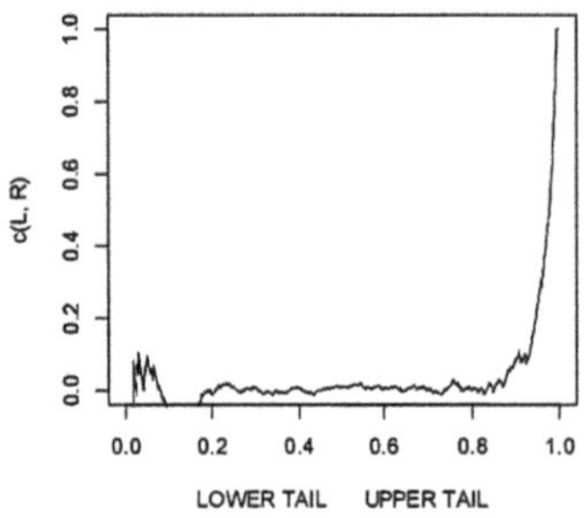

BTC vs. Sh.

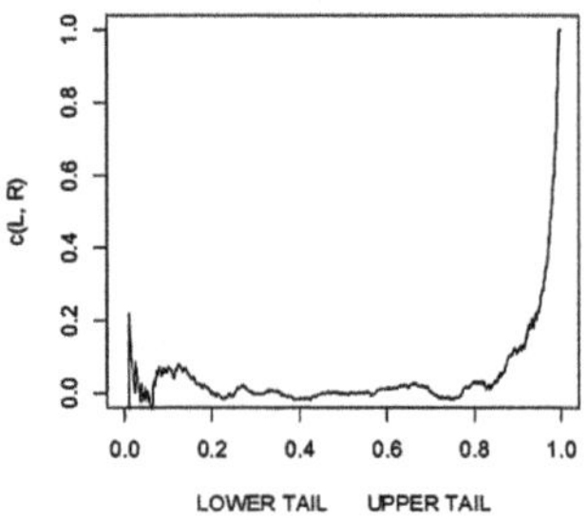

2) BTC vs. EUR

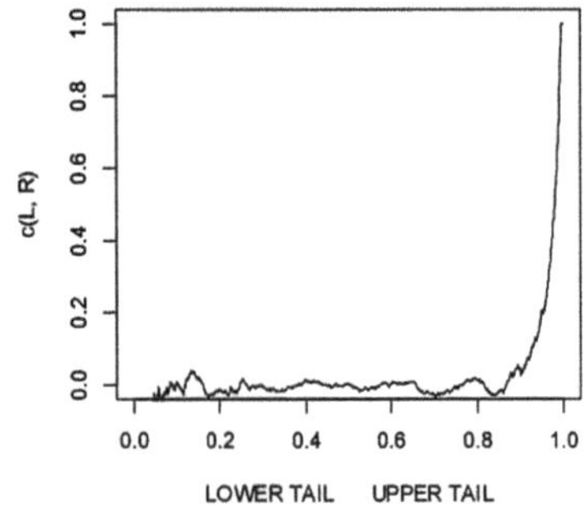

BTC vs. JPY

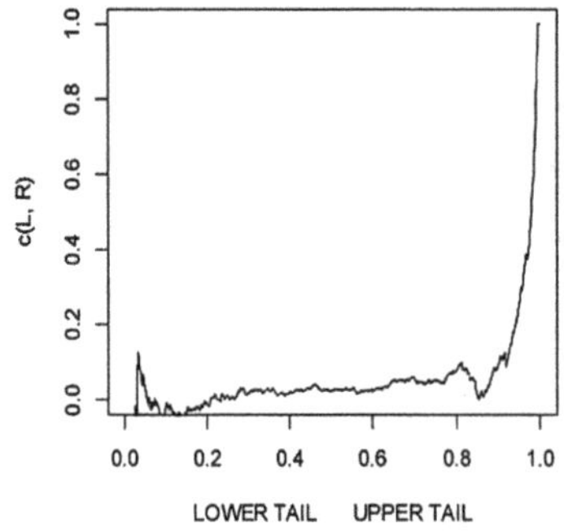

BTC vs. GBP

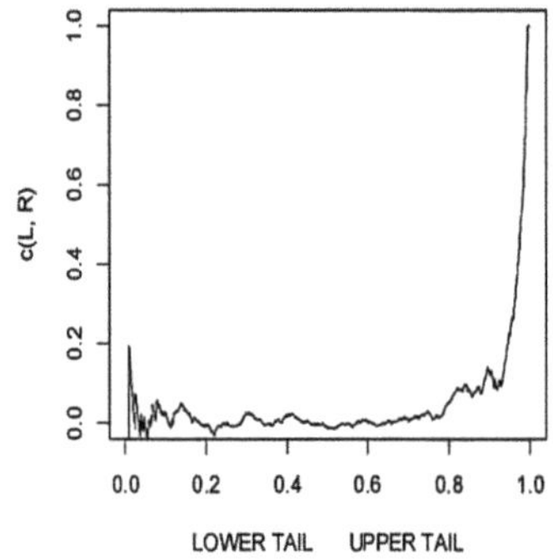

3) BTC vs. TN10Y

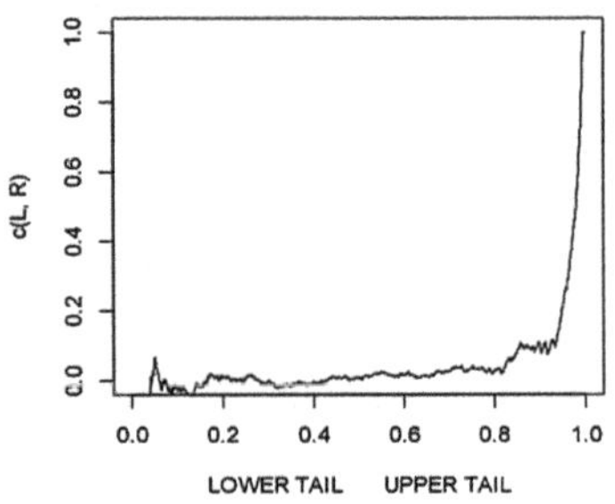

BTC vs. WTI

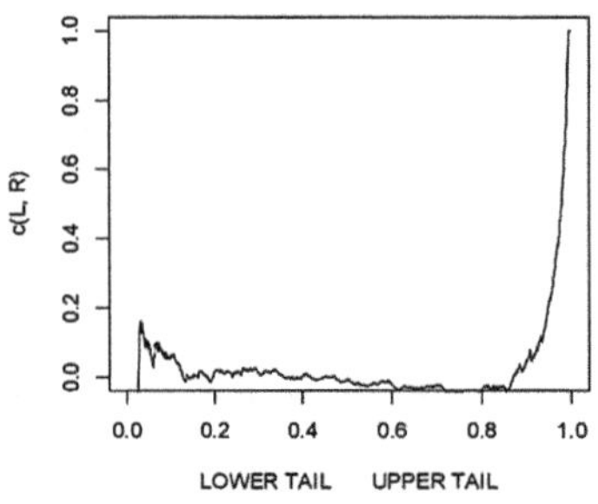

BTC vs. Gold

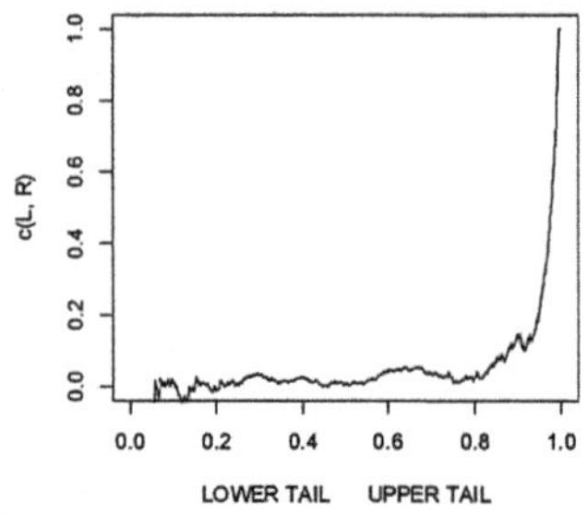

Table 4. Parametric estimation of the selected bivariate copula

	Par1 (SE)	Par2 (SE)	Tau	Family
DW30	-0.04	0.00	-0.02	23
SP500	0.00	0.00	0.00	0
Sh	0.00	0.00	0.00	0
EUR	-1.02	0.00	-0.02	34
JPY	0.05	0.00	0.02	3
GBP	-1.30	0.03	-0.02	234
Gold	0.00	0.00	0.00	0
WTI	-0.07*	0.00	-0.04*	1
US TN-10Y	20.00	0.00	0.00	214

Note: Standardized residuals are from ARMA-GARCH estimation. Par1 and par2 are the scalar parameters of the model. Test of independence significance (*). 0 (Independent copula), (1) Gaussian copula, (3) Clayton copula, (23) Rotated Clayton 90°, (34) Rotated Gumbel 270°, (214) Rotated Tawn type2 180° and (234) Rotated Tawn type2 270°.

To measure the contribution of the virtual market to the systemic risk, we use the dynamic VaR, CoVaR and ΔCoVaR measures. We select these measures because they have been substantially discussed in the recent literature and can be easily used by regulators and other practitioners to monitor day-to-day financial stability.

To perform the daily ΔCoVaRs, we use the DCC-MGARCH model and for the robustness check, we will focus on the GO-GARCH (MLS) model. Here, the financial system distress is defined by the $VaR^{s}_{0.05,t}$ of each selected traded assets. $VaR^{BTC}_{0.05,t}$ denotes, however, the loss of the virtual market for a probability level 0.05. According to Adrian and Brunnermeier (2016), ΔCoVaR captures the virtual market's contribution to systemic risk. This also measures how the VaR of the system changes when BTC becomes financially distressed.

Following table 5, the results related to DCC and GO-GARCH models are quite similar. From the panel "a" it is easy to observe that the mean values of VaR and CoVaR are negatives and differ among markets. The crude oil market has, on average, a significant excess (in absolute values) of VAR, CoVaR, and ΔCoVoR; this is probably due to the long period of energy price instability starting in mid-2014.

ΔCoVaR measure indicates the contribution of the virtual market to each asset exposure risk, i.e., how sensitive the ordinary system is when the virtual market going into distress. In other words, it is an estimation of how much a virtual market adds for instance to VaR of equity index when moving from

Table 5. VaR, CoVaR and ΔCoVaR

	DW	SP500	Sh	EUR	JPY	GBP	Gold	WTI	USTN10Y
Panel a. DCC Method									
VaR(0.05)	-1.26	-1.65	-2.07	-0.78	-0.86	-0.82	-1.69	-3.30	-0.47
CoVaR	-1.27	-1.99	-3.68	-0.44	-0.57	-0.56	-2.04	-7.38	-0.13
ΔCoVaR	-0.02	-0.07	-0.06	0.01	0.01	0.00	-0.04	0.23	0.00
Panel b. GO-GARCH Method									
VaR(0.05)	-1.26	-1.65	-2.07	-0.78	-0.86	-0.82	-1.69	-3.30	-0.47
CoVaR	-1.06	-1.67	-3.54	-0.42	-0.54	-0.44	-1.89	-6.49	-0.13
ΔCoVaR	0.00	0.04	-0.36	0.01	0.00	0.04	-0.09	0.45	0.00

the median state to the 5% VaR level. Following table 5, we show that ΔCoVaR statistics are however mixed. The negative sign and the higher values of ΔCoVaR indicate a higher contribution of the virtual market to the instability of the ordinary system. This is associated for instance with the examined equity index and the gold market. However, the positive sign corresponds in general to the stability effects. This is the situation of the EUR, JPY, and WTI data.

The bottom panel of Table 5 reports mean statistics relative to CoVaR and ΔCoVaR with respect to the estimation of GO-GARCH model. The statistics improve the robustness of our results based on the DCC model that demonstrate the presence of many cases where the mean of CoVaRs is slightly more than their isolation VaRs. Hence, it is possible to draw here the conclusion that the virtual market can trigger, on average, the instability of the real economy. This conclusion seems important to regulators' who underestimate the risks of the crypto market until today. Moreover, this conclusion is in the opposite to previous studies that support the point that it couldn't happen contagion effects through both systems (see Trabelsi, 2018).

Figures 4, 5 and 6 report the dynamic evolution of VaRs, CoVaRs, and ΔCoVaRs. This is important to better understand the dependence between the virtual and real systems during calm and distress periods

The graphs of figure 4 show that there are several periods of significantly larger loss in the virtual market and the selected traded assets such as the energy markets. Indeed, a deeper investigation of these results reveals that the virtual market showed non-persistence downturn trend with a large one at near mid-2016. This seems different from other markets which show persistent volatility in the general distress periods. On the other side, there is a significantly larger loss of virtual market during the periods of real economic downturn (e.g., correspond mainly to the 2013 decline price of gold and mid-2014

Figure 4.

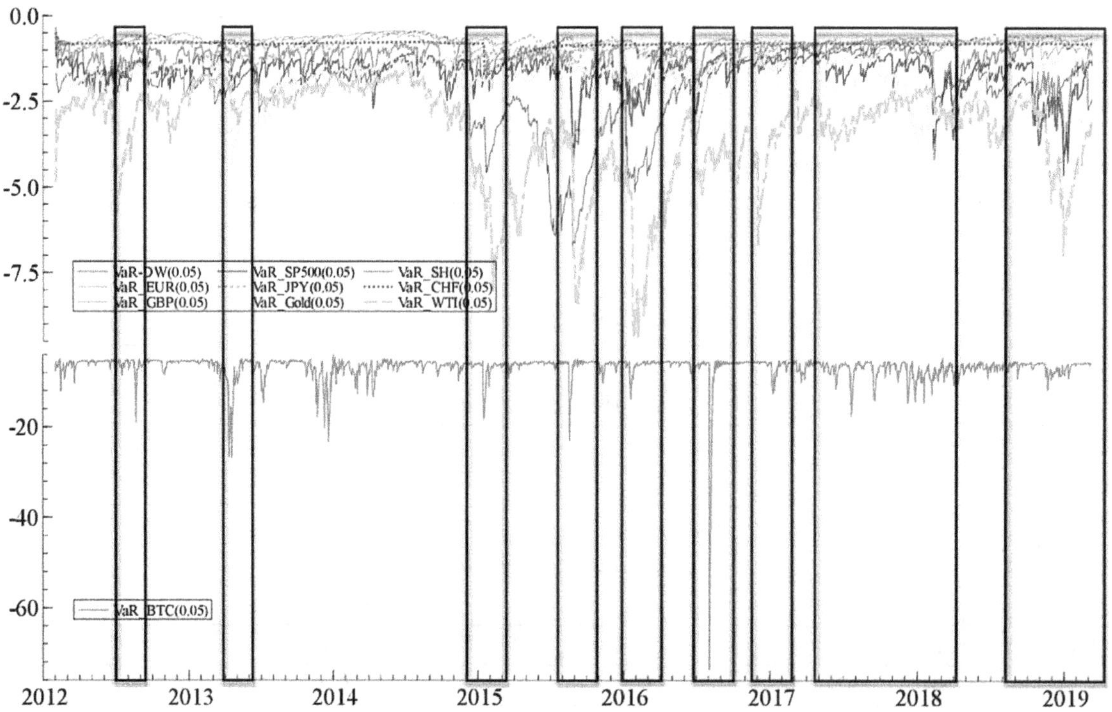

decline of oil prices). These periods are designed by rectangles in the figure and appear more frequent after 2016. The latter effectively implies the contribution of the virtual market sudden change to raise the whole real system losses.

The graphs of figure 5 show that there is a similarity between VaR and CoVaR time-varying of each series, but with a larger difference in magnitude. Except for US TN 10Y, EUR and JPY series, one can easily show strong pick down of CoVaRs compared to their isolated VaRs during distress periods. These differences between conditional and unconditional losses reflect the contribution of the virtual system to intensify the crisis. Hence contrary to, as can be expected (i.e., no spillover effects), the virtual market has a significant adverse effect on the stability of the US and China equity markets, as well as the gold market. The debt market is, however, less affected by the virtual traded.

Figure 6 shows the evolution of the ΔCoVaR over the sample following the DCC and GO-GARCH models. The result confirms our previous analysis that supports the adverse effects of the virtual trade on the China equity market during turmoil periods. The adverse effect on the US equity markets detected by the DCC estimation is, however, non-robust (i.e., non-confirmed by the GO-GARCH model). On the other side, one can see a positive trend in ΔCoVaR series, which may be a sign of health. Precisely, the virtual market could pose robustness stability effects onto the energy market as it can limit and resolve its imbalances.

CONCLUSION

In sum, the growth of crypto-asset trading platforms, the introduction of crypto derivatives, and the growing interest by retail investors have rendered crypto markets more related to ordinary markets. Precisely, we have shown from the copula approach that there is a significant dependence between Bitcoin and WTI daily changes defined by a normal copula model. Given the results related to systemic measures, we retain also the presence of a significant reaction of the regular system when the virtual market is going into distress. This reaction differs from one market to another, where it is, on average, negative (i.e., destabilize effects) to equity and gold markets and positive (i.e., stability effects) with the EUR, JPY, and WTI data. Given a dynamic analysis of VaRs, CoVaRs, and ΔCoVaRs over the sample period, we have also shown that after 2016 the virtual market sudden changes are more likely to raise the whole regular financial system losses, except for the energy market that exhibits positive spillover effects from the virtual system. The debt market appears without reaction in the face to Bitcoin price losses. These results are consistent with Selmi et al. (2018) who show that both Bitcoin and gold would serve the roles of a hedge, a safe haven and a diversifier for oil price movements.

These results seem important to better understand the dependence between the virtual and real systems during calm and distress periods. It appears mainly that the risk for crypto markets to destabilize the global financial system has become more relevant after 2016. This can result in the exponential growth of their size and number of users, and the huge increase in their prices. Before this date, our results seem in line with the conclusions of several central banks and other regulatory authorities (e.g. Reserve Bank of Australia (2014) and Federal Advisory Committee(2014). The European Central Bank's position is similar to that of other central banks (ECB,2015)) which conclude that crypto-currencies do not pose a serious danger to the operation of payment systems, monetary policy, price stability and financial stabil-

Figu

Pa

ity, in part because mainstream financial systems continue to predominate. Moreover, the use of virtual currencies remains limited and the European Central Bank (ECB) feels no immediate threat (For more details see report of Reserve Bank of New Zealand published by Kumar and Smith (2017)).

These results have several implications for (i) investors in their risk management practices. Precisely, they should be aware of the negative co-movements with the crypto-assets and equity markets in the turmoil periods. (ii) regulators and policymakers who should act now to monitor the financial stability implications of developments in crypto-asset markets and put in place prudential measures to identify early or predictive signs of a shock and palliative actions in the event a global financial shock.

REFERENCES

Acharya, V. V., Engle, R., & Richardson, M. (2012). Capital shortfall: A new approach to ranking and regulating systemic risks. *The American Economic Review*, *102*(3), 59–64. doi:10.1257/aer.102.3.59

Acharya, V. V., Pedersen, L. H., Philippon, T., & Richardson, M. (2010). *Measuring systemic risk*. NYU Working Paper.

Agenor, P.-R. (2003). Benefits and Costs of International Financial Integration: Theory and Facts. *World Economy*, *26*(8), 1089–1118. doi:10.1111/1467-9701.00564

Andrian, T., & Brunnermeier, M. (2016). CoVaR. *The American Economic Review*, *106*(7), 1705–1741. doi:10.1257/aer.20120555

Baek, C., & Elbeck, M. (2015). Bitcoins as an investment or speculative vehicle? A first look. *Applied Economics Letters*, *22*(1), 30–34. doi:10.1080/13504851.2014.916379

Bariviera, A. F. (2017). The Inefficiency of Bitcoin Revisited: A Dynamic Approach. *Economics Letters*, *161*, 1–4. doi:10.1016/j.econlet.2017.09.013

Benoit, S., Colliard, J.-E., Hurlin, C., & Perignon, C. (2015). *Where the risks lie: A survey on systemic risk*. Unpublished Working Paper.

Bessembinder, H., & Paul, J. (1992). Futures-Trading Activity and Stock Price Volatility. *The Journal of Finance*, *47*(5), 2015–2034. doi:10.1111/j.1540-6261.1992.tb04695.x

Blau, B. M. (2018). Price dynamics and speculative trading in Bitcoin. *Research in International Business and Finance, Elsevier*, *43*(C), 15–21. doi:10.1016/j.ribaf.2017.07.183

Bollerslev, T., Chou, R. Y., & Kroner, K. F. (1992). ARCH modeling in finance: A selective review of the theory and empirical evidence. *Journal of Econometrics*, *52*(1-2), 5–59. doi:10.1016/0304-4076(92)90064-X

Bouri, E., Azzi, G., & Dyhrberg, A. H. (2017b). On the return-volatility relationship in the Bitcoin market around the price crash of 2013. Economics-The Open-Access. *Open-Assessment E-Journal*, *11*, 1–16.

Bouri, E., Das, M., Gupta, R., & Roubaud, D. (2018). Spillovers between Bitcoin and other assets during bear and bull markets. *Journal of Applied Econometrics*, *50*(55).

Bradley, B., & Taqqu, M. S. (2005). How to Estimate Spatial Contagion between Financial Markets. Finance Letters, 3(1), 64–76. Retrieved from https://ssrn.com/abstract=714143

Brownlees, C. T., & Engle, R. F. (2015). *Srisk: A Conditional Capital Shortfall Measure of Systemic Risk*. ESRB Working Paper Series from European Systemic Risk Board.

Cheah, E., & Fry, J. (2015). Speculative bubbles in Bitcoin markets? An empirical investigation into the fundamental value of Bitcoin. *Economics Letters, 130*, 32-36.

Conrad, J. (1989). The Price Effect of Option Introduction. *The Journal of Finance, 44*(2), 487–498. doi:10.1111/j.1540-6261.1989.tb05068.x

Corbet, S., Lucey, B., & Yarovaya, L. (2018a). Datestamping the bitcoin and ethereum bubbles. *Finance Research Letters, 26*, 81–88. doi:10.1016/j.frl.2017.12.006

Diebold, F. X., & Yilmaz, K. (2009). Measuring Financial Asset Return and Volatility Spillovers, With Application to Global Equity Markets. *Economic Journal (London), 119*(534), 158–171. doi:10.1111/j.1468-0297.2008.02208.x

Durante, F., & Jaworski, P. (2008). Absolutely continuous copulas with given diagonal sections. *Communications in Statistics. Theory and Methods, 37*(18), 2924–2942. doi:10.1080/03610920802050927

Dwyer, G. P. (2015). The economics of Bitcoin and similar private digital currencies. *Journal of Financial Stability, 17*, 81–91. doi:10.1016/j.jfs.2014.11.006

Gkillas, K., & Katsiampa, P. (2018). An application of extreme value theory to cryptocurrencies. *Economics Letters, 164*, 109–111. doi:10.1016/j.econlet.2018.01.020

Hansen, B. (1994). Autoregressive Conditional Density Estimation. *International Economic Review, 35*(3), 705–730. doi:10.2307/2527081

Jang, H., & Lee, J. (2017). An empirical study on modeling and prediction of bitcoin prices with Bayesian neural networks based on blockchain information. *IEEE Access: Practical Innovations, Open Solutions, 6*, 5427–5437. doi:10.1109/ACCESS.2017.2779181

Joe, H. (1997). *Multivariate Models and Dependence Concepts*. London: Chapman and Hall. doi:10.1201/b13150

Kumar, A., & Smith, C. (2017). *Crypto-currencies – An introduction to not-so-funny moneys*. Reserve Bank of New Zealand Analytical Note Series.

Kumar, A. S., & Suvvari, A. (2019). Volatility spillover in crypto-currency markets: Some evidences from GARCH and wavelet analysis. *Physica A, 524*.

Liu, Y., & Tsyvinski, A. (2018). *Risks and Returns of Cryptocurrency* (Working Paper No. 24877). National Bureau of Economic Research. doi:10.3386/w24877

Nakamoto, S. (2008). *Bitcoin: A Peer-to-Peer Electronic Cash System*. Unpublished working paper. Retrieved from https://bitcoin.org/bitcoin.pdf

Nelsen, R. B. (2006). *An Introduction to Copulas* (2nd ed.). New York: Springer Verlag.

DOI: 10.4018/978-1-7998-0039-2.ch012

The declining use of cash[9] in advanced economies and financial inclusion in emerging market and developing economies are considered as the two main reasons of the CBDC issuance (Mancini-Griffoli et al., 2018). The central banks that are more seriously considering issuing CBDCs are those that face a reduction in the use of cash (De Lis, 2018). The CBDC is not designed to replace cash but rather to be an additional digital option for non-banks to hold money. As demonstrated by Engert and Fung (2017), the use of cash relative to others payment is declined in many developed countries notably in Sweden[10]. Thereby, there is a need for adequate central bank money for the public. However, Panetta (2018) and Judson (2018) consider that the cash as physical central bank money remains the dominant mean of payment in many countries like the euro area and thereby the CBDC issuance with its characteristics remains an open question. Khiaonarong and Humphrey (2019), note that the level and trend in cash use in a country will influence the demand for CBDC. They explain that the demand for CBDC is weak in countries where cash use is already very low, due to a preference for cash substitutes (cards, electronic money, mobile phone payments), however, where cash use is very high, demand should be stronger, due to a lack of cash substitutes.

There are several roles that CDBC can play such as the improvement of the efficiency of the payment system, being an additional tool to control the financial system stability, allowing access to central bank currencies for individuals and firms. CBDC would have to ensure the fulfillment of anti-money laundering, counter-terrorism financing (AML/CFT) requirements, as well as limiting tax evasion (Coeuré and Loh, 2018)[11]. CBDC can be an alternative safe payment instrument, it ensures more contestability in retail and large value payments and increases the efficiency in payments. CBDC guarantees the speed of transactions and low transaction costs (Oubdi and Raghibi, 2018). Thereby, the efficiency of blockchain technology can be improved if the system is centralized as the decentralized system is more expensive. In addition, CBDC is considered as "helicopter money"[12] and could facilitate a direct transfer of central bank funds to general people and encourages aggregate demand (Dyson and Hodgson, 2016).

Design and Features of CBDC

CBDC is defined as a monetary value stored electronically and can be used to make payments (Fung and Halaburda, 2016). Like cash, the CBDC is a liability of the central bank and would be widely accessible to the general public as legal tender. CBDC is a new form of money, issued digitally by the central bank and intended to serve as legal tender and designed for retail payments (Mancini-Griffoli et al., 2018). The idea of CBDC accessible to the general public in the form of a deposit at the central bank was mentioned by Tobin (1987)[13]. Tobin (1987) recommend that the government create "deposited currency accounts" (DCAs) at the central bank: "*I think the government should make available to the public a medium with the convenience of deposits and the safety of currency, essentially currency on deposit, transferable in any amount by check or other order*." Coeuré and Loh (2018) distinguished various design choices for CBDC in terms of access (restricted e.g. limit access to predefined group vs widely e.g. accessible to users); the degree of anonymity (from complete to none); interest bearing characteristics (or interest-free) and operational availability (ranging from current opening hours to one day to a week). A stable, trusted, and fully anonymous CBDC could be ideally suited for illicit transactions (Agur, 2018). Unlike fiat and metal money, digital currencies cannot be altered, forged, or manipulated (Muedini, 2018). CBDC is better in storing currencies as it is done digitally, and people can access anywhere with private keys.

The CBDC establishes a monetary relationship between the central bank and economic agents. As a legal tender, the CBDC can be held by all or a restricted set of economic agents for retail or wholesale payment. The key innovation with CBDC is to allow non-banks (individuals and firms) to hold direct accounts with the central banks (centralized technology) or to transact directly with one another (state-backed token) without the direct involvement of the central bank (Decentralized technology) (Ahmat and Bashir, 2017). Regarding the technology, the payment through CBDC can be supported by distributed ledger technology and cryptography technologies. The distributed ledger technology allows a digital currency to be used in a decentralised payment system. Thereby, as central bank digital liability, CBDC can be exchanged directly through decentralised system or peer-to-peer characterized by its anonymity and the absence of intermediary. In this case, the design of the CBDC is quite similar to physical cash except the fact that the CBDC is digital. However, when CBDC is exchanged through centralised system it is similar to bank deposit or central bank reserves, with the presence of an intermediary and the absence of anonymity. In both payment systems, the CBDC can be limited to a set of economic agents and with or without interest bearing.

Furthermore, the CBDC can be interest- bearing with positive, zero or negative rates or a non-interest-bearing which could be considered as e-cash. The interest-bearing form of CBDC hold by individuals and firms involves the central bank directly in the intermediation banking activity which means a new role of the central banks in the banking system and in economic activities. The CBDC could solve the "zero lower bound" problem because when money circulates in the physical form it is difficult to implement policy interest rates below zero (Rogoff, 2014)[14]. When CBDC is interest bearing, it can be a substitute of money market instruments, such as government bills, reverse repos. If it is not interest bearing, CBDC would be analogous to physical cash. A non-interest bearing CBDC would be a better substitute for cash (He et al., 2017). When CBDC looks like cash it enjoys many characteristics such as anonymity[15], immediate settlement, non-interest bearing, non-exclusive access, make retail payments without fees for distributing/exchanging or storing and a distributed ledger system. CBDC maybe like cash if it is used in token form and like bank deposits if it is in the form of account-based. For digital cash to be a success, there has to be an incentive to adopt it compared to others instruments of payment. One possible incentive could be for central banks to provide it at no cost to those that use it or retailers and billers that accept payments from it (Khiaonarong and Humphrey, 2019).

The CDBC can serve as a stable unit of account over time facilitating the effectiveness of economic and financial decisions, a costless medium of exchange accepted for all payment transactions, and a secure store of value with interest bearing allowing the central bank to adjust the interest rate to ensure

Table 1. Main differences between money forms

Money	Form	Interest Bearing	Accessibility	Payment Mechanism	Anonymity	Issuer
Cash	Physical	No	All economic agents	Decentralized or peer-to-peer	Token-based	Central bank
Bank deposit	Electronic	Yes/No	All economic agents	Centralized	Account-based	Banks
CB reserves	Electronic	Yes/No	Limited to financial institutions	Centralized	Account-based	Central bank
CBDC	Digital	Yes/No	All or limited economic agents	Centralized or decentralized	Token or account-based	Central bank

CBDC Implications and Challenges for Banking Intermediation and Financial Stability

Issues have been raised about the impact of the CBDC on the payment system, monetary policy, banking intermediation and financial stability (Ketterer and Andrade, 2016; Bech and Garrat, 2017; Gouveia et al., 2017; Mancini-Griffoli et al., 2018, Ward and Rochemont, 2019). In a dual banking system, where Islamic banks coexist alongside with the conventional banks under the umbrella of the central bank, the Islamic banking system will face the consequences as the conventional banks in term of competition with the CBDC and the stability of the funding and financing activities. The competition between CBDC and banks deposit should have implications for the banking business model and financial stability (Barrdear and Kumhof 2016; Stevens, 2017; Coeuré and Loh, 2018; Meaning, Dyson, Barker and Clayton, 2018). However, the extent to which CBDC would impact the banking sector and financial stability remains uncertain and depend on the widespread of the substitution of bank deposit by CBDC (Stevens, 2017). Engert and Fung (2017) precise that "*The overall impact of CBDC on financial stability would depend on the behaviour of economic agents over time, which probably depends also on the specific attributes of the CBDC*". The impact and risks of CBDC on the financial system, the real economy and society depend on its specific design characteristics (Panetta, 2018). Furthermore, Grym et al., (2017) note that there is no experience of CBDC which allows to well assess the macroeconomic effects of CBDC. The potential benefit of CBDC divides opinion in the international community, with a variety of positions (Ward and Rochemont 2019). Agur (2018) summarizes through a survey of literature the CBDC pros arguments considering the elimination of the effective lower bound on monetary policy, the improvement of monetary control, the containing of the growth of private crypto-currencies and the fulfilling a societal need. Yet, Cons are focused on financial disintermediation risks, illicit activities and operational risks. In this section, we contribute to the literature regarding the impact of CBDC on the banking intermediation and financial stability especially banking deposit, lending activity and the inherent risks in a dual banking system.

CBDC Affects Banks Intermediation and Financial Stability

Potentials threats may impact the banking intermediary role and financial stability. Precisely, CBDC can affect the structure of financial intermediation and influence both the liability and asset sides of banks. In this context, the volume of deposits could be weakened by CBDC and thereby the credit supply become more costly affecting economic activity (Ketterer and Andrade, 2016). "*If transactions balances could migrate to digital currency, how would banks compete? Would there be any implications for the availability of credit?*" (Bank of England, 2015, p 31). With CBDC, the central bank will be more present in the financial system and there may be a withdrawal funding from commercial banks given the larger central bank balance sheet[18].

According to Sharia principles, Islamic banks are not concerned by the CBDC interest bearing but by CBDC interest free or CBDC PLS-based. In this regard, the effect of CBDC on Islamic banks will depend on their *Sharia* compliance and *Sharia* purposes (*Maqasid Sharia*). Moreover, it is worth mentioning that Islamic banking intermediation has some similarities with conventional banks in term of fund collect and debt assets. Through this similarity and for competition pretext, Islamic banks can mimetic the conventional bank's products (Belabes, 2014) which make Islamic banks far away from *Sharia* principles. In consequence, the Islamic banks will undergo the same consequences as conventional banks regarding CBDC impact in term of banking disintermediation and financial instability. Islamic banks can increase or decrease the negative effect of CBDC on the whole bank system, this obviously depends, as presented previously, on the *Sharia* compliance and the CBDC design.

The introduction of the CBDC will likely involve a switch of deposits away from commercial banks towards the central bank. The significance of the switch causes a decline in banks deposits versus an increase of central bank liabilities, with a parallel increase in seigniorage gains. For central banks in many emerging markets and developing economies, seigniorage is the main source of revenue and an important safeguard of their independence (He, 2018). If there is a substantial and permanent deposit switch, base money would increase sharply and the central bank could realize higher seigniorage gains, in this regard, the expected increase in central bank revenue mirrors the fact that commercial banks would lose a major source of cheap funding (Fiedler et al., 2017). In addition, the decline of banks deposits limits to some extent the practice of fractional reserve banking which is a prelude of a narrow banking system. The latter support financial stability but impairing banks funding sources with negative spillovers effects on credit creation and economic activity if the switch is large and easy (Stevens, 2017). If there is a large flow from deposit accounts to CBDC, this significantly affects the liquidity ratios of individual commercial banks and all banking system. Then, CBDC leads to financial surplus for the central bank but a financial deficit for commercial banks (Grym et al., 2017). Consequently, the central bank is invited to increase its refinancing to commercial banks[19].

A CBDC could affect the banking system by limiting the fractional reserve system practiced by commercial banks. In fact, the access of the general public to CBDC and by consequence the competition with commercial bank deposits might result in the unbundling of the banking functions and the reshape of financial system according to the idea of narrow banks or full reserve banks (Ketterer and Andrade, 2016). The narrow banking system could lead to a more important role of securities in the banking funding. The deposit switch from commercial banks to CBDC might narrow the banking intermediation in terms of funding and lending where the reduction of deposit, as a main funding source, will shrink lending activity and force banks to issue new securities probably costlier than deposit (Raskin and Yermack, 2016). Giving the potential transfer of deposit to central bank, commercial banks will prevent this loss of deposit, even in the presence of deposit insurance, by raising interest rates or seek other funding to replace such outflows which would likely be costlier and affect the riskiness and the volume of their lending and creating more financial stability risks (Coeuré and Loh, 2018). Thereby, the impact of CBDC on bank resources structure is linked to the funding stability, funding cost, and lending growth. If a significant share of bank deposits shifted to the central bank, the bank supply of low cost funding would fall, raise funding cost, and lower bank credit creation (Khiaonarong and Humphrey, 2019).

An interest-bearing CBDC may impact the transmission mechanism and financial stability more than the non-interest bearing CBDC (He et al., 2017). If CBDC is interest bearing it will affect the competitiveness of the bank deposit. The banks are supposed to increase the attractiveness of their deposit by raising the deposit rates which in turn involve higher lending rates or a decrease of interest margin. Given the increase in funding cost and lower profitability, the bank intermediation and lending decrease (Engert and Fung, 2017). Actually, CBDC affects the banks' revenues and constitute a serious threat for banks profitability in the long run. In stress conditions, disturbances on financial system are more important and they are more important in the case of CBDC with interest bearing. Interest rates on retail CBDCs have to be carefully geared to avoid financial disintermediation effects (Agur, 2018). With CBDC, the role of central bank evolves through having a more important role in banking intermediation and CBDC becomes an alternative source of credit which reduces the bank credit. There are risks combined with the potential adverse economic impact of reduced lending (Stevens, 2017) leading to more instability risk. Engert and Fung (2017) sustain that less financial intermediation increase volatility. However, they note that disturbances and volatility are probably more important for interest-bearing CBDC.

At another level, the switching from bank deposit to CBDC has implications for bank funding and liquidity which make a challenge to the sustainability of current bank business models (Meaning, Dyson, Barker and Clayton, 2018). The conversion of deposit bank into CBDC by the general public could cause risks to the business models of commercial banks which will be disintermediated, and hence less able to perform essential economic functions, such as monitoring borrowers (Bech and Garrat, 2017). Besides, the competition between CBDC and commercial bank deposits could lead to the volatility in fund flows from commercial banks toward the central bank, which may hamper financial stability if CBDC is incorrectly designed (He and Khan, 2018). CBDC could affect the financial stability and banking intermediation if it competes with bank deposits with the possibility of a run from bank deposits to CBDC (Mancini-Griffoli et al., 2018; Barrdear and Kumhof, 2016). CBDC could give rise to higher instability of commercial bank deposit funding, this, in turn, leads to a greater role for central banks in allocating economic resources (Coeuré and Loh, 2018). Banks facing competition regarding resources mobilization consider that CBDC is more attractive than their deposits. The increase of supply for CBDC which is high liquid and safe increments led to a "near-money premium" in wholesale markets, i.e yields on short-term, agents are then likely to fund longer-term assets with short-term liabilities (e.g repo or commercial paper), which are notably associated with rollover risks and consequently this hampers the financial stability.

It is worth noting that the impact significance of the CBDC on bank funding in terms of volume, cost and deposit stability depends on the market power and the size of each bank. Although CBDC could increase the cost of funding for deposit-taking institutions and intensify run risk in some jurisdictions, design choices and policies can help ease such concerns (Mancini-Griffoli et al., 2018). The potential reaction of the banks to the introduction of CBDC depends on the design of CBDC and could involve a rethinking of the banking business model which experiences a strong change due to the development of the private cryptocurrency and Fintech. In fact, banks have to face the competition from CBDC in order to maintain their deposit market share and to some extent to avoid a bank run. In a competitive area, commercial banks are tended to raise interest rate (offer high interest rate on banking saving) to avoid the loss of deposits, which will be more costly. Commercial banks could also engage riskier forms of lending to offset the higher cost of funding, this may cause financial stability risks, they can also increase transactions fees and spread to keep their returns (Coeuré and Loh, 2018). According to Engert and Fung (2017), the commercial bank could offer spread above the (policy) interest rate to face the CBDC in order "to reflect the marginal credit risk". The flow of funds from banks to CBDC results in liquidity problems for the banks and forcing them to raise the deposit rate to stop the flow (Ben Dyson and Hodgson, 2016). The design of CBDC by the central bank should take in consideration the banking system stability. The central bank could limit the decline in bank deposits and lending by setting limits on individual CBDC holdings and bank deposits conversion to CBDC, and in addition, deposit insurance could alleviate the effects of banks run (Mancini-Griffoli et al., 2018).

CBDC Supports Banking Intermediation and Financial Stability

Due to the CBDC, the new shape of banking intermediation characterized by the central bank as a new banking intermediary is likely to incite banks to:

- Focus and attract other sources of funding like long term deposits, equity, bonds, *Sukuk*[20]. This funding mix or financing structure may potentially stabilize the banking resources and affect positively the lending activity. The Islamic banking system is more able to be in compatibility with the CBDC[21] given that bank intermediation is not primarily credit-driven but it offers products based on risk sharing and asset backing.
- Reinforce their equity capital and thereby increase the capital adequacy ratio which promotes financial stability.
- Promote increasingly the investment in the financial market and banking services in their asset strategy which might promote narrow banking system.

Given the elements above, Islamic banks might be more able than conventional banks to face the CBDC effects. Indeed, the development of the *Sukuk* market provides more liquidity and funding. The *Sukuk* could be with long maturity enabling banks to have stable funding. In addition, the long-term investment deposit based on risk sharing may reduce the excessive maturity transformation. The current maturity mismatch of banks' assets and liabilities would be reduced by the substitution of short-term funding through deposits with longer-term financing instruments. As a result, the structural stability of the banking sector would be an improved system (Fiedler et al., 2017). The importance of equity capital in Islamic banks is another factor that may contribute to better face the risk of financial instability. In fact, the Islamic banks are characterized by higher capital adequacy which helps them to stabilize their resources. Accordingly, the Islamic banks business model is able to absorb the shock of deposit switch given their capital buffer. It is worth noting that narrow banking is in conformity with the Islamic economic principals regarding money attributes. The Islamic monetary system which gives to the State the authority for money creation supports the narrow banking and doing so is against the fractional reserve system. In a dual bank system, the CBDC will give more role to the central bank which reinforces the Islamic monetary system view.

With the introduction of CBDC in the banking system, the fractional reserve system used for money creation will be less relevant and the business banking model might converge to narrow-banking or full reserve system which limits excessive lending[22]. This change in banking intermediation is likely to allow increasingly the long-term resources to finance bank assets which in turn add more stability to the financial system. CBDC-based narrow banking and loanable-funds intermediaries could ensure a better and more stable financial system (Roubini, 2018). Moreover, the scenario of narrow banking involves increasingly the central bank in the banking system due to the CBDC competition with the banking intermediaries and could help macroprudential policymakers to reach their objectives of risks regulation and supervision.

The CBDC will challenge the present fractional reserve system through the shift of liquidity, by market participants, from banks deposit to CBDC, thereby, commercial banks would increasingly have to rely on other funding sources than deposits which change the fractional reserve system and could finally lead to a more stable financial system (Fiedler et al., 2017). Tobin (1987) defend the relevance of the deposit currency account at central banks for the general public in order to have a safe currency, to diminish the reliance on deposit insurance and to avoid the risk of bank failure. If deposits are shifting from commercial banks to central bank, this contributes to *"narrow banking"* where assets are as liquid as liabilities and thus deposits become more safer without the need for deposits insurance[23].

The design and regulation of CBDC and thereby its competition with other forms of money is relevant to understand if CBDC will be a complement or a substitute to these monies. Even if introduced in the future, CBDC would likely be a complement rather than a substitute to cash and bank deposits (Ahmat and Bashir, 2017; Judson, 2018). If digital currencies are sufficiently similar to commercial bank deposits, banks can compete with higher interest rates and better services (Lagarde, 2018). In this regard, associate services offered by commercials banks with deposits such as loans, wealth management, mortgage finance, financial advice can be bundled by banks. Engert and Fung (2017) highlight that if CBDC does not pay interest, there is not a significant shift from commercial deposits and saving in banking to CBDC in normal conditions since customers choose banks deposits to enjoy associated financial services and higher spread. If CBDC is designed interest free it will compete most likely with physical cash rather than deposits especially term deposit, thereby there might be fewer implications on banking intermediation and financial stability. In this regard, the *Sharia* compliant CBDC interest free based sustains more the financial stability in a dual banking system. CBDC *Sharia* compliant can contribute to reach the objectives of Islamic law by avoiding excessive money creation by banks and its adverse effects on indebtedness and solvency risk. Thereby, CBDC *Sharia* compliant can enjoy more value stability which may guarantee a non-discretionary monetary policy.

Kumhof and Noone (2018) find that if the introduction of CBDC follows a set of core principles, bank funding is not necessarily reduced, credit and liquidity provision to the private sector need not contract, and the risk of a system-wide run from bank deposits to CBDC is addressed. They added that with CBDC banks can continue to play their traditional intermediation role and with these core principals the financial instability risk of CBDC can be managed. For instance, if a central bank defines a rule or a limit for the switching between deposit and CBDC the consequences on financial stability will be less important. Under digital cash as a form of CBDC, the financial system will be safer by reducing the concentration of liquidity and credit risk in payment systems, moreover, the supply of credit may increase and the access to the payments services market will be possible for non-banks institutions which will increase the competition and the service quality (Dyson and Hodgson, 2016). All non-bank institutions (pension funds and insurers) do not have access to central bank reserves and assume the risk of the bank where they have their deposits. This risk will be avoided if there is access to CBDC and account at central banks which in return reduces credit and liquidity risk in the payment system.

According to Greenwood et al., (2016), financial stability could be improved with the provision of a safe and ultra-liquid asset (CBDC) thanks to the reduction of risks and excessive maturity transformation. In the conventional system, commercial banks are highly leveraged and are important transformers of liquidity and maturity. When agents rely more on CBDC as a store of value and means of payment, this may reduce aggregate risk and improve financial stability (Engert and Fung, 2017). Ben Dyson and Hodgson (2016) argue that direct access to CBDC for individuals, private sector companies, and non-bank financial institutions (compared to bank deposits) is able to reduce the concentration of liquidity and credit risk in payment systems. With the change from bank deposits to CBDC, there is less need for government guarantee on deposits and doing so this reduces the moral hazard in the financial system. In fact, the system of deposit insurance leads authorities to guarantee the liabilities of commercial banks. However, banks are so encouraged to undertake important risk[24] and the government guarantees assume the mistake of private[25]. In this context, CBDC reduces the need for deposit insurance (Ben Dyson and Hodgson, 2016).

CONCLUSION

CBDC is designed as a new digital currency to be used with other forms of money and private digital currencies. CBDC allows broad access to the liability side of central banks' balance sheets for the general public. The key motivation of CBDC issuance is to face the competition of the private digital currencies and to improve the payment system efficiency. How CBDC should be designed in terms of accessibility, degree of anonymity, free of interest or not, and centralized or decentralized payment system is essential to understand the potentials effects on the banking intermediation and financial stability.

In the literature, two main opinions exist regarding the necessity of CBDC issuance and its effects on the banks and financial stability. The first, notes that while CBDC leads to better efficiency of the payment system, it may cause instability for banking and financial system importantly when the shift of bank deposit to CBDC is significant. The second opinion encourages the CDBC issuance for different reasons mainly the idea of narrow banking which limits the excessive lending and encourages banking system to rely more on long term resources which in return contributes to the banking and financial stability.

From an Islamic perspective, the *Sharia* compliant CBDC with interest free form leads to less competition with banking deposits which sustains more financial stability in a dual banking system. The CBDC PLS-based form will involve the central bank in the real economic activity. In addition, given the principals of risk sharing and asset backing, Islamic banks should be more able to be in compatibility with the CBDC interest free and CBDC PLS-based which limits threats to bank intermediation and financial stability. Further, Islamic banks which enjoy more stable funds with investment deposits and *Sukuk* may face less challenge with CBDC than conventional ones. Opportunities can also be exploited in the regard of the using of CBDC PLS-based in a smart-contract platform in order to enhance the link between currency and real transactions. Nevertheless, it can be assumed that CBDC PLS-based could present specific implementation challenges such as privacy, scalability, value fluctuation, huge energy consumption, which constitutes a central issue in Islamic perspective.

Finally, in a dual banking system, the issuance and design of the CBDC as new money in addition to cash, deposit, reserves and private digital currencies is a challenge for the monetary authority. It is important that the implementation of CBDC take into consideration the efficiency of banking intermediation, specificities of Islamic banks, financial stability, and regulation of private digital currencies.

REFERENCES

Abu Bakar, N., Rosbi, S., & Uzaki, K. (2017). Cryptocurrency Framework Diagnostics from Islamic Finance Perspective: A New Insight of Bitcoin System Transaction. *International Journal of Management Science and Business Administration*, *4*(1), 19–28. doi:10.18775/ijmsba.1849-5664-5419.2014.41.1003

Agur, I. (2018). Central bank digital currencies: An overview of pros and cons. In *SUERF Conference Proceedings 2018/2: Do We Need Central Bank Digital Currency? Economics, Technology and Institutions.* Bocconi University and Baffi Carefin.

Ahmat, N., & Bashir, S. (2017). *Central Bank Digital Currency: A Monetary Policy Perspective.* Bank Negara. Monetary Policy Department/Staff Insights 2017/11.

Al-Masri, Y. R. (2013). *Money in Islamic Economy* (1st ed.). Damascus: Dar Almaktabi. (in Arabic)

Al-Sabhani, A. H. O. (1998). Money as it should be, in an Islamic system. [in Arabic]. *Journal of King Abdulaziz University: Islamic Economics*, *10*, 3–38.

Albahouth, A. S. A. (2018). Crypto-currency: concept, typology and economic impacts, *Scientific Journal of Economics and Trade*, 1. (in Arabic)

Ali, R., Barrdear, J., Clews, R., & Southgate, J. (2014). The economics of digital currencies. Bank of England. *Quarterly Bulletin*, *54*(3), 276–286.

Bank of England. (2015). *One Bank Research Agenda - Discussion Paper*. Bank of England.

Barontini, C., & Holden, H. (2019). *Proceeding with caution – a survey on central bank digital currency*. BIS Papers No 101.

Barrdear, J., & Kumhof, M. (2016). *The macroeconomics of central bank issued digital currencies*. Bank of England. Staff Working Paper No. 605.

Bech, M. L., & Garratt, R. (2017). *Central Bank Cryptocurrencies*. BIS Quarterly Review. September.

Belabes, A. (2014). Maqasid dimensions of finance in a complex world: Methodological comparison between Islamic and conventional economic literature. [in Arabic]. *Journal of King Abdulaziz University: Islamic Economics*, *27*(3), 2014.

Belouafi, A., Bourakba, C., & Saci, K. (2015). Islamic Finance and Financial Stability: A Review of the Literature. *Journal of King Abdulaziz University: Islamic Economics*, *28*(2), 3–44.

Bjerg, O. (2017). *Designing New Money: The Policy Trilemma of Central Bank Digital Currency*. Copenhagen Business School Working Paper.

Bordo, M., & Levin, A. (2018). *Central Bank Digital Currency and the Future of Monetary Policy*. NBER Working Paper No. 23711

Caporal, G. M., Gil-Alana, L., & Plastun, A. (2018). Long-term price overreactions: Are markets inefficient? *Journal of Economics and Finance*. doi:10.100712197-018-9464-8

Chapra, M. U. (1996). Monetary Policy in an Islamic Economy. In Z. Ahmed, M. Iqbal, & M. Fahim Khan (Eds.), *Money and Banking in Islam* (pp. 27–46). Islamabad, Pakistan: Institute of Policy Studies.

Coeuré, B., & Loh, J. (2018). Central bank digital currency. Committee on payment and market infrastructures. Market committee, BIS (Bank for International Settlement).

De Lis, S. F. (2018). Central bank digital currencies: features, options, pros and cons. In *SUERF Conference Proceedings 2018/2: Do We Need Central Bank Digital Currency? Economics, Technology and Institutions*. Bocconi University and Baffi Carefin.

Dhaliwal, S. (2017). Is Bitcoin Halal? How Cryptocurrency Conforms with Shariah. *Coin Telegraph*. Available Online: https://cointelegraph.com/news/is-bitcoin-halal-how-cryptocurrency-conforms-with-islam-and-sharia

Dyson, B., & Hodgson, G. (2016). *Digital cash: Why Central Banks Should Start Issuing Electronic Money*. Positive Money.

Engert, W., & Fung, B. S. C. (2017). *Central Bank Digital Currency: Motivations and Implications.* Bank of Canada Staff Discussion Paper, 2017-16. Available at https://www.bankofcanada.ca/wp-content/uploads/2017/11/sdp2017-16.pdf

Fiedler, S., Gern, K., Kooths, S., & Stolzenburg, U. (2017). *Financial innovation and monetary policy: Challenges and prospects. Directorate general for internal policies.* Policy department a: economic and scientific policy. IP/A/ECON/2017-02.

Fung, B., & Halaburda, H. (2016). *Central Bank Digital Currencies: A Framework for Assessing Why and How.* Bank of Canada Staff Discussion Paper 2016–22.

Gouveia, O.C., Dos Santos, E., De Lis, S.F., Neut, A., & Sebastian, J. (2017). *Central Bank Digital Currencies: assessing implementation possibilities and impacts.* BBVA Research, Document Number 17/04.

Green, E. (2008). Some challenges for research in payment systems. In A. Haldane, S. Millards, & V. Saporta (Eds.), *The Future of Payment Systems.* Milton Park: Routhledge.

Greenwood, R., Hanson, S., & Stein, J. (2016). *The Federal Reserve's balance sheet as a financial stability tool.* Paper presented at the Economic Policy Symposium. Available at https://scholar.harvard.edu/files/stein/files/jackson_hole_ghs_20160907_final.pdf

Grym, A., Heikkinen, P., Kauko, K., & Takala, K. (2017). *Central bank digital currency, Bank of Finland, 5. BoF economics Review.* Bank of Finland.

He, D. (2018). *Monetary policy in the digital age. Finance and Development. June 2018.* Washington, DC: International Monetary Fund.

He, D., Habermeier, K., Leckow, R., Haksar, V., Almeida, Y., Kashima, M., … Verdugo-Yepes, C. (2016). *Virtual Currencies and Beyond: Initial Considerations.* IMF Staff Discussion Note 16/03.

He, D., & Khan, A. (2018). Central bank digital currencies. In Global Financial Stability Report. International Monetary Fund.

He, D., Leckow, R., Haksar, V., Mancini-Griffoli, T., Jenkinson, N., Kashima, M., ... Tourpe, H. (2017). *Fintech and Financial Services: Initial Considerations. IMF Staff Discussion Note 17/05.* Washington, DC: International Monetary Fund.

Heller, D. (2017). *The implications of digital currencies for monetary policy.* European Parliament's Committee on Economic and Monetary Affairs. Directorate general for internal policies. Policy department a: economic and scientific policy. IP/A/ECON/2017-02.

Jackson, A., & Dyson, B. (2013). *Modernising Money: Why Our Monetary System is Broken and How it can be fixed.* London: Positive Money.

Kahf, M. (2014). *Fatwa on Bitcoin.* Retrieved from http://lightuponlight.com/blog/fatwa-on-bitcoin-by-monzer-kahf/

Kahn, C. M., Rivadeneyra, F., & Wong, T. (2019). *Should the Central Bank Issue E-Money?* FRB St. Louis. Research Division. Working Paper No. 2019-003A.

Ketterer, J. A., and Andrade, G. (2016). *Digital Central Bank Money and the Unbundling of the Banking Function.* Inter-American Development Bank.

Khiaonarong, T., & Humphrey, D. (2019). *Cash Use Across Countries and the Demand for Central Bank Digital Currency*. IMF working paper 19/46.

Kumhof, M., & Noone, C. (2018). *Central bank digital currencies — design principles and balance sheet implications*. Bank of England. Staff Working Paper No. 725.

Lagarde, C. (2018). Winds of Change: The Case for New Digital Currency. *Singapore Fintech Festival*. Retrieved from https://www.imf.org/en/News/Articles/2018/11/13/sp111418-winds-of-change-the-case-for-new-digital-currency

Mancini-Griffoli, T., Soledad Martinez Peria, M., Agur, I., Ari, A., Kiff, J., Popescu, A., & Rochon, C. (2018). Casting Light on Central Bank Digital Currency. IMF Staff Discussion Note 18/08. International Monetary Fund. doi:10.5089/9781484384572.006

Meaning, J., Dyson, B., Barker, J., & Clayton, E. (2018). *Broadening Narrow Money: Monetary Policy with a Central Bank Digital Currency*. Bank of England Staff Working Paper 724.

Mersch, Y. (2017). *Digital base money: an assessment from the ECB's perspective*. Speech at the Bank of Finland.

Muedini, F. (2018). The Compatibility of Cryptocurrencies and Islamic Finance. *European Journal of Islamic Finance*, *10*, 1-10.

Oubdi, L., & Raghibi, A. (2018). La perception des cryptomonnaies selon la loi islamique: Une analyse critique. *Recherches et Applications en Finance Islamique*, *2*(2), 161–173.

Panetta, F. (2018). 21st Century cash: Central banking, technological innovation and digital currencies. In *SUERF Conference Proceedings 2018/2: Do We Need Central Bank Digital Currency? Economics, Technology and Institutions*. Bocconi University and Baffi Carefin.

Raskin, M., & Yermack, D. (2016). *Digital Currencies, Decentralized Ledgers, and the Future of Central Banking*. NBER Working Paper No. 22238.

Rogoff, K. S. (2014). *Costs and Benefits to Phasing Out Paper Currency*. NBER Working Paper 20126. National Bureau of Economic Research.

Rogoff, K. S. (2016). *The curse of cash*. Princeton University Press. doi:10.1515/9781400883219

Roubini, N. (2018). *Why central bank digital currencies will destroy bitcoin*. Retrieved from https://www.theguardian.com/business/2018/nov/19/why-central-bank-digital-currencies-will-destroy-bitcoin

Ruth, J. (2018). Big note, small note: Central bank digital currency and cash. In *SUERF Conference Proceedings 2018/2: Do We Need Central Bank Digital Currency? Economics, Technology and Institutions*. Bocconi University and Baffi Carefin.

Skingsley, C. (2016). *Should the Riksbank issue e-krona?* Speech at FinTech Stockholm. Available online: https://www.bis.org/review/r161128a.pdf

Stevens, A. (2017, June). Digital currencies: Threats and opportunities for monetary policy. *NBB Economic Review*.

Thompson, D. (2017). What On Earth Is Going On With Bitcoin? *Atlantic (Boston, Mass.)*, *30*(November). Available online https://www.theatlantic.com/business/archive/2017/11/bitcoindelusion-conquer-world/547187/

Tobin, J. (1987). The case for preserving regulatory distinctions. In *Restructuring the Financial System, Proceedings of the Economic Policy Symposium*. Federal Reserve Bank of Kansas City. 10.1080/05775132.1987.11471196

Villaverde, J. F. (2018). Cryptocurrency Competition and the U.S. Monetary System. Penn Wharton.

Ward, O., & Rochemont, S. (2019). *Understanding Central Bank Digital Currencies (CBDC), An addendum to "A Cashless Society- Benefits, Risks and Issues (Interim paper)*. Academic Press.

ENDNOTES

1 The general public already holds central bank liabilities or physical fiat money in the form of banknotes and coins.

2 Profit and loss sharing principle is the basic mechanism in the Islamic banking intermediation.

3 The rapid growth of assets held by Islamic banks around the world during the last decades deserve more attention concerning their business model which is interest free-based system and fundamentally different compared to conventional banks.

4 For a literature review survey on Islamic bank stability see Belouafi, Bourakba, and Saci (2015).

5 The blockchain is a decentralized and automatic database maintained by nodes that ensure the confirmation and storage of transactions. There is a robustness of the system based on a P2P verification of the whole community as well as a secure storage on the Blockchain which prevents any malicious modification of the transaction register.

6 However, the absence of a financial intermediary in the transactions may make the traceability of the transactions more difficult.

7 Settlement account balances held by commercial banks and other financial institutions at the central bank.

8 For instance, the private cryptocurrency is used to regulate the money issue and to secure the transfer of funds independently of the central banks (Abu Bakar, Rosbi and Uzaki, 2017).

9 Paper currency has become a major impediment to the smooth functioning of the global financial system (Rogoff, 2016).

10 Skingsley (2016) argues that in Sweden, "there is currently a need among the general public and companies to have access to central bank money and this need will still be there in the future."

11 Cash has many drawbacks: it is the main instrument of tax evasion, money laundering and the financing of illegal activities (Gouveia, Dos Santos, De Lis, Neut and Sebastian, 2017).

12 The idea of helicopter money is attributed to the economist Milton Friedman (1969) in his paper 'The Optimum Quantity of Money'.

13 Tobin (1987) calls this digital money *deposited currency accounts* (DCA), p172-173

14 Cash limits the scope for monetary policies based on negative interest rates, since it provides a zero-rate alternative that can be stored (Gouveia, Dos Santos, De Lis, Neut and Sebastian, 2017).

15 A preference for anonymity does not necessarily stem from a desire to conduct illicit activities (Bech and Garratt, 2017).

16 The survey asked central banks about their current work on CBDCs, what motivates that work, and how likely their issuance of a CBDC is.

17 Account based interest free.

18 Central authorities can limit the substitutions by imposing quantitative limits (Coeuré and Loh, 2018).

19 Since central banks provide liquidity against collateral, commercial banks would need more securities as collateral. This could increase e.g. securitization of bank loans.

20 The Accounting and Auditing Organization for Islamic Financial Institutions (AAOIFI) defines Sukuk as follow: "Certificates of equal value representing undivided shares in the ownership of tangible assets, usufructs and services or (in the ownership of) the assets of particular projects or special investment activities, however, this is true after receipt of the value of sukuk, the closing of subscription and the employment of funds received for the purpose for which the sukuk were issued." The AAOIFI *Sharia* Standard number 17 on investment Sukuk, item2.

21 CBDC interest free or CBDC PLS-based. If it is CBDC interest bearing, the investment depositor with Sharia motive would keep their fund at Islamic banks rather than switch them to CBDC.

22 Under narrow banking, deposits are fully backed by central bank reserves.

23 After the depression of 1929, economists of "Chicago plan" called for the end of fractional reserve banking.

24 See Jackson and Dyson (2013) for critics the perverse effects of deposit insurance

25 "Deposit insurance simply creates the illusion that deposits are risk free" as they are in reality, risk-bearing.

Chapter 13
The Impact of FinTech on Economic Performance and Financial Stability in MENA Zone

Souhaila Kammoun
IHEC, CODECI, University of Sfax, Tunisia

Sahar Loukil
University of Sfax, Tunisia

Youssra Ben Romdhane Loukil
University of Sfax, Tunisia

ABSTRACT

This chapter deliberates on the effects of FinTech on economic performance in the context of political instability in MENA zone countries. Using a multiple regression model to estimate time series data based on a sample of 10 MENA zone countries for 2011, 2014, and 2017, the study contends that FinTech's lending activities increase inflation and that this effect could be interestingly moderated by sound policies and regulations. In addition, the authors find empirical support for the FinTech's role as a driver of economic growth and a breeding ground for innovative projects in a context of freedom of expression, association, and media. In terms of practical implications, decision makers are asked to formulate and implement sound policies and regulations that permit and promote the positive role of FinTech in terms of economic performance.

DOI: 10.4018/978-1-7998-0039-2.ch013

INTRODUCTION

This chapter examines the impact of digital finance on financial inclusion and the stability of the financial system. In the past decade, the information technology (IT) revolution and advancement in encryption and network computing have transformed every aspect of human life, including banking and the financial services industry knew a supreme transformation in banking activities related to innovation and technologies. Indeed, with the emergence of virtual currencies, also known as crypto-currencies or digital currencies, the way goods, services, and assets are exchanged faced a fundamental transformation. IT acts as a catalyst for growth in the banking sector; in particular, it supports banking, productivity growth and risk management. IT is a driver of activity and can therefore be used to enhance competitiveness (Porter and Millar, 1985).

As a breakthrough innovation, financial technologies, nowadays known under the term of Fintech, denote companies that combine financial services with innovative technologies (Dorfleitner et al, 2017). More precisely, Fintech was coined to mean innovative financial solutions that have harnessed technologies and new and creative ways[1]. Even if, there is not a universally definition, Fintech is seen as a redesign of the financial services sector using entirely new business models for payment, wealth management, crowdfunding, lending and capital markets. Zavolokina et al. (2016) postulate that 'Fintech" is a living body with a flexible and changing nature, rather than a stable notion that is transparent and clearly understood by both academia and the media' (p 12). They further postulate that the emergence of Fintech is the result of three main factors simultaneously interacting and challenging the status quo at the same time: organizations, people and geographical locations (markets). That being said, it must be recognized that Fintech lending was first created around the financial crisis and then has been growing quickly in the last decade. Today, Fintech are experiencing an increasing popularity in the financial markets and in portfolio management as they can be classified as financial assets or commodities to pure store of value advantages. Consequently, banking sector has increasingly moved to a shadow banking sector. According to Matvos, Piskorski, and Seru (2018) the market share of shadow banks in originating residential mortgages nearly doubled from 2007 to 2015.

As in other countries, the MENA Fintech sector is booming, with dozens of new start-ups launching every year. Such changes are expected to have an impact on countries' economic performance. In this context, digital finance promises to increase the gross domestic product (GDP) of digitized economies by providing convenient access to a wide range of financial products and services (and credit facilities) for individuals, as well as small, medium and large businesses, which can boost overall growth and spending, thereby improving GDP levels. Digital finance can also lead to greater economic stability and increased financial intermediation for both customers and economy. Meanwhile, some other countries are often facing periods of political instability which would influence the relationship between Fintech and economic performance. Previous researches were conducted to study the relationship between digital finance, economic performance and financial stability e.g. [Han, R., & Melecky, M. (2013), Accenture, (2013), GSMA, (2014), McKinsey, (2015), Dermine (2016), Young (2017), Buchak et al. (2017) and Fuster et al. (2018). Our study intends to extend literature on the impact of Fintech on economic performance moderated by political instability. Focusing on digital finance, this chapter offers a discussion on digital finance and explores the impact of digital finance on economic performance in a context of financial instability; a problem that has not been addressed in the literature.

In this light, the main purpose of the chapter is to analyze the impact of Fintech on the economic performance and some contingency factors in MENA zone countries. We discuss the evidence of the Fintech impact on a country's economic performance. Building on previous researches, this chapter reviews how the Fintech literature tried to address these issues. In section II, we briefly review empirical literature as regards to the determinants of Fintech and their impact on economic and financial environment in order to provide the theoretical basis for the study. The next section focuses on Fintech state in MENA countries. Section IV presents methodology and data sources and some summary statistics of the variables used in our empirical work where we highlight the empirical results and formulate our conclusions. The concluding remarks are presented in Section V.

THE ECONOMIC IMPACT OF THE FINTECH OPPORTUNITY

The increased use of Big data and alternative data analytics combined with increased use of mobile phones and internet in the developing countries creates a potential for anyone to be included in the financial system. Artificial intelligence (AI) and machine learning (ML) allow researchers to analyze this big amount of data from internet sites and mobile phones. Moreover, digital financial services have great potential to extend the provision of basic financial services through an affordable, convenient and secure environment to the general public (especially the poor) through innovative technologies such as mobile-enabled solutions, electronic money models and digital payment platforms. The figure below presents the different types of digital financial technologies, digital finance business functions and digital finance institutions.

Figure 1. Digital finance; technological concepts, business functions and institutions.

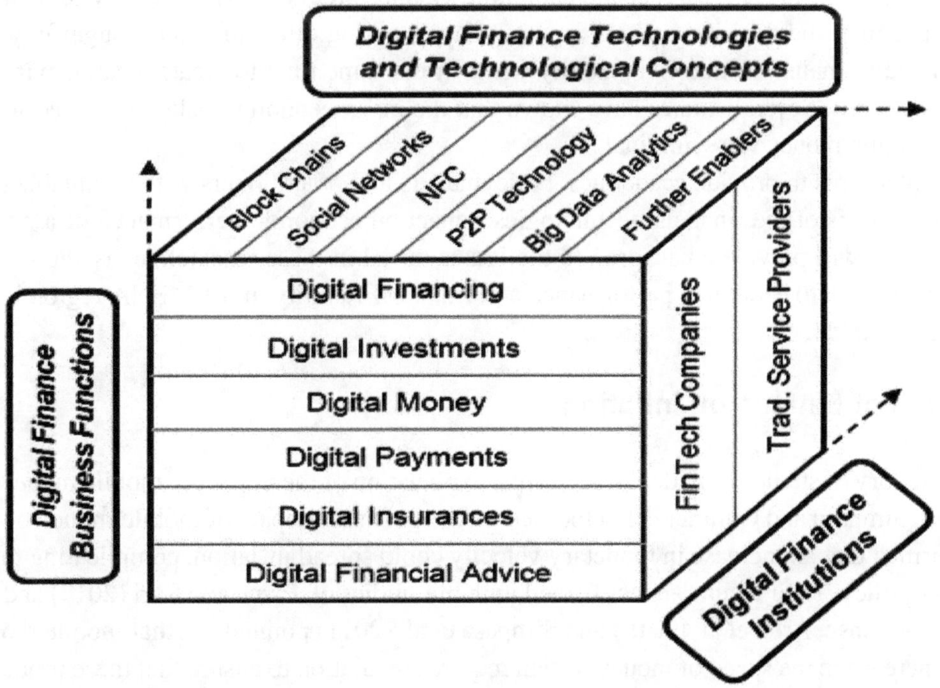

Many research studies have focused on the benefits and risks of digital finance, digital financial inclusion and financial inclusion. Indeed, digital finance and financial inclusion offer several benefits for financial service users, digital finance providers, governments and the economy such as expanding access to finance among the poor, reducing the cost of financial intermediation for banks and technology providers, and overall spending for governments, White et al, (2016). According to Gomber et al, (2017), since 2010, the G-20 and the World Bank have led the initiative to increase financial inclusion in developing countries to help reduce poverty levels in developing and emerging economies (GPFI, 2011).

As a result of its distributed ledgers based on blockchain, Fintech not only offer some unique advantages to the economy, investors, and consumers, but also pose considerable risks to users and challenges for regulators when fitting the new technology into the old legal framework. Using new technology, Fintech advancement is expected to have huge ramifications over the next decade2, particularly in the less developed part of the world in all financial services like saving, loans, investments, payments. Jagtiani and Lemieux (2018) find that Fintech penetrate both highly concentrated and relatively underserved banking and areas where the local economy is not performing well. Weil et al. (2014) argue that mobile money is a mean of transfer and savings and that the speed of mobile money has increased over time, indicating increased use of mobile money in transactions. Adam and Walker (2015) postulate that mobile money should increase the macroeconomic stability of the countries in which it is spread, contrary to popular expectations that this would lead to destabilization of the currency.

Additionally, Kamukama and Tumwine (2012) conclude that the proliferation of mobile payments can disadvantage commercial banks by weakening their liquidity positions. According to Jagtiani and Lemieux (2018), that Fintech lenders such as Lending Club are able to provide loans to clients in areas underserved by traditional banks or defined by limited economic activity, Bromberg, Godwin and Ramsay, (2017). While advanced technology provides benefits to both consumers and lenders, these financial technologies have potential to disrupt and to create new types of risk. Indeed, financial innovation generally leads to higher credit creation, which increases systemic risk. This means that financial innovations, such as Fintech, markets and economic systems are more exposed to systemic risk, Chui, (2017). Academics and decision-makers are nowadays working diligently and thoughtfully to protect consumers and to maintain financial stability while at the same time to create a safe environment for Fintech innovations. Several studies have shown that the macroeconomic risks associated with the expansion of mobile money were minimal.

This chapter aims to provide academics, policymakers and practitioners with a valuable discussion and critical analysis of the financial technologies impact on economic performance of a country. The literature review will provide a backdrop to the issues raised in these research areas and highlight the relevance of Fintech to economic performance and financial stability in the MENA region in a context of political instability.

The Impact of Fintech on Inflation

The first category of studies provides an economic explanation of the impact of mobile money (Fintech) on inflation. Simpasa and Gurara (2012) focused on the potential impact of mobile money on inflation. They confirmed that an increase in monetary velocity could spread inflation, complicating the conduct of monetary policy. Their results are confirmed with the studies of Tavne and Suri (2017) and Iazzolino (2015). In this sense, Aron et al. (2015) and Simpasa et al. (2011) pointed out that mobile money could lead to an increase in the speed of money, which requires regulation to ensure that these products do not detract from the effectiveness of monetary policy. Aron and Sebudde (2015) emphasized the relationship between mobile money and inflation for Uganda during 1994-2003 using multivariate models across equilibrium correction terms. According to them, mobile money is a recent financial innovation offering financial transaction services via a mobile phone, including unbanked people.

In the same vein, Ondabu et al (2015) analyzed the relationship between effective inflation control and mobile money in Somaliland through a sample of 119 respondents selected from the population (managers and staff of Zaad) using a stratified random sampling technique. The study used the quantitative theory of money and modern monetary theory to explain the behaviour of inflation control. The results show that the mobile money service (Zaad) can be an inflation control tool helping central banks to control inflation. These authors proposed recommendations on mobile money transfer and effective inflation control as the use of carefully crafted policies and procedures to maintain client satisfaction. In the same country, Walker (2016) confirmed that mobile phones play a very important role at micro and macro levels. Through a modeling of the emergence of mobile money, this author has introduced a more and more advanced technology of payment of funds in a Dynamic Stochastic General Equilibrium (DSGE) framework with two sectors (urban producer households and rural). Empirical results show that financial innovations help to reduce the incompleteness of markets, and monetary authorities could usefully move from headline inflation to core inflation. These results should encourage policymakers to continue to support and encourage the spread of mobile phones in the countries of the East African Community (EAC).

For Mawejje and Lakuma (2017), the use of mobile money does not lead to high inflationary risks. In addition, Mehrotra and Yetman (2014) examined the effect of financial inclusion on the maximization of monetary policy. Their results showed the existence of a positive relationship between the number of households included financially and the relationship between output and the volatility of inflation. Furthermore, Nampewo and Opolot (2016) have found that in the case where mobile money greatly facilitates transactions, and not the creation of added value, this results in an increase in the speed of money. To combat this problem, Carrick (2016) noted that Bitcoin is a global virtual currency that is not regulated by the government and therefore is very effective to gradually eliminate the risk of inflation.

The introduction and widespread use of credit cards promotes the efficiency of transactions but results in inflation in the absence of monetary intervention. In the event that the monetary authority attempts to restore pre-credit price levels by reducing the money supply, it may have to sacrifice efficiencies. In case of default on credit cards, there is still more inflation and less efficiency gains, Geanakoplos, (2010) and Alvarez and Lippi (2017). According to Zhang et al, (2013) mobile money can affect interest rates as it leads to the creation of credit by commercial banks. The role of mobile money in credit creation has been studied by Nampewo et al (2016), who emphasize the crucial role of savings and deposit mobilization. This author has asserted in his hypothesis that if mobile money leads to economic efficiency through a reduction in transaction costs and a better allocation of resources and credit, it follows that the overall economic activity will be supported. The empirical results show that whenever money and credit coexist, the equilibrium is generally ineffective and that an optimal policy implies a rate of inflation strictly superior to the Friedman rule. Similarly, Smith et al (2006) have argued that the inflation fall does increase the use of cash and credit in low-inflation countries. From Erosa and Ventura's (2002) point of view, financial innovation determines the choice of households' portfolio in relation to monetary and non-monetary assets / liabilities, which reduces the cost of holding assets, non-monetary debts. Their results are confirmed with the studies of Mulligan and Sala-i. Martin (2000) and Attanasio and al (2002).

The Impact of Fintech on Business and Investment Freedom

The second category of studies provides an economic explanation of the relationship between business freedom and Fintech. According to Ruberti et al (2018), the evolution of financial technology is based on innovations in processes, applications, products and business models such as Fintech. This author has studied the effect of Fintech on private investment in sub-Saharan Africa. The results show that Fintech supports private investment by leveraging existing mobile platforms to reduce the frictions of fund intermediation between savers and investors. Although the growth of mobile payments in this region is not directly related to financial intermediation services, providers of this method of payment are beginning to rely on the maturity of the technology platform. These results are confirmed by BRI, (2012) and CBSB, (2017), who said that Fintech promotes investment growth in the region by improving the efficiency of financial market infrastructure, including regulation and clearing in sub-Saharan Africa compared to other regions of the world. In addition, Pejkovska (2018) examined the effect of Fintech on the global financial services sector for two countries: India and the United States. Due to the extensive scope of Fintech, the paper focuses solely on three elements, namely blockchain, cryptocurrencies, alternative payment methods and investment and banking, it uses arguments and empirical evidence referring to three different geographical and political regions in EU. The results show that the current regulation of Fintech in the above-mentioned regions is inappropriate and could have potential negative effects on the global financial services sector, such as cyber-security corruption, data breach and the use of data. Fintech services for illegal purposes. Therefore, EU, India and US authorities need to focus on creating appropriate regulation for Fintech to mitigate potential negative effects.

From the point of view of Gomber et. al (2018), Nicoletti (2017) and Haan (2015), Fintech has begun to attract significant investments, which are expected to increase in the future as more technologies are deployed in the financial services business. However, there are also threats related to these elements of Fintech, which are rarely addressed but which could have a negative impact on the entire financial services sector. Potential negative effects are mainly explained by the lack of appropriate regulation with respect to the activities of Fintech companies. The study of Athey and. al (2016) showed that Bitcoin had already been used as a means of payment to buy drugs and weapons on dark-web platforms worth $ 11 billion. Due to the anonymity of Bitcoin, those guilty of these acts could not be identified. The inability to trace the origin and destination of transactions facilitates the commission of financial offenses such as money laundering and tax evasion. Such actions could further reduce public confidence in the financial services sector and aggravate its already fragile reputation. In this sense, Prescott & Larose (2016) argue that the United States is a concrete example of corrupt cyber-security and breach of data privacy. A Fintech start-up, offering alternative payment solutions, assured its customers that their data was safe, but when a cyber-attack corrupted their cyber-security system, the company compromised the financial and personal data of its customers. This example shows why it is important for the EU, US and India authorities to engage the Fintech companies with the regulations in force and ask them to provide first class cyber-security to ensure data confidentiality.

The Impact of Fintech on Unemployment

The third category of studies offers an economic explanation of the relationship between unemployment and Fintech. The Broby study (2017) analyzes the impact of collaboration in financial technologies on production and productivity. The results show that collaboration in this sector will increase the production and productivity of labours and is also very positive for employment. This study is confirmed with the studies of Clarke and Broby (2017) and Davine and Dickson, (1983). A Citigroup study in 2016 predicts a decline in US bankrolls by 30% in ten years from 2.6 million in 2015 to 1.8 million in 2025. In Europe, the downsizing would reach 37% and even 50% in UK. In the Canadian example, the banking system experienced disruptions in 2008, particularly because of a rigorous regulatory framework; financial innovation has not seen the growth that has been observed in other countries. In London, for example, the many layoffs following the 2008 crisis enabled former employees who understood the challenges of the financial sector to innovate, which favored the emergence of Fintech.

Such phenomena have the potential to change business models, bring about structural changes, and/or change any other aspect of the system under investigation. It is about real change with real Managerial and research implications, Balyuk, (2017). Based on the previous theoretical and empirical underpinnings, this study addresses the two following research questions: What is the impact of Fintech on economic performance in MENA zone? And how can political instability moderate the relationship between Fintech and the economic development of MENA countries?

MENA ZONE: AN EVER-EVOLVING FINTECH SPACE

Across the Middle East, Fintech is driven by technology-enabled innovation that improves existing financial services, but also provides routes for unbanked populations to access financial services. In fact, for emerging economies whose banking penetration is low, financial inclusion is relevant theme. Across the Middle East and North Africa (MENA) banking penetration, measured by the percentage of adults that have bank accounts is on average slow. The MENA zone countries have the worldwide top percentage of unbanked population. In fact, in 2014, only 14% of population owns a bank account. Simultaneously, the region boasts a huge proportion of youth tech-savvy. Moreover, in 2017, 365 million unique subscribers accounting for 63% of the population in 2017 reveal a high penetration mobile-phone rate while mobile-Internet penetration stand at 38% as of 2016. It is expected to grow to 48% by 2020. According to Sanne Wass (2018), a global trade hub and home to regulators with big Fintech ambitions, the Middle East could be the next location for trade finance technology to bloom. By 2022, the Fintech market is estimated to reach a value of US$2.5 billion across the broader MENA region.

In this section, we highlight key trends and developments in financial technology (Fintech) across 10 different MENA jurisdictions. Digital transformation of financial services across the region remains a hot topic on the agenda of industry participants and decision makers looking for the economic development and modernization in order to diversify from natural resources. Globally, we are seeing the first signs of regulatory sandboxes seeking to work together and many new initiatives of public and private institutions to work together. The market is recognizing the power and speed of collaborative approaches in Fintech.

UAE

The governments of Dubai and Abu Dhabi have focused on ‘smart’ technologies. UAE banks and financial institutions are creating digital platforms and launching electronic innovative solutions. They vary from e-payments, electronic wallet services to robo-advice platforms. It offers computerized and algorithm-driven financial services with little human supervision. The fast uptake of smartphone payment in the UAE in 2018 is remarkable. The Emirates Digital Wallet initiative is a joint project amongst a large

Table 1. Current regulatory environment[3]

	Cryptocurrency Trading/ICOs	Payment Services/ Mobile Wallets	Crowdfunding	Sandbox/Regulatory Testing License?
ADGM*	1	1	1	Yes
UAE	2	1	1	Yes
DIFC*	2	2	1	Yes
BAHRAIN	3	2	1	Yes
KSA	4	3	2	Yes
KUWAIT	4	1	4	Yes
JORDAN	4	1	2	No
EGYPT	4	1	2	No
LEBANON	4	1	1	No
MOROCCO	4	1	2	No

1. Regulations implemented 2. Regulations planned 3. No specific regulations, but conducted under regulatory supervision 4. No specific regime now or anticipated in the near future.

Figure 2. Fintech start-up by MENA Zone country[45]

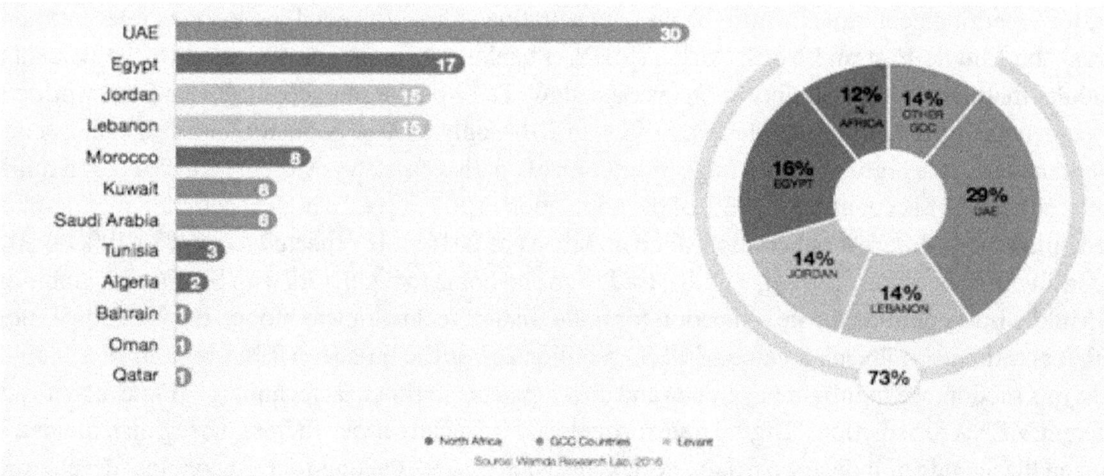

number of UAE banks to create a mobile cash wallet available to customers. These projects are likely to hit the market in the near future in this area. The country launched the Fintech Innovation Centre in Abu Dhabi in late 2017. Moreover, the DUBAI INTERNATIONAL FINANCIAL CENTRE "DIFC" continues to support a growing Fintech industry with several firms gaining international funding and introducing products and services to the market. The Dubai Land Department announced in Mai 2018 the creation of a "Real Estate Self Transaction" platform for digital transactions in land for 2020.

Saudi Arabia

A big chunk of the Saudi government's Vision 2030 is about digital transformation in Fintech. In February 2018, the Saudi Authority signed a deal with Ripple, a US-based technology company, to help banks in the kingdom settles payments using blockchain technology. Fintech Saudi has been launched, with both the Saudi Arabian Monetary Authority (SAMA) and the Capital Markets Authority (CMA) as partners along with a host of banks, service providers and Fintechs. The CMA also created a Fintech lab and is issuing permits for financial technology experimentation.

Bahrain

Bahrain is actively developing a Fintech industry involving different governmental authorities. First, the central bank entered into MoUs with the Monetary Authority of Singapore and the ADGM to facilitate cooperation on innovation projects. Second, the CBB has introduced a regulatory framework for Fintech and a sandbox for tech firms to test their innovations. It has had success in the crypto-space by hosting one of the first licensed crypto-exchanges. Moreover, the Economic Development Board (EDB) created earlier in 2018 the Bahrain Fintech Bay. According to Rasheed Mohammed Al Maraj, governor of the bank, BCB and BF form together a part of a "strategy towards positioning Bahrain as a regional leader in Fintech". This Fintech Bay launched the Global Islamic & Sustainable Fintech Center (GISFC) consisting of local, regional and international members with the aim to encourage "sustainable, social and responsible innovation".Recently the Bahrain Development Bank and Economic Development Board have each announced funds of USD100m to invest in tech start-ups.

Egypt

The Egyptian Government and the Central Bank of Egypt's (CBE) intention to upgrade payment systems and to get to cashless system is the reason behind the growing number of Fintech start-ups. In April 2018, the first blockchain-focused incubator opened in collaboration with Egyptian firms. CBE issued new regulations for cashless payments using smartphones. But, Fintech start-ups can work in partnership with the banks to provide financial services for banked and unbanked customers. Since Fintech companies act as payment services providers, there was a widespread growth of in online payment gateway services. It is still necessary to adopt e-commerce law and other financial regulatory reforms to respond to the growth in digital credit lending and crowdfunding.

Jordan

The majority of Jordanians does not have bank accounts and use cash to settle their bills and make payments. Fintech in Jordan is in its infancy, but is slowly growing. At firm's level, they are still implementing systems to settle electronic bills and make payments through smartphones. At Jordanian Government level, it is actively encouraging the introduction of Fintech in various public and private sectors. The CBJ anticipate the rise of Fintech in Jordan and is gradually issuing regulations and instructions for Fintech providers and users. The CBJ partnered with Fintech company Madfoo'atcom launched e-FAWATEER.

com in 2015 as an electronic bill presentation and payment system. In order to provide the "unbanked" with access to financial services, the CBJ provide electronic mobile wallet that enables people to pay bills and make person-to-person or personto-merchant transfers.

Lebanon

Lebanese local banks have introduced Fintech like mobile and online banking, payment and deposit platforms and money transfer platforms which have had a significant impact on the Lebanese financial sector. The Capital Markets Authority (CMA) regulates crowdfunding and CBL regulates electronic banking. In order to obtain a crowdfunding licence, the CMA conducts "Know Your Customer" (KYC) verification. Doing so, it investigates relations between the crowdfunding operation and the underlying companies. The CMA canceled the prohibition on promoting or dealing with electronic currencies for their own account or for the account of their clients and on issuing electronic money. BDL (la banque du Liban) prohibits all institutions from providing advice of any kind to the investors or the company and applies to all institutions authorized to carry on securities trading. But, in the last two years, the BDL applied plans allowing the central bank to launch its own digital currency.

Kuwait

Before the ET Law (Electronic Transactions) issued by the Kuwaiti national assembly in January 2015, only a small number of Fintech start-ups are operating in Kuwait. This typical law governs electronic contractual agreements and electronic signatures, and covers electronic payments. Under this ET law, electronic payment is an acceptable payment method so long as it complies with the ET Law and the provisions set out by the CBK and an electronic signature is binding and admissible as evidence if it complies with the provisions of Law. In November 2018, the CBK (central bank of Kuwait) announced the launch of a regulatory sandbox for start-ups. But, this sandbox is not yet implemented.

Figure 3. Digital readiness[6]
Source: Fintech ecosystem playbook (2018).

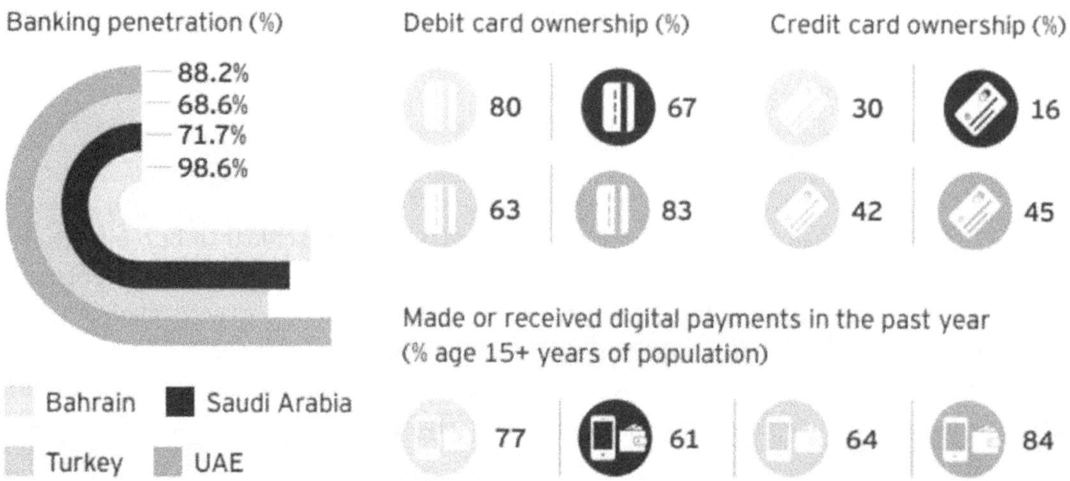

Figure 4. Financial parameters
Source: Fintech ecosystem playbook (2018).

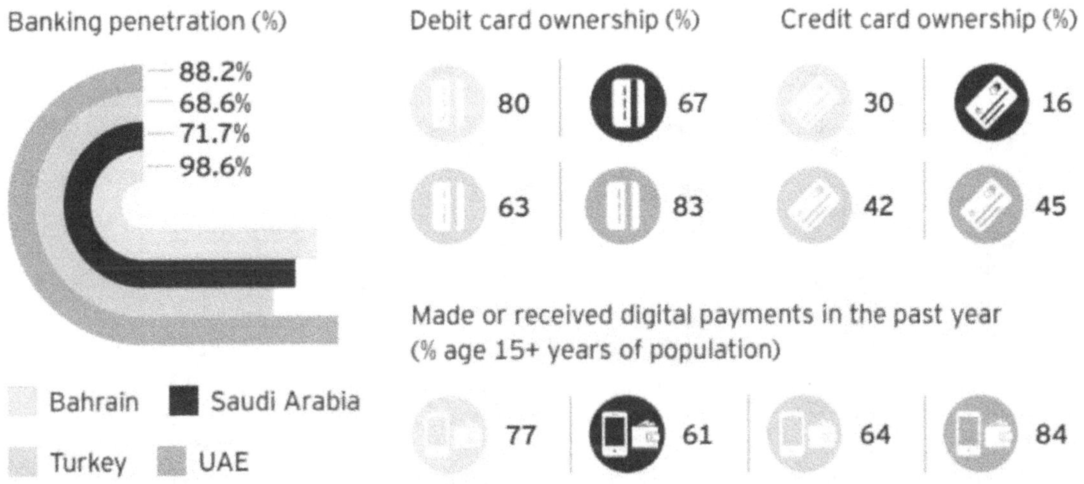

Oman

The Fintech sector in the Sultanate of Oman is in a continuing development at a slow rhythm due to a lack of consumer awareness and confidence. People in Oman are used to settle their payments and bills with cash at banks or teller machines. Recently, the first Omani Fintech company "Thawani Pay" is established. It is a mobile digital platform. The Omani government announced a blockchain collaboration initiative with the Oman Banks Association in April 2018. Despite the diversified existing laws of Fintech transactions, there is no clear law that provides clear terms of Fintech transaction as it is not expressly covered under the existing laws. In fact, all Fintech transactions are subject to the ETL that governs all forms of electronic transaction. While aspects of Fintech are regulated by these general laws, there is a need for a comprehensive regime which governs Fintech in Oman.

Tunisia

Tunisia is a Greenfield opportunity for Fintech. Mobile payments have revolutionized the financial industry, where more than two thirds of people are subscripted to mobile telephone networks[7] and 55% are connected to internet[8], but only around one-quarter[9] have bank accounts. Some countries like South Africa are among the fastest growing Fintech markets in the world. In Tunisia[10], more than 3/4 of population lives in less than 10% of the territory where 80% of the economic activities take place. Most of the people own a mobile phone and more than the half use internet. The Fintech revolution can reach these people and change the current status of the financial services industry in Tunisia. In fact, the number of valid electronic transaction tripled since 2010 to 2018 and reached above 18557 deals[11]. Nevertheless, the ecosystem for digitizing content and services is not developed, as projects have often relied only on the public sector's abilities (E-Culture, E-Education, E-Agriculture, E-etc.). In addition, the ICT budgets allocated to digitization projects are rather low[12]. The innovation ecosystem is inefficient and the logistic system is not competitive and is unable to support e-commerce, except the post. Similarly, the new digital

Figure 5. Smartphone penetration and mobile broadband subscriptions by country[14]
Base: National only; n=4,529.
Source: Mobile Broadband Subscriptions - World Economic Forum (2015), Network readiness index.

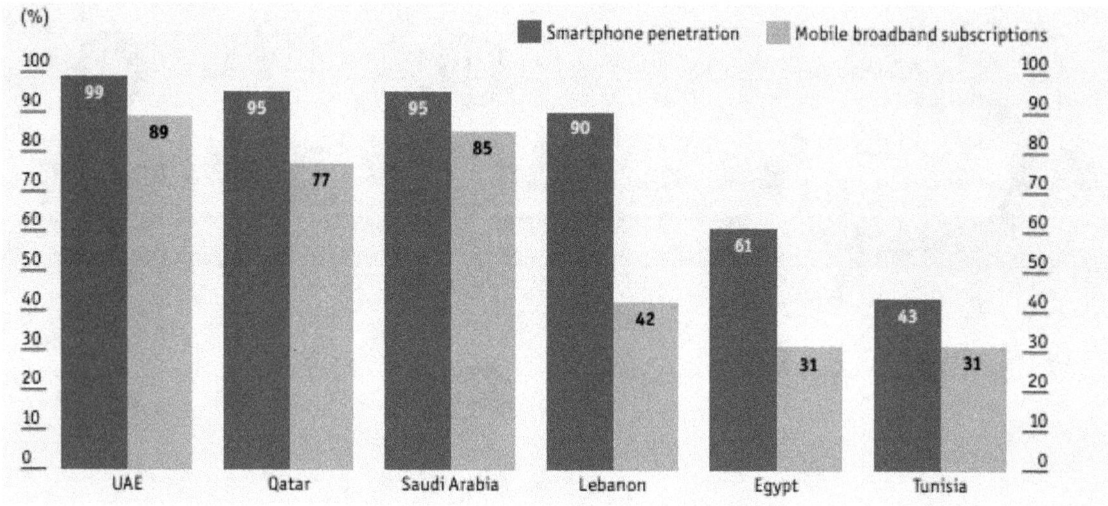

regulatory framework is not yet set up (digital code) to replace the current framework (telecommunications code) while the incentive framework for off-shoring is slowly implemented in practice. Moreover, there is a lack of coordination between economic and social departments in the implementation of the National Strategic Plan Tunisia Digital (Industry, Health, etc.) getting to a lower level of ICT integration in companies, health institutions, etc. According to the report of the Ministry of Communication Technologies and the Economy, we note that the added value of digital increased from 45150 in 2014 to 10000 (MDT) in 2018. This increase has a positive effect on the economy. The digital export rises from 950 in 2014 up to 3000 (MDT) in 2018and the number of jobs in the digital sector from 2.5% to 20%[13].

We can conclude that digital banking, cryptocurrencies, ecommerce and Fintech start-ups knew recently record years for digital investments in the MENA region. But there's wide variation between countries.

DATA AND STUDY METHODOLOGY

In this chapter, we use data from Datastream, data bank platform as representative of Fintech concerning MENA Zone countries during 2011, 2014 and 2017. Our choice is explained by the fact that emerging countries especially Arab ones are Greenfield opportunity for the expansion of financial technologies. To approximate Fintech, we use Mobile Money, Digital Payment, Debit card and Regulatory quality. We study Fintech's impact on macroeconomic variables such as inflation rate and unemployment rate (Broby 2017, Deloitte 2017, Gomber et al 2018, Nicoletti 2017, Pejkovska 2018, Alvarez and Lippi, 2017 and Tavne and Suri, 2017) and investment and financial freedom, etc. We also use the World Bank's governance indicators to assess the quality of the Arab institutional framework such as political instability, corruption, and government effectiveness, rule of law and voice and accountability as contingency factors explaining the probable effect of Fintech on a country's economy. The table below presents all variables measures used in our study. Based on a multiple regression model to estimate, the study uses the ordinary least squares (MLS) technique. Political risk variables were used as indices or percentages. The multiple regression models for estimating the main effects of the Fintech have the following form:

$$Yi = \beta_0 + \beta_{i1} FINTECHi + \beta_{i2} CVi + \varepsilon$$

Where;

β_0 : is the intercept or constant amount
β_{i1} : are coefficients of the explanatory variables
β_{i2} : are coefficients of the control variables
ε : stands for the error term

Table 2 reports the variables indications and measurements used in this research.

EMPIRICAL RESULTS

The impact of Fintech on Inflation

Before analyzing the relationship between Fintech and inflation, we admit that FinTechs are disruptive and are not free of risk. These technologies offer financial services to customers using technology-integrated business models more effectively and convenient than traditional ones. In fact,

the potential impact of mobile money on inflation has been addressed for the first time by Simpasa and Gurara (2012), who argued that the increase in monetary speed could spread inflation, thus complicating the implementation of monetary policy. According to Aron and Sebudde (2015), forecasting the relationship between mobile money and inflation is difficult in emerging markets, where trade and monetary regimes have changed and foreign exchange prices, energy and food prices are highly volatile. Our empirical results show that Mobile Money approximated by Debit Card and Digital payment through mobile phone does significantly increase Inflation in MENA zone countries, as illustrated in Table 3.

This result is convergent with several previous empirical studies, Simpasa et al. (2011), Mas and Klein (2012), Mehrotra and Yetman (2014), Aron et al. (2015) and Tavneet Suri (2017). The widespread use of credit cards promotes the efficiency of transactions but results in inflation in the absence of monetary intervention. In case of default on credit cards, there is still more inflation and less efficiency gains, Geanakoplos, (2010) and Alvarez and Lippi (2017). On the other hand, Zhang et al, (2013) postulates that mobile money can affect interest rates as it leads to the creation of credit by commercial banks. The role of mobile money in credit creation has been studied by Nampewo et al (2016), who emphasize the crucial role of savings and deposit mobilization. This author has asserted in his hypothesis that if mobile money leads to economic efficiency through a reduction in transaction costs and a better allocation of resources and credit, it follows that the overall economic activity will be supported. In fact, our findings just support previous academic results suggesting the importance of the effectiveness of authorities and decision-makers. We interestingly empirically prove that the ability of the government to formulate and

Table 2. Presentation of variables

Variables	Indication	Measure
Annual inflation rate	INFLATION	The percentage of annual inflation.
Bank account	ACCOUNT	The percentage of respondents who report having an account at a bank or another type of financial institution or report personally using a mobile money service in the .past 12 months (see definition for mobile money account).
Debit card ownership		The percentage of respondents who report having a debit card.
Digital payment	DIGITAL PAIEMENT	The percentage of respondents who report using mobile money, a debit or credit card, or a mobile phone to make a payment from an account, or report using the internet to pay bills or to buy something online, in the past 12 months. It also includes respondents who report paying bills, sending or receiving remittances, receiving payments for agricultural products, receiving government transfers, receiving wages, or receiving a public sector pension directly from or into a financial institution account or through a mobile money account in the past 12 months
Regulatory quality	REGULATORY	Regulatory Quality captures perceptions of the ability of the government to formulate and implement sound policies and regulations that permit and promote private sector development. Estimate gives the country's score on the aggregate indicator, in units of a standard normal distribution, i.e. ranging from approximately -2.5 to 2.5.
Unemployment rate	UNEMPLOYMENT	The percentage of annual unemployment.
Voice and Accountability	VOICE	Voice and Accountability captures perceptions of the extent to which a country's citizens are able to participate in selecting their government, as well as freedom of expression, freedom of association, and a free media. Estimate gives the country's score on the aggregate indicator, in units of a standard normal distribution, i.e. ranging from approximately -2.5 to 2.5.
The freedom if investment	Investment Freedom	The business freedom component measures the extent to which the regulatory and infrastructure environments constrain the efficient operation of businesses. The quantitative score is derived from an array of factors that affect the ease of starting, operating, closing a business
The freedom if finance	Financial Freedom	Financial freedom is a measure of banking efficiency as well as a measure of independence from government control and interference in the financial sector. State ownership of banks and other financial institutions such as insurers and capital markets reduces competition and generally lowers the level of available services
Social revolution	REVOLUTION	A dummy variable that capture the existence of a social revolution.
POLIICAL INSTABILITY	INSTABILITY	Political Stability and Absence of Violence/Terrorism measures perceptions of the likelihood of political instability and/or politically-motivated violence, including terrorism. Percentile rank indicates the country's rank among all countries covered by the aggregate indicator, with 0 corresponding to lowest rank, and 100 to highest rank. Percentile ranks have been adjusted to correct for changes over time in the composition of the countries covered by the WGI.
Gross domestic production	GDP	The logarithm of gross domestic production per capital.

Table 3. Effect of Fintech on inflation (Empirical results of the OLS regression)

Inflation	Coef.	Std. Err.	t	P>|t|	[95% Conf.	Interval]
ACCOUNT	-1.035978***	0.2463666	-4.21	0.000	-1.54338	-0.5285765
DEBIT CARD	0.5704459**	0.251695	2.27	0.032	0.0520702	1.088822
DIGITAL PAIEMENT	0.4063905**	0.1656345	2.45	0.021	0.0652598	0.7475211
REGULATORY * DIGITAL PAIEMENT	-0.3127777*	0.1548258	-2.02	0.054	-0.6316473	0.006092
cons	135.8908***	7.207181	18.85	0	121.0473	150.7343
F(P-value)	5.98 (0.0016)					
R-squared	0.4888					

Notes: * P<0.1,** p < 0.05, *** p < 0.01

implement sound policies and regulations significantly permit to promote development through inflation reduction. In this regard, Narayan and Sahminan (2018) argue that FinTech is able to reduce inflation since these innovative solutions bring down costs and improve the quality of financial services. Ondabu et al. (2015) analyze the relationship between effective inflation control and mobile money and found that mobile money service can be an inflation control tool that allows central banks to control inflation. These authors proposed recommendations on mobile money transfer and effective inflation control as the use of carefully crafted policies and procedures to maintain client satisfaction.

Our result is very important since it takes into consideration the moderating effect of social factors. Empirical results of several regressions show that, as expected, in the context of regulation, approximated by the ability of the government to formulate and implement sound policies and regulations that permit and promote private sector development, inflation significantly decreases. As we present below, there are many studies concerning the relationship between Fintech and economic indicator but this research is the first according to our knowledge to integrate social factors.

Tavneet Suri (2017) argued that mobile money systems could accelerate the speed of the currency and inflation. They also facilitate trade, remittances and transactions in US dollars. On the other hand, Mas and Klein (2012) confirm that the speed of money increases in a normal way is above all the electronic money which is based on a safe model. In this sense, Aron et al. (2015) and Simpasa et al. (2011) pointed out that mobile money could lead to an increase in the speed of money and therefore the need for regulation to ensure that these products do not undermine the effectiveness of monetary policy. Walker (2016) confirmed that financial innovations help to reduce the incomplete nature of markets, and monetary authorities could usefully move from headline inflation to core inflation. These results encourage policymakers to continue to support and encourage the spread of mobile phones. Even Mawejje (2017) argued that the use of mobile money does not lead to high inflationary risks. In this sense, Mehrotra and Yetman (2014) showed the existence of a positive relationship between the financial inclusion and the volatility of inflation. However, since the Fintech share in the economy and financial markets remains small, it's too early to draw a policy implication especially in a fast growing market.

The Impact of Fintech on Unemployment

With existing robotics and artificial learning technologies, about half of all paid activities could be automated. It is clear that significant disappearances and job changes are likely to be observed. It would be better to accept and improve the digital revolution than to ignore it and counter it so the reorganization of the economy around revolutionary technologies is extremely beneficial in the long run.

Since little research exists to find correlation between FIintech and the general economy and society, we rely mostly on economic intuition to choose variables as indicators for social and economic environment. Given that Dietrich & Wernli (2016) and Foo et al. (2017)[15] found that higher unemployment rates were correlated with higher Fintech rates, we include the annual unemployment rate. In our case, we analyze the potential effect of Fintech moderated by social factors on unemployment as a country's welfare measures (see Table 3).

In fact, there are serious pressure related to Fintech, which are not efficiently and sufficiently because they still could have a negative impact on production and productivity. Several studies examined the effect of Fintech on the global economic and social environment. While most of countries attempt to reduce unemployment through Fintech, the hiring rate remains low, especially in the MENA zone countries. Unemployment among young people and holder of higher certificates was the principal reason of social movements in those countries. Therefore, authorities should focus on creating appropriate regulation for Fintech to moderate potential negative effects.

Empirical results reveal that banking account creating and Fintech approximated by digital payment decrease significantly unemployment. This result is relevant since it is in harmony with country's objectives. So, Fintech is a driver of economic growth for MENA zone countries and a breeding ground for innovative projects and jobs. Moreover, we interestingly find that the context of voice and accountability where country's citizens are able to participate in selecting their government, as well as freedom of expression, freedom of association, and a free media, unemployment rate significantly decrease. This result suggests the importance of role of the government to formulate and implement sound policies and regulations significantly permit to promote development through job creation.

Table 4. Impact of Fintech on unemployment (Empirical results of the GLS regression)

Unemployment	Coef.	Std. Err.	t	P>|t|	[95% Conf.	Interval]
CREDIT CARD	-0.0849186	0.0863276	-0.98	0.335	-0.26309	0.0932529
DIGITAL PAYMENT	-0.1143828*	0.0578573	-1.98	0.060	-0.2337944	0.0050289
DIGITAL PAYMEENT *VOICE	-0.1081099**	0.043865	-2.46	0.021	-0.1986427	-0.0175771
ACCOUNT	-0.1377893**	0.0548975	-2.51	0.019	-0.2510921	-0.0244865
GDP	0.1635161	0.6087936	0.27	0.791	-1.092972	1.420004
_cons	17.40928***	1.658756	10.5	0.000	13.98578	20.83278
F(P-value)	9.99(0.000)					
R-squared	0.6754					

Notes: * P<0.1,** p < 0.05, *** p < 0.01

THE IMPACT OF FINTECH ON INVESTMENT AND FINANCIAL FREEDOM

Recent years were good vintage for fintech. Globally, 2018 marks a record for investments in fintech, which reached $ 27.5[16] billion in the first six months, notably thanks to Asia. However, while Fintech investment in Mena zone is building fast, it remains modest compared to other parts of the world, especially as mentioned in Asia. In fact, according to the Magnitt report, a Dubai-based entrepreneurs' network, last year was a record with 366 deals, attracting $893 million in investment. Of all deals in the region, digital startups account for 12% followed be e-commerce. Almost absent few years ago, MENA fintech is now a $2 billion market. The Beirut-based consultants MENA Research Partners expect annual growth to reach $125 million by 2022 with more new firms launching every year[17].

A regulatory approach to financial technology should assure that consumers and investors are safe from fraud and the state can fight against tax evasion, money laundering and terrorist financing while ensuring that that risks are well understood and managed. When developing a regulatory framework decision-makers should look to the future while being more creative and flexible. According to Gomber and. al (2018), Finteh has begun to attract significant investments, which are expected to increase in the future as more technologies are deployed in the financial services business. Many positive features justify people's willingness to adopt encryption and encrypted currencies, alternative payment solutions, and Fintech investment and banking services. However, there are also threats related to these elements of Fintech, which are rarely addressed but which could have a negative impact on the entire financial services sector. Pejkovska (2018) examined the effect of Fintech on the global financial services sector. The results show that the current regulation of Fintech is inappropriate and could have potential negative effects on the financial sector, such as corruption of cyber security, breach of data privacy and use of Fintech services for illegal purposes. Therefore, authorities should focus on creating appropriate regulation for Fintech to mitigate potential negative effects. That's why Nicoletti (2017) argue that financial technology companies do not yet have to establish themselves as a force of influence in the financial services sector.

In our case, empirical results on MENA zone countries highlights interesting findings. We show that Digital Payment and Credit Card, as Fintech's proxy, significantly increase investment and financial freedom while it significantly decreases when we consider Political Instability (see Table 4). This result is expected since in case of political stability decision-makers do not opt for innovative technologies and protect the interests of economic lobbies. This is the case of several Arab countries. This is clear for dictators ones and could be explained by the long duration of democratic transition steps. On the other hand, and in line with our findings, we interestingly find that revolution in MENA zone countries do positively and significantly affect both investment and financial freedom. Indeed, after revolution country's citizens participate in selecting their government and then get freedom of expression in all sectors including financial and investment ones. Technology enabled lending platforms could enhance the resilience and stability of credit in the financial system and contain liquidity risks in the economy to pure liquidity shocks, provided that: (i) investors are educated with an understanding that such networks are not direct providers of liquidity, and (ii) that the end investors are not traditional banks. Fintech platforms are currently less exposed to system-wide shocks compared to traditional banks since on aggregate and by scale they are more domestically driven in their operations. Large exogenous shocks and spill-over effects might be further moderated by the degree of low system interconnectedness compared

Table 5. Impact of Fintech on Investment and financial freedom (Empirical results of the GLS regression)

	Investment Freedom			Financial Freedom		
	Coef.	**T**	**P>|t|**	**Coef.**	**T**	**P>|t|**
REVOLUTION	17.68951	2.42	0.024	14.29646	2.14	0.043
DIGITAL PAYMENT * POLIICAL STABILITY	-0.199481	-1.93	0.066	-0.2388399	-2.53	0.019
CREDIT CARD	0.2995667	1.14	0.265	0.4785135	2	0.057
DIGITAL PAYMENT	0.2489989	1.68	0.106	0.071741	0.53	0.601
GDP	-2.11135	-0.85	0.404	-1.49215	-0.66	0.516
_cons	33.79442	4.21	0	27.94862	3.82	0.001
F(p-value)	3.14(0.000)			11.13(0.000)		
R-squared	0.4198			0.4054		

Notes: * P<0.1, ** p < 0.05, *** p < 0.01

to banks. Yet, this degree of low connection may potentially gradually decline as Fintechs become more interconnected with banks (FSB, 2018). This is an aspect for competition and regulatory authorities to consider further.

Figure 6 displays the main empirical results of the moderating effect of political stability, regulation and voice on the relationship between Fintech and economic performance.

The moderating effect of political stability, regulation and voice on the relationship between fintech and economic performance.

CONCLUDING REMARKS AND SUGGESTIONS FOR FUTURE RESEARCH

Fintech companies have produced a public market for consumer debt, analogous to the bond market; this market did not exist prior to 2006 and it was largely owed to financial and informational frictions on the part of banks, Balyuk, (2017). Fintechs are a new, fast-growing part of the financial services domain, and as such, they are characterized by limited understanding due to new phenomena emerging. While a well-documented and established amount of research concentrates on the field of financial services and the banking sector, only a few academic researchers have investigated the Fintech business. This chapter tried to study the effect of Fintech on macroeconomic conjuncture in MENA zone countries in times of political and social upheaval. Doing so, we attempt to demystify the creative disruption arena and the gradually widespread presence of digital platforms within the financial community. We also attempted to shed more light on the moderating effect of social and political factors, an issue which was rarely addressed. Our empirical results emphasize previous researches supporting that Fintech increase Inflation, Simpasa et al. (2011), Simpasa and Gurara (2012), Iazzolino (2015), Aron et al. (2015) and Tavne and Suri (2017). Indeed, the creation of crypto-currencies increases inflation which is at the origin of the speed of the currency in the absence of the intervention of the governmental authority through a monetary policy and the appropriate regulations. Hence the need for the central bank to resume its role, support the evolution of the currency and control inflation in the presence of Fintech.

Figure 6.

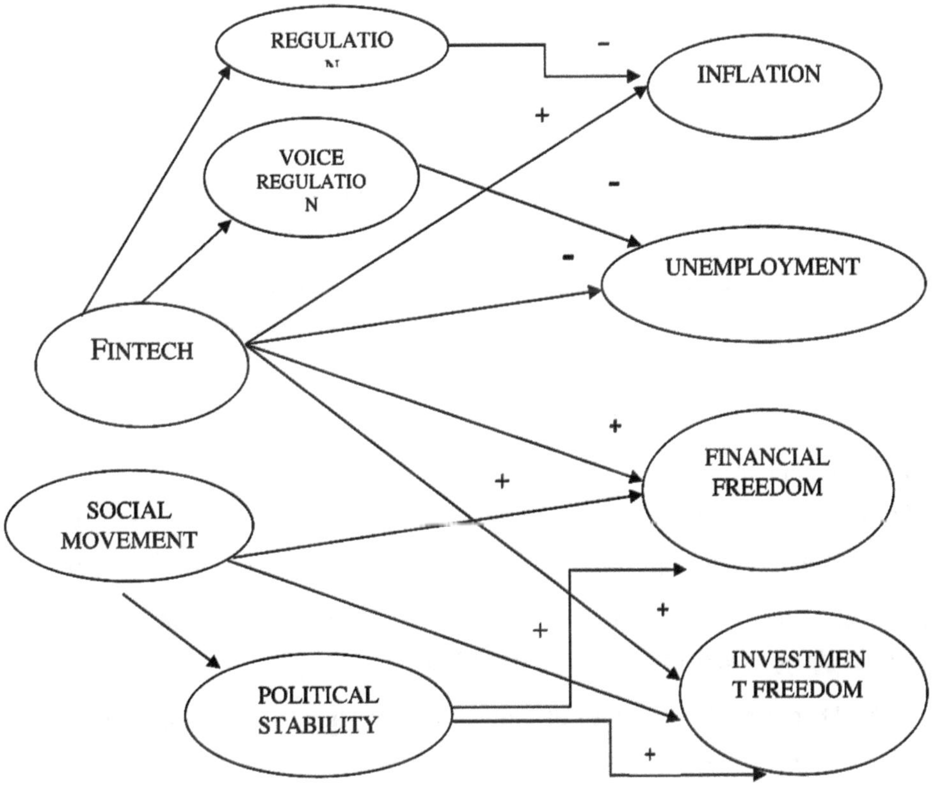

In this chapter, we interestingly prove that the ability of the government to formulate and implement sound policies and regulations significantly allow to promote economic development through inflation reduction. So, appropriate regulations allow mitigating those potentials negative impacts. Moreover, at the social level, we prove that Fintech decrease unemployment. Furthermore, in a context of voice and accountability where country's citizens enjoy freedom of expression, freedom of association, and a free media, and therefore are able to participate in selecting their government, this positive effect is validated. We conclude that, Fintech is a driver of economic growth for MENA zone countries and a breeding ground for innovative projects and jobs and that the role of government to formulate and implement sound policies and regulations allow promoting social and development through job creation, Ruberti et al. (2018). Finally, we highlight interesting findings. In line with the results of Gomber and. al (2018), Nicoletti (2017) and Haan (2015), we show that Fintech's increase investment and financial freedom by attracting investments. But, while social revolution is an improving factor, political stability is negatively correlated with increase investment and financial freedom. This result could be explained by the fact that decision-makers do not opt for innovative technologies and want to protect the interests of economic lobbies. This is the case of several countries in MENA zone region where some countries are characterized by dictator political regime and others are in a process of setting up new democratic regimes going through a long transition steps. It would also be interesting to study the degree of correlations and interactions between bank and Fintech activity as evolving companies. In order to extend empirical literature on Fintech, further study is warranted to examine the impact of the maturity of infrastructure like digital platforms to attract Fintechs in emerging countries.

REFERENCES

Adam & Walker. (2016). *Mobile Money and Monetary Policy in East African Countries*. University of Oxford.

AFI. (2016). *Applications for Future Internet*. International Summit, Puebla, Mexico.

Alvarez, L., & Lippi, F. (2017). Cash burns: An inventory model with a cash-credit choice. *Italy Journal of Monetary Economics*, *90*, 99–112. doi:10.1016/j.jmoneco.2017.07.001

Aron, Janine, Muellbauer, & Sebudde. (2015). *Inflation Forecasting Models for Uganda: Is Mobile Money Relevant?* CSAE Working, Paper 2015–17, Centre for the Study of African Economies.

Aron, Rivadeneyra, & Sohal. (2017). *Fintech: Is This Time Different? A Framework for Assessing Risks and Opportunities for Central Banks*. Bank of Canada Staff Discussion Paper.

Athey, Susan, Chetty, Imbens, & Kang. (2016). *Estimating Treatment Effects Using Multiple Surrogates: The Role of the Surrogate Score and the Surrogate Index*. arXiv: 1603.09326

Brody. (2017). *Un impact positif sur la société en soutenant l'économie*. rapport d'activité.

Carrick. (2016). Bitcoin as a Complement to Emerging Market Currencies. *Emerging Markets Finance and Trade, 52*(10). doi:10.1080/1540496X.2016.1193002

Chiu. (2017). The Disruptive Implications of Fintech-Policy Themes for Financial Regulators. *Journal of Technology Law & Policy, 21*(1).

Claessens, Frost, Turner, & Zhu. (2018). *Les marchés du crédit Fintech à travers le monde: taille, moteurs et enjeux de politique publique*. BRI.

Clarke & Broby. (2017). How to foster co-operation between the Scottish and Irish Asset Management industries. *Scottish and Irish Finance Initiative Conference*.

Deloitte. (2017). The Connecting Global Fintech. *Interim Hub Review*.

Demirgüç-Kunt. Leora, Ansar, & Jagati. (2017). *Making It Easier to Apply for a Bank Account: A Study of the Indian Market*. Policy Research Working Paper 8205. World Bank.

Dorefleitner, Shmitt, & Weber. (2017). Fintech in Germany. Springer International Publishing.

Erosa, A., & Ventura, G. (2002). On inflation as a regressive consumption tax. *Journal of Monetary Economics*, *49*(4), 761–795. doi:10.1016/S0304-3932(02)00115-0

Foo, Lim, & Wong. (2017). *Macroeconomics and FinTech: Uncovering Latent Macroeconomic Effects on Peer-to-Peer Lending*. Papers 1710.11283, arXiv.org.

Gabor & Brooks. (2016). The digital revolution in financial inclusion: International development. *New Political Economy*, *4*, 23–436.

Geanakoplos. (2010). Credit cards and inflation. *Games and Economic Behavior.*

Global Partnership for Financial Inclusion. (2011). *The G20 Principles for Innovative Financial Inclusion: Bringing the Principles to Life.* Author.

Godwin, Kourabas, & Ramsay. (2017). Financial Stability Authorities and Macroprudential Regulation. *Banking & Finance Law Review, 32*(2), 223–254.

Gomber, K., Koch, J.-A., & Siering, M. (2017). Digital Finance and FinTech: Current research and future research directions. *Journal of Business Economics, 87*(5), 537–580. doi:10.100711573-017-0852-x

Haan, Oosterloo, & Schoenmaker, (2015), 'Financial markets and institutions: A European perspective)'. Cambridge University Press 978-1-107-02594-3.

Jagtiani & Lemieux. (2018). *Do Fintech Lenders Penetrate Areas That Are Underserved by Traditional Banks?* Working Paper, org/papers/w20899.pdf.

Lee, I., & Shin, Y. J. (2018). Fintech: Ecosystem, business models, investment decisions and challenges. *Business Horizons, 61*(1), 35–46. doi:10.1016/j.bushor.2017.09.003

Maier. (2016). Supply and demand on crowdlending platforms: connecting small and medium sized enterprise borrowers and consumer investors. *Journal of Retailing and Consumer Services, 33*, 143-153.

Manyika, Lund, Singer, White, & Berry. (2016). *Digital Finance for All: Powering Inclusive Growth In Emerging Economies.* McKinsey Global Institute.

Mas & Klein. (2012). *A note on macro-financial implications of mobile money schemes.* Working Paper Series 188.

Mawejje & Lakuma. (2017). *Macroeconomic Effects of Mobile Money in Uganda.* Economic Policy Research Centre. doi:10.13140/RG.2.2.24254.18244

Mbiti & Weil. (2014). *Mobile Banking: the Impact of M-PESA in Kenya.* NBER Working Paper Series.

Mulligan, C. B., & Sala-i-Martin, X. (2000). Extensive Margins and the Demand for Money at Low Interest Rates. *Journal of Political Economy, 108*(5), 961–991. doi:10.1086/317676

Narayan, Rahman, & Setiawan. (2018). Bitcoin Price Growth and Indonesia's Monetary System. *Emerging Markets Review.*

Nepote-Cit, Ruberti, & Tran. (2018). *Perspectives économiques régionales: Afrique subsaharienne.* International Monetary Fund.

Nicoletti. (2017). *The Future of Fintech.* Integrating Finance and Technology in Financial Services.

Ondabu, Mohamed Sheikh, & Oyagi. (2015). Assessment of Non-Financial Motivation on Employee Productivity: Case of Ministry of Finance Headquarters in Hargeisa Somaliland. *International Journal of Business Management and Economic Research, 6*(6), 400–416.

Pejkovska. (2018). *Potential negative effects of Fintech on the financial services sector Examples from the European Union, India and the United States of America*. Applied Sciences Bachelor of Business Administration Double Degree in European Business Administration Thesis.

Porter & Millar. (1985). How information gives you competitive advantage. *Harvard Business Review*, 149–160.

Prescott & Larose. (2016). Fintech Companies Face Big Privacy Challenges in 2016. *VC Experts Blog*. Available at: https://blog.vcexperts.com/2016/08/09/Fintech-companies-face-big-privacy-challenges

Puschmann. (2017). Business & Information Systems Engineering. *The International Journal of wirt schafts informatik*, *59*(1), 69-76.

Simpasa & Gurara. (2012). Inflation Dynamics in selected East African countries: Ethiopia, Kenya, Tanzania and Uganda. AFDB Brief 2012. African Development Bank.

Smith. (1997). Financial markets in development, and the development of financial markets. *Journal of Economics Dynamics and Control*.

Suri, T. (2017). Mobile Money. *Annual Review of Economics*, *9*, 497–520.

Turkish. (2014). *Turkey/GCC Economic Relations*. Franco-Turkish Paper, No. 12.

Yang, G., Lu, Y., Gupta, S., Cao, Y., & Zhang, R. (2012). Mobile payment services adoption across time: An empirical study of the effects of behavioral beliefs, social influences, and personal traits. *Computers in Human Behavior*, *28*(1), 129–142. doi:10.1016/j.chb.2011.08.019

ENDNOTES

1. Singapore Fintech Festival 2018.
2. Approximately 3 billion unbanked consumers around the globe could potentially be connected to the financial system.
3. CLIFFORD CHANCE, Fintech in Middle East – Developments across MENA, 2018. available for free download at https://www.cliffordchance.com/briefings/2018/12/fintech_in_the_middleeast-developmentsacros.html
4. Wamda research Lab, 2016.
5. Fintech Flourishes in MENA: Report by Fintechnews Middle East 6. January 2018
6. Report of Singapore Association., "FinTech ecosystem playbook", (2018).
7. See figure 6.
8. See figure 7.
9. There are "8 516 992" bank account in 2016 according to the Tunisian central bank report.
10. https://www.webmanagercenter.com/2018/04/09/418301/taux-durbanisation-70-de-la-population-tunisienne-vit-dans-seulement-10-du-territoire/

11 See figure 8.

12 ICTs represent only 0.6% of investments in 2015.

13 Note that the digital positioning of Tunisia in advanced; first in Africa and 40th in the world.

14 The Economist Corporate Network report (2016).

15 Jessica Foo & Lek-Heng Lim & Ken Sze-Wai Wong, 2017. "Macroeconomics and FinTech: Uncovering Latent Macroeconomic Effects on Peer-to-Peer Lending," Papers 1710.11283, arXiv.org.

16 Investments in the first half of 2018 totaled $ 27.5 billion, exceeding the 2017 total of $ 20.5 billion, according to a note from the Boston Consulting Group (BCG).

17 McKinsey Global Institute (2016).

APPENDIX

Figure 7. Tunisian people subscripted to mobile telephone networks

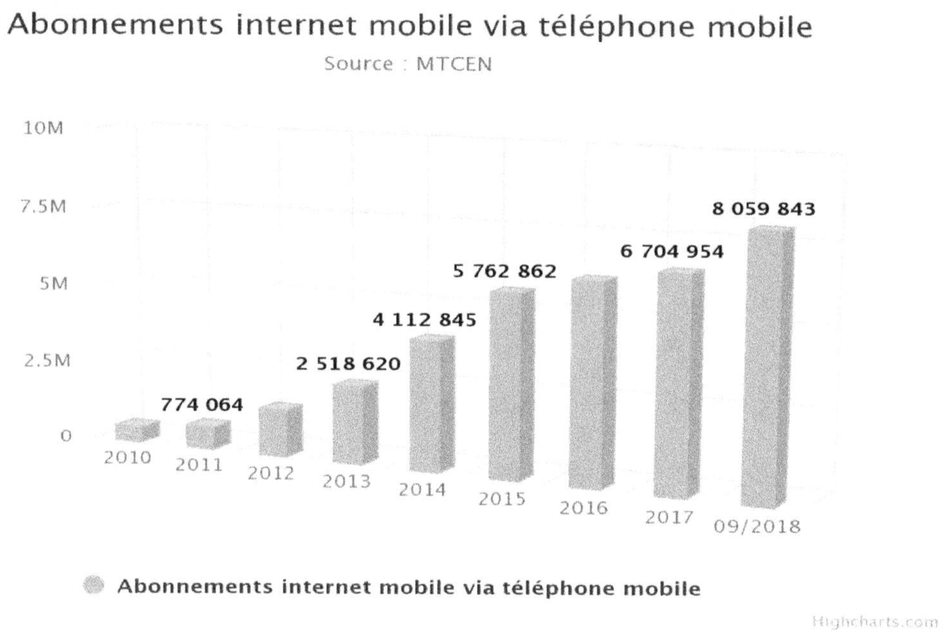

Figure 8. Tunisian people using internet

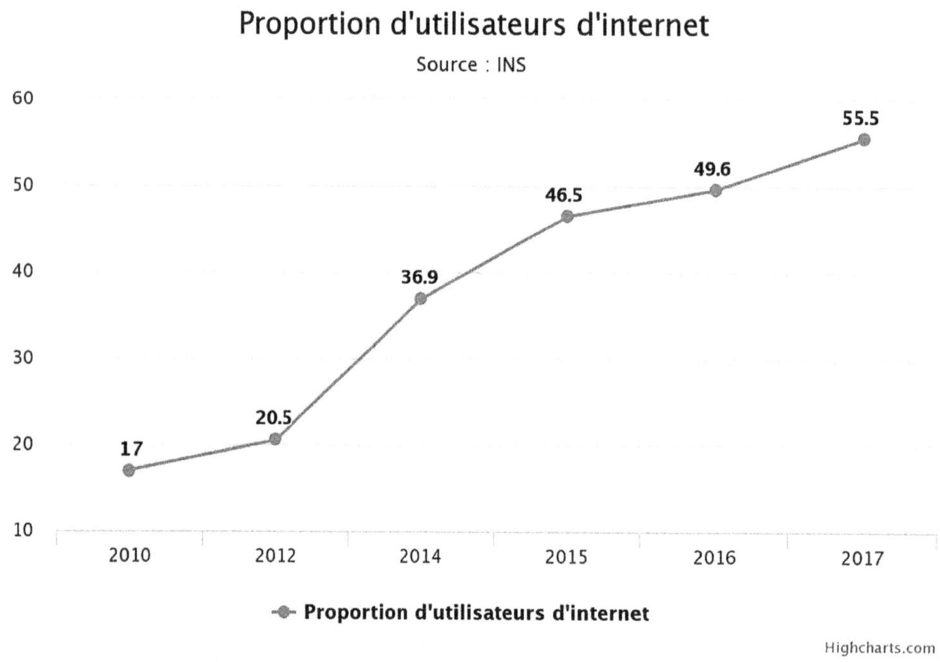

Figure 9. Progress of valid electronic transaction (2010-2018)

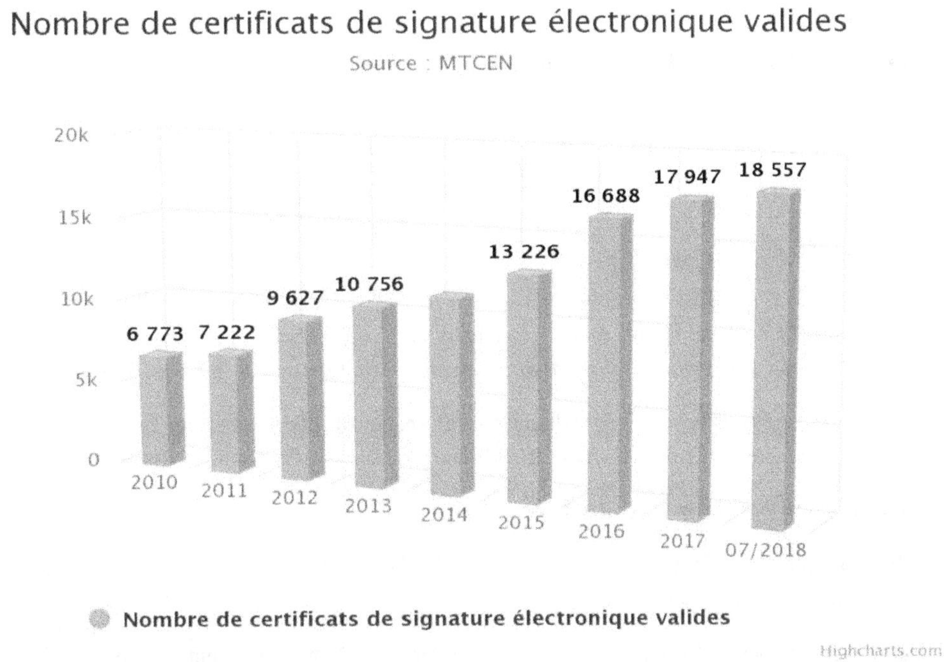

Compilation of References

Abidin, Alwi, & Ariffin. (2011). A case Study on the Implementation of Qardhul Hasan Concept as a Financial Product for Islamic Banks in Malaysia. *International Journal of Economics, Management & Accounting, 19*, 18-100.

Abojeib, M., & Habib, F. (2019). Blockchain for Islamic Social Responsibility Institutions. In *FinTech as a Disruptive Technology for Financial Institutions* (pp. 221–240). IGI Global. doi:10.4018/978-1-5225-7805-5.ch010

Abozaid, A. (2004). *Fiqh Al-Riba*. Beirut: Al-Risalah.

Abozaid, A. (2016). Critical Review of the Tools of Ijtihad Used in Islamic Finance. *Journal of Islamic Economic Studies, The Islamic Research and Training Institute, 24*, 31.

Abozaid, A. (2016). The Impact of Currencies Value Depreciation on Debt Repayment, (Arabic) *Al-Tajdid Journal. International Islamic University Malaysia, 20*, 40.

Abrams, J., Carraro, M., & Ahmed, W. (2016). *Alternate Delivery Channels for Financial Inclusion: Opportunities and Challenges in African Banks and Microfinance Institutions*. The MasterCard Foundation and Bankable Frontier Associates.

Abu Bakar, N., Rosbi, S., & Uzaki, K. (2017). Cryptocurrency Framework Diagnostics from Islamic Finance Perspective: A New Insight of Bitcoin System Transaction. *International Journal of Management Science and Business Administration, 4*(1), 19–28. doi:10.18775/ijmsba.1849-5664-5419.2014.41.1003

Acharya, V. V., Pedersen, L. H., Philippon, T., & Richardson, M. (2010). *Measuring systemic risk*. NYU Working Paper.

Acharya, V. V., Engle, R., & Richardson, M. (2012). Capital shortfall: A new approach to ranking and regulating systemic risks. *The American Economic Review, 102*(3), 59–64. doi:10.1257/aer.102.3.59

Achsien, I. H., & Purnamasari, D. L. (2016). Islamic Crowd-funding as The Next Financial Innovation in Islamic Finance : Potential and Anticipated Regulation in Indonesia. *European Journal of Islamic Finance Voluntary, 5*, 1–11. doi:10.13135/2421-2172/1771

Adam & Walker. (2016). *Mobile Money and Monetary Policy in East African Countries*. University of Oxford.

AFI. (2016). *Applications for Future Internet*. International Summit, Puebla, Mexico.

Agenor, P.-R. (2003). Benefits and Costs of International Financial Integration: Theory and Facts. *World Economy, 26*(8), 1089–1118. doi:10.1111/1467-9701.00564

Agrawal, A., Gans, J. S., & Goldfarb, A. (2019b). Artificial intelligence: The Ambiguous Labour Market Impact of Automating Prediction. *The Journal of Economic Perspectives, 33*(2), 31–50. doi:10.1257/jep.33.2.31

Agrawal, A., Gans, J., & Goldfarb, A. (2019a). Economic Policy for Artificial Intelligence. *Innovation Policy and the Economy, 19*(1), 139–159. doi:10.1086/699935

Agur, I. (2018). Central bank digital currencies: An overview of pros and cons. In *SUERF Conference Proceedings 2018/2: Do We Need Central Bank Digital Currency? Economics, Technology and Institutions.* Bocconi University and Baffi Carefin.

Ahmat, N., & Bashir, S. (2017). *Central Bank Digital Currency: A Monetary Policy Perspective.* Bank Negara. Monetary Policy Department/Staff Insights 2017/11.

Aitken, R. (2018). *Global Financial Services Bullish on AI, the 'Disruptive Tech' Frontrunner.* Retrieved from https://www.forbes.com/sites/rogeraitken/2018/11/28/global-financial-services-bullish-on-ai-the-disruptive-tech-frontrunner/?source=post_page---------------------------#5ed3b85f2311

Ajzen, I. (1991). The theory of planned behaviour. *Organizational Behavior and Human Decision Processes, 50*(2), 179–211. doi:10.1016/0749-5978(91)90020-T

Ajzen, I., & Fishbein, M. (1980). *Understanding Attitudes and Predicting Social Behavior.* Englewood Cliffs, NJ: Prentice-Hall.

Akter, S., D'Ambra, J., & Ray, P. (2011). An Evaluation of PLS Based Complex Models : The Roles of Power Analysis, Predictive Relevance and GOF Index. In 7th AMCIS Proceedings (pp. 1–7). Academic Press.

Al Janabi, M. A. M. (2008, Summer). Integrating Liquidity Risk Factor into a Parametric Value at Risk Method. *Journal of Trading*, 76-87.

Al Janabi, M. A. M. (2009). Market Liquidity and Strategic Asset Allocation: Applications to GCC Stock Exchanges. *Middle East Development Journal, 1*(2), 227–254. doi:10.1142/S1793812009000115

Al Janabi, M. A. M. (2010). Incorporating Asset Liquidity Effects in Risk-Capital Modeling. *Review of Middle East Economics and Finance, 6*(1), 60–89. doi:10.2202/1475-3693.1258

Al Janabi, M. A. M. (2011). Modeling coherent trading risk parameters under illiquid market perspective. *Studies in Economics and Finance, 28*(4), 301–332. doi:10.1108/10867371111171555

Al Janabi, M. A. M. (2012). Optimal Commodity Asset Allocation with a Coherent Market Risk Modeling. *Review of Financial Economics, 21*(3), 131–140. doi:10.1016/j.rfe.2012.06.007

Al Janabi, M. A. M. (2013). Optimal and Coherent Economic-Capital Structures: Evidence from Long and Short-Sales Trading Positions under Illiquid Market Perspectives. *Annals of Operations Research, 205*(1), 109–139. doi:10.100710479-012-1096-3

Al Janabi, M. A. M. (2014). Optimal and Investable Portfolios: An Empirical Analysis with Scenario Optimization Algorithms under Crisis Market Prospects. *Economic Modelling, 40*, 369–381. doi:10.1016/j.econmod.2013.11.021

Al Janabi, M. A. M., Arreola-Hernández, J. A., Berger, T., & Nguyen, D. K. (2017). Multivariate dependence and portfolio optimization algorithms under illiquid market scenarios. *European Journal of Operational Research, 259*(3), 1121–1131. doi:10.1016/j.ejor.2016.11.019

Ala, A. A. (2014). *Islamic Banking and Finance in the Philippines.* Retrieved from Inclusive Insurance Asia Website: https://www.inclusiveinsuranceasia.com/docs/landscape-study-2013/session6/MLSAO_S6_Takaful_BSP_Arifa.pdf

Alaabed, A., & Mirakhor, A. (2017). Accelerating Risk Sharing Finance via FinTech: NextGen Islamic Finance. *The 1st International Colloquium on Islamic Banking and Islamic Finance*, 1–10.

Alaeddin, O., & Altounjy, R. (2018). Trust, technology awareness and satisfaction effect into the intention to use cryptocurrency among generation Z in Malaysia. *International Journal of Pure and Applied Mathematics, 120*(2), 7–10. doi:10.14419/ijet.v7i4.29.21588

Albahouth, A. S. A. (2018). Crypto-currency: concept, typology and economic impacts, *Scientific Journal of Economics and Trade*, 1. (in Arabic)

Alim, E. A. (2014). *Global Leaders in Islamic Finance: Industry Milestones and Reflections*. John Wiley & Sons.

Ali, R., Barrdear, J., Clews, R., & Southgate, J. (2014). The economics of digital currencies. Bank of England. *Quarterly Bulletin, 54*(3), 276–286.

Allen, F., & Gu, X. (2018). The Interplay between regulations and financial stability. *Journal of Financial Services Research, 53*(2-3), 233–248. doi:10.100710693-018-0296-7

Al-Maqrizi, T. (2011). *Ighathat al-Umma bi Kashf al-Ghumma*. Cairo: Al-Manarah Al-Azhariyah Publilsher.

Al-Masri, Y. R. (2013). *Money in Islamic Economy* (1st ed.). Damascus: Dar Almaktabi. (in Arabic)

Almgren, R., & Chriss, N. (1999). *Optimal Execution of Portfolio Transaction*. Working Paper. Department of Mathematics, The University of Chicago.

Alnajdi. (2010). *Accounting and Auditing Organization for Islamic Financial Institutions "Shari'ah Standards."* Al-imtiyaz Investment.

Al-Nawawi, Y. (1995). *Al-Majmouh, Jaddah*. Irshad Publisher.

Alonso. (2015). Crowdfunding in Islamic Finance and Microfinance: A Case Study of Egypt. In *Access to Finance and Human Development – Essays on Zakah, Awqaf and Microfinance.* (Vol. 1, pp. 85–94). Academic Press.

Al-Sabhani, A. H. O. (1998). Money as it should be, in an Islamic system. [in Arabic]. *Journal of King Abdulaziz University: Islamic Economics, 10*, 3–38.

Alvarez, L., & Lippi, F. (2017). Cash burns: An inventory model with a cash-credit choice. *Italy Journal of Monetary Economics, 90*, 99–112. doi:10.1016/j.jmoneco.2017.07.001

Amihud, Y., Mendelson, H., & Pedersen, L. H. (2005). Liquidity and Asset Prices. *Foundations and Trends in Finance, 1*(4), 269–364. doi:10.1561/0500000003

Andrian, T., & Brunnermeier, M. (2016). CoVaR. *The American Economic Review, 106*(7), 1705–1741. doi:10.1257/aer.20120555

Angelidis, T., & Benos, A. (2006). Liquidity adjusted value-at-risk based on the components of the bid-ask spread. *Applied Financial Economics, 16*(11), 835–851. doi:10.1080/09603100500426440

Anonymous. (2013, December 4). *Bitcoin hype worse than 'tulip mania' says dutch central banker.* https://www.theguardian.com/technology/2013/dec/04/bitcoin-bubble-tulip-dutch-banker

Anonymous. (2013, November 29). Man Throws Away 7,500 Bitcoins, Now Worth $7.5 Million. *CBS DC.* Retrieved from https://washington.cbslocal.com/2013/11/29/man-throws-away-7500-bitcoins-now-worth-7-5-million/

Anonymous. (2015 January 13). The magic of mining. *The Economist.* Retrieved from https://www.economist.com/business/2015/01/08/the-magic-of-mining

Anonymous. (2015 October 31). The great chain of being sure about things. *The Economist.* Retrieved from https://www.economist.com/briefing/2015/10/31/the-great-chain-of-being-sure-about-things

Anonymous. (2015, January16). Deep Web Drug Dealers Are Freaking Out About the Bitcoin Crash. *Business Insider.* Retrieved from https://www.businessinsider.com/bitcoin-crash-drug-dealers-2015-1

Antonopoulos, A. M. (2014). *Mastering Bitcoin. Unlocking Digital Crypto-Currencies.* O'Reilly Media.

Aqidah, N., Mohd, S., & Palil, R. (2016). Crowdfunding: a Collaborative Waqf Based Internet Platform. *International Journal of Business, Economics and Law, 11*(5), 41–46. Retrieved from http://ijbel.com/wp-content/uploads/2017/03/IJBEL-57.pdf

Arner, D. W., Barberis, J. N., & Buckley, R. P. (2015). *The Evolution of Fintech: A New Post-Crisis Paradigm? Academic Press.*

Aron, Janine, Muellbauer, & Sebudde. (2015). *Inflation Forecasting Models for Uganda: Is Mobile Money Relevant?* CSAE Working, Paper 2015–17, Centre for the Study of African Economies.

Aron, Rivadeneyra, & Sohal. (2017). *Fintech: Is This Time Different? A Framework for Assessing Risks and Opportunities for Central Banks.* Bank of Canada Staff Discussion Paper.

Arreola-Hernández, J., Al Janabi, M. A. M., Hammoudeh, S., & Nguyen, D. K. (2015). Time lag dependence, cross-correlation and risk analysis of U.S. energy and non-energy stock portfolios. *Journal of Asset Management, 16*(7), 467–483. doi:10.1057/jam.2015.33

Arreola-Hernandez, J., Hammoudeh, S., Khuong, N. D., Al Janabi, M. A. M., & Reboredo, J. C. (2016). Global financial crisis and dependence risk analysis of sector portfolios: A vine copula approach. *Applied Economics, 49*(25), 2409–2427. doi:10.1080/00036846.2016.1240346

Asian Development Bank. (2018). *Republic of the Philippines: Islamic Finance for the Philippines.* Retrieved from https://www.adb.org/sites/default/files/project-documents/50325/50325-001-tar-en.pdf

Association of Southeast Asian Nations (ASEAN). (2017). *Facilitating Equity Crowdfunding in the ASEAN Region.* Author.

Asutay, M. (2013). The development of Islamic banking in Turkey: regulation, performance and political economy. In V. Cattelan (Ed.), *Islamic finance in Europe: Towards a plural financial system* (pp. 213–226). Cheltenham, UK: Elward Elgar Publishing. doi:10.4337/9781781002513.00026

Athey, Susan, Chetty, Imbens, & Kang. (2016). *Estimating Treatment Effects Using Multiple Surrogates: The Role of the Surrogate Score and the Surrogate Index.* arXiv: 1603.09326

Australian Government Treasury. (n.d.). *Economic benefits of fintech.* Retrieved from https://treasury.gov.au/publication/backing-australian-fintech/economic-benefits-of-fintech/

Auzzir, Z., Haigh, R., & Amaratunga, D. (2018). Impacts of Disaster to SMEs in Malaysia. *Procedia Engineering, 212,* 1131–1138. doi:10.1016/j.proeng.2018.01.146

Aziz, M. A., & Che Wan, B. A. (2016). Platform Akaun Pelaburan – IAP Alternatif Baharu Usahawan Raih Teroka. *Berita Harian.*

Aziz, S., Md Husin, M., Hussin, N., & Afaq, Z. (2019). Factors that influence individuals' intentions to purchase family takaful mediating role of perceived trust. *Asia Pacific Journal of Marketing and Logistics*, *31*(1), 81–104. doi:10.1108/APJML-12-2017-0311

Bacha, O. I. (2008). The Islamic interbank money market and a dual banking system: The Malaysian experience. *International Journal of Islamic and Middle Eastern Finance and Management*, *1*(3), 210–226. doi:10.1108/17538390810901140

Bacon, J., Michels, J. D., Millard, C., & Singh, J. (2018). Blockchain Demystified: A Technical and Legal Introduction to Distributed and Centralised Ledgers. *Richmond Journal of Law and Technology*, *25*(1), 1–106.

Baek, C., & Elbeck, M. (2015). Bitcoins as an investment or speculative vehicle? A first look. *Applied Economics Letters*, *22*(1), 30–34. doi:10.1080/13504851.2014.916379

Bagozzi, R. P., & Yi, Y. (1988). On the evaluation of structural equation models. *Journal of the Academy of Marketing Science*, *16*(1), 74–94. doi:10.1007/BF02723327

Bakar, N. A., & Rosbi, S. (2018). Robust Framework Diagnostics of Blockchain for Bitcoin Transaction System : A Technical Analysis from Islamic Financial Technology (i -FinTech) Perspective. *International Journal of Business and Management*, 2(3), 22–29. doi:10.26666/rmp.ijbm.2018.3.4

Bakar, N. A., & Rosbi, S. (2018). Robust Framework Diagnostics of Blockchain for Bitcoin Transaction System: A Technical Analysis from Islamic Financial Technology (i-FinTech) Perspective. *International Journal of Business and Management*, 2(3), 22–29.

Bangia, A., Diebold, F.X., Schuermann, T., & Stroughair, J.D. (2002). *Modeling liquidity risk with implications for traditional market risk measurement and management.* Academic Press.

Bank Negara Malaysia and Securities Commission. (2018). *Press release: Joint statement on the regulation of digital assets in Malaysia.* Retrieved from http://www.bnm.gov.my/index.php?ch=en_press&pg=en_press&ac=4783

Bank Negara Malaysia. (2016). *Financial technology regulatory sandbox.* Retrieved from http://www.bnm.gov.my/index.php?ch=57&pg=137&ac=533&bb=file

Bank Negara Malaysia. (2018). *Qard Application to Islamic Banks and other Islamic Financial Institutions.* Bank Negara Malaysia.

Bank Negara Malaysia. (2019*). Laws and guidelines.* Retrieved from www.bnm.gov.my

Bank of England. (2015). *One Bank Research Agenda - Discussion Paper.* Bank of England.

Barberis, J. (2014). *The rise of Fintech: Getting Hong Kong to lead the digital financial transition in APAC.* Academic Press.

Bariviera, A. F. (2017). The Inefficiency of Bitcoin Revisited: A Dynamic Approach. *Economics Letters*, *161*, 1–4. doi:10.1016/j.econlet.2017.09.013

Barontini, C., & Holden, H. (2019). *Proceeding with caution – a survey on central bank digital currency.* BIS Papers No 101.

Barrdear, J., & Kumhof, M. (2016). *The macroeconomics of central bank issued digital currencies.* Bank of England. Staff Working Paper No. 605.

Basilico, P., & Attanasio, R. (2018). *A preliminary overview of RegTech.* Retrieved from https://www.politesi.polimi.it/bitstream/10589/142407/5/A%20preliminary%20overview%20of%20RegTech.pdf

Bass, B. M. (2000). The Future of Leadership in Learning Organizations. *The Journal of Leadership Studies*, *7*(3), 18–40. doi:10.1177/107179190000700302

Bech, M. L., & Garratt, R. (2017). *Central Bank Cryptocurrencies.* BIS Quarterly Review. September.

Belabes, A. (2014). Maqasid dimensions of finance in a complex world: Methodological comparison between Islamic and conventional economic literature. [in Arabic]. *Journal of King Abdulaziz University: Islamic Economics*, *27*(3), 2014.

Belanche, D., Casaló, L. V., & Flavián, C. (2019). Artificial Intelligence in FinTech: Understanding Robo-Advisors Adoption among Customers. *Industrial Management & Data Systems*, IMDS-08-2018-0368. doi:10.1108/IMDS-08-2018-0368

Belouafi, A., Bourakba, C., & Saci, K. (2015). Islamic Finance and Financial Stability: A Review of the Literature. *Journal of King Abdulaziz University: Islamic Economics*, *28*(2), 3–44.

Benoit, S., Colliard, J.-E., Hurlin, C., & Perignon, C. (2015). *Where the risks lie: A survey on systemic risk.* Unpublished Working Paper.

Berkowitz, J. (2000). *Incorporating Liquidity Risk into VaR Models.* Working Paper. Graduate School of Management, University of California, Irvine, CA.

Bessembinder, H., & Paul, J. (1992). Futures-Trading Activity and Stock Price Volatility. *The Journal of Finance*, *47*(5), 2015–2034. doi:10.1111/j.1540-6261.1992.tb04695.x

Best, M. J., & Grauer, R. R. (1991). On the sensitivity of mean-variance-efficient portfolios to changes in asset means: Some analytical and computational results. *Review of Financial Studies*, *4*(2), 315–342. doi:10.1093/rfs/4.2.315

Bitcoin Wiki. (2018). Retrieved from https://en.bitcoin.it/wiki/Main_Page

Bjerg, O. (2017). *Designing New Money: The Policy Trilemma of Central Bank Digital Currency.* Copenhagen Business School Working Paper.

BKM. (2018). *General Statistical Reports.* Retrieved from https://bkm.com.tr/en/reports-and-publications/reports-2/

Blau, B. M. (2018). Price dynamics and speculative trading in Bitcoin. *Research in International Business and Finance, Elsevier*, *43*(C), 15–21. doi:10.1016/j.ribaf.2017.07.183

Block, J. H., Colombo, M. G., Cumming, D. J., & Vismara, S. (2018). New players in entrepreneurial finance and why they are there. *Small Business Economics*, *50*(2), 239–250. doi:10.100711187-016-9826-6

Bloomio. (n.d.). *The State of Equity Crowdfunding: Equity Crowdfunding Insights and Analysis.* Author.

Bollerslev, T., Chou, R. Y., & Kroner, K. F. (1992). ARCH modeling in finance: A selective review of the theory and empirical evidence. *Journal of Econometrics*, *52*(1-2), 5–59. doi:10.1016/0304-4076(92)90064-X

Bordo, M., & Levin, A. (2018). *Central Bank Digital Currency and the Future of Monetary Policy.* NBER Working Paper No. 23711

Bouri, E., Azzi, G., & Dyhrberg, A. H. (2017b). On the return-volatility relationship in the Bitcoin market around the price crash of 2013. Economics-The Open-Access. *Open-Assessment E-Journal*, *11*, 1–16.

Bouri, E., Das, M., Gupta, R., & Roubaud, D. (2018). Spillovers between Bitcoin and other assets during bear and bull markets. *Journal of Applied Econometrics*, *50*(55).

Bradley, B., & Taqqu, M. S. (2005). How to Estimate Spatial Contagion between Financial Markets. Finance Letters, 3*(1)*, 64–76. Retrieved from https://ssrn.com/abstract=714143

Britannica. (2019). *Artificial Intelligence*. Retrieved from https://www.britannica.com/technology/artificial-intelligence

Brody. (2017). *Un impact positif sur la société en soutenant l'économie*. rapport d'activité.

Brownlees, C. T., & Engle, R. F. (2015). *Srisk: A Conditional Capital Shortfall Measure of Systemic Risk*. ESRB Working Paper Series from European Systemic Risk Board.

Brudirect. (2016). *Brunei-Korea ICT Conference held to promote new industry*. Retrieved from https://brudirect.com/news.php?id=11167

Brummer, C., & Yadav, Y. (2019). Fintech and the Innovation Trilemma. *The Georgetown Law Journal*, *107*, 235–307.

Cain, B., & Zurbruegg, R. (2010). Can switching between risk measures lead to better portfolio optimization? *Journal of Asset Management*, *10*(6), 358–369. doi:10.1057/jam.2009.20

Cairnscross, F. (1997). *The death of distance*. Harvard Business Review Press.

Campenon, B. (2016). Fintech and the Future of Securities Services. *Journal of Securities Operations and Custody*, *8*(2), 107–112.

Canaday, T. (2017). Evolving a Payments Business to Meet the Demands of a Distributed Economy. *Journal of Payments Strategy and Systems*, *11*(1), 15–22.

Capgemini, LinkedIn, & Efma. (2018). *World Fintech Report 2018*. Authors.

Capital, F. (2018). *Fintech Prediction. 3rd annual edition for financial technology prediction*. Author.

Caporal, G. M., Gil-Alana, L., & Plastun, A. (2018). Long-term price overreactions: Are markets inefficient? *Journal of Economics and Finance*. doi:10.100712197-018-9464-8

Caramela, S. (2017). 4 ways to define leadership. *Business News Daily*. Retrieved from https://www.businessnewsdaily.com/3647-leadership-definition.html

Carney, M. (2017, January). *The promise of Fintech–something new under the sun*. Speech at Deutsche Bundesbank G20 Conference, by Bank of England Governor Mark Carney.

Carrick. (2016). Bitcoin as a Complement to Emerging Market Currencies. *Emerging Markets Finance and Trade, 52*(10). doi:10.1080/1540496X.2016.1193002

Central Bank of Malaysia. (2016). *Financial Technology Regulatory Sandbox Framework. Central Bank of Malaysia*. Retrieved from http://www.bnm.gov.my/index.php?ch=57&pg=137&ac=533&bb=file

Cham, T. H., Low, S. C., Lim, C. S., Aye, A. K., & Raymond, L. L. Bin. (2018). Preliminary Study on Consumer Attitude towards FinTech Products and Services in Malaysia. *International Journal of Engineering & Technology, 7*(2.29), 166. doi:10.14419/ijet.v7i2.29.13310

Chapra, M. U. (1996). Monetary Policy in an Islamic Economy. In Z. Ahmed, M. Iqbal, & M. Fahim Khan (Eds.), *Money and Banking in Islam* (pp. 27–46). Islamabad, Pakistan: Institute of Policy Studies.

Cheah, E., & Fry, J. (2015). Speculative bubbles in Bitcoin markets? An empirical investigation into the fundamental value of Bitcoin. *Economics Letters, 130*, 32-36.

Chin, W. W. (1998). The partial least squares approach to structural equation modeling. In *Modern methods for business research* (pp. 295–336). Mahwah, NJ: Lawrence Erlbaum Associates.

Chiu. (2017). The Disruptive Implications of Fintech-Policy Themes for Financial Regulators. *Journal of Technology Law & Policy, 21*(1).

Cho, Y. C., & Sagynov, E. (2015). Exploring Factors That Affect Usefulness, Ease Of Use, Trust, And Purchase Intention In The Online Environment. *International Journal of Management & Information Systems, 19*(21–36), 7763–7769. doi:10.1021/acs.inorgchem.8b00815

Chohan, U. (2017). Assessing the Differences in Bitcoin & Other Cryptocurrency Legality Across National Jurisdictions. *Information Systems & Economics eJournal, Social Science Research Network, 6*, 4.

Chu, T. H., & Chen, Y. Y. (2016). With Good We Become Good: Understanding e-learning adoption by theory of planned behavior and group influences. *Computers & Education, 92–93*, 37–52. doi:10.1016/j.compedu.2015.09.013

Claessens, Frost, Turner, & Zhu. (2018). *Les marchés du crédit Fintech à travers le monde: taille, moteurs et enjeux de politique publique*. BRI.

Claessens, S., Frost, J., Turner, G., & Zhu, F. (2018). *Fintech credit markets around the world: size, drivers and policy issues. BIS Quarterly Review.*

Clarke & Broby. (2017). How to foster co-operation between the Scottish and Irish Asset Management industries. *Scottish and Irish Finance Initiative Conference.*

Coeuré, B., & Loh, J. (2018). Central bank digital currency. Committee on payment and market infrastructures. Market committee, BIS (Bank for International Settlement).

Cohen, J. (1988). *Statistical Power Analysis for the Behavioral Sciences*. Hillsdale, NJ: Lawrence Earlbaum Associates.

Cohen, W. A. (1990). *The Art of a Leader*. Englewood Cliffs, NJ: JosseyBass.

Commission Européenne, Eurostat. (1996). La mesure des activités scientifiques et technologiques: Principes directeurs proposés pour le recueil et l'interprétation des données sur l'innovation technologique. In *Manuel d'Oslo*. OCDE.

Computerweekly. (2016). *Royal Bank of Scotland to use A.I. platform for customer services.* Retrieved from https://www.computerweekly.com/news/450400525/Royal-Bank-of-Scotland-to-use-AI-platform-for-customer-services

Conrad, J. (1989). The Price Effect of Option Introduction. *The Journal of Finance, 44*(2), 487–498. doi:10.1111/j.1540-6261.1989.tb05068.x

Contreras, G. (2008). *Internet transactions and business models*. Investigación Review.

Corbet, S., Lucey, B., & Yarovaya, L. (2018a). Datestamping the bitcoin and ethereum bubbles. *Finance Research Letters, 26*, 81–88. doi:10.1016/j.frl.2017.12.006

Crosby, M., Pattanayak, P., Verma, S., & Kalyanaraman, V. (2016). Blockchain technology: Beyond bitcoin. *Applied Innovation*, *2*(6-10), 71.

Daj, A. (2018). Beyond Cryptocurrencies: Economic and Legal Facets of the Disruptive Potential of Blockchain Technology. *Bulletin of the Transilvania University of Brasov. Series V, Economic Sciences*, *11*(2), 207–216.

Daka, V. R., & Basu, S. (2016). Assessing performance of liquidity adjusted Value at Risk models. *International Journal of Financial Research*, *7*(5), 87–98. doi:10.5430/ijfr.v7n5p87

Danielsson, J., & Zigrand, J.-P. (2006). On time-scaling of risk and the square-root-of-time rule. *Journal of Banking & Finance*, *30*(10), 2701–2713. doi:10.1016/j.jbankfin.2005.10.002

Davis, F. (1989). Perceived Usefulness, Perceived Ease of Use, and User Acceptance of Information Technology. *Management Information Systems Quarterly*, *13*(3), 319–340. doi:10.2307/249008

Davis, F. D., Bagozzi, R. P., & Warshaw, P. R. (1989). User acceptance of computer technology: A comparison of two theoretical models. *Management Science*, *35*(8), 982–1003. doi:10.1287/mnsc.35.8.982

Dawkins, D. (2018, Feb 9). The HACK that could break bitcoin - '51% attack' concerns mainstream 'banking bunnies'. *Sunday Express*.

De Buysere, K., Gajda, O., Kleverlaan, R., Marom, D., Klaes, M., & De Buysere, K. (2012). *A framework for European crowdfunding. European Crowdfunding Network (ECN)*. Retrieved from https://d21buns5ku92am.cloudfront.net/26522/documents/17930-1351284179-FRAMEWORK_EU_CROWDFUNDING.pdf

De Lis, S. F. (2018). Central bank digital currencies: features, options, pros and cons. In *SUERF Conference Proceedings 2018/2: Do We Need Central Bank Digital Currency? Economics, Technology and Institutions*. Bocconi University and Baffi Carefin.

Delmond, M.H., Coelho, F., Keravel, A., & Mahl, R. (2016). *How Information Systems Enable Digital Transformation: A focus on Business Models and Value Co-production*. CIGREF foundation (the French association of CIOs), hal-01369141v2.

Deloitte. (2016). *Disaggregating Fintech: Brighter shades of disruption*. Deloitte Centre for Financial Services.

Deloitte. (2016). *Islamic megabank. The redeemer? A Middle East Point of View*. Available at: https://www2.deloitte.com/content/dam/Deloitte/xe/Documents/AboutDeloitte/mepovdocuments/mepov21/islamic-megabank_mepov21.pdf

Deloitte. (2017). The Connecting Global Fintech. *Interim Hub Review*.

Demirgüç-Kunt. Leora, Ansar, & Jagati. (2017). *Making It Easier to Apply for a Bank Account: A Study of the Indian Market*. Policy Research Working Paper 8205. World Bank.

Demirguc-Kunt, A., Klapper, L., Singer, D., Ansar, S., & Hess, J. (2018). *The Global Findex Database 2017: measuring financial inclusion and the Fintech revolution*. The World Bank. doi:10.1596/978-1-4648-1259-0

Desai, F. (2015). *The Evolution of FinTech*. Retrieved from https://www.forbes.com/sites/falgunidesai/2015/12/13/the-evolution-of-fintech/#16ac4a847175

DESİYAB. (1981). *The Role and Future of Workers Companies in the Industrialization of Turkey*, State Industry and Worker's Bank (DESİYAB) 2nd Symposium, Ankara, Turkey.

Dhaliwal, S. (2017). Is Bitcoin Halal? How Cryptocurrency Conforms with Shariah. *Coin Telegraph*. Available Online: https://cointelegraph.com/news/is-bitcoin-halal-how-cryptocurrency-conforms-with-islam-and-sharia

Diebold, F. X., & Yilmaz, K. (2009). Measuring Financial Asset Return and Volatility Spillovers, With Application to Global Equity Markets. *Economic Journal (London)*, *119*(534), 158–171. doi:10.1111/j.1468-0297.2008.02208.x

Dillon, A.P., & Morris, M. G. (1996). User Acceptance of Information Technology: Theories and Models. *Annual Review of Information Science and Technology*, *31*, 3-32.

DiNizo, A. M. Jr. (2018). From Alice to Bob: The Patent Eligibility of Blockchain in a Post-CLS Bank World. *Journal of Law. Technology and the Internet*, *9*, 1–28.

Dorefleitner, Shmitt, & Weber. (2017). Fintech in Germany. Springer International Publishing.

Dowd, K., Blake, D., & Cairns, A. (2004, Winter/Spring). Long-Term Value at Risk. *Journal of Risk Finance*, 52-57.

Durante, F., & Jaworski, P. (2008). Absolutely continuous copulas with given diagonal sections. *Communications in Statistics. Theory and Methods*, *37*(18), 2924–2942. doi:10.1080/03610920802050927

Dwyer, G. P. (2015). The economics of Bitcoin and similar private digital currencies. *Journal of Financial Stability*, *17*, 81–91. doi:10.1016/j.jfs.2014.11.006

Dyson, B., & Hodgson, G. (2016). *Digital cash: Why Central Banks Should Start Issuing Electronic Money*. Positive Money.

Engel, C. (2018). *Artificial Intelligence: The Weapon of Choice in Banks' Fight for Survival*. Retrieved from https://thefinancialbrand.com/71108/artificial-intelligence-banking-machine-learning/

Engert, W., & Fung, B. S. C. (2017). *Central Bank Digital Currency: Motivations and Implications*. Bank of Canada Staff Discussion Paper, 2017-16. Available at https://www.bankofcanada.ca/wp-content/uploads/2017/11/sdp2017-16.pdf

Ernst & Young. (2017). *Luxembourg: the gateway for Islamic finance and the Middle East*. Retrieved from https://www.ey.com/Publication/vwLUAssets/Luxembourg:_the_gateway_for_Islamic_finance_and_the_Middle_East_-_May_2017/$FILE/Islamic%20Finance%20-%20May%202017-LR.pdf

Erosa, A., & Ventura, G. (2002). On inflation as a regressive consumption tax. *Journal of Monetary Economics*, *49*(4), 761–795. doi:10.1016/S0304-3932(02)00115-0

Evans, C. W. (2015). Bitcoin in Islamic Banking and Finance. *Journal of Islamic Banking and Finance.*, *3*(1), 5. doi:10.15640/jibf.v3n1a1

EY. (2017). *EY FinTech Adoption Index 2017: The Rapid Emergence of Fintech*. Author.

Eyal, I. (2017). Blockchain Tecnology: Transforming Libertarian Cryptocurrency Dreams to Finance and Banking Realities. *Computer*, *50*(9), 38–49. doi:10.1109/MC.2017.3571042

FAQ - Bitcoin. (2018). Retrieved from https://bitcoin.org/en/faq#what-about-bitcoin-and-consumer-protection

Federal Council of Switzerland. (2014, June 25). *Swiss Confederation*.

Federal Government Gazette. (2019). *Capital Markets and Services (Prescription of Securities) (Digital Currency and Digital Token) 2019*. Retrieved from http://www.federalgazette.agc.gov.my/outputp/pua_20190114_PUA12.pdf?fbclid=IwAR3RG1vaiM3MSd_lONZl4jyuVeAUt_anYTJmI08GhVB0kb8IAWKhhTaV1rQ

Ferrari, R. (2016). FinTech Impact on Retail Banking–From a Universal Banking Model to Banking Verticalization. *The FinTech Book: The Financial Technology Handbook for Investors, Entrepreneurs and Visionaries*, 248-252.

Fiedler, S., Gern, K., Kooths, S., & Stolzenburg, U. (2017). *Financial innovation and monetary policy: Challenges and prospects. Directorate general for internal policies*. Policy department a: economic and scientific policy. IP/A/ECON/2017-02.

Financial Action Task Force. (2014). *Virtual currencies – Key definitions and potential AML/CFT risks*. Retrieved from http://www.fatf-gafi.org/media/fatf/documents/reports/Virtual-currency-key-definitions-and-potential-aml-cft-risks.pdf

Financial Stability Board. (2017). *Artificial Intelligence and Machine Learning in Financial Services: Market Developments and Financial Stability Implications*. Financial Stability Board. Retrieved from http://www.fsb.org/2017/11/artificial-intelligence-and-machine-learning-in-financial-service/

Financial Technology Enabler Group. (2017). *Approved Participants in Sandbox*. Retrieved from https://www.myfteg.com/?page_id=1131

Finck, M. (2018). Blockchains: Regulating the Unknown. *German Law Journal*, *19*(4), 665–692. doi:10.1017/S2071832200022847

Finews Asia. (2016). *Ant Fortune: Wealth Management with Several Scenarios*. Retrieved from https://www.finews.asia/finance/22965-ant-fortune-offers-wealth-management-with-scenarios

Fintech, I. F. N. (2019). *Islamic Bank becomes the First in Kuwait to integrate AI*. Retrieved from http://www.ifnfintech.com/eng/article-detail.php?guid=26EE62DB-F106-4880-851C-1ACB022FB5C6

Firmansyah, E. A., & Anwar, M. (2019). Islamic Financial Technology (Fintech): Its Challenges and Prospect. In *Achieving and Sustaining SDGs 2018 Conference: Harnessing the Power of Frontier Technology to Achieve the Sustainable Development Goals (ASSDG 2018)*. Atlantis Press.

Firmansyah, H. B., & Ramdani, A. L. (2018). The Role of Islamic Financial Technology (FinTech) Start-Up in Improving Financial Inclusion in Indonesia Case: Angsur. *3rd International Conference of Integrated Intellectual Community (ICONIC) 2018*. Available at SSRN: https://ssrn.com/abstract=3194546

Flanagan, K. (2017). *TimeTrade 2017 State of Retail survey report*. Retrieved from https://www.timetrade.com/blog/state-of-retail-2017-infographic/

Flavián, C., Guinalíu, M., & Torres, E. (2006). How bricks-and-mortar attributes affect online banking adoption. *International Journal of Bank Marketing*, *24*(6), 406–423. doi:10.1108/02652320610701735

Foo, Lim, & Wong. (2017). *Macroeconomics and FinTech: Uncovering Latent Macroeconomic Effects on Peer-to-Peer Lending*. Papers 1710.11283, arXiv.org.

Fornell, C., & Larcker, D. F. (1981). Evaluating Structural Equation Models with Unobservable Variables and Measurement Error. *JMR, Journal of Marketing Research*, *18*(1), 39–50. doi:10.1177/002224378101800104

Fung, B., & Halaburda, H. (2016). *Central Bank Digital Currencies: A Framework for Assessing Why and How*. Bank of Canada Staff Discussion Paper 2016–22.

Gabor & Brooks. (2016). The digital revolution in financial inclusion: International development. *New Political Economy*, *4*, 23–436.

Gai, K., Qiu, M., & Sun, X. (2017). A Survey on FinTech. *Journal of Network and Computer Applications*, *103*, 262–273. doi:10.1016/j.jnca.2017.10.011

Gamal Aboelmaged, M. (2010). Predicting e-procurement adoption in a developing country: An empirical integration of technology acceptance model and theory of planned behaviour. *Industrial Management & Data Systems*, *110*(3), 392–414. doi:10.1108/02635571011030042

Geanakoplos. (2010). Credit cards and inflation. *Games and Economic Behavior.*

Gejke, C. (2018). A New Season in the Risk Landscape: Connecting the Advancement in Technology with Changes in Customer Behaviour to Enhance the Way Risk is Measured and Managed. *Journal of Risk Management in Financial Institutions*, *11*(2), 148–155.

Gervais, A. (2016). Is Bitcoin a Decentralized Currency? *InfoQ & IEEE Computer Society.*

Gervais, A. (2016, October 10). Is Bitcoin a Decentralized Currency? *InfoQ & IEEE Computer Society.*

Getting started with Bitcoin mining. (2018). Retrieved from https://www.bitcoinmining.com/getting-started/

Ghazali, N. H., & Yasuoka, T. (2018). Awareness and Perception Analysis of Small Medium Enterprise and Start-up Towards FinTech Instruments-Crowdfunding and Peer-to-Peer Lending in Malaysia. *International Journal of Finance and Banking Research*, *4*(1), 13–24. doi:10.11648/j.ijfbr.20180401.12

Gkillas, K., & Katsiampa, P. (2018). An application of extreme value theory to cryptocurrencies. *Economics Letters*, *164*, 109–111. doi:10.1016/j.econlet.2018.01.020

Glass, J. (2017). What is a Digital Currency. *IDEA – The Journal of the Franklin Pierce Center for Intellectual Property*, *57*(3), 455 – 517.

Global Partnership for Financial Inclusion. (2011). *The G20 Principles for Innovative Financial Inclusion: Bringing the Principles to Life*. Author.

Godwin, Kourabas, & Ramsay. (2017). Financial Stability Authorities and Macroprudential Regulation. *Banking & Finance Law Review*, *32*(2), 223–254.

Goh Thean Eu. (2016*). Malaysia first to regulate P2P financing, after SC introduced six P2P operators.* Retrieved from https://www.sc.com.my/api/documentms/download.ashx?id=cb6aedad-aa7b-43fc-8a34-a1061f0554f5

Gokul, B. (2018). Artificial Intelligence in Financial Services. *Sansmaran Research Journal*, *8*(1), 3–5.

Gomber, K., Koch, J.-A., & Siering, M. (2017). Digital Finance and FinTech: Current research and future research directions. *Journal of Business Economics*, *87*(5), 537–580. doi:10.100711573-017-0852-x

Gomber, P., Kauffman, R. J., Parker, C., & Weber, B. W. (2018). On the Fintech Revolution: Interpreting the Forces of Innovation, Disruption, and Transformation in Financial Services. *Journal of Management Information Systems*, *35*(1), 220–265. doi:10.1080/07421222.2018.1440766

González-Páramo, J. M. (2017). Financial innovation in the digital age: Challenges for regulation and supervision. *Revista de estabilidad financiera, 32*(9), 37.

Google. (2016a). *Google Adwords-Keywords.* Retrieved from https:/www.google.com/adwords

Google. (2016b). *Google Trends - fintech search term.* Retrieved from https://www.google.com/trends/

Gouveia, O.C., Dos Santos, E., De Lis, S.F., Neut, A., & Sebastian, J. (2017). *Central Bank Digital Currencies: assessing implementation possibilities and impacts.* BBVA Research, Document Number 17/04.

Granic, A., & Marangunic, N. (2015). Technology Acceptance Model : A Literature Review from 1986 to 2013. *Universal Access in the Information Society, 14*(1), 81–95. doi:10.100710209-014-0348-1

Green, E. (2008). Some challenges for research in payment systems. In A. Haldane, S. Millards, & V. Saporta (Eds.), *The Future of Payment Systems.* Milton Park: Routhledge.

Greenwood, R., Hanson, S., & Stein, J. (2016). *The Federal Reserve's balance sheet as a financial-stability tool.* Paper presented at the Economic Policy Symposium. Available at https://scholar.harvard.edu/files/stein/files/jackson_hole_ghs_20160907_final.pdf

Griffin, A. (2018). *Tackling the risks of the FinTech boom - AML considerations.* Retrieved from https://www.lexology.com/library/detail.aspx?g=5f081a53-caf3-46f6-9d57-e1958dca977d

Grym, A., Heikkinen, P., Kauko, K., & Takala, K. (2017). *Central bank digital currency, Bank of Finland, 5. BoF economics Review.* Bank of Finland.

Guérineau, S., & Jacolin, L. (2014). L'inclusion financière en Afrique subsaharienne: faits stylisés et déterminants. In *Revue d'économie financière, N° 116* (pp. 57–80). Cairn. doi:10.3917/ecofi.116.0057

Gulamhuseinwala, I., Hatch, M., Lloyd, J., Bull, T., & Chen, S. (2017). *EY FinTech Adoption Index 2017: The rapid emergence of Fintech.* Ernst & Young Global Limited.

Haan, Oosterloo, & Schoenmaker, (2015), 'Financial markets and institutions: A European perspective)'. Cambridge University Press 978-1-107-02594-3.

Hair, J. F., Hult, G. T. M., Ringle, C. M., & Sarstedt, M. (2017). *A primer on partial least squares structural equation modeling (PLS-SEM).* Academic Press. doi:10.1016/j.lrp.2013.01.002

Hair, J. F., Risher, J. J., Sarstedt, M., & Ringle, C. M. (2018). When to use and how to report the results of PLS-SEM. *European Business Review.* doi:10.1108/ebr-11-2018-0203

Halaburda, H. (2018). Economic and Business Dimensions: Blockchain Revolution Without the Blockchain? *Communications of the ACM, 61*(7), 27–29. doi:10.1145/3225619

Hamid, A. A., Razak, F. Z. A., Bakar, A. A., & Abdullah, W. S. W. (2016). The Effects of Perceived Usefulness and Perceived Ease of Use on Continuance Intention to Use E-Government. *Procedia Economics and Finance, 35*, 644–649. doi:10.1016/S2212-5671(16)00079-4

Hansen, B. (1994). Autoregressive Conditional Density Estimation. *International Economic Review, 35*(3), 705–730. doi:10.2307/2527081

Harel, R., & Kaufmann, D. (2016). Financing innovative SMEs of traditional sectors: The supply side. *EuroMed Journal of Business, 11*(1), 84–100. doi:10.1108/EMJB-02-2015-0007

Härle, P., Havas, A., & Samandari, H. (2006). *The Future of Bank Risk Management.* Retrieved from https://www.fintech.finance/featured/the-future-of-bank-risk-management/

Haron, Saniza, & Ishak. (2015). Factors Influencing Small Medium Enterprises (SME) in obtaining Loan. *International Journal of Business and Social Science, 4*(15).

Harrison, R., Jaumandreu, J., Mairesse, J., & Peters, B. (2014). Does innovation stimulate employment? A firm-level analysis using comparable micro-data from four European countries. *International Journal of Industrial Organization, 35*, 29–43. doi:10.1016/j.ijindorg.2014.06.001

Hassan, M. U., Iqbal, A., & Iqbal, Z. (2018). Factors affecting the adoption of internet banking in Pakistan: An integration of technology acceptance model and theory of planned behaviour. *International Journal of Business Information Systems, 28*(3), 342–370. doi:10.1504/IJBIS.2018.092530

He, D., & Khan, A. (2018). Central bank digital currencies. In Global Financial Stability Report. International Monetary Fund.

He, D., Habermeier, K., Leckow, R., Haksar, V., Almeida, Y., Kashima, M., … Verdugo-Yepes, C. (2016). *Virtual Currencies and Beyond: Initial Considerations*. IMF Staff Discussion Note 16/03.

He, D. (2018). *Monetary policy in the digital age. Finance and Development. June 2018.* Washington, DC: International Monetary Fund.

He, D., Leckow, R., Haksar, V., Mancini-Griffoli, T., Jenkinson, N., Kashima, M., ... Tourpe, H. (2017). *Fintech and Financial Services: Initial Considerations. IMF Staff Discussion Note 17/05.* Washington, DC: International Monetary Fund.

Heller, D. (2017). *The implications of digital currencies for monetary policy*. European Parliament's Committee on Economic and Monetary Affairs. Directorate general for internal policies. Policy department a: economic and scientific policy. IP/A/ECON/2017-02.

Henly, C., Hartnett, S., Endemann, B., Tejblum, B., & Cohen, D. S. (2018). Energizing the Future with Blockchain. *Energy Law Journal, 39*, 197–232.

Henseler, J., Ringle, C. M., & Sarstedt, M. (2015). A new criterion for assessing discriminant validity in variance-based structural equation modeling. *Journal of the Academy of Marketing Science, 43*(1), 115–135. doi:10.100711747-014-0403-8

Hileman, G., & Rauchs, M. (2017). *Global Cryptocurrency Benchmarking Study*. Cambridge University Press.

Hines, P. (2018). *APIs in Banking: Unlocking Business Value with Banking as a Platform*. BAAP.

Hisata, Y., & Yamai, Y. (2000). *Research Toward the Practical Application of Liquidity Risk Evaluation Methods*. Discussion Paper, Institute for Monetary and Economic Studies, Bank of Japan.

Hong, L. C. (2018). Crowdfunding: Issues pertaining to financial reporting and assurance in Malaysia. *Journal of Wealth Management and Financial Planning, 5*, 17–24.

Iansiti, M., & Lakhani, K. R. (2017). The truth about blockchain. *Harvard Business Review, 95*(1), 118–127.

Ibn Al-Qayyem, J. (1991). *I'lam al-Muwaqe'*. Beirut: Dar al-Kutub al-Elmiyya.

ICLG. (2018). *The International Comparative Legal Guide to: Fintech 2018*. ICLG.

Ikpefan, O. A., & Agwu, M. E. (2015). Leadership of modern financial institutions and the changing paradigm of Banking in Nigeria. *Journal of Internet Banking and Commerce, 20*(3), 1–17.

IMF Communication Department. (2018). The Bali Fintech Agenda: A Blueprint for Successfully Harnessing Fintech's Opportunities. *International Monetary Fund*. Retrieved from https://www.imf.org/en/News/Articles/2018/10/11/pr18388-the-bali-fintech-agenda

ING Internationali. (2015). *Mobile Banking, New Technologies and Financial Behaviour*. ING International Survey.

International Trade Administration. US department of Commerce. (2016). Top Markets reports financial Technology. International Trade Administration, US.

Islamic Financial Services Board (IFSB). (2015). *Islamic Financial Services Industry Stability Report 2015*. Retrieved from http://www.ifsb.org/docs/IFSB%20Islamic%20Financial%20Services%20Industry%20Stability%20Report%20 2015_final.pdf

Islamic Financial Services Board. (2017). Islamic Financial Services Industry. *Stability Report, 2017*. doi:10.1017/CBO9781107415324.004

Ismail, M. B. (2001). *Albukhari "Aljami' Alsahih" [The book of debt]. In Husn al-Qada' Dar Duruq al-Najah*. Al-Qahira.

Jackson, A., & Dyson, B. (2013). *Modernising Money: Why Our Monetary System is Broken and How it can be fixed*. London: Positive Money.

Jagtiani & Lemieux. (2018). *Do Fintech Lenders Penetrate Areas That Are Underserved by Traditional Banks?* Working Paper, org/papers/w20899.pdf.

Jakarta Post. (2018). *Indonesia leads Asia-Pasific in AI implementation, study shows*. Retrieved from https://www.thejakartapost.com/news/2018/09/05/indonesia-leads-asia-pacific-in-ai-implementation-study-shows.html

Jang, H., & Lee, J. (2017). An empirical study on modeling and prediction of bitcoin prices with Bayesian neural networks based on blockchain information. *IEEE Access: Practical Innovations, Open Solutions*, *6*, 5427–5437. doi:10.1109/ACCESS.2017.2779181

Jarrow, R., & Subramanian, A. (1997). Mopping up Liquidity. *Risk (Concord, NH)*, *10*(12), 170–173.

Jin, C. C., Seong, L. C., & Khin, A. A. (2019). Factors Affecting the Consumer Acceptance towards Fintech Products and Services in Malaysia. *International Journal of Asian Social Science*, *9*(1), 59–65. doi:10.18488/journal.1.2019.91.59.65

Joe, H. (1997). *Multivariate Models and Dependence Concepts*. London: Chapman and Hall. doi:10.1201/b13150

Julia Horowitz, C. (2017). *JPMorgan's move into crypto puts the rest of the industry on notice*. Retrieved from https://edition.cnn.com/2019/02/19/business/jpmorgan-jpm-coin-banks-blockchain/index.html

Jun, J., & Yeo, E. (2016). Entry of FinTech Firms and Competition in the Retail Payments Market. *Asia-Pacific Journal of Financial Studies*, *45*(2), 159–184. doi:10.1111/ajfs.12126

Kahf, M. (2014). *Fatwa on Bitcoin*. Retrieved from http://lightuponlight.com/blog/fatwa-on-bitcoin-by-monzer-kahf/

Kahn, C. M., Rivadeneyra, F., & Wong, T. (2019). *Should the Central Bank Issue E-Money?* FRB St. Louis. Research Division. Working Paper No. 2019-003A.

Kamalul Ariffin, S., Mohan, T., & Goh, Y. N. (2018). Influence of consumers' perceived risk on consumers' online purchase intention. *Journal of Research in Interactive Marketing*, *12*(3), 309–327. doi:10.1108/JRIM-11-2017-0100

Kaplan, J. (2016). *Artificial Intelligence: What everyone needs to know*. Oxford University Press.

Karim, N. A. A. (2016). *Islamic crowdfunding for social-impact housing (Pt 1)*. The Edge Malaysia.

Karlan, D., Kendall, J., Mann, R., Pande, R., Suri, T., & Zinman, J. (2016). *Research and impacts of Digital Financial Services*. HKS Faculty Research Working paper series, RWP14-037.

Kassim, N. M., & Ramayah, T. (2015). Perceived Risk Factors Influence on Intention to Continue Using Internet Banking among Malaysians. *Global Business Review*, *16*(3), 393–414. doi:10.1177/0972150915569928

Katz L. (2017). *Bitcoin Acceptance Among Retailers Is Low and Getting Lower.* Bloomberg.com.

Kaushik B. (2014). *Ponzis: The Science and Mystique of a Class of Financial Frauds.* Worldbank.org.

Kavitha, P., & Baag, P. K. (2018). *Crowdfunding for Entrepreneurs- Analysis of the Institutional Work.* Academic Press.

Kerényi, Á., & Molnár, J. (2017). The Impact of the Fintech Phenomenon–Radical Change Occurs in the Financial Sector? *Financial and Economic Review*, *16*(3), 32–50.

Ketterer, J. A., and Andrade, G. (2016). *Digital Central Bank Money and the Unbundling of the Banking Function.* Inter-American Development Bank.

Khalilov, M. C. K., & Gündebahar, M. (2012). XTM: An Alternative Delivery Channel in Turkish Banking Sector. *Procedia: Social and Behavioral Sciences*, *57*, 373–380. doi:10.1016/j.sbspro.2012.09.1200

Khan, S. J. M., & Anuar, A. R. (2018). Access to Finance: Exploring Barriers to Entrepreneurship Development in SMEs. In Global Entrepreneurship and New Venture Creation in the Sharing Economy (pp. 92-111). IGI Global.

Khiaonarong, T., & Humphrey, D. (2019). *Cash Use Across Countries and the Demand for Central Bank Digital Currency.* IMF working paper 19/46.

Kim, S., & Kim, C.-B. (2018). A Study on the Factors Affecting the Continuous Use Intention of Easy Payment Services. In *International Academic Conference* (p. 216). Academic Press. 10.20472/IAC.2018.042.030

Kim, Y., Park, Y. J., Choi, J., & Yeon, J. (2016). The adoption of mobile payment services for "Fintech". *International Journal of Applied Engineering Research*, *11*(2), 1058–1061.

Kim, Y., Park, Y.-J., & Choi, J. (2016). The Adoption of Mobile Payment Services for Fintech. *International Journal of Applied Engineering Research*, *11*(2), 1058–1061.

Kmeid, R. (2017). Will Artificial Intelligence Rejuvenate Islamic Finance. *Wahed Invest.* Retrieved from https://journal.wahedinvest.com/will-artificial-intelligence-rejuvenate-islamic-finance/

Koontz, H. (1978). *Essentials of Management.* New Delhi: Tata McGraw Hill Publishing Co. Ltd.

Kouzes, J., & Posner, B. (2003). *The Leadership Challenge.* San Francisco: Jossey-Bass.

Kovas, A. (n.d.). *Understanding the risks of fintech.* Retrieved from https://legal.thomsonreuters.com/en/insights/articles/understanding-the-risks-of-fintech

KPMG. (2017). *Forging the Future: How Financial Institutions are Embracing Fintech to Evolve and Grow.* KPMG International. doi:10.1093/acprof:oso/9780199742745.003.0007

KPMG. (2018). *The pulse of fintech 2018.* Retrieved from https://assets.kpmg/content/dam/kpmg/xx/pdf/2018/07/h1-2018-pulse-of-fintech.pdf

KPMG. (2018). *The Pulse of Fintech 2018: Biannual Global Analysis of Investment in Fintech.* Author.

Kumar, A., & Smith, C. (2017). *Crypto-currencies – An introduction to not-so-funny moneys.* Reserve Bank of New Zealand Analytical Note Series.

Kumar, A. S., & Suvvari, A. (2019). Volatility spillover in crypto-currency markets: Some evidences from GARCH and wavelet analysis. *Physica A*, 524.

Kumhof, M., & Noone, C. (2018). *Central bank digital currencies — design principles and balance sheet implications.* Bank of England. Staff Working Paper No. 725.

Kunt, D. A., Klapper, L., Singer, D., & Oudheusden, P. V. (2015). *E-global findex database 2014 measuring financial inclusion around the world.* World Bank Policy Research Working Paper, (7255).

KuveytTurk Participation Bank. (2018). *BOA Banking Plat*form. Retrieved from https://www.kuveytturk.com.tr/en/about-us/about-kuveyt-turk/news/boa-banking-platform-the-local-software-of-kuveyt-turk-is-to-be-used-in-20-countries

Lacasse, R. M., Lambert, B. A., Osmani, E., Couture, C., Roy, N., Sylvain, J., & Nadeau, F. (2016). A Digital Tsunami : FinTech and Crowdfunding. In *International Scientific Conference on Digital Intelligence* (pp. 1–5). Academic Press.

Lacity, M., Willcocks, L. P., & Craig, A. (2017). *Service automation: cognitive virtual agents at SEB Bank.* Retrieved from http://www.umsl.edu/~lacitym/LSEOUWP1701.pdf

Lagarde, C. (2018). Winds of Change: The Case for New Digital Currency. *Singapore Fintech Festival.* Retrieved from https://www.imf.org/en/News/Articles/2018/11/13/sp111418-winds-of-change-the-case-for-new-digital-currency

Lam, E. (2017). *What the World's Central Banks Are Saying About Bitcoin.* Bloomberg.com.

Lane, K. (2013). *Overview Of The Backend as a Service (BaaS) Space.* Retrieved from http://www.integrove.com/wp-content/uploads/2014/11/api-evangelist-baas-whitepaper.pdf

Larios-Hernandez, G. J. (2017). Blockchain Entrepreneurship Opportunities in the Practices of the Unbanked. *Business Horizons*, *60*(6), 865–874. doi:10.1016/j.bushor.2017.07.012

Lee, T. (2013, August 21). Five surprising facts about Bitcoin. *The Washington Post.*

Lee, T., & Kim, H. (2015). An Exploratory Study on Fintech Industry in Korea : Crowdfunding Case. In *2nd International conference on Innovative Engineering Technologies* (pp. 58–64). Academic Press.

Lee, I., & Shin, Y. J. (2018). Fintech: Ecosystem, business models, investment decisions and challenges. *Business Horizons*, *61*(1), 35–46. doi:10.1016/j.bushor.2017.09.003

Lee, M. C. (2009). Factors influencing the adoption of internet banking: An integration of TAM and TPB with perceived risk and perceived benefit. *Electronic Commerce Research and Applications*, *8*(3), 130–141. doi:10.1016/j.elerap.2008.11.006

Lee, S. (2016). User Behavior of Mobile Enterprise Applications. *Transactions on Internet and Information Systems (Seoul)*, *10*(8), 3972–3985.

Lee, S. Y., & Park, J. (2016). A Study on the Intention of the Use of Mobile Payment Services: Application of the Technology Acceptance Model. *Korean Management Science Review*, *33*(2), 65–74. doi:10.7737/KMSR.2016.33.2.065

Life.SREDA. (2015). *Overview of APIs and Bank-as-a-Service in FINTECH.* Author.

Lines, B. (2016). How FinTech Is Shaping Financial Services. *PwC Global Fin-Tech Report.*

Lipsky, J. (2012). Session III: Introductory remarks. BIS Papers No 62 Financial sector regulation for growth, equity and stability. *Proceedings of a conference organised by the BIS and CAFRAL in Mumbai.* Retrieved from https://www.bis.org/publ/bppdf/bispap62.pdf

Liu, Y., & Tsyvinski, A. (2018). *Risks and Returns of Cryptocurrency* (Working Paper No. 24877). National Bureau of Economic Research. doi:10.3386/w24877

Lou, A. T. F., & Li, E. Y. (2017). Integrating Innovation Diffusion Theory and the Technology Acceptance Model : The Adoption of Blockchain Technology from Business Managers ' Perspective. In *International Conference on Electronic Business* (pp. 298–302). Academic Press.

Low, R. K. Y., Alcock, J., Faff, R., & Brailsford, T. (2013). Canonical vine copulas in the context of modern portfolio management: Are they worth it? *Journal of Banking & Finance, 37*(8), 3085–3099. doi:10.1016/j.jbankfin.2013.02.036

Lutfi, M. A., & Ismail, M. A. (2016). Sadaqah-Based Crowdfunding Model for Microfinancing and Health Care. *The Journal of Muamalat and Islamic Finance Research, 13*(December), 32–51.

Ma'lum, M. (2016, February 11). ACCC investigating why banks are closing bitcoin companies' accounts. *Financial Review.*

Mackenzie. (2015, December 15). The future military artificial intelligence complex? *Financial Times.*

Mackenzie, A. (2015). The Fintech Revolution. *London Business School Review, 26*(3), 50–53. doi:10.1111/2057-1615.12059

Macky, M. (2018). Artificial Intelligence 2017: AI age has begun in the Philippines. *Imark International.* Retrieved from https://www.imarkintl.com/artificial-intelligence-philippines/

Maddox, T. M., Rumsfeld, J. S., & Payne, P. R. (2019). Questions for Artificial Intelligence in Health Care. *Journal of the American Medical Association, 321*(1), 31–32. doi:10.1001/jama.2018.18932 PMID:30535130

Madoroba, S. B. W., & Kruger, J. W. (2014). Liquidity effects on value-at-risk limits: Construction of a new VaR model. *Journal of Risk Model Validation, 8*(4), 19–46. doi:10.21314/JRMV.2014.127

Maier. (2016). Supply and demand on crowdlending platforms: connecting small and medium sized enterprise borrowers and consumer investors. *Journal of Retailing and Consumer Services, 33,* 143-153.

Maierbrugger, A. (2018). *Fintech on Track to Shape Future of Islamic Finance.* Gulf Times.

Malay Mail. (2017). *Funding societies eyes institutional investors in 3 years.* Retrieved from http://epaper.mmail.com.my/2017/09/05/funding-societies-eyes-institutional-investors-in-3-years/

Malaysia International Islamic Financial Centre. (2016). *Financial Technology (FinTech) in Islamic Finance.* Available at: https://www.islamicfinance.com/wpcontent/uploads/2016/05/Islamic-FinanceTechnology-and-Innovation.pdf

Malaysian Reserve. (2017). *A.I. and Islamic Financial Institutions.* Retrieved from https://themalaysianreserve.com/2017/12/18/ai-islamic-financial-institutions/

Mancini-Griffoli, T., Soledad Martinez Peria, M., Agur, I., Ari, A., Kiff, J., Popescu, A., & Rochon, C. (2018). Casting Light on Central Bank Digital Currency. IMF Staff Discussion Note 18/08. International Monetary Fund. doi:10.5089/9781484384572.006

Manyika, Lund, Singer, White, & Berry. (2016). *Digital Finance for All: Powering Inclusive Growth In Emerging Economies.* McKinsey Global Institute.

Markowitz, H. (1959). *Portfolio Selection: Efficient Diversification of Investments.* New York: John Wiley.

Marous, J. (2018). *Innovation in Retail Banking Digital Banking Report*. Retrieved from https://www.efma.com/assets/content/study/2018/Innovation_In_Retail_Banking_2018_preview.pdf

Mas & Klein. (2012). *A note on macro-financial implications of mobile money schemes*. Working Paper Series 188.

Matute, J., Polo-Redondo, Y., & Utrillas, A. (2016). The influence of EWOM characteristics on online repurchase intention: Mediating roles of trust and perceived usefulness. *Online Information Review*, *40*(7), 1090–1110. doi:10.1108/OIR-11-2015-0373

Mawejje & Lakuma. (2017). *Macroeconomic Effects of Mobile Money in Uganda*. Economic Policy Research Centre. doi:10.13140/RG.2.2.24254.18244

Mbiti & Weil. (2014). *Mobile Banking: the Impact of M-PESA in Kenya*. NBER Working Paper Series.

McCloskey, D. W. (2011). The Importance of Ease of Use, Usefulness, and Trust to Online Consumers: An Examination of the Technology Acceptance Model with Older Consumers. *Journal of Organizational and End User Computing*, *18*(3), 47–65. doi:10.4018/joeuc.2006070103

McKenzie, B. (2017). *Malaysia welcomes two new participants to fintech regulatory sandbox*. Retrieved from https://www.lexology.com/library/detail.aspx?g=8f3948d0-e82a-4d1f-8af2-ef2aac7214af

Meaning, J., Dyson, B., Barker, J., & Clayton, E. (2018). *Broadening Narrow Money: Monetary Policy with a Central Bank Digital Currency*. Bank of England Staff Working Paper 724.

Meera, A. K. (2018). Cryptocurrencies from Islamic Perspective: The Case of Bitcoin. *Bulletin of Monetary Economics and Banking*, *20*, 475–491.

Memminger, M., Baxter, M., & Lin, E. (2016). *Banking regtechs to the rescue*. Retrieved from www. bain. com/Images/BAIN_BRIEF_Banking_Regtechs_to_ the_Rescue. pdf

Mersch, Y. (2017). *Digital base money: an assessment from the ECB's perspective*. Speech at the Bank of Finland.

Meucci, A. (2009). Managing Diversification. *Risk (Concord, NH)*, *22*(5), 74–79.

Milne, A. (2016). Competition policy and the financial technology revolution in banking. *DigiWorld Economic Journal*, *103*, 145–161.

Mishra, D., Akman, I., & Mishra, A. (2014). Theory of reasoned action application for green information technology acceptance. *Computers in Human Behavior*, *36*, 29–40. doi:10.1016/j.chb.2014.03.030

Mobiloitte Blog. (2018). *Public Vs Private Blockchain: What's Right For your Business?* Retrieved from https://www.mobiloitte.com/blog/public-vs-private-blockchain-whats-right-for-your-business/

Mohamed Asmy, M. T. T., & Hassanudin, M. T. T. (2017). The Behavioural Intention of Investors to Use Islamic Banking's Investment Account Platform (IAP) As A Source of Investment Portfolio: A Structural Equation Modeling Approach. *Journal of Islamic Monetary Economics and Finance*, *3*(1), 113–138. doi:10.21098/jimf.v3i1.712

Moneymatch. (2018). *Rethinking finance.* Retrieved from https://moneymatch.co/#WhatWeDo

Moore, G.C. & Benbasat. (1991). Development of an Instrument to Measure the Perceptions of Adopting an Information Technology Innovation. *Information Systems Research, 2*(3), 192-222.

Moore, G. C., & Benbasat, I. (1996). Integrating diffusion of innovations and theory of reasoned action models to predict utilization of information technology by end-user. In *Diffusion and adoption of information technology* (pp. 132–146). Boston, MA: Springer. doi:10.1007/978-0-387-34982-4_10

Morabito, V. (2017). *Business innovation through blockchain*. Cham: Springer International Publishing. doi:10.1007/978-3-319-48478-5

Morgan Guaranty Trust Company. (1994). *RiskMetrics-Technical Document*. New York: Morgan Guaranty Trust Company, Global Research.

Moslehpour, M., Pham, V., Wong, W.-K., & Bilgiçli, İ. (2018). e-Purchase Intention of Taiwanese Consumers : Sustainable Mediation of Perceived Usefulness and Perceived Ease of Use. *Sustainability*, *10*(1), 1–17. doi:10.3390u10010234 PMID:30607262

Muedinai, F. (2018). The Compatibility of Cryptocurrencies and Islamic Finance. *EJIF – European Journal of Islamic Finance, 10,* 12-19.

Muedini, F. (2018). The Compatibility of Cryptocurrencies and Islamic Finance. *European Journal of Islamic Finance*, *10*, 1-10.

Mulligan, C. B., & Sala-i-Martin, X. (2000). Extensive Margins and the Demand for Money at Low Interest Rates. *Journal of Political Economy*, *108*(5), 961–991. doi:10.1086/317676

Munch, J. (2015). *What is fintech and why does it matter to all entrepreneurs*. Retrieved from https://www.hottopics.ht/3182/what-is-fintech-and-why-it-matters/

Munier, L., & Kemball-Cook, A. (2019). *Blockchain and the General Data Protection Regulation: Reconciling Protection and Innovation*. Academic Press.

Muslim, H. (1990). Sahih Muslim. Beirut: Dar Ehia' al-Turath al-'Arabi.

Nakamoto, S. (2008). *Bitcoin: A peer-to-peer electronic cash system*. Available at: https://bitcoin.org/bitcoin.pdf

Nakamoto, S. (2008). *Bitcoin: A Peer-to-Peer Electronic Cash System*. Unpublished working paper. Retrieved from https://bitcoin.org/bitcoin.pdf

Narayan, Rahman, & Setiawan. (2018). Bitcoin Price Growth and Indonesia's Monetary System. *Emerging Markets Review*.

National Digital Research Centre. (2014). *So what is FinTech? March 2014*. Available at: www.ndrc.ie/2014/03/fintech

Navaretti, G. B., Calzolari, G., Mansilla-Fernandez, J. M., & Pozzolo, A. F. (2018). *Fintech and Banking. Friends or Foes?* Available at SSRN: https://ssrn.com/abstract=3099337

Neftci, S. F. (2000). Value at Risk Calculations, Extreme Events and Tail Estimations. *Journal of Derivatives*, *7*(Spring Issue), 23–37. doi:10.3905/jod.2000.319126

Nelsen, R. B. (2006). *An Introduction to Copulas* (2nd ed.). New York: Springer Verlag.

Nepote-Cit, Ruberti, & Tran. (2018). *Perspectives économiques régionales: Afrique subsaharienne*. International Monetary Fund.

Nicoletti. (2017). *The Future of Fintech*. Integrating Finance and Technology in Financial Services.

Nicoletti, B. (2017). Regulations. In *The Future of FinTech* (pp. 195–209). Cham: Palgrave Macmillan.

Nicols, J. P. (2016). *The Fintech Grief Cycle for Bankers*. Retrieved from http://jpnicols.com/2016/07/12/fintech-grief-cycle-bankers/

Nienaber, R. (2016). Banks need to think collaboration rather than competition. *The FinTech Book: The Financial Technology Handbook for Investors, Entrepreneurs and Visionaries*, 20-21.

NST. (2017a). *Al Rajhi to roll out Malaysia's first Artificial Intelligence programme for Anti-Money Laundering*. Retrieved from https://www.nst.com.my/business/2017/10/287718/al-rajhi-bank-roll-out-malaysias-first-artificial-intelligence-programme

NST. (2017b). *Malaysia introduces the first Islamic digital framework*. Retrieved from https://www.nst.com.my/business/2017/12/316538/malaysia-introduce-first-islamic-digital-framework

NST. (2019). *PM: Islamic Banking Players must Invest in Technologies*. Retrieved from https://www.nst.com.my/news/nation/2019/04/478016/pm-islamic-banking-players-must-invest-technologies

Nusa Kapital. (2017). *About us*. Retrieved from https://www.nusakapital.com/about-us/

Ogubunka, M. U. (2004). *Corporate Management and Leadership Challenges*. Lagos: The Nigerian Banker CIBN.

Ojo, O. (2018). Disruptive Technology and the Fintech Industry in Nigeria: Imperatives for Legal and Policy Responses. *Gravitas Review of Business and Property Law, 9*(3).

Ondabu, Mohamed Sheikh, & Oyagi. (2015). Assessment of Non-Financial Motivation on Employee Productivity: Case of Ministry of Finance Headquarters in Hargeisa Somaliland. *International Journal of Business Management and Economic Research*, *6*(6), 400–416.

Organization for Economic Co-operation and Development. (2015). *New approached to SME and Entrepreneurship Financing: Broadening the Range of Instruments*. OECD.

Organization for Economic Co-operation and Development. (2017). *Financing SMEs and Entrepreneurs 2017 and OECD Scoreboard*. OECD.

Oubdi, L., & Raghibi, A. (2018). La perception des cryptomonnaies selon la loi islamique: Une analyse critique. *Recherches et Applications en Finance Islamique*, *2*(2), 161–173.

Özcan, M.E., & Hazıroğlu, T. (2000). *A new dimension in banking, participation banking, private financial institutions theory and practice in Turkey*. İstanbul: AlBaraka Turk Publications.

Ozili, P. K. (2018). *Impact of digital finance on financial inclusion and stability*. Borsa Istanbul Review.

Padmanaban, P., & Soo, H. K. Y. (2016). *Catching the Fintech Wave: A Survey on FinTech in Malaysia*. Retrieved from https://www.pwc.com/my/en/assets/publications/2016-pwc-aicb-catching-the-fintech-wave.pdf

Paluch, D. (2018). *CryptoMonday: Russia, Ukraine, France, And Thailand | Blockchain24.co*. Retrieved from https://www.blockchain24.co/cryptomonday-russia-ukraine-france-and-thailand/

Panetta, F. (2018). 21st Century cash: Central banking, technological innovation and digital currencies. In *SUERF Conference Proceedings 2018/2: Do We Need Central Bank Digital Currency? Economics, Technology and Institutions*. Bocconi University and Baffi Carefin.

Park, S. Y. (2009). An Analysis of the Technology Acceptance Model in Understanding University Students' Behavioral Intention to Use e-Learning. *Journal of Educational Technology & Society*, *12*(3), 150–162. doi:10.1145/3108421.3108432

Pejkovska. (2018). *Potential negative effects of Fintech on the financial services sector Examples from the European Union, India and the United States of America*. Applied Sciences Bachelor of Business Administration Double Degree in European Business Administration Thesis.

Peng, Y., Albuquerque, P. H. M., Camboim de S_a, J. M., Padula, A. J. A., & Montenegro, M. R. (2018). The best of two worlds: Forecasting high frequency volatility for cryptocurrencies and traditional currencies with Support Vector Regression. *Expert Systems with Applications, 97*, 177-192. doi:10.1016/j.eswa.2017.12.004

Perrin, J. (2001). *Innovation et analyse fonctionnelle*. Congrès AFAV.

Pikri, E. (2019). *SC Malaysia clarifies: A crypto-asset is only a security if used in specific ways*. Retrieved from https://fintechnews.my/19737/blockchain/securities-commission-malaysia-status-tokens-coins-utility-bitcoin/

Pikri, E. (2018). *StashAway is The First Robo-Advisor The SC Has Approved for The Malaysian Market*. WEALTHTECH.

Pollari, I. (2016). The rise of Fintech opportunities and challenges. *Jassa*, (3), 15-21.

Porter & Millar. (1985). How information gives you competitive advantage. *Harvard Business Review*, 149–160.

Prescott & Larose. (2016). Fintech Companies Face Big Privacy Challenges in 2016. *VC Experts Blog*. Available at: https://blog.vcexperts.com/2016/08/09/Fintech-companies-face-big-privacy-challenges

Prime Minister Office. (2019). *Media Release the 15th KLIFF*. Retrieved from https://www.pmo.gov.my/wp-content/uploads/2019/04/Media-Copy-Speech-YAB-Tun-Mahathir-Mohamad-at-the-Kuala-Lumpur-Islamic-Finance-Forum-2019-on-10-April-2019.pdf

Puschmann. (2017). Business & Information Systems Engineering. *The International Journal of wirt schafts informatik, 59*(1), 69-76.

PwC. (2016). *Global FinTech Report: How FinTech is shaping Financial Services*. Author.

PwC. (2018). The fight against economic crime and corruption: Aligning people, processes and technology to emerge stronger. *Global Economic Crime and Fraud Survey 2018 (Malaysia Report)*. Retrieved from https://www.pwc.com/my/en/assets/publications/2018/gecfs-2018-pwc-malaysia-2.pdf

PwC. (2019). *Budget 2019 overview: What's in store for the economy and impacted sectors*. Author.

Raskin, M., & Yermack, D. (2016). *Digital Currencies, Decentralized Ledgers, and the Future of Central Banking*. NBER Working Paper No. 22238.

Rasoolimanesh, S. M., & Ali, F. (2018). Guest editorial. *Journal of Hospitality and Tourism Technology, 9*(3), 238–248. doi:10.1108/JHTT-10-2018-142

Ratten, V. (2008). Technological innovations in the m-commerce industry: Aconceptual model of WAP banking intentions. *Journal of High Technology Management Research, 18*, 111–117.

Ray, S. (2018). Blockchains: The Technology of Transactions – Towards Data Science. *Towards Data Science*. Available at: https://towardsdatascience.com/blockchains-the-technology-of-transactions-9d40e8e41216

Reboredo, J. C., & Ugolini, A. (2015). Systemic risk in European sovereign debt markets: A CoVaR-copula approach. *Journal of International Money and Finance, 51*, 214–244. doi:10.1016/j.jimonfin.2014.12.002

Reuters. (2014). *Planned Malaysia investment platform to expand role of Islamic banks*. Author.

Reuters. (2018). *Fintech, a global boost for Islamic Finance?* Retrieved from https://www.reuters.com/article/idUS-WAOAPHREBLWW18A3

Ripple. (2019). *Solutions to Send Money Globally, Using Blockchain Technology*. Retrieved from https://ripple.com/ripplenet/

Risen, J. (2017). *Bank Negara kicks off fintech sandbox*. Retrieved from https://www.thestar.com.my/business/business-news/2017/05/29/bank-negara-kicks-off-fintech-with-licences-issued/#aajmZoCBJdbgOkaB.99

Roch, A., & Soner, H. M. (2013). Resilient price impact of trading and the cost of illiquidity. *International Journal of Theoretical and Applied Finance*, *16*(6), 1–27. doi:10.1142/S0219024913500374

Rogers, E. M. (1962). *Diffusion of innovations*. New York: Free Press of Glencoe.

Rogoff, K. S. (2014). *Costs and Benefits to Phasing Out Paper Currency*. NBER Working Paper 20126. National Bureau of Economic Research.

Rogoff, K. S. (2016). *The curse of cash*. Princeton University Press. doi:10.1515/9781400883219

Romānova, I., & Kudinska, M. (2016). Banking and Fintech: A Challenge or Opportunity? In Contemporary Issues in Finance: Current Challenges from Across Europe (pp. 21-35). Emerald Group Publishing Limited. doi:10.1108/S1569-375920160000098002

Romānova, I., Grima, S., Spiteri, J., & Kudinska, M. (2018). The Payment Services Directive 2 and competitiveness: The perspective of European FinTech Companies. *European Research Studies Journal*, *21*(2), 5–24.

Rosli, L. (2019). *Securities Commission amends guidelines for digital assets trading*. Retrieved from https://www.nst.com.my/business/2019/01/456233/securities-commission-amends-guidelines-digital-assets-trading

Ross, E. S. (2017). Nobody Puts Blockchain in a Corner: The Disruptive Role of Blockchain Technology in the Financial Services Industry and Current Regulatory Issues. *The Catholic University Journal of Law and Technology*, *25*(2), 353–386.

Roubini, N. (2018). *Why central bank digital currencies will destroy bitcoin*. Retrieved from https://www.theguardian.com/business/2018/nov/19/why-central-bank-digital-currencies-will-destroy-bitcoin

Roy, N. C., & Viswanathan, T. (2018). *Impact of Technological Disruption on Workforce Challenges of Indian Banks-Identification*. Assessment & Mitigation.

Ruozi, R., & Ferrari, P. (2013). *Liquidity Risk Management in Banks: Economic and Regulatory Issues*. Springer Briefs in Finance. doi:10.1007/978-3-642-29581-2

Rusydiana, A. S. (2018). Developing Islamic financial technology in Indonesia. *Hasanuddin Economics and Business Review*, *2*(2), 143–152. doi:10.26487/hebr.v2i2.1550

Ruth, J. (2018). Big note, small note: Central bank digital currency and cash. In *SUERF Conference Proceedings 2018/2: Do We Need Central Bank Digital Currency? Economics, Technology and Institutions*. Bocconi University and Baffi Carefin.

Saiti, B., Afghan, M., & Noordin, N. H. (2018). Financing agricultural activities in Afghanistan: A proposed salam-based crowdfunding structure. *ISRA International Journal of Islamic Finance*, *10*(1), 52–61. doi:10.1108/IJIF-09-2017-0029

Saiti, B., Hasan, A., & Ali, E. R. A. E. (2016). Islamic interbank money market: Contracts, instruments and their pricing. In *Islamic Capital Markets* (pp. 67–100). Cham: Palgrave Macmillan. doi:10.1007/978-3-319-33991-7_5

Saksonova, S., & Kuzmina-Merlino, I. (2017). Fintech as Financial Innovation–The Possibilities and Problems of Implementation. *European Research Studies, 20*(3A), 961.

Salyer, K. (2013, March 20). *Fleeing the Euro for Bitcoins.* Bloomberg L.P.

Saunders, A., & Cornett, M. (2008). *Financial Institutions Management* (6th ed.). Singapore: McGraw Hill.

Schueffel, P. (2016). Taming the Beast: A Scientific Definition of Fintech. *Journal of Innovation Management, JIM, 4*, 32–54.

Schumpeter, J. (1951). *Capitalism, Socialism and Democracy*. Payot Edition.

Securities Commission. (2017). *Media release: The SC initiates aFINity Innovation Lab for alternative trading*. Retrieved from https://issuance.sc.com.my/digital/ats/

Securities Commission. (2018). *Licensing handbook*. Retrieved from https://www.sc.com.my/api/documentms/download.ashx?id=1f230c0d-988e-4b34-b497-71d8372a3998

Securities Commission. (2019a). *Regulations*. Retrieved from www.sc.com.my

Securities Commission. (2019b). *List of market operators*. Retrieved from https://www.sc.com.my/development/digital/list-of-registered-recognized-market-operators

Securities Commission. (2019c). *List of digital asset exchanges in transitional period.* Retrieved from https://www.sc.com.my/regulation/guidelines/recognizedmarkets/list-of-digital-asset-exchanges-in-transitional-period

Securities Commission. (2019d). *Consultation paper (No 1/2019) on proposed regulatory framework for the issuance of digital assets through ICO.* Retrieved from https://www.sc.com.my/api/documentms/download.ashx?id=d3067bf4-ba39-4bce-8dc4-1b660ff37977

Selmi, R., Mensi, M., Hammoudeh, S., & Bouoiyour, J. (2018). Is Bitcoin a hedge, a safe haven or a diversifier for oil price movements? A comparison with gold. *Energy Economics, 74*, 787–801. doi:10.1016/j.eneco.2018.07.007

Senach, B. (1990). *Evaluation ergonomique des interfaces homme-machine: une revue de la littérature*. Rapport de recherche, RR-1180, INRIA.

Shiller, R. (2014, March 1). In Search of a Stable Electronic Currency. *New York Times.*

Sidlo, K. W. (2017). *Islamic Finance 2017: State of the Art and Outlook for the Future, K4D Helpdesk Report*. Brighton, UK: IDS.

Silva, R. L. S., & Laboratório, J. C. de O. (2003). Introduction to Augmented Reality. *National Laboratory for Scientific Computation*, 1–11. doi:10.3169/itej.66.53

Simpasa & Gurara. (2012). Inflation Dynamics in selected East African countries: Ethiopia, Kenya,Tanzania and Uganda. AFDB Brief 2012. African Development Bank.

Skingsley, C. (2016). *Should the Riksbank issue e-krona?* Speech at FinTech Stockholm. Available online: https://www.bis.org/review/r161128a.pdf

SME Corporation. (2016). *Guideline for New SME Definition.* SME Corporation.

SME Corporation. (2017a). *Economic Census 2016: Profile of SMEs*. Retrieved from http://www.smecorp.gov.my/images/SMEAR/latest/2/Census English_FINAL.pdf

SME Corporation. (2017b). *SME Annual Report 2017/18*. Author.

SME. (2016a). *Access to Finance*. Retrieved from http://www.smecorp.gov.my/images/SMEAR/latest/Chapter6.pdf

SME. (2016b). *SME Annual Report 2016*. SME.

Smith. (1997). Financial markets in development, and the development of financial markets. *Journal of Economics Dynamics and Control*.

Srokosz, W. (2015). The use of cryptocurrencies for tax evasion and tax fraud. *Tax Law vs Tax Frauds and Tax Evasions. Non – conference proceedings of scientific papers, 2*.

Stevens, A. (2017, June). Digital currencies: Threats and opportunities for monetary policy. *NBB Economic Review*.

Stogdill, R. M. (1974). *Handbook of Leadership: A Survey of the Literature*. New York: Free Press.

Subramanian, H. (2018). Decentralized Blockchain Based Electronic Marketplaces. *Communications of the ACM*, *61*(1), 78–84. doi:10.1145/3158333

Suri, T. (2017). Mobile Money. *Annual Review of Economics*, *9*, 497–520.

Surujnath, R. (2017). Off the Chain! A Guide to Blockchain Derivatives Markets and the Implications on Systemic Risk. *Fordham Journal of Corporate and Financial Law*, *23*, 257–304.

Susskind, J. (2017). Decrypting Democracy: Incentivizing Blockchain Voting Technology for an Improved Election System. *The San Diego Law Review*, *54*, 785–827.

Swan, M. (2015). *Blockchain: Blueprint for a new economy*. O'Reilly Media, Inc.

Takahashi, D., & Alexander, S. (2002). Illiquid Alternative Asset Fund Modeling. *Journal of Portfolio Management*, *28*(2), 90–100. doi:10.3905/jpm.2002.319836

Tanduklangi, A. (2017). Determinants of User Intention in Using e-Learning Technology in Indonesian Context: An Empirical Study. *Mediterranean Journal of Social Sciences*, *8*(3), 69–77. doi:10.5901/mjss.2017.v8n3p69

Teece, D. J. (2010). Business Models, Business Strategy and Innovation. *Long Range Planning, Elsevier*, *43*(2–3), 172–194. doi:10.1016/j.lrp.2009.07.003

Tenenhaus, M., Amato, S., & Esposito Vinzi, V. (2004). A global goodness-of-fit index for PLS structural equation modelling. In *Proceedings of the XLII SIS scientific meeting* (pp. 739–742). Academic Press.

Tenenhaus, M., Vinzi, V. E., Chatelin, Y. M., & Lauro, C. (2005). PLS path modeling. *Computational Statistics & Data Analysis*, *48*(1), 159–205. doi:10.1016/j.csda.2004.03.005

Thakor, A. V. (2019). *Fintech and Banking*. Available at SSRN: https://ssrn.com/abstract=3332550

The Banks Association of Turkey. (2019). *Banks and Banking Sector Information, Statistical Reports*. Available at: https://www.tbb.org.tr/en/banks-and-banking-sector-information/statistical-reports/20

The Digital Finance Institute. (2018). *Global Review of Commercial A.I.: Artificial Intelligence and Machine Learning Report for Business*. Retrieved from Digital Finance Institute Website: http://www.digitalfinanceinstitute.org/?post_documents=ai-report

The Star Online. (2018). *Coincheck begins allowing yen withdrawals ahead of FSA deadline.* Retrieved from https://www.thestar.com.my/business/business-news/2018/02/13/coincheck-begins-allowing-yen-withdrawals-ahead-of-fsa-deadline/#vkDQydOdk3yBPDAu.99

Thenuan, P., & Raina, A. (2016). Data privacy congress for big data monetization in mobile application. *Researchgate.* Retrieved from https://www.researchgate.net/publication/309012928_DATA_PRIVACY_CONCERNS_FOR_BIG_DATA_MONETIZATION_IN_MOBILE_APPLICATION

Thompson, D. (2017). What On Earth Is Going On With Bitcoin? *Atlantic (Boston, Mass.), 30*(November). Available online https://www.theatlantic.com/business/archive/2017/11/bitcoindelusion-conquer-world/547187/

Tobin, J. (1987). The case for preserving regulatory distinctions. In *Restructuring the Financial System, Proceedings of the Economic Policy Symposium.* Federal Reserve Bank of Kansas City. 10.1080/05775132.1987.11471196

Tole, F. (2017, Dec. 12). Drug Dealers Laundering their Money at Bitcoin ATMs. *Business Insider.*

Trabelsi, N. (2018). Are There Any Volatility Spill-Over Effects among Cryptocurrencies and Widely Traded Asset Classes? *Journal of Risk and Financial Management., 11*(4), 66. doi:10.3390/jrfm11040066

Tsai, W. H., Huang, B. Y., Liu, J. Y., Tsaur, T. S., & Lin, S. J. (2010). The application of Web ATMs in e-payment industry: A case study. *Expert Systems with Applications, 37*(1), 587–597. doi:10.1016/j.eswa.2009.05.058

Turkish. (2014). *Turkey/GCC Economic Relations.* Franco-Turkish Paper, No. 12.

Ulya, N. U. (2018). Peer to Peer Lending on Financial Technology under Perspective Positive Law and Islamic Law. *Journal of Islamic Business Law, 2*(1).

Venkatesh, V., Morris, M.G., Davis, G.B., & Davis, F.D. (2003). User Acceptance of Information Technology: Toward a Unified View. *MIS Quarterly, 27*(3), 425-478.

Villaverde, J. F. (2018). Cryptocurrency Competition and the U.S. Monetary System. Penn Wharton.

Vives, X. (2017). The impact of FinTech on banking. *European Economy,* (2), 97-105.

Wahed. (2017). *Will Artificial Intelligence Rejuvenate Islamic Finance.* Retrieved from https://journal.wahedinvest.com/will-artificial-intelligence-rejuvenate-islamic-finance/

Wahjono, S. I., & Marina, A., & Widayat. (2015). Islamic Crowdfunding : Alternative Funding Solution. In *1st World Islamic Social Science Congress* (pp. 1–12). Academic Press.

Walch, A. (2017). The Path of the Blockchain Lexicon (and the Law). *Review of Banking and Financial Law, 36,* 713–765.

Waldo, J. (2019). A Hitchhiker's Guide to the Blockchain Universe. *Communications of the ACM, 62*(3), 38–42. doi:10.1145/3303868

Ward, O., & Rochemont, S. (2019). *Understanding Central Bank Digital Currencies (CBDC), An addendum to "A Cashless Society- Benefits, Risks and Issues (Interim paper).* Academic Press.

Weber, R. (2018). An Advisor's Introduction to Blockchain. *Journal of Financial Service Professionals, 72*(6), 49–53.

Weiß, G. N. F., & Supper, H. (2013). Forecasting liquidity-adjusted intraday Value-at-Risk with vine copulas. *Journal of Banking & Finance, 37*(9), 3334–3350. doi:10.1016/j.jbankfin.2013.05.013

Welling, M. (2019). *Artificial Intelligence Versus Intelligence Engineering.* Harvard Data Science Review.

White, L. H. (2015). The Market for Cryptocurrencies. *The Cato Journal, 35*(2), 383–402.

Wilcocks, L., & Plant, R. (2001). Getting from bricks to clicks. *Sloan Management Review*, 50–59.

Wilhelm, A. (2017). *Popular Bitcoin Mining Pool Promises to Restrict its Compute Power to Prevent Feared '51%' Fiasco.* TechCrunch.com.

Williams, M. T. (2014). *The New York State Department of Financial Services: Hearing on Virtual Currencies.* Academic Press.

Williams, M. T. (2014). Virtual Currencies – Bitcoin Risk. In *World Bank Conference*. Boston University.

Wilson, M. G., & Yelowitz, A. (2014). *Characteristics of Bitcoin Users: An Analysis of Google Search Data.* Social Science Research Network. Working Papers Series.

Wonglimpiyarat, J. (2017). FinTech banking industry: A systemic approach. *Foresight, 19*(6), 590–603. doi:10.1108/FS-07-2017-0026

Wonglimpiyarat, J. (2018). Challenges and dynamics of FinTech crowd funding: An innovation system approach. *The Journal of High Technology Management Research, 29*(1), 98–108. doi:10.1016/j.hitech.2018.04.009

Workie, H., & Jain, K. (2017). Distributed Ledger Technology: Implications of Blockchain for the Securities Industry. *Journal of Securities Operations and Custody, 9*(4), 347–355.

World Bank Group. (2018). *Malaysia Economic Monitor: Navigating Change*. Author.

World Islamic Banking Competitiveness Report 2013-2014. (n.d.). *The transition begins*. Available at: https://www.ey.com/Publication/vwLUAssets/EY_-_World_Islamic_Banking_Competitiveness_Report_2013%E2%80%9314/$FILE/EY-World-Islamic-Banking-Competitiveness-Report-2013-14.pdf

World Islamic Banking Competitiveness Report. (2016). *New realities, new opportunities*. Available at: https://www.ey.com/Publication/vwLUAssets/ey-world-islamic-banking-competitiveness-report-2016/%24FILE/ey-world-islamic-banking-competitiveness-report-2016.pdf

Yang, D., & Li, M. (2018). Evolutionary Approaches and the Construction of Technology-Driven Regulations. *Emerging Markets Finance & Trade, 54*(14), 3256–3271. doi:10.1080/1540496X.2018.1496422

Yang, G., Lu, Y., Gupta, S., Cao, Y., & Zhang, R. (2012). Mobile payment services adoption across time: An empirical study of the effects of behavioral beliefs, social influences, and personal traits. *Computers in Human Behavior, 28*(1), 129–142. doi:10.1016/j.chb.2011.08.019

Yermack, D. (2013). *Is Bitcoin a real currency? An economic appraisal* (No. w19747). National Bureau of Economic Research. Retrieved from http://www.nber.org/papers/w19747

Yılmaz, C. (1993). Supporting the rural industry and the case of workers companies in Turkey. *Ondokuz Mayıs University Journal of Faculty of Education, 8*(1), 305–334.

Yin, H. H. S., Langenheldt, K., Harlev, M., Mukkamala, R. R., & Vatrapu, R. (2019). Regulating Cryptocurrencies: A Supervised Machine Learning Approach to De-Anonymizing the Bitcoin Blockchain. *Journal of Management Information Systems, 36*(1), 37–73. doi:10.1080/07421222.2018.1550550

Yousafzai, S. Y., Foxall, G. R., & Pallister, J. G. (2010). Explaining internet banking behavior: Theory of reasoned action, theory of planned behavior, or technology acceptance model? *Journal of Applied Social Psychology, 40*(5), 1172–1202. doi:10.1111/j.1559-1816.2010.00615.x

Zahid, A. Z. M. (2018). *Assistant Governor's Welcoming Remarks at the Islamic Finance Rendezvous Series*. Academic Press.

Zetzsche, D. A., Buckly, R. P., & Arner, D. W. (2018). The Distributed Liability of Distributed Legers: Legal Risks of Blockchain. *University of Illinois Law Review, 4*, 1361–1406.

Zyskind, G., & Nathan, O. (2015, May). Decentralizing privacy: Using blockchain to protect personal data. In *2015 IEEE Security and Privacy Workshops* (pp. 180-184). IEEE.

About the Contributors

Nader Naifar is currently a professor of finance at Imam Mohammad Ibn Saud Islamic University in Riyadh, Saudi Arabia and the University of Sfax. In 2009, he received his Ph.D. in Finance from the University of Sfax, Tunisia. He has published a large number of papers on reputable journals indexed in Web of Science and Scopus databases. His main research fields are Islamic finance, credit derivatives, financial crisis, and energy markets. Currently, his research interests focus on Fintech, Blockchain, and Artificial Intelligence for business. In 2019 he received the "Oxford Fintech programme" certificate from Said Business School at Oxford University.

* * *

Abdulazeem Abozaid holds BA and higher studies Diploma in Islamic law and its principles, MA and PhD in Islamic financial law, all from Damascus University. He has been teaching since 1998 at different universities, and also advising Islamic banks since 2006. Abdulazeem has more than 30 published papers, 7 books and 4 book chapters. Currently, he is teaching at Hamad bin Khalifa University since 2013.

Mazin A. M. Al Janabi is Full Professor of Finance at Tecnologico de Monterrey, EGADE Business School, Santa Fe Campus, Mexico City, Mexico. Professor Al Janabi holds a Ph.D. degree from the University of London, UK, and has over 30 years of real-world experience in diverse academic institutions and financial markets, and in many different roles. Professor Al Janabi has strong interest for research, publications and developments within emerging economies. Professor Al Janabi has published in top-tiered journals such as: International Review of Financial Analysis, European Journal of Operational Research, Annals of Operations Research, Applied Economics, Economic Modelling, Review of Financial Economics, Journal of Asset Management, Service Industries Journal, Studies in Economics and Finance, International Journal of Financial Engineering, Journal of Emerging Market Finance, Emerging Markets Finance and Trade, Review of Middle East Economics and Finance, Journal of Economic Research, Journal of Risk Finance, Journal of Banking Regulation, Journal of Financial Regulation and Compliance, Journal of Derivatives & Hedge Funds, Annals of Nuclear Energy, among others.

Shahab Aziz is a practicing Islamic banker having more than 10 years' experience of Islamic banking industry. He has worked in different roles in Islamic banking including risk management, facility approval, branch credit etc. He has been involved in executing major Islamic finance modes for corporate and SME and consumer sectors. Shahab has recently completed his PhD in Islamic Finance from Azman Hashim International Business School, Universiti Teknologi Malaysia, Kuala Lumpur, Malaysia. Prior to that, he had obtained master's degree in Islamic Banking and Finance from Loughborough University, UK, MS Finance from Capital University of Science and Technology Islamabad Pakistan and MA Economics from University of Punjab Lahore, Pakistan. Shahab also has published research articles in various international journals and attended numerous international conferences. His area of research interests are Islamic banking, Islamic Marketing, consumer behavior and behavioral finance.

Khoutem Ben Jedidia is associate Professor of economics at The High Institute of Accounting (ISCAE) (Tunisia) and a Research associate in the research unit in development Economics (URED, Faculty of economics and management of Sfax, Tunisia). She completed her undergraduate studies in the Faculty of economics and management of Sfax in 1993 and taught there. She received an honorary presidential Prize in economics. Then, she received a master's degree of Advanced Studies in Money, Finance and Banks from University Lumière Lyon II, France in 1994, and completed a Ph.D in Economics at University Lumière Lyon II in 1998. Her first academic job was as an Assistant Professor at the Faculty of economics and management of Sfax from 1999-2004. Dr. Ben Jedidia's research focuses on financial intermediation, monetary economics and Islamic finance. Many of Ben Jedidia's papers are interested in financial development of Tunisia, and Islamic financial intermediation.

Musa Gün is an Assistant Professor of Finance at Recep Tayyip Erdoğan University. He holds a PhD in Finance from Istanbul University. His areas of research interest include Islamic finance, financial economics, international financial markets, capital markets, economics and nonlinear econometric analysis and modelling in finance.

Hichem Hamza holds a Ph.D. in Economics from the University of Economics and Management in Clermont-Ferrand, France. He started his career at Tunis higher School of Business in 2003. Currently, he is a researcher at the Islamic Economics Institute- King Abdulaziz University. His research interests include Islamic finance and banking, monetary policy and financial economics.

Razali Haron is a Researcher at IIUM Institute of Islamic Banking and Finance with area of interest in corporate finance.

Rusni Hassan is a Professor and was the Deputy Dean at the IIUM Institute of Islamic Banking and Finance, IIUM. She graduated with LLB (Honours), LLB (Shariah) (First Class), Master of Comparative Laws (MCL) and Ph.D. in Law. She is a registered Shariah Advisor with the Securities Commission Malaysia. She joins EXIM Bank as the member of Shariah Committee on 2 January 2018. She is also active in the Association of Shariah Advisors in Islamic Finance Malaysia (ASAS) and the International Council of Islamic Finance Educators (ICIFE) where she is the Secretary and the Assistant Secretary for both associations respectively. Her works and contribution to Islamic Finance has also been recognized internationally when she was listed among the Top 10 Women in Islamic Finance by CPI Financial in 2013 and been awarded as Most Talented Women Professional in Islamic Banking, Asia Islamic Banking Excellence Awards, CMO Asia, 2014; and Women of Distinction in her contribution in the field of Islamic Finance and law by Venus International Women Awards (VIWA 2016). She is also listed as one of the 50 Most Influential Women in Islamic Finance by ISFIRE in 2017.

Azman Ismail is the President, IIFIN Consulting Sdn Bhd. He has been in the Islamic finance industry since 1985 and has provided training and consultancy services to companies in Malaysia, Singapore, Indonesia, Saudi Arabia, Qatar, Brunei, Iran, Somaliland and France and presented papers in Kuala Lumpur, Manama, New York, Tokyo, Brunei, Singapore, Cairo, London, Milan, Taipei, Taroudant and Abu Dhabi. He was an external lecturer for the Master in Islamic Banking and Finance program at the Institute of Islamic Banking and Finance (IIiBF), International Islamic University Malaysia (IIUM). He was also a Course Consultant and Member, Board of Studies at the Institute. He has been commissioned by the International Centre for Education in Islamic Finance (INCEIF) and the International Shari'ah Research Academy for Islamic Finance (ISRA). Azman was a Member of the Information Panel, AmanahRaya, the Public Trustee of Malaysia and currently a Shariah Advisor to several Islamic institutions in Malaysia and Singapore. He has written and translated a total of fourteen books. Currently, he is active in providing Shariah advisory and consultancy.

Sherin Kunhibava is a Senior Lecturer at the University Malaya Law faculty. Her area of expertise is in commercial law and Islamic banking and finance law. Apart from her fifteen years of teaching experience in academia, Dr. Sherin has also worked at Pacific Bank Bhd. and at International Shariah Research Academy (ISRA). At Pacific Bank Bhd she was attached with the legal department. At ISRA she headed research in Islamic banking and finance and was Editor of the ISRA International Journal of Islamic Finance. Dr. Sherin was also for a number of years an Examiner for two external bodies namely the Malaysian Association of Company Secretaries and the Malaysian Institute of Chartered Secretaries and Administrators. Dr. Sherin writes extensively. Her articles on law have appeared in newspapers, magazines, International and local refereed journals. Dr. Sherin has written chapters in a number of prominent books on Islamic finance. Dr. Sherin's latest area of research project has been green banking framework, and regulatory framework for blockchain and fintech.

Maizaitulaidawati Md Husin is a senior lecturer at Azman Hashim International Business School (AHIBS) Universiti Teknologi Malaysia. Registered as a certified Islamic Financial Planner, she holds a PhD in Islamic Economics from Universiti Malaya, a Master of Science in Banking and a Bachelor of Business Administration in Finance. Her PhD was focusing on adoption of family takaful among Muslim in Malaysia. Mai had a successful career in banking industry before fulfilling her dream of becoming a lecturer. She started her teaching career when she joined UTM in 2009. Within her 10 years of service in UTM, she has been involved in more than 10 consultancy and research projects as either a leader or a team member with total value of involving RM7 Million. Mai have also authored and co-authored more than 60 research papers, book chapters for businesses, universities, seminars, conferences and journal publications. She has served AHIBS as the research manager in 2017 and held several other managerial positions in the faculty. From 2018 to 2019, she pursued her post-doctoral study at International Islamic University Malaysia at which she conducted research specifically on Islamic fintech, takaful and Small and Medium Enterprises. Now back in AHIBS, Mai continues her research interest in the area of Islamic banking and finance. She is a member of Malaysian Finance Association (MFA), Malaysian Economic Association (MEA) and Financial Planning Association of Malaysia (FPAM). In her spare time, Mai enjoys a good happy hour with family and friends, the sounds of a great music playlist, reading, travelling and seeking adventure in the outdoors. Visit her profile at https://www.maizaitulaidawati.com.

Nor Razinah Binti Mohd. Zain is currently an Assistant Professor at the IIUM Institute of Islamic Banking and Finance (IIiBF), International Islamic University Malaysia (IIUM). She actively participated and published on Dispute Resolution, Islamic Banking, and Islamisation of Knowledge since 2013. She was trained in mediation for conflict solution and trauma conciliation by Prof Dr. Johan Galtung, the Founder of Peace Research Institute, Oslo in 2014. Prior to joining IIUM, she was an Advocate and Solicitor of the High Court of Malaya (Non-Practising). She is an acting Editor for Journal of Islamic Finance and Islamisation Coordinator for IIiBF. She is also an active member of the International Council of Islamic Finance Educators (ICIFE) and Association of Shariah Advisors in Islamic Finance (ASAS). Recently, she and her team successfully proposed the use of dispute resolution to the Malaysian Government, which leads to the establishment of the National Unity and Reconciliation Council in overcoming interfaith and interracial disputes. In relation to fintech, she is among the earliest researchers that contribute to the discussion on smart contracts and their impacts on regulations and Shariah principles. She also has lectured in companies, contracts, governance, business, and commercial transaction laws.

Aishath Muneeza is an Associate Professor at INCEIF. She is the first female Deputy Minister of Ministry of Islamic Affairs and is the Deputy Minister of Ministry of Finance & Treasury of Republic of Maldives. She is also the chairwoman of Maldives Center for Islamic Finance. She is considered as the founder of Islamic finance in Maldives. Her contribution to Islamic finance include structuring of the corporate sukuks and sovereign private sukuk of the country including the Islamic treasury instruments. She also drafted the Islamic Capital Market framework of the country and is the only registered shariah adviser for Islamic capital market in the country since 2013. She played a key role in setting up of the Tabung Haji of Maldives, Maldives Hajj Corporation and was the first chairperson of it. She sits in various shariah advisory bodies nationally and internationally and is chairman for many of these Shariah advisory bodies including the apex Shariah Advisory Council for capital market in Maldives. She holds a doctorate in law from International Islamic University of Malaysia.

Anwar Allah Pitchay is a senior lecturer at School of Management, Universiti Sains Malaysia. He joined the university upon completing his PhD in 2015 from the International Islamic University Malaysia (IIUM). His research interests are in the areas of Islamic Banking and Finance and, Non-Banking Islamic Finance Institutions (NBFI). He has published several articles related to Waqf, Islamic Banking, and governance in various indexed and refereed journals, both locally and internationally.

Auwal Adam Sa'ad is an Assistant Professor at IIUM Institute of Islamic Banking and Finance, (IIiBF) International Islamic University Malaysia. Prior to his appoint at IIiBF, Dr. Auwal worked with the Islamic Banking and Finance Section, School of Management, University Sains Malaysia (USM). Dr. Auwal acquired his PhD from Ahmad Ibrahim Kulliyyah of Laws, (AIKOL) International Islamic University Malaysia in 2016. In 2009, he obtained Master of Comparative Laws from AIKOL as well. He was also a part time lecturer at the same faculty between 2011 to 2016. Dr. Auwal acquired his LLB_Shari'ah from Islamic University Madina in 2006. His areas of specialization and research are Sukuk Markets Development, Islamic Commercial law, Islamic Economics, Islamic Capital Markets, Smart Sukuk, Islamic Fintech and Islamic Entrepreneurship & Halal Innovation.

Buerhan Saiti is currently an Associate Professor of Department of Islamic Economics and Finance of the Istanbul Sabahattin Zaim University. Recently, he earned Outstanding Young Researcher Award by Turkey Academy of Sciences (TÜBA) (2018-2021). Previously, he was full-time Associate and Assistant Professor of Institute of Islamic Banking and Finance of the International Islamic University Malaysia (IIUM) where he won the highest number of publications in citation-indexed journals in social science category in the year 2017. As a young academician, he has published 2 books, 6 book chapters, almost 50 refereed journal publications (most of them are citation-indexed journals) and attended more than 35 Intentional and local conferences. He teaches both at the Post Graduate and Undergraduate levels. His research interest is both theoretical and empirical studies of Islamic Banking and Finance.

Index

I

L

M

O

P

R

S

T

www.ingramcontent.com/pod-product-compliance
Lightning Source LLC
LaVergne TN
LVHW062143300926
849161LV00010B/2614